Ireland and
the Americas

Other Titles in ABC-CLIO's

Transatlantic Relations Series

Ireland and
the Americas

Culture, Politics, and History

A Multidisciplinary Encyclopedia

VOLUME III

EDITED BY

James P. Byrne

Philip Coleman

Jason King

Transatlantic Relations Series

Will Kaufman, Series Editor

A B C ⬥ C L I O

Santa Barbara, California   Denver, Colorado   Oxford, England

Library of Congress Cataloging-in-Publication Data
Ireland and the Americas / edited by James P. Byrne, Philip Coleman, and Jason King.
    p. cm. — (Transatlantic relations series)
 Includes bibliographical references and index.
 ISBN 978-1-85109-614-5 (hard copy : alk. paper) — ISBN 978-1-85109-619-0 (ebook : alk. paper) 1. America—Relations—Ireland—Encyclopedias. 2. Ireland—Relations—America—Encyclopedias. 3. America—History—Encyclopedias. 4. Ireland—History—Encyclopedias. 5. North America—History—Encyclopedias. 6. Latin America—History—Encyclopedias. 7. South America—History—Encyclopedias. 8. America—Politics and government—Encyclopedias. 9. Ireland—Politics and government—Encyclopedias. I. Byrne, James P., 1968– II. Coleman, Philip Michael Joseph, 1972– III. King, Jason Francis, 1970–

E18.75.I74 2008
327.730417—dc22

                                                              2007035381

12   11   10   09   08   1   2   3   4   5   6   7   8

Senior Production Editor: *Vicki Moran*
Editorial Assistant: *Sara Springer*
Production Manager: *Don Schmidt*
Media Editor: *Jason Kniser*
Media Resources Coordinator: *Ellen Brenna Dougherty*
Media Resources Manager: *Caroline Price*
File Management Coordinator: *Paula Gerard*

ABC-CLIO, Inc.
130 Cremona Drive, P.O. Box 1911
Santa Barbara, California 93116-1911

This book is also available on the World Wide Web as an ebook.
Visit www.abc-clio.com for details.

This book is printed on acid-free paper ∞
Manufactured in the United States of America

CONTENTS

NATIONALISM, IRISH-AMERICAN

Beginnings

In *American Opinion and the Irish Question,* Thomas Carroll defines "Irish-American" as "referring to the Catholic Irish who immigrated to the United States in large numbers during the nineteenth century." Three million Irish emigrated to America between the onset of the Great Famine in 1846 and the death of Charles Stewart Parnell in 1891. Although some came from Protestant Ulster, the majority came from the Catholic provinces of Munster and Connacht. This influx provided the impetus for the spread of Irish-American nationalism.

The roots of Irish-American nationalism can be traced to early Irish republican movements, which looked to America for inspiration. In 1782, the Ascendancy Patriots, inspired by the American revolutionaries, assembled a militia known as the "Irish Volunteers," which wrested from George III's government an acceptance of Irish freedom under the crown. In the 1790s, Theobald Wolfe Tone used both America and France for inspiration for his attempt to establish an Irish Republic with his abortive Wexford Rising of 1798. Tone, among others, was sentenced to death, but other patriots fled to America. Meanwhile Pitt the Younger's British government pushed through the 1801 Act of Union, abolishing the independent Irish parliament and merging the kingdoms of England and Ireland.

Irish nationalists needed to look to America once more for support. From the 1820s to the 1840s, Daniel O'Connell found funds and supporters in America for his campaigns for Catholic Emancipation—which was achieved in 1829—and to repeal the union. In this relatively welcoming environment, Irishmen were able to debate Irish issues before a sympathetic American audience. But American-Irish relations would become strained with the onset of mass immigration in the late 1840s.

Status Anxiety

The Irish immigrants carried with them not just their homesickness but also the scars of their painful history. Arriving in America meant exposing those scars to the world. Moreover, although the Irish were angry with the English for creating the circumstances that forced them out of Ireland, they were also ashamed of themselves for letting it happen. As Thomas Brown emphasizes in *Irish-American Nationalism,* "for those living amongst Americans—the people of get-up-and-go to whom poverty was sinful—there was no escaping a sense of humiliation in reflecting on so much suffering so passively endured." Anti-Irish feeling, which in America had been bubbling below the surface even before mass immigration, worsened with the establishment in America of the anti-Irish Know-Nothing movement of the 1850s.

Coupled with this was the problem that, as Francis Hackett underlines in *Ireland: A Study in Nationalism*, "Americans were frequently unable to reconcile the nationalistic Irishman's account of England with their own impression of the English race and even the British empire. Such Americans may like their Irishman, they may want to be hospitable to his emotions, but they cannot belie the admiration and respect they have long given to England." In this light, it is unsurprising that some of the most important Irish-American nationalist figures were second- or third-generation Irish. Being both geographically and temporally removed from the anxieties of Irish history, they nevertheless identified with the ideal of an Irish national struggle.

Conflicting Nationalisms

When Henry Grattan, leader of the Ascendancy Patriots, declared in 1782 that now "Ireland is a nation," he gave voice to an ideal that would be interpreted and reinterpreted by subsequent generations of Irish nationalists. In 1840s Ireland, the nationalist movement was divided between the realistic constitutional aims of the aging, Catholic Daniel O'Connell and the potentially revolutionary idealism of a new group of middle-class Protestants calling themselves "Young Ireland." This division would influence future generations of nationalists on both sides of the Atlantic. In 1846 Young Irelanders broke with the O'Connellites when O'Connell's Repeal Association resolved to condemn taking violent action. It all ended in 1848 with another abortive rising, hastily arranged by the Young Ireland leaders, at Ballingarry, Co. Tipperary. Several of the conspirators fled, arriving eventually in the United States.

Revolutionary Nationalism

In 1858, two members of Young Ireland, John O'Mahony and Michael Doheny, established the secret Fenian Brotherhood, the first significant movement in Irish-American nationalism. Members of the Brotherhood pledged allegiance to the Irish Republic and swore to take up arms when needed. The Fenian Movement was a precursor to Clan na Gael, the American sister organization of the Irish Republican Brotherhood. O'Mahony had escaped abroad after the Rising of 1848, settling in New York in 1952. During the American Civil War (1861–1865), the Fenians masterminded plans for insurrection while taking refuge in the United States. The 1867 Rising failed almost as disastrously as the last.

The 1870s saw the emergence of new heroes of Irish-American revolutionary nationalism. Galway-born Patrick Ford became editor of *Irish World*. Although John O'Cleary called Ford a "totally ignorant, highly unscrupulous, and thoroughly ill-conditioned fanatic," his idealism for the cause could not be mistaken. In 1871, Jeremiah O'Donovan Rossa and John Devoy arrived in New York, having been released from prison by the British government under the Amnesty Act of 1870. Rossa would boast of being in charge of dynamite attacks in English cities in the 1880s, while Devoy would found the influential *Irish*

Nation (1881–1885) and later the *Gaelic American* (1903–1951). In 1878, Michael Davitt was released from prison after serving eight years for Fenian activities. Although he never lived in America, he visited it often and, like Ford, was eulogized for his attempts to understand the anxieties of the average Irish American.

In the 1880s, revolutionary figures began to emerge from second- and third-generation Irish groups. Canadian-born Alexander Sullivan became known publicly as the leading American Irish supporter of the Republican Party and privately as the head of the "Triangle" responsible for the campaign of dynamite terrorism in Britain. Captain John McCafferty from Ohio was reputed to be chief of the Invincibles who assassinated Lord Frederick Cavendish in Phoenix Park in 1882. Then, in 1884 William Mackey Lomasney from Cincinnati was blown up while attempting to dynamite London Bridge.

By the beginning of the twentieth century, revolutionary groups were still smarting from the Parnell divorce scandal of 1890–1891, which had divided nationalist opinion. Apathy began to set in when in 1914 Irish republican groups failed to achieve Home Rule. The situation improved in March 1916, when the Friends of Irish Freedom (FOIF), the public face of Clan na Gael, became the main player in Irish nationalism. Clansmen used the huge membership of the FOIF—it had 270,000 at its peak—to muster popular support for those executed by the British after the Easter Rising of 1916 and later for the Irish Republican Army (IRA). However, in 1921 the Clan and the FOIF, like Sinn Féin in Ireland, split over the merits of the Anglo-Irish treaty. Whereas Irish Catholic nationalism gathered pace after the establishment of the Irish Free State in 1921–1922, Irish-American nationalism began to lose momentum. As Andrew Wilson remarks in *Irish America and the Ulster Conflict,* "The degree of independence achieved by the twenty-six counties satisfied most of the diaspora."

Nevertheless, militant nationalists continued to play a part in Irish politics, particularly following the eruption of the Troubles in Ulster in 1968. In 1977 the Ad Hoc Committee on Irish Affairs was formed; it, along with other organizations, including the Irish National Caucus, Irish American Unity Conference, and the American Irish Political Education Committee, had barely concealed revolutionary sympathies. These groups, however, had little influence in Washington, and so they concentrated instead on publicizing human rights abuses by British forces in Ulster and working for a British withdrawal.

By the late 1980s, however, influential figures in Irish-American republican organizations had concluded that the Ulster conflict had reached a stalemate: it was becoming increasingly unlikely that the British could be forced to withdraw. In Ireland, Sinn Féin was beginning to perceive the negative impact of the IRA's military operations on its electoral support. Republican leaders began to look to negotiation rather than violence, signaling the beginning of the end for revolutionary Irish-American groups.

Cultural Nationalism

Cultural nationalism was originally born out of the loneliness of Irish immigrants who came together in social clubs and firefighting brigades, literary clubs, militia companies, and corner saloons. Older allegiances found expression in Irish neighborhoods in American cities through Kerry Patches, Donegal Squares, and Corkmen's Hollows. Meanwhile individuals tried, sometimes unsuccessfully, to establish literary communities for Irish-Americans. In 1848, Thomas D'Arcy McGee, another member of Young Ireland who had escaped after the rising, established a new *Nation,* but it was criticized by New York's Catholic bishop John Hughes. In 1868 he was assassinated by a Fenian in Ottawa for his involvement in Canadian politics. Meanwhile, in 1854 John Mitchel, an Irishman who had been imprisoned in a penal colony for comments made in the *United Irishman,* arrived in New York. Like McGee, he also brought out a newspaper, the *Citizen,* and encountered the New York bishop's enmity. In 1862 he returned to New York to publish the *Irish Citizen* but infuriated Fenians with his grandiloquent claims. John Boyle O'Reilly had more success. In 1869, O'Reilly, a convicted Fenian, arrived in Philadelphia after escaping from the British penal colony at Bunbury, Australia, via an American whaling ship. Within a few months of his arrival in Boston he had established himself as a lecturer, poet, and staff member of the *Boston Pilot.* By 1875 he had become editor and co-owned the paper with Archbishop John J. Williams.

In the early part of the twentieth century, Irish-American literary communities continued to take an interest in Irish events. American periodicals like the *Literary Digest* debated the issue of Home Rule. After the Easter Rising in Dublin in 1916, the *Washington Post* carried short biographical sketches of some of the known leaders and an analysis of the rebellion by Pádraic Colum, an Irish writer living in New York. The poet Eleanor Cox arranged a meeting of New York poets to express sympathy for the rebels and Irish Americans in New York, and the FOIF collaborated with Clan na Gael to set up an "Irish Bazaar" to welcome Irish refugees like Nora Connolly, daughter of the executed rebel James Connolly. The Colums brought out *The Irish Rebellion of 1916 and Its Martyrs,* a book of short portraits of the leaders of the Rising, and Marianne Moore, an American poet of Irish heritage, published a pro-republican poem, "Sojourn in the Whale," in 1917. Moore continued to promote Irish politics and culture when, editing the New York-based literary magazine *The Dial* from 1925–1929, she published original pieces by Irish and Irish-American writers, some of which had been banned by the Irish government. The 1920s also saw Irish writers such as James Joyce, Liam O'Flaherty, and Seán O'Faoláin turn to American publishers to publish their books that had been banned in Ireland. Irish-American sympathies had turned away from the newly established Sinn Féin government toward the individual Irish voice.

With successive generations, Irish Americans began to be incorporated further into mainstream American society: a trend reflected in the election of President John F. Kennedy in 1960. But this incorporation generated a desire on the part of cultural nationalists to try to recreate something of their ancestral homeland. They contributed to the growing popularity of university courses in Irish literature and history in the 1970s. Some cultural societies also encouraged a revival of interest in traditional music and the Irish language. This trend persists today, and Irish-American societies exist in many towns and cities, and university courses offer programs in Irish language, literature, and culture.

Constitutional Nationalism

The beginning of the Troubles in Ulster in 1968 meant the increase of political involvement by more moderate Irish Americans. Most supported Irish unification but disagreed with the violent tactics of the IRA. From the mid-1970s this view was represented by Irish-American senators Edward Kennedy and Daniel Moynihan, Speaker of the House Thomas "Tip" O'Neill, and Governor Hugh Carey of New York—known, somewhat ambiguously, as the "Four Horsemen" of Irish politics. In 1971, Senator Kennedy courted political controversy by demanding the immediate withdrawal of troops from Ulster. John Hume, of the Social Democratic and Labour Party (SDLP), contacted Kennedy to encourage him to adopt a more moderate approach. Ultimately the Four Horsemen, persuaded by such arguments, became a source of support for constitutional nationalism on Capitol Hill.

Throughout the 1970s and 1980s American political pressure continued to affect British policy in Northern Ireland. On Saint Patrick's Day 1977, the Four Horsemen issued the first of their annual joint statements, which they used to exert their influence in Washington to work for a new political initiative in Ulster. Then, in March 1981, the Four Horsemen formed the congressional group "Friends of Ireland." Its membership included some of the most powerful politicians in America and marginalized the influence of the more revolutionary agenda of the Ad Hoc Committee on Irish Affairs. Although both groups would work together on certain campaigns, for example working for the release of the Birmingham Six in the 1980s, the Friends' more moderate approach would win it considerable influence in American and Anglo-Irish political matters.

Indeed, the Friends proved instrumental in repairing Anglo-Irish relations in the 1980s and 1990s. When a November 1984 summit between Margaret Thatcher and Garret FitzGerald broke down, Fitzgerald's Irish government appealed to the Friends for assistance. The Friends in turn obtained Ronald Reagan's intervention, despite his close friendship with Thatcher, and Anglo-Irish discussions were resumed in January 1985. The Friends meanwhile helped block a potentially serious challenge to the forthcoming agreement from Fianna Fáil leader Charles Haughey. When the Anglo-Irish Agreement was signed in November, it represented not only a major achievement for Fitzgerald and the SDLP but also for the Friends. In 1989, the Ad Hoc Committee also achieved a degree of success when its "MacBride Principles Campaign," which won support from a wide spectrum of political groups, and pushed the British government toward reforming its fair employment legislation in Northern Ireland.

In the 1990s, Irish-American political groups also influenced U.S. policy concerning Northern Ireland. In April 1992, Bill Clinton pledged that if elected to the White House he would appoint a special envoy for Northern Ireland and grant a United States visa to Sinn Féin leader Gerry Adams. However during the first few months of his presidency, bowing to strong opposition from Unionists and the British government, Clinton shelved plans for a special envoy and refused Adams's plans for a U.S. book tour. Irish Americans were disgruntled, but they were able to use the events of 1993, beginning with the "blueprint for peace" drawn up by Gerry Adams and John Hume in April and the Downing Street Declaration of December, to drive home their advantage. Kennedy,

Moynihan, and others, acting on behalf of Hume, suggested to Clinton that progress might be made by offering Adams a visa. Despite strong opposition from the British government, U.S. Attorney General Janet Reno, and Secretary of State Warren Christopher, Clinton allowed Adams into New York for forty-eight hours to address the National Committee on American Foreign Policy. Andrew Wilson argues that "Adams' treatment as an international statesman in New York reinforced his position within the republican movement and helped generate greater momentum for peace." On August 31, 1994, the IRA announced a complete cessation of violence, at least partly in response to an Irish-American delegation led by Bruce Morrison, chairman of the lobbying group Americans for a New Irish Agenda, which pressed for an unconditional ceasefire. Irish-American politicians had clearly been instrumental in constructing and maintaining the foundations for peace.

Postscript: Finance, Fireworks, and Forgery

Between 1850 and 1900, steady collections of remittances were sent to families and Catholic parishes and institutions in Ireland. The Fenian Brotherhood also founded its own treasury to finance revolutionary work. In the 1880s, American contributions to Charles Stewart Parnell's Land League greatly advanced his drive to obtain land reform. Although Americans of many backgrounds gave money to Parnell's various funds, the actual subscription network was composed of immigrant Irish.

Irish-American aid peaked again following the beginning of the Troubles in Ulster in 1968. As Dennis Clark puts it in *Irish Blood,* the Irish looked to America once more because "the American connection was traditional—almost habitual." In 1968 the Irish-American republican George Harrison sent the first consignment of American rifles to Ireland: these were used during the sectarian riots of 1969. Then, in 1969, the Provisionals sent Seán Keenan to America to coordinate the gun-running network. In 1970, the Irish Northern Aid Committee (Noraid) was formed, which Wilson describes as the "most prominent and controversial militant nationalist group in America." Noraid's reports to the U.S. Justice Department indicate that it sent nearly $3 million to republican agencies in Ireland from 1971 to 1990. The Justice Department also claimed that unspecified amounts of larger sums had been sent secretly to the Provisional IRA. In 1977, the British government claimed that 80 percent of the IRA's weapons came from the United States; meanwhile, the Royal Ulster Constabulary released figures showing that American guns were used in 70 percent of Provisional IRA killings. American authorities acknowledged the problem but played down its significance.

Ironically, 1977 was also the year that the Four Horsemen of Irish-American politics issued a joint statement suggesting that grassroots approaches, such as economic investment, would be the best means of bringing peace to Ulster. Their attitude heralded a gradual decline in funding in the late 1970s and 1980s. The IRA turned to Eastern Europe and the Middle East for weapons. Nevertheless, American weaponry still played an important part. In the 1980s, the Irish-American republican network worked to develop weapons to help the IRA's new plan of trying to shoot down British helicopters. Meanwhile,

Irish-American republicans gave assistance to the IRA through other means. In 1983, Noraid started the first of its annual tours of Northern Ireland. Militant nationalist organizations also smuggled IRA fugitives into the United States. For example, in 1983 IRA inmates Jimmy Smyth, Pol Brennan, Kevin Barry Artt, and Terence Kirby escaped from the Maze Prison and were supplied with forged identities, employment, and housing. They established ordinary lives in California until the Federal Bureau of Investigation (FBI) caught up with them in 1992. Indeed, American financing still constituted a significant proportion of IRA funding until the cease-fire was declared on August 31, 1994.

More moderate Irish Americans, such as the congressional group Friends of Ireland, provided promises of financial assistance to speed up the peace process. During the Anglo-Irish discussions of February 1985, the leader of the Friends traveled to Dublin and gave assurances of U.S. financial support for a political settlement. Following the signing of the Anglo-Irish agreement in November 1985, the Friends ensured the continuation of American financial contributions to the International Fund for Ireland. House Speaker Thomas Foley also gave much-needed assistance. After the cease-fire of August 1994, President Bill Clinton announced that a package of $30 million would be given to the International Fund for Ireland and in December appointed an adviser for Economic Initiatives for Ireland. A major conference was held in Washington, D.C., in May 1995 to lure American businesses to Ulster, cementing a financial relationship between Northern Ireland and America that continues today.

Tara Stubbs

See also: CLINTON, William Jefferson; COLUM, Padraic; DAVITT, Michael; DEVOY, John; FENIANS; FORD, Patrick; HUGHES, Archbishop John; IRISH REPUBLICAN ARMY; IRISH REPUBLICAN BROTHERHOOD; KENNEDY FAMILY; MCGEE, Thomas D'Arcy; MITCHEL, John; MOORE, Marianne; MOYNIHAN, Daniel Patrick; NATIONALISM IN THE TWENTIETH CENTURY, IRISH AMERICAN; NATIVISM AND ANTI-CATHOLICISM; NORAID; O'MAHONY, John; O'NEILL, Thomas P. "Tip"; O'REILLY, John Boyle; PRESS, THE ETHNIC IRISH

References

Brown, Thomas. *Irish-American Nationalism 1870–1890.* New York: Lippincott, 1966.

Callan, Charles. *America and the Fight for Irish Freedom, 1866–1922.* New York: Devon Adair, 1957.

Carroll, F. M., *American Opinion and the Irish Question 1910–1923: A Study in Opinion and Policy.* Dublin: Gill & Macmillan, 1978.

Clark, Dennis J. *Irish Blood: Northern Ireland and the American Conscience.* New York: Kennikat, 1977.

Hackett, Francis. *Ireland: A Study in Nationalism.* New York: Huebsch, 1918.

Holland, Jack. *The American Connection.* Swords: Poolbeg, 1989.

Kenny, Kevin, ed. *New Directions in Irish-American History.* Madison: University of Wisconsin Press, 2003.

O'Clery, Connor. *The Greening of the White House: The Inside Story of How America Tried to Bring Peace to Ireland.* Dublin: Gill & Macmillan, 1996.

Wilson, Andrew. *Irish America and the Ulster Conflict 1968–1995.* Belfast: Blackstaff, 1995.

NATIONALISM IN THE TWENTIETH CENTURY, IRISH-AMERICAN

The story of Irish-American nationalism during the twentieth century encompasses a number of stages, with fluctuating fortunes that partially reflected the ebb and flow of Irish immigration to the United

States. The common academic diagnosis of "ethnic fade" offers only a superficial understanding of the internal trends that took place within this transatlantic connection and fails to explain the continued fascination that so many millions of Americans continue to have with the fate of their ethnic homeland. The continued relevance of Irish-American nationalism on both sides of the Atlantic is best explained as a deeply ingrained result of American ethnic pluralism itself, reflecting American influences nearly as much as Irish events.

The movement for Irish autonomy in the United States during the earliest years of the twentieth century was remarkably similar to that of its domestic counterpart in Ireland. Still recovering from the dashed hopes of Charles Parnell's Home Rule movement, most expatriate nationalists adopted the cultural and political arguments of their transatlantic counterparts during the first decades of the twentieth century. Militant republican groups like Clan na Gael continued to struggle with internal bickering and transatlantic feuds, while the growing emergence of middle-class leadership in Irish America helped to channel energies toward most "respectable" pursuits through organizations such as the American Irish Historical Society and American branches of the Gaelic League. The Irish-American entrance into the middle class also encouraged well-educated nationalists to combine the hopes for a free Ireland with a number of other well-heeled causes, such as the campaign for women's suffragism and anti-imperialist pursuits. When Padraig Pearse read his Declaration of an Irish Republic during the Easter Rising of 1916, few Irish Americans knew what to make of this seemingly futile effort.

The British treatment of these Irish rebels soon produced a unique moment of convergence among expatriate nationalists, however, much like in Ireland. The predominantly Catholic cause took on an ecumenical flavor, generating support from previously uninterested groups. While the most outspoken advocates of physical force found themselves constrained by state censorship after the United States entered World War I in 1917, other groups of activists rallied to the cause to protest the execution of the leaders of the Easter Rising and the brutal British reprisals during the ensuing Anglo-Irish War. Irish-American leaders gathered more than 5,000 delegates in Philadelphia in 1919 under the auspices of the Third Irish Race Convention, raising more than $1 million in pledges. The new-found spirit of unanimity was even more striking than the generosity, given a wide variety of attendees that included sympathetic Irish Protestants, members of U.S. Catholic hierarchy, and Clan na Gael militants. The convention also drew letters of support from nationalists in San Francisco and Butte, Montana, as well as institutional endorsements from nonethnic bodies like the American Federation of Labor.

This newfound cohesiveness was short-lived, however, and by the early 1920s the movement had splintered once again. The arrival of Eamon de Valera, the elected leader of the Irish Dáil, to lead a fund-raising campaign for the fledgling Republic started out with great fanfare. But de Valera soon became embroiled in a dispute with the elder leaders of Clan na Gael, who insisted that any American contributions should be used to secure official recognition of the Irish Republic by the U.S. government. When de Valera seemed to make public concessions about the complete independence of the newly formed Irish Republic, Judge Daniel F. Cohalan called together a group of approximately 100 fellow nationalists to unceremoniously request that de Valera return to Ireland. De Valera's stubborn refusal prompted the creation of separate and competing nationalist bodies: the American-led Friends of Irish Freedom (FOIF) and the pro–de Valera American Association for the Recognition of the Irish Republic (AARIR). The split even ran through the American Catholic clergy, and when both sides sent representatives to the Democratic and Republican national conventions during the summer of 1920, neither party even mentioned Irish freedom in their respective platforms. The subsequent controversy over the Anglo-Irish Treaty of 1921 only worsened matters. In 1922, Irish-American sympathizers were further frustrated and confused by an embarrassing spectacle when anti-treaty partisans launched an unsuccessful assault on the Irish Free State's consulate in New York City. American activism soon gave way to confusion and apathy, and by the end of the decade the only legacy of the once-spirited campaign was an ongoing legal battle between the FOIF and the AARIR over the money that had been raised during de Valera's contentious tour.

The onset of the Great Depression during the early 1930s continued this dispiriting trend, depleting the rolls and resources of even the most venerable Irish-American ethnic institutions. As transatlantic ties waned, the leadership of the movement passed into the hands of an increasingly shrill group of Anglophobes who targeted not only Britain but also the longest-running president in American history, Franklin Roosevelt. Driven to the political margins by waning interest in overseas events, the decimated leadership of Irish-American nationalist groups eventually pursued an association with the isolationist leadership of the America First organization.

The outbreak of European hostilities in 1939 soon produced a rallying cause for expatriate nationalists, but this effort was soon cut short by more immediate American concerns. When British Prime Minister Winston Churchill reacted to Ireland's refusal to budge from its prewar declarations of official neutrality, Eamon de Valera called to the remaining leadership of the AARIR to help protect Ireland against a possible British invasion. Irish-American leaders responded with impressive alacrity, reuniting the disparate branches of the movement in New York City under the new banner of the American Friends of Irish Neutrality. This time, however, Irish-American nationalists and Anglophobes encountered serious opposition from within their own ethnic circles. Within months a group of prominent Irish-American figures like boxer Gene Tunney and World War I hero William "Wild Bill" O'Donovan (the former commander of the famous "Fighting Irish" 69th Regiment) formed the American Irish Defense Association (AIDA), which called for increased direct assistance to Britain. The impact of a later congressional discovery that the AIDA received direct support from the Roosevelt administration in the fall of 1941 was soon muffled by the Japanese attack on Pearl Harbor. The ensuing sea change in American popular opinion even affected erstwhile supporters of Irish neutrality, who were now left with the embarrassing and nearly impossible task of explaining Ireland's stubborn neutrality to a frustrated and unsympathetic American public.

While Irish-American apologists were left to split hairs in their apology for Irish neutrality, a new generation of Irish-American leadership came of age during the war and achieved national prominence in the new battle against communism during the late 1940s. Stressing their Catholic, anticommunist credentials, the ethnic patriotism championed by dynamic young men like Jack Kennedy left little time for the continuation of the seemingly petty feuds of the Old World. Militant nationalists attempted to return to their Anglophobic appeals throughout the late 1940s and early 1950s. These leaders convened a series of annual Irish Race Conventions starting in 1947, but Irish-American attentions were elsewhere, and these partisans were faced with the daunting task of supporting claims that the Anglo-Irish struggle remained relevant with the new struggle against communism. The steadily diminishing circulation of the *Gaelic American* led to a reckless allegation in 1951 that Roosevelt had tricked the United States at the behest of the British Empire, and the ensuing furor over this claim only seemed to hasten the demise of this weekly after more than a half century of publication. Even mainstream Irish-American ethnic groups such as the Ancient Order of Hibernians reinvented themselves, stepping further away from the unseemly matter of Irish wartime neutrality. Abandoned by the Irish Republic as well as their upwardly mobile coethnics, the Anglophobes of the interwar era soon based their argument for continued relevance on the fortunes of doomed demagogues like General Douglas MacArthur and Senator Joseph McCarthy.

Combined with a sustained decline in Irish transatlantic migration during the mid-twentieth century, this dispiriting turn helped account for the pitiable state of the Irish-American nationalist movement when the modern-day Troubles emerged in the late 1960s. The outbreak of violence that greeted Northern Irish civil rights marchers during the mid-1960s (who incidentally modeled themselves on African-American leaders rather than their ethnic counterparts) quickly drew an emotional response from Irish America. Newsreels of violent attacks on Irish Catholic communities in Belfast and Derry provoked a mixture of outrage laced with guilt among later-generation ethnics, and American dollars flowed into the coffers of thinly disguised militant organizations.

Yet even American dollars could not bridge the generational divide between American ethnic nationalists and younger Irish activists. The gap soon created a telling moment in the transatlantic nationalist relationship when young Irish activist Bernadette Devlin visited the United States in 1969. Feted by Chicago Mayor Richard J. Daley during one fund-raiser, Devlin alleged that her host resembled her unionist opponents more than her fellow compatriots. As she professed an identification with the American radicals like those who had caused so much trouble in Daley's city the year before, Devlin charged that Irish-American leaders had taken on the role of reactionary oppressors. Faced with this divisive charge that seemed substantiated by radical republican identification with Marxist revolutionary rhetoric, many Irish-American nationalists soon grew estranged from the Irish republican cause, especially after the increasingly violent tactics adopted by the Irish Republican Army (IRA) by the mid-1970s.

Open support for militant nationalism receded to the marginalized ethnic neighborhoods of Boston, New York City, and other Irish-American urban areas. Meanwhile middle-class Irish Americans turned to the decidedly moderate leadership of the "Four Horsemen" (Daniel Patrick Moynihan, Hugh Carey, Thomas P. "Tip" O'Neill, and Ted Kennedy), all of whom marshaled their political energies to insist on the recognition of equal rights for Northern Irish Catholics at the same time as they decried IRA violence. Following in the footsteps of Irish-American cold warriors in the late 1940s, these moderates offered a respectable voice for the increasingly suburbanized, middle-class population of Irish America. Even the Hunger Strikers' protests in 1981 failed to substantially change Irish-American minds on the matter of Northern Ireland, apart from some emotional appeals immediately after the death of Bobby Sands. Ronald Reagan was left free to capitalize on his Irish-American ancestry without answering any challenges to his close cooperation with British Prime Minister Margaret Thatcher.

Nevertheless, the 1990s offered an epilogue to the story of Irish-American nationalism in the twentieth century, one that contradicted the notion that the passage of time had reduced this sentiment to entirely superficial importance. This episode came as part of the larger story of Sinn Féin's movement into the political arena, which drew particular assistance from Bill Clinton's pledge to allow Gerry Adams admission to the United States during the 1992 U.S. presidential campaign. Clinton's promise provoked vehement protests from the British diplomatic corps as well as indirect interference in the election by British Prime Minister John Major to aid Clinton's opponent, President George H. W. Bush.

Nevertheless, once elected, President Clinton followed through on this pledge, providing a transatlantic forum from which Adams could make the case for a republican nationalist movement that would be weaned from militarism. Adams's 1994 visit and subsequent American tours by other Sinn Féin leaders has been seen as encouraging the advocates of the IRA declaration of a unilateral ceasefire later that year.

In fact, this transatlantic influence has even extended into the twenty-first century. The terrorist attacks of September 11, 2001, in New York City soon cast republican resistance to complete disarmament in ominous light, even among Irish-American nationalists. Combined with allegations about collaboration between former IRA members and Marxist revolutionaries in Colombia, a large bank robbery in December 2004 that was assumed to be carried out by the IRA, and the murder of Robert McCartney shortly afterwards, the pressure exerted by Irish-American nationalists has been seen as an important force in convincing the IRA to announce a complete and permanent decommissioning of weaponry in August 2005.

Matthew J. O'Brien

See also: ANCIENT ORDER OF HIBERNIANS; CLINTON, William Jefferson; COHALAN, Daniel F.; DE VALERA, Eamon; KENNEDY, John Fitzgerald; IRISH REPUBLICAN ARMY; IRISH REPUBLICAN BROTHERHOOD; McCARTHY, Joseph; NATIONALISM, IRISH-AMERICAN; O'NEILL, Thomas P. "Tip"; PRESS, THE ETHNIC IRISH; TUNNEY, James Joseph "Gene"

References

Blessing, Patrick. "The Irish." In *The Harvard Encyclopedia of American Ethnic Groups,* edited by Stephen Thernstrom, 524–545. Cambridge, MA: Harvard University Press, 1980.

Carroll, Francis. *American Opinion and the Irish Question: A Study of Irish Opinion and Policy*. Dublin: Gill and Macmillan, 1978.

Clark, Dennis. *Erin's Heirs: Irish Bonds of Community*. Lexington: University of Kentucky Press, 1991.

Cuddy, Joseph. *Irish America and National Isolationism, 1914–1920*. New York: Arno, 1976.

Dwyer, T. Ryle. *Strained Relations: Ireland at Peace and the U.S.A. at War, 1941–1945*. Dublin: Gill and Macmillan, 1988.

Funchion, Michael, ed. *Irish-American Voluntary Organizations*. Westport, CT: Greenwood Press, 1983.

Kenny, Kevin. *The American Irish: A History*. New York: Pearson, 2000.

McCartan, Patrick. *With de Valera in America*. New York: Brentano, 1932.

Shannon, William. *The American Irish*. New York: Macmillan, 1963.

Wilson, Andrew. *Irish America and the Ulster Conflict, 1968–1995*. Washington, DC: Catholic University Press, 1995.

NATIVISM AND ANTI-CATHOLICISM

Nativism is a generic term for a cultural phenomenon, which though not particular to the nineteenth century and not restricted in its discrimination to just the Irish immigrants, certainly became defined by its response to the postfamine immigration of the peasant, pauperized Irish Catholics. Deriving from the term "native," nativisim essentially espouses an antiforeign sentiment that, for the American republic from the nineteenth century to the present day, manifests itself in public anti-immigration sentiment and certain anti-immigration policies. Begun as a reactionary response to the fears of the native population that they would be overrun by immigration, nativism, in fact, came to reveal itself in a number of similar recurring movements.

In 1798, faced with the problem, and fear, of mass immigration supplanting the "native" order (through wresting control of the public institutions) the Federalists, then in office, extended the term of residence before naturalization to 14 years. Once the Republicans—then seen as the party of the immigrant—were returned to office in 1801, they quickly repealed the law and reduced the term to five years. Thus began a debate over the rights of immigrants that would continue throughout the next century. By 1830, as the fledgling nation grew increasingly wary of the communion of church and state witnessed in the Catholic capitals of Europe, the "native" American spirit was fast becoming decidedly anti-Catholic. During the 1830s, a decade of increasing immigration and rising anti-immigrant feeling, the debate over immigrants' rights often descended into rioting and religious violence. In one incident in 1834, a convent was attacked and burned to the ground by "defenders of the Protestant faith."

Finally, in 1841, the American Republic Party, or, as it soon came to be called, the Native-American Party was founded (from which the term "nativism" comes) at a Louisiana State convention. The cardinal principles of the party were (1) to extend the term of naturalization to 21 years, (2) that the Catholic religion was dangerous to the country, (3) that the Protestant scriptures should be the foundation of all common-school education, and (4) to nominate no man to office who was not native born. At this stage, the party was still a secret order whose membership increased in fits and starts over the coming years, whenever the threat of immigration became public discussion; its members were often seen calling for the "No Catholic

Irish Ticket" at polls. As immigration numbers waned, however, the party's membership also fell off.

By the 1850s, immigration had begun to climb rapidly again—reaching almost the total number for the previous decade in just three years—and, driven by the fear of having their public and charitable institutions swamped by pauperized Catholics, the native population rushed to join this anti-Catholic movement. Also at this time, the arrival in America of Father Gavazzi, an apostate Barnabite Monk, marked the beginning of a new anti-papal crusade. He declared that Sisters of Charity were prostitutes the world over and that priests were given to every form of debauchery. Under his influence street preaching was revived, and by 1854 most major cities had an antipopery preacher holding forth from the street corners. This greatly increased the feeling of fear and resentment toward the new immigrants, particularly the Irish, and swayed many uncommitted Americans over to the side of the nativists.

In 1854, thanks in large part to its rapidly growing numbers, the organization declared itself publicly and politically as the Native-American party and, subsequently, carried elections in Massachusetts and Delaware, as well as securing congressmen elsewhere. At this time, it also got the name by which it became popularly known, "The Know-Nothings"—so-called because when members of the lower degrees were questioned about the Order's purpose their usual response was, "I don't know." The success of the Know-Nothing Party was short-lived, however, and after little more than two years, with the threat of immigration receding again, it had gone into decline.

From this point on, though often a party with little or no political strength, the Native American movement was recognized in the public arena and "nativism" became a byword for any and all anti-immigrant feeling. The postfamine period, which produced masses of brutalized Irish peasantry overloading the unskilled workforce and overcrowding the poorest quarters of the cities, crystallized for an American public the need for a nativist movement to regulate immigration and control the immigrants that had already arrived.

In fact, it was a move to control the immigrants that had already arrived that initiated the next significant, public display of nativism. In 1891, driven by the increasing election of immigrants to political office and the subsequent fear this produced in the native population, a lawyer from Maryland named Henry F. Bowers formed a new secret society—the American Protective Association—to protect the public institutions from being overrun by foreigners. This order most affected the Irish immigrants, as they constituted the main body of immigrants of this period, and as this new nativist movement perceived the biggest threat to American identity as coming from their Catholicism. Though it spread slowly, from 1893 to 1896 it gained and retained varying degrees of political influence in many states, from California to Massachusetts.

The main tenets of the American Protective Association were derived from the oath that the members of the order were bound to take and observe: first, that no member shall ever favor or aid the nomination, election, or appointment of a Roman Catholic to any political office; second, that he shall never employ a Roman Catholic in any capacity if a Protestant may be obtained to render the service required.

Though declaring publicly that the organization "attack(s) no man's religion so long as he does not attempt to make his religion an element of political power," it is clear from the secret oath that this was, in fact, a hypocritical statement and that the American Protective Association actively sought the elimination of any and all Catholic men from public office, solely on the grounds of their religion, and, further than this, actually sought to deny men and women gainful employment, again based solely on their religious preferences.

Due in large part to this order's vilification of the immigrant Irish on the grounds of their religion, racism directed against the Irish became refined to a particular, distinguishable aspect of their character, their Catholicism. This is evident in the large body of articles printed in political and popular journals—such as "The Irish Conquest of our Cities" (1894), "The Threatening Conflict with Romanism" (1894), and "The Irish in American Life" (1896)—which all associated the corrupting nature of Irish immigrants with their absolute devotion to the Catholic creed. As well as this, noted political cartoonists, such as Thomas Nast, depicted the miters of Catholic bishops as coming to life as crocodiles to devour children, an obvious allusion to what he saw as Catholicism's potential to corrupt the youth of America.

By 1896, the American Protective Association had begun to disappear from public and political life, emphasized by the failure of its representative in Congress, William S. Linton, to secure reelection. However, even though its reign was brief, it had, along with the earlier incarnations of nativist sentiment, bound forever nativism and anti-Catholicism as almost synonymous movements and had registered Catholicism as the identifiable nonnative characteristic of the immigrant Irish.

James P. Byrne

See also: CATHOLIC CHURCH, the

References
"American Protective Association." *Catholic Encyclopedia.* www.newadvent.org/cathen/01426a.htm (accessed November 26, 2003).
Coudert, Frederic R. "The American Protective Association." *Forum* (July 1894): 513–523.
Higham, John. *Strangers in the Land: Patterns of American Nativism, 1860–1925.* New York: Atheneum, 1963.
Lee, John Hancock. *The Origin and the Progress of the American Party in Politics.* New York: Books for Libraries Press, 1970.
"The Riotous Career of the Know-Nothings." *Forum* (July 1894): 524–537.

NEESON, LIAM (1952–)

Liam Neeson was born in Ballymena, Northern Ireland, in 1952. His interest in drama developed during his studies to become a teacher. In 1976, he joined the Belfast Lyric Players' Theatre and made his professional acting debut in the play *The Risen People* by Joseph Plunkett. In 1979, he joined the Abbey Theatre, Dublin, where he appeared in Brian Friel's *Translations.* He won the Best Actor Award at the Royal Exchange Theatre for his role in Seán O'Casey's *The Plough and the Stars.* In 1981, Neeson appeared in *Excalibur,* a film directed by John Boorman. Throughout the 1980s, he enjoyed steady work as a film actor, appearing in supporting roles in films such as *Krull* (1983), *The Bounty* (1984), and *The Mission* (1986). His breakthrough came when he appeared in a Broadway production of *Anna Christie* in 1992, for which he received a Tony Award nomination (1993). As well as receiving critical acclaim for his performance, Neeson met his

Actor Liam Neeson (center) on the set of Michael Collins *with Alan Rickman (left) and Aidan Quinn (right) in 1996. (Geffen/Warner Bros./The Kobal Collection)*

future wife Natasha Richardson during the production. His performance was also seen by Stephen Spielberg, who offered him the leading role in *Schindler's List* (1993). This role finally brought Neeson to the attention of the public. He was nominated for both an Academy Award and a Golden Globe for his performance. Neeson then took leading roles in two historical films, *Rob Roy* (1995) and *Michael Collins* (1996). In 1998 Liam starred as Jean Valjean in the screen adaptation of the Broadway hit *Les Miserables*. In 1999, he starred as a Jedi Knight in the *Star Wars* film *Episode One: The Phantom Menace*. Recent films include *Gangs of New York* (2002) and *Love Actually* (2003). He also starred in the 2002 revival of Arthur Miller's *The Crucible,* a performance that earned him a second Tony Award nomination for Best Actor.

Aoileann Ní Eigeartaigh

References

Klein, Fred, and Ronald Dean Nolen, eds. *The Macmillan International Film Encyclopaedia.* London: Macmillan, 2001.

Lalor, Brian, ed. *The Encyclopaedia of Ireland.* Dublin: Gill and Macmillan Ltd., 2003.

McRedmond, Louis, ed. *Modern Irish Lives.* Dublin: Gill and Macmillan Ltd., 1996.

Pettitt, Lance. *Screening Ireland: Film and Television Representation.* Manchester, UK: Manchester University Press, 2000.

Quinlan, David. *Quinlan's Illustrated Directory of Film Stars.* London: B. T. Batsford Ltd., 1996.

NEILSON, JOHN (CA. 1770–1827)

Born in Ballycarry, Co. Antrim, John Neilson served an apprenticeship with an architect in Belfast. The three Neilson/Nelson brothers became active in the United Irishman uprising: teenage Willie was hanged, and John and Sam were banished to the West Indies. Sam died en route; John escaped, to arrive in Philadelphia where in 1804 he was naturalized and was soon hired by President Thomas Jefferson.

Neilson oversaw the building plans at two of Jefferson's classical projects: Monticello, his home, and the University of Virginia where a Pantheon-like Rotunda heads a large quadrangle that is highlighted by spaced, two-story pavilions. Neilson's best efforts here are seen at Pavilions IX and X. Overall, his finest work is manifest at Upper Bremo plantation in nearby Fluvanna County, where Neilson's name as the architect is mentioned in the cornerstone.

Alongside fellow Antrim builder James Dinsmore, Neilson did considerable work at Montpelier, estate of President James Madison. On the grounds, they erected a domed garden temple, encircled with 10 unfluted Doric columns with bases, which support an entablature of triglyphs and unadorned metopes, with guttae below and dentil molding above. The design stems from that of the Temple of Venus at Versailles.

At his death, his effects included fiddle strings, a large library of classical and Restoration literature, many books on Irish culture, and his own paintings and architectural drawings. By the terms of his will, a "likeness" of Neilson was to have been sent to his Ballycarry widow, Mary. Another beneficiary was Mary Ann McCracken, "the friend of my family and sister of the late Henry Joy McCracken."

A cenotaph was erected in 1999 in Maplewood Cemetery in Charlottesville, Virginia, near the Vinegar Hill area where Neilson had lived. Among his several Irish friends in the community was the nephew of Robert Emmet, Professor John Patten Emmet, who had been appointed by Thomas Jefferson to the university faculty.

Kevin Donleavy

References
Durey, Michael. *Transatlantic Radicals and the Early American Republic.* Lawrence: University Press of Kansas, 1997.
Hume, David, ed. *The Broadisland Journal.* Vol. 3. Ballycarry: 1997.
Hume, David, ed. *The Broadisland Journal.* Vol. 5. Ballycarry: 1999.
Lay, K. Edward. *The Architecture of Jefferson Country.* Charlottesville: University Press of Virginia, 2000.
Madden, Richard R. *Antrim and Down in '98.* Glasgow: Cameron, Ferguson, 1844.

NELLIGAN, ÉMILE (1879–1941)

Born out of the union of a modest Irish postal employee, David Nelligan, and a French Canadian housewife, Émilie Amanda Hudon, in 1879, Émile Nelligan became over time the uncontested pillar around which French Canadian and later Quebecois poetry flourished. Influenced by Paul Verlaine, Charles-Pierre Baudelaire, and Edgar Allan Poe, he was in many ways closer to John Keats, as his best and most voluminous work was written within a very short period when he was 17 to 19 years old.

As his name illustrates, the Irish community in Quebec was well integrated into the host French-Canadian society. Being a poor student, Nelligan had embarked on a poetic career by the age of 16. By 17, he had already gained some notoriety; as a result of this, he was accepted by l'École littéraire de Montréal, where he became very quickly their best and most noted poet. His bohemian lifestyle led also to the mysticism of his poetry.

Before Nelligan, French Canadian poetry relied heavily on the picturesque, on substantive realistic themes, which left very little to the imagination. Nelligan introduced the aesthetic of symbolism that projected and explored the imaginative world. With Nelligan, French-Canadian poetry and Canadian poetry in general became highly acclaimed. Unfortunately, one of the reasons Nelligan wrote with such intensity is because he suffered from a degenerative mental illness, which was diagnosed when he was 20.

From the age of 20, Nelligan was committed by his father to various mental institutions, until his death in 1941. Even though his productive years were very short, his reputation as Quebec's most influential poet has grown over the years. In 1979 le prix Émile Nelligan—Quebec's most prestigious poetry award—was established, for young poets under the age of 35. As is the case for all distinguished people of Irish descent, there is a plaque in Montreal's Saint Patrick Basilica commemorating the life and genius of Émile Nelligan. "Ah! Comme la neige à neigé!"

Donald Cuccioletta

See also: MONTREAL, QUEBEC CITY

Reference

Nelligan, Émile. *Poésies Complètes (1896–1899)*. Montreal: Fides, 1952.

NEW BRUNSWICK

During the nineteenth century, the Irish contribution to the Canadian province of New Brunswick was immense: the Irish became the largest ethnic group and, proportionately, New Brunswick was the most Irish province in British North America. One of the proposed names for the province (created in 1784) was "New Ireland."

There were several waves of Irish immigration to New Brunswick. The Irish were among the very sparse and scattered settlers in the seventeenth century, when the region was still part of Nova Scotia. Overall, numbers were bolstered significantly when the Loyalists arrived during and after the American War of Independence; some of the Loyalists who fled the 13 colonies had Irish surnames. Many more came from Ireland after the Napoleonic Wars ended in 1815. Initially, most of the Irish migrated as families but many more individuals came in the 1820s and 1830s. Before the 1840s most Irish immigrants were skilled Protestants from the northern counties.

The largest single influx was from 1845 to 1854, during the Potato Famine: many of those who arrived were sick and impoverished. In 1847 alone approximately 2,000 died en route while another 15,000 sought entry through the port of Saint John. The local population was just over 30,000. The province was ill prepared for the onslaught and overwhelmed by it. During the 1840s most of those who arrived were poor Catholics from Ireland's south and west.

The Loyalists are credited as founding New Brunswick, but the Irish are recognized for building it. The Irish provided much of the workforce for the province's major industries, whether in timber, the docks, foundries, mills, shipyards or railways. A large number became farmers, and New Brunswick had the reputation as "a good poorman's country." To a lesser extent they distinguished themselves in the professions. Many of the children of the first settlers became prominent in the political, religious, and economic life of the province.

Several used New Brunswick as an entry point for other destinations, notably the United States. Those who stayed developed Irish religious institutions and Irish national societies. The Irish in New Brunswick were diverse: there were significant differences based on religion, skill set, place of origin, and where they settled. Just as in their homeland, denominationalism proved a source of conflict in New Brunswick. This is especially true of the 1840s when Irish Catholics began to swamp the Irish Protestants who had arrived earlier. By 1871 the Irish of New Brunswick numbered 100,000 out of a total population of 285,000 (35.2 percent). The majority lived in the main urban center, Saint John, which still claims to be the most Irish city in Canada. Many settled on the Miramichi, with various other pockets around the province. Catholics tended to predominate in the cities and the north shore while southwestern New Brunswick was mostly "Orange territory" with a sizable Irish Catholic population. There are many Irish place names in New Brunswick.

By 1941 (the last census to deal with the Irish as a distinct ethnic group), those of Irish birth or descent had dropped to 20 percent of the population. The reasons for this have yet to be studied. It may be a reflection of the high degree of intermarriage and assimilation of Irish Protestants with the English and Scots. The Irish Catholics retained their ethnicity to a greater degree.

The study of the Irish in New Brunswick is still in its infancy. This is one reason for the formation of the Irish Canadian Cultural Association of New Brunswick (ICCANB) in 1983. Its mission is to commemorate and celebrate the very significant Irish contribution in New Brunswick. Its six chapters undertake various projects such as Heritage Parks at Partridge Island, Middle Island, and Hospital Island, and the Belfast children's vacation. The ICCANB works closely with the popular Miramichi Irish Festival as well.

Cheryl Fury

See also: AMERICAN WAR OF INDEPENDENCE; EMIGRATION

References

Houston, Cecil J., and William J. Smyth. "New Brunswick and Irish Shipping: The Commissioning of the *Londonderry,* 1838." *Acadiensis* 16, no. 2 (1987): 95–106.

Mannion, John J. *Irish Settlements in Eastern Canada: A Study of Cultural Transfer and Adaptation.* Toronto: University of Toronto Press, 1974.

O'Driscoll, Robert, and Lorna Reynolds, eds. *The Untold Story: The Irish in Canada.* 2 vols. Toronto: Celtic Arts of Canada, 1988.

Toner, P. M., ed. *New Ireland Remembered.* Fredericton, New Brunswick: New Ireland Press, 1988.

Toner, P. M. "The Origins of the New Brunswick Irish, 1851." *Journal of Canadian Studies* 23 (1988):104–119.

NEW IRISH IN AMERICA

The roots of the so-called "New Irish" migration extend to the international economic recession of the late 1970s and early 1980s, which drove Irish unemployment to record levels. Faced with few prospects at home, young Irish men and women turned to overseas opportunities once again. But this outflow seemed to be qualitatively different from the "push forces" that drove out earlier generations, as most commentators shared the perception that these latest émigrés were better educated and more personally ambitious than earlier leavers. Whether

NEW IRISH IN AMERICA 665

it was the fiscal conservatives bemoaning the lost fruits of Ireland's recently expanded educational system, or career politicians who meant to reassure the parents of emigrants by attributing the outflow to wanderlust, there was a general consensus that the emigrants of the 1980s were qualitatively different than their predecessors.

The novelty of the New Irish was much less apparent to the later-generation ethnics on the other side of the Atlantic, however. Irish Americans saw these immigrants as the latest installment in their proud tradition of immigrant contributors to the United States. Projecting their ethnic notions of the past onto this new influx, they eagerly welcomed the new arrivals as a much-needed infusion of new blood into their graying community.

The true significance of this inflow defied both sets of expectations, however. The disproportionately well-educated outflow of the mid-1980s soon gave way to a more balanced exodus by the later years of that decade. Driven underground by their undocumented status, many New Irish immigrants set aside their educational qualifications to follow their predecessors with manual positions in familiar fields such as construction and bartending. On the other hand, most New Irish migrants resisted the invitation to take their places in traditional Irish-American institutions and instead formed their own groups to assert their more contemporary view of Irish identity.

The struggle over naturalization initially papered over this division between immigrants and ethnics during the late 1980s and early 1990s. The 50-year hiatus in Irish immigration to the United States occasioned significant changes in American immigration policy that effectively denied legal residency for most of the New Irish.

After an initial outburst of frustration with allegedly complacent Irish-American ethnic institutions, a new generation of Irish activists formed their own lobbying groups, such as the Irish Immigration Reform Movement (IIRM) and the Emerald Isle Immigration Center. The generational difference between young immigrants and older ethnics also manifested itself in the cultural expressions of New Irish immigrants, many of whom resisted and criticized ethnic views of Ireland as outdated and patronizing. This friction even broke out in public by the early 1990s with the highly charged controversy between the Irish Lesbian and Gay Organization and the Ancient Order of Hibernians regarding inclusion in the Saint Patrick's Day parade during the early 1990s. Instead of new blood, Irish-American leaders found themselves presented with new wine, which would not be easily contained in the old skins of their ethnic institutions.

Nevertheless, the political acumen of the New Irish leaders soon led them to cooperate with the more experienced Irish-American lobby, and intergenerational tensions gave way to interagency cooperation in the campaign to secure entrance visas for the estimated 40,000 undocumented immigrants living subterranean lives in the United States. IIRM activists often adopted the rhetorical appeal advanced by their ethnic hosts, presenting the New Irish as young men and women who were willing to give up their old life to pursue their ambitions in the Land of Opportunity, much like their predecessors had done during the late nineteenth and early twentieth centuries, helping to build the United States along the way. The campaign combined youthful energy with political sagacity to convince the United States Congress to set aside special visas for Irish applicants. This effort reached its apex in 1994 with the special recognition afforded to Irish applicants in the Diversity Visas program, which set aside 40,000 slots for would-be registrants from the Republic of Ireland.

Ironically, the realization of these American dreams during the mid-1990s coincided with a domestic trend in the Republic of Ireland that rendered such political achievements anticlimactic. The emergence of the "Celtic Tiger" during the early 1990s soon stifled the net outflow from Ireland. Continued growth actually reversed migratory trends, and there was consistent net immigration during the rest of the decade. While many young Irish men and women continued to leave the Republic, their travels were now much more temporary: aimed at garnering professional experience in white-collar fields, rather than securing a permanent home and career in North America or elsewhere. The demand for American entrance visas soon slackened among the New Irish in the United States, and many visa holders, including one of the cofounders of the IIRM, actually returned to the Republic after securing a green card through the legalization programs.

While the Irish commentators of the 1980s focused on the highly qualified backgrounds of recent migrants, and the Irish Americans of the early 1990s characterized Irish arrivals through their untraditional assertiveness, these attributes are best seen as reflections of the redefinition of the Irish migration experience by the New Irish. This new understanding of the transatlantic passage as transitory movement rather than permanent resettlement has shaken Irish nationality at home as well as expatriate ethnicity in the United States, providing a momentous point of departure in the ongoing relationship between these two communities.

Matthew J. O'Brien

See also: ANCIENT ORDER OF HIBERNIANS; SAINT PATRICK'S DAY PARADES

References
Almeida, Linda Dowling. *Irish Immigrants in New York City, 1945–1995.* Bloomington: University of Indiana Press, 2001.
Corcoran, Mary. *Irish Illegals: Transients between Two Societies.* Westport, CT: Greenwood Press, 1993.
Kenny, Kevin. *The American Irish: A History.* New York: Pearson, 2000.
O'Hanlon, Ray. *The New Irish Americans.* Niwot, CO: Roberts Rinehart, 1998.
Sexton, J. J. "Recent Changes in the Irish Population and the Pattern of Emigration." *Irish Banking Review* (Autumn 1987): 45–54.

NEW JERSEY

The Irish have been traced to the earliest days in the history of New Jersey following its establishment as a colony in 1664. Throughout the seventeenth century, individual Irish skilled workers came to New Jersey and settled there. Immigration to the state at this time was not confined to the Scots-Irish or Ulster Protestants but drew from all those living in Ireland. In spite of this, Catholics were barred from holding public office by the state constitution of 1776. It was only with the drawing up of a new constitution in 1844 that this prohibition was removed. In the 1790 census, 11 percent of the white population was counted as being either Irish or Scots-Irish, and the majority came from Ulster. Compared with a state like Pennsylvania, this number was quite small. However, the Scots-Irish in particular were to play an important role in the Revolutionary War with Britain and many of them occupied important positions in George Washington's army.

It was with the Great Famine that the Irish really became a visible and tangible presence in New Jersey life; the largest influx of Irish took place during the 1840s. Unlike before, the majority of Irish immigrants at this time were Catholic and from rural Ireland. This led to more than 31,000 Irish, out of a total number of immigrants of 56,000, settling in New Jersey. In 1870, out of a total population of nearly one million in New Jersey, more than 80,000 had been born in Ireland. In 1900, 94,848 people in New Jersey had been born in Ireland. New Jersey's proximity to New York, the principal port of entry to America, combined with the fact of a high demand for labor, motivated many to settle there. While many of the women were employed as domestic servants, there were high numbers of Irish men constructing canals and railroads as well as working in the textile mills in Paterson. Among these immigrants in Paterson an organization was formed called the Friends of Ireland. This group campaigned for Catholic Emancipation in Ireland and the abolition of slavery in the District of Columbia. However, with increasing Irish immigration to New Jersey, tensions increased between the Irish and the native population and clashes frequently broke out between them. In opposition to the Know-Nothing Party, which campaigned against immigration, the Irish supported the Democratic Party, which rewarded them with positions.

With the increase in immigration from Italy and Eastern Europe the status of the Irish slowly began to change. Soon the Irish became identified with positions of power in local government. "Little Bob" Davis of Jersey City, "Big Jim" Smith of Newark, Thomas McCran of Paterson, and Frank Hague of Jersey City controlled political machines that dominated local politics. The fact that the Irish had a long presence in New Jersey, spoke English, and were used to political deal making in the Democratic Party meant that they were readily suited for this system. From 1917 to 1947, Mayor Frank Hague of Jersey City ran Hudson County. Born in 1876, he had risen through local politics in city hall to become mayor. He appealed to the Catholic sensibilities of the voters and was courted by both priests and state politicians. His slate for the city commission never changed and always consisted of five Irishmen—four Catholics, and one Protestant. He resigned in 1947, and, in a move that smacked of nepotism, he handed power to his nephew, Frank Hague Eggers. Two years later, Eggers was defeated by an anti-Hague ticket supported by more recent immigrants. This symbolized the end of untrammeled Irish dominance of local politics in the city. With the rise in living standards among the Irish, they began to move out of the cities and to the suburbs after World War II. This upward movement was symbolized by the fact that from 1961 to 1970 the governor of New Jersey was Richard Hughes, who was the grandchild of an emigrant from County Clare who had first arrived in New Jersey in 1856.

David Doyle

NEW ORLEANS

The majority of academic histories of Irish immigrants to North America focus on the major cities of the East Coast and New England. However, the Irish immigrant experience does not conform to one uniform pattern and the story of the Irish experience in New Orleans provides an important counterpoint to the dominant narratives of the Irish in New York City, Philadelphia, and Boston. The Irish settled in Louisiana in the French colony's founding years and this early presence included military mercenaries, trappers, scouts, and transatlantic slave traders. During the Spanish phase of colonial rule, Irish priests were sent to Louisiana to minister to the region's growing English-speaking Catholic population, and Irish-born Alejandro (Alexander) O'Reilly ruled as governor.

In the opening three decades of the nineteenth century, many of the Irish immigrants arriving in New Orleans belonged to the professional or merchant class. Irish teachers, lawyers, doctors, architects, and printers practiced throughout Louisiana. Many Irish in the city of New Orleans managed boardinghouses, hotels, and other small businesses, while others, such as John McDonogh, became cornerstones of the city's slave-owning plantocracy. These new arrivals helped establish the Crescent City's first Saint Patrick's Day celebration in 1809 and founded Saint Patrick's Church, the city's second Catholic parish, on Camp Street in 1834.

The major infusion of Irish, however, came after 1830, especially after the potato blight of the 1840s. By 1860 the Irish in New Orleans numbered more than 24,000, about one-fourteenth of the city's total population. As the largest port city in the American South, and the second largest in the United States, New Orleans offered Irish immigrants the opportunity of plentiful food, a great variety of employment, and a much quicker and cheaper route to the interior, via the Mississippi River, than overland from New York, Boston, or Baltimore. Many of these new Irish arrivals in the Crescent City were employed building roads, levees, canals, and railroads. They also labored on the docks and warehouses, coming into direct competition with and often replacing African-American workers, both free and slave, in a number of waterfront trades. Mid-nineteenth-century Irish waterfront workers in New Orleans lived in a neighborhood known as the Irish Channel District, several blocks of streets bounded by the Mississippi River in the city's lower Garden District. The area was allegedly controlled by a variety of gangs and contained some of the city's most notorious brothels and saloons.

New Orleans's reputation as the necropolis of the New World was well-earned, and repeated disease outbreaks in the 1840s and 1850s claimed the lives of thousands of Irish victims already drained by earlier trials in their diaspora journey. New Irish arrivals also suffered high rates of mortality because of their dangerous work. The Irish builders of the New Basin Canal, which connected the downtown American sector of New Orleans with Lake Pontchartrain, often labored in water up to their hips and were susceptible to typhus, malaria, and cholera. A Celtic Cross Monument was erected in 1990 by the Irish Cultural Society of New Orleans to honor an estimated 30,000 Irishmen who died while digging the New Basin Canal.

Many young Irish women who migrated to New Orleans in the mid-nineteenth century worked as domestic servants. The most celebrated Irish female immigrant of this era was entrepreneur and philanthropist Margaret Haughery. Earning her reputation as a businesswoman through the success of her bakery, Haughery also helped establish and maintain several charitable institutions in the city, including the New Orleans Female Orphan Asylum and the Poydras Orphan Asylum. Known throughout the city by her nickname "the bread woman of New Orleans," or more simply as "Margaret," Haughery was commemorated by a statue erected in 1884, one of the first in North America to honor a woman. It stands in a small park two blocks away from the Ogden Museum of Southern Art on Camp Street.

During the Civil War, large numbers of New Orleans Irish joined the Confederate ranks in defending the institution of slavery, forming volunteer companies and regiments, such as the "Louisiana Irish." Irish immigration to New Orleans dramatically declined in the post–Civil War period and the distinctive Irish-born community was gradually replaced by a more anonymous white Southern identity, an ethnic transformation facilitating substantial political and economic gains from African Americans in the city after Reconstruction.

Irish culture in New Orleans in the late twentieth and early twenty-first century was most visibly expressed in community festivals and parades, most notably those held in the Irish Channel on Saint Patrick's Day. The city's commodity culture and tourist economy also evidence a strong Irish theme by the numerous Irish-named public houses, such as Pat O'Brien's in the French Quarter, which serves the celebrated Hurricane drink, and the Irish Shop of New Orleans on Toulouse Street.

Stephen C. Kenny

References

Niehaus, Earl F. *The Irish in New Orleans, 1800–1850.* Baton Rouge: Louisiana State University Press, 1965.

Roediger, David R. *The Wages of Whiteness: Race and the Making of the American Working Class.* London: Verso, 1999.

NEW YORK CITY

Introduction

By the late nineteenth century, both the number of Irish in New York and their cultural presence exceeded that of any city in the world, even Dublin. By 1890 not only did the Irish-born population of New York exceed that of both Belfast and Dublin, but their cultural intrusion had been felt to such a degree in the city that both high and popular culture had recognized and responded to their presence: by 1842 one of the more popular attractions in Phineas T. Barnum's American Museum, on the corner of Broadway and Printing House Row, was a scale model of Dublin; by 1861 New York's great poet, Walt Whitman, had included a poem to "Old Ireland" in his homage to American culture, *Leaves of Grass.*

Early Irish Involvement in New York

The Irish presence in New York began almost with the origin of the city itself. In 1638, when it was still simply a trading post of the Dutch West India Company, Irish men were listed among its employees stationed in New Amsterdam. In 1683, Irish Catholic Thomas Dongan's appointment as governor of the colony of New York (renamed after the Duke of York) would be the first occurrence of Irish involvement in the city's municipal government, an involvement that would later come to characterize the Irish immigrant experience in New York and America. A native of Co. Kildare, Dongan brought both progressive reform (in the "Charter of Libertyes") and public Catholic worship to New York (celebrating the first public Mass, in Fort James on October 30, 1683).

His plans to bring colonists from Ireland never materialized; in 1688 he was removed from office, and in 1689 he fled the anti-Catholic backlash consuming New York. Irish immigration to New York would continue to be largely Protestant and numerically insignificant well into the next century.

The Irish presence in New York began to resurface publicly in the latter half of the eighteenth century. On March 17, 1762, a group of Irish-born soldiers staged an impromptu march through the streets of colonial New York and, thus, initiated a celebration that would become the largest public display of ethnic identity in the United States in the next two centuries: New York's Saint Patrick's Day Parade. In 1784, James Duane, the son of an Irish immigrant, became the first mayor of New York City. The opening of Saint Peter's Church on Barclay Street in 1786 marked the resurgence of Catholicism within the city. The failed Irish Rising of 1798 sent a number of political exiles, such as Thomas Addis Emmet, William Sampson, and William MacNeven, to New York; their arrival would precipitate the rise of Irish nationalism in the city and the country. In 1803, De Witt Clinton, the son of an Ulster immigrant, became first mayor (1803–1815) and then governor of New York (1817–1832, 1825–1828); he oversaw the building of the Erie Canal and ushered in New York as the commercial capital of the United States. By 1810, the first weekly Irish paper, *The Shamrock,* or *Hibernian Chronicle,* had appeared in the city to comment on life for the Irish immigrants in America and the continuing struggle for independence in Ireland.

After the Napoleonic Wars, Irish immigration to New York not only increased significantly in numbers but also showed a marked change in religious denomination, shifting from the primarily Protestant emigration of the previous century to a more Catholic exodus. By 1815, New York had a bishop and its second church, Saint Patrick's on Mott Street; a Catholic population of about 15,000 centered in the neighborhoods around the two churches. In just 10 years the numbers of Irish in the state swelled to 100,000, most of them poor laborers who found work in the city or on the Erie Canal. This increase in numbers excited anti-Irish and anti-Catholic feeling among the predominantly Protestant population of the city. Initially tame, Anglo-American nativist demonstrations grew more serious as the Irish community increased. Disturbances began to escalate soon after Catholics were legally allowed to hold elective office in the state (1806), and clashes were often most severe around symbolic edifices or days. On July 12, 1824, Orangeman's Day, a serious clash occurred in the Irish enclave of Greenwich Village; while in 1831 Saint Mary's on Grand Street in the Lower East Side was destroyed by arson.

Violent anti-Catholic and anti-Irish demonstrations were a sporadic feature of the early 1800s, as the city continued to expand to accommodate the "new" immigrants. In 1842, John Hughes, an immigrant from Co. Tyrone, became bishop of New York and began to organize the Catholic Irish into a politically distinctive and powerful voting bloc. Using similar organizational techniques to those of Daniel O'Connell in Ireland, Hughes molded the various Irish communities from Vinegar Hill to the Five Points into a significant political unit that could agitate for Catholic advancement. He oversaw a significant increase in the number of Catholic churches in New York and the erection of a spectacular new Saint Patrick's Cathedral on Fifth Avenue, and he was instrumental in creating a Catholic parochial school system (paid for by Catholic parishioners) and the founding of Fordham University and Mount St. Vincent College. By 1850, reflecting both the importance of New York to the Vatican and Hughes' impressive achievements, the city was picked to be an archdiocese and Hughes was appointed its first archbishop.

The Famine Immigrants and Beyond

Hughes's growing power coincided with the Great Famine and the subsequent massive Irish Catholic immigration to North America and New York. Fleeing the devastation in Ireland, the famine immigrants poured into New York, for a time radically altering its demographic makeup. Not only did they arrive in numbers far exceeding those of any previous immigration, but they were also, in general, much more destitute than their predecessors. They soon overwhelmed charitable organizations, such as the Irish Emigrant Society (1841), which had been established to aid them. In 1855, in an effort to regulate immigrant reception, Castle Garden was converted into the Emigrant Landing Depot. Coming into the city, these largely destitute Irish immigrants found work in the lowest positions, often displacing African Americans. By 1855, Irish immigrants accounted for 87 percent of New York's unskilled laborers. The famine immigrants also found themselves living in the poorest sections of the city, such as the Five Points, alongside and in competition with African Americans. This proximity would create harmony as well as discord, and American tap dance is reckoned to have originated from the fusion of Irish and African dance styles in the Five Points area.

As the century progressed, however, New York would grow more ethnically diverse and more socially disharmonious. Fear that the Catholic Irish could wrest control of municipal and federal institutions led to the public and political success of the Native American party or the Know-Nothing Party in 1854. This fear also led to anti-Irish riots on the streets as part of the larger recurrence of social unrest throughout the 1840s and 1850s. To support their anti-Irish platform nativists would point to Fernando Wood's (and later William Tweed's) manipulation of the large Irish voting bloc to gain power and, subsequently, corrupt public and city charters for personal ends. They also pointed to the Irish reputation for violence and criminality; in one citation 59 percent of all people arrested in New York City in 1859 were Irish.

By the beginning of the Civil War, in 1861, almost a quarter of the city's population was Irish. Unlike their Irish hero, O'Connell, they were probably largely anti-abolitionist and, as such, held mixed views about the impending conflict. However, once the war began, they volunteered in large numbers, seeing it as their duty to help preserve the Union. An estimated 51,000 Irish volunteered from New York State, the majority serving under either Col. Michael Corcoran in the 69th Regiment or Thomas Francis Meagher (an exiled Young Ireland leader) in an Irish Brigade. They joined for many reasons—to repudiate nativist charges that they were unworthy of citizenship, to strike a blow against the English (as the supposed ally of the Confederate "cotton lords"), or simply for the adventure—but they fought and died as heroes of the Union.

However, as the war progressed and the casualties mounted, initial Irish enthusiasm quickly began to wane. With the passing of the federal Conscription Act by Congress in March 1863, the Irish thought that in effect they were being victimized by the government. When the first list of draftees was posted on Saturday, July 11, in the uptown Ninth District of New York, it became clear that the Irish wards would supply the largest numbers of recruits. By Monday, when the draft office reopened, resentment had grown into anger and, led by the Black Joke Volunteer Fire Company, the gathered crowd attacked and destroyed the office. Over the next three days, New York City fell into anarchy, and the worst destruction was visited on those who could do least to defend themselves—African Americans. The chief part played by the Irish in the Draft Riots would undo a lot of the goodwill generated toward them by their impressive service and immense sacrifice in the Civil War.

The failure of the 1848 Rising in Ireland had resulted in a number of important Irish nationalists being exiled in New York: Michael Doheny, John Mitchel, John O'Mahony, and Thomas Francis Meagher, among others. With the end of the Civil War, their thoughts turned once again to Irish freedom. The Fenian Brotherhood, a secret society that had been formed in 1859 for the purpose of bringing about a revolution in Ireland, now turned its thoughts toward invading Canada as a way of involving America in a war with England. Beginning in 1866, many New York Civil War veterans became involved in a series of minor and unsuccessful raids in Canada. After another failed rebellion in Ireland in

1867 and the exile of two prominent nationalist leaders to New York—Jeremiah O'Donovan Rossa and John Devoy—the Fenian movement was reorganized and remerged as Clan na Gael. After his arrival in New York in 1871, Devoy emerged as the dominant leader of Irish nationalist politics in America. He founded two newspapers, the *Irish Nation* (1882) and the *Gaelic American* (1903) and, along with Michael Davitt, began the shift in the Irish and Irish-American national movement to the "New Departure"—an informal alliance among constitutional and physical force nationalists to work together peacefully under the leadership of Charles Stewart Parnell.

Postbellum New York witnessed the rise of the Irish in Democratic politics. While "Boss" Tweed had used the Irish vote to win power, privilege, and wealth for himself, after the Civil War the Irish emerged to take over the reigns of the "Tammany machine" and, through it, to manipulate the Democratic politics in New York. With "Honest" John Kelly's ascension to Tammany "boss" in 1872, control of Tammany Hall in New York fell into Irish hands and remained there well into the twentieth century, producing such renowned New York figures as "Commissioner" Murphy, Jimmy Walker, and Al Smith. While infamous for its corruption, Tammany provided the Irish immigrants with a way out of the slums and into civil service and public employment. In 1880 New York elected its first Irish Catholic mayor, William R. Grace, and by the turn of the century the Irish were well on the rise out of the ghettos and into the parlors of middle-class New York.

With Irish female immigration equaling and even, at times, exceeding Irish male immigration to the United States, Irish women were a major part of New York's Irish population; by the turn of the century almost 60 percent of Irish immigrants would be female, and most of these would come through New York. On January 1, 1892, Annie Moore, an emigrant from Cork, was the first immigrant to set foot on New York's new federal immigration facility, Ellis Island. Domestic service offered the best opportunity for employment for Irish women in New York; by 1855 almost three quarters of all domestics in New York City were Irish. However, women were also employed outside the home, primarily in the "needle trades," and they were often deeply involved in union and political organizations. In 1880 Fanny and Anna Parnell (sisters of Charles Stuart Parnell) formed the New York Branch of the Ladies' Irish National Land League, in support of the Land League movement in Ireland. The Ladies' Land League Association, as it became known, quickly spread across the country and even into Ireland in 1881. Although its tenure would be brief, the Ladies' Land League was a stepping-stone to further involvement for Irish American women in political and labor organizations. By the twentieth century, Irish-American women like Elizabeth Gurley Flynn (who ran as a Communist candidate for New York State representative) would become organizers and leading figures in New York labor and political movements, formerly exclusively male domains.

The Irish in Twentieth-Century New York

By the early twentieth century, the New York Irish were moving from the margins to the mainstream of society and involving themselves in culture and sport. In 1897,

Celtic Park was opened in Queens, New York; it offered a combination of track, field, and traditional Gaelic sports. By the start of World War I, the Gaelic Athletic Association was organized in the city, and it continues to operate as an active organization in the city to this day. Cultural perception of the New York (and American) Irish was influenced by theatrical representations of the Irish by playwrights such as Dion Boucicault (who took his major plays to New York) and Edward Harrigan and Tony Hart (whose *The Mulligan Guard Ball,* in 1879, was one of the first plays to show the Irish Americans in their urban environment); by popular Irish character actors from Tyrone Power to James O'Neill; and by popular Irish performers such as Chauncey Olcott and John McCormack. By the 1920s, with F. Scott Fitzgerald's celebration as a great American writer, the second- and third-generation New York Irish were acknowledging themselves and being acknowledged as American.

Two wars would clarify this for them: World War I and the Irish War of Independence. Although the New York Irish would again involve themselves in large numbers in a war not of their making, they would do so as American soldiers and not as Irishmen trying to affirm their American identity. While the New York Irish still joined the 69th Regiment of New York—now a nationally renowned fighting unit—in large numbers, they did so now more for local pride than for ethnic validation. The War of Independence, in certain ways an opportunistic endeavor on the part of the Irish (to rise up against the English while their forces were engaged in a major conflict in Europe), certainly energized the exiled nationalists in New York: John Devoy and Judge Cohalan formed the Friends of

Irish Freedom (to gather American support for Irish Independence) at the first Irish Race Convention of March 4–5, 1916, just weeks before the Easter Rising. New York–born Irishman Eamon de Valera, whose death sentence was commuted because of his American citizenship, would go on to head the Irish Free State and become the most prominent figure in Ireland and Irish politics for the next half century.

While de Valera was making history in Ireland, the New York Irish had their own "Irish" political figure to rally around: Al Smith. Born in 1873 on the Lower East Side, Smith was the champion of the working class because of his interest in labor legislation and social reform. Elected governor of New York in 1918, he would hold the office for four terms and become one of New York's great governors. In 1928, he ran for president of the United States—the first Irish Catholic ever to do so—but lost to Herbert Hoover. After this loss, Smith became disillusioned and largely dropped out of politics. With the onset of the Depression in the 1930s, Irish immigration to New York diminished to almost imperceptible levels and did not recover until after World War II. But even then it was only a fraction of what it had been in the nineteenth century. During World War II, New York Irish Americans, once again, served bravely and honorably, while they were privately and publicly rankled that Ireland and the Irish government under de Valera remained neutral.

In 1945, William O'Dwyer, a former native of Bohola, Co. Mayo, was elected mayor of New York City. But what looked like a glorious return to political power for the Irish proved to be nothing more than an aftershock to the Tammany Hall reign. Dogged by accusations of corruption (which had blighted the careers of so many New York Irish political figures before him), O'Dwyer resigned his mayoralty in 1950. O'Dwyer's election as mayor of New York is a significant event in the history of Irish political power in the city; he stands as possibly the last Irish immigrant ever to win election to New York's highest elective office.

By the end of World War II, the Irish population of the city was greatly reduced. After 1945, as a result of new immigration from Ireland, it began to increase, but it would never again achieve the numbers or public presence of the late nineteenth and early twentieth century. Immigrants in the 1940s and 1950s proved largely invisible to the broader New York population as they settled into already well-established Irish neighborhoods within the city. The older generations of Irish Americans in the city had largely made the transition from working-class to middle-class and even upper-class citizens. With the help of the Catholic Church and their strong political base they had moved from laboring jobs into mercantile and professional careers and had moved their homes into the Upper West Side, the Bronx, and across the East River to Queens. They were defined by their parish, their church, and their faith, and ethnicity was no longer a primary register; they were now comfortably Catholic Americans.

Although immigration died off in the 1960s and 1970s, the 1980s brought another significant wave of Irish immigrants to America and New York. These "new Irish" as they were known, were noticeably different from their earlier compatriots. In general, they were better educated than previous immigrants and consisted of more skilled laborers and professionals. They also proved to be more mobile than their predecessors (not committing themselves to established Irish neighborhoods but rather settling all over New York) and introduced to the city a modern Irish identity, not confined by the traditional markers of religion and nationalism. Because of new immigration restrictions, a significant percentage of these new Irish immigrated illegally and remained as undocumented aliens. In this and many ways, the new Irish have more in common with other new immigrant communities, such as those from Latin American and Asia, than they do with the older-generation Irish Americans. They have rejuvenated the Irish presence in New York and regenerated debate about what it means to be Irish American. One of the city's oldest demonstrations of traditional Irish pride—the Saint Patrick's Day Parade—has in recent times become the center of contentious debates surrounding Irish nationalism and the right of the Irish Lesbian and Gay Organization to march in the parade. These debates have generally ranged the older generations of Irish Americans against the younger Irish Americans and newer immigrants.

As New York moves into the twenty-first century, the Irish continue to be a vital part of the intricate ethnic makeup of the city. From more traditional Irish symbols such as the Waterford crystal ball (which, since 2000, drops every year from the top of One Times Square to signal the start of the New Year) to a more active engagement in fostering a deepening understanding of Ireland and Irish America (signaled by New York University's opening of Glucksman Ireland House at Washington Mews and Fifth Avenue in 1993), the Irish presence in New York continues to this day to be an active one.

James P. Byrne

See also: AMERICAN CIVIL WAR; CATHOLIC CHURCH, the; DE VALERA, Eamon; DEVOY, John; DONGAN, Thomas; DRAFT RIOTS; GREAT FAMINE, The; HARRIGAN, Edward, and HART, Tony; HUGHES, Archbishop John; MEAGHER, Thomas Francis; MITCHEL, John; NATIVISM AND ANTI-CATHOLICISM; SAINT PATRICK'S CATHEDRAL; SAINT PATRICK'S DAY PARADES

References

Almeida, Linda Dowling. *Irish Immigrants in New York City, 1945–1995.* Bloomington: Indiana University Press, 2001.

Bayor, Ronald H., and Timothy J. Meagher, eds. *The New York Irish: Essays toward a History.* Baltimore, MD: John Hopkins University Press, 1995.

Burrows, Edwin G., and Mike Wallace. *Gotham: A History of New York City to 1898.* New York: Oxford University Press, 1999.

Casey, Marion R. "Irish." In *The Encyclopedia of New York City,* edited by Kenneth T. Jackson. London: Yale University Press, 1995.

Ridge, John. "New York City." In *The Encyclopedia of the Irish in America,* edited by Michael Glazier, 678–686. Notre Dame, IN: University of Notre Dame Press, 1999.

NEWFOUNDLAND AND LABRADOR

England's oldest colony and now Canada's most recent province, Newfoundland and Labrador sits on the most easterly edge of the North American continent. The tenth province to join Confederation with Canada in 1949, it consists of the island of Newfoundland, the adjacent islands (except St. Pierre and Miquelon, which are French possessions), and the coastal area of Labrador, which borders the province of Quebec.

Aboriginal peoples have lived in the area since at least 7000 B.C. Today, Newfoundland and Labrador is home to four peoples of Aboriginal ancestry: the Inuit, the Innu, the Micmac, and the Métis. The island Beothuk became extinct in the early nineteenth century when Shanawdithit, the last known of her people, died in the capital city of St. John's. According to some interpretations of Icelandic sagas, Newfoundland and Labrador was visited by Leif Eriksson who established a short-lived colony around A.D. 1010 in what is now a UNESCO (United Nations Educational, Scientific, and Cultural Organization) World Heritage Site at L'Anse aux Meadows, on the tip of the island's northern peninsula. There are also strong indications that Newfoundland was the site of John Cabot's landfall during his first voyage to North America in 1497. England's King Henry VII awarded Cabot £10 for "finding the new isle." In 1583, Sir Humphrey Gilbert, with a charter from Queen Elizabeth I, landed and took possession of the island in the name of England. Throughout the sixteenth century French, Portuguese, Spanish, and Basque fishers established seasonal communities, harvesting the cod-rich waters off the coast of Newfoundland. Since the early seventeenth century, Newfoundland was a strategic geographic prize over which rival British and French interests fought in order to control and regulate the profitable fishery.

Ancestors of most contemporary Newfoundlanders and Labradorians came from southeast Ireland (counties Wexford and Waterford, mostly) or the southwest of England, in one of the most significant waves of immigration in the nineteenth century. Most Irish migrants were young men working on temporary contract for English merchants, but eventually more permanent settlements developed. Almost all were Catholic and only spoke Irish on arrival. Significant aspects of Newfoundland and Labrador culture—music, art, folklore, linguistic peculiarities—remain a testament to these Irish immigrants.

Newfoundland and Labrador's colorful political history began in 1832 with the granting of representative government. A British-appointed governor and council held most of the power, but a House of Assembly was elected by open ballot. This unworkable arrangement was replaced in 1855 with responsible government based on the British parliamentary system. In 1934, after devastating losses in World War I and the crushing economic disaster of the Great Depression, the Dominion of Newfoundland reverted to crown colony status, governed by a British Commission. This political situation proved equally unworkable, and a contentious and bitter political referendum was held in 1949. The people of Newfoundland and Labrador were offered three choices: continuation of Commissional Government, return to Dominion status and responsible government, or confederation with Canada. Joseph R. Smallwood, who led the campaign for confederation, became Newfoundland and Labrador's first premier when the close vote resulted in confederation with Canada.

The late twentieth century has arguably seen the greatest changes in Newfoundland and Labradorian culture and society. After confederation with Canada, the new provincial government of Premier Smallwood pursued a number of modernization projects: building roads, water and sewer systems, hospitals, schools, and electric power lines. Many initiatives designed to diversify the industrial sector and economy proved less successful. The most controversial policy, however, was the Community Resettlement Program of the 1960s, under which people living in the small, outport fishing communities were induced to leave for larger centers. Many Newfoundlanders viewed this program with resentment, as the destruction of distinct culture and traditions. In the larger communities, most notably in the capital city of St. John's, generations who grew up as Canadians began a revitalization of that culture, mostly in theater and music: a revitalization that questioned Newfoundland and Labrador's past and its present role in Canada.

In 1992 the centuries-old cod fishery collapsed and a moratorium on all cod fishing was established, resulting in economic crisis in many rural communities. A change in the political landscape of Labrador was seen in 2004, with the establishment of a new territory, Nunatsiavut, under a land claims agreement between the Inuit and the provincial government. The province as a whole has been forced to look beyond the fishery, and tourism and offshore oil are seen as the keys to economic development in the twenty-first century.

Danine Farquharson

See also: ETHNIC AND RACE RELATIONS, Irish and Indegenous Peoples

References

Hiller, James K., and Peter Neary, eds. *Newfoundland in the Nineteenth and Twentieth Centuries.* Toronto: University of Toronto Press, 1980.

Johnston, Wayne. *The Colony of Unrequited Dreams.* Toronto: Knopf, 1998.

Mannion, John J., ed. *The Peopling of Newfoundland: Essays in Historical Geography.*

The Newfoundland and Labrador Heritage website. www.heritage.nf.ca/home.html (accessed October 4, 2007).

Prowse, D.W. *A History of Newfoundland.* London: Macmillian, 1895.

Social and Economic Papers, 8. St. John's, Newfoundland: Institute of Social and Economic Research, 1977.

NIBLO, WILLIAM B. (1789–1878)

William Niblo (whose name was probably originally Niblock) came to New York from Ireland as a young man around 1813, and he left an indelible mark on the city as one of the great pioneers of Broadway family entertainment. He initially worked in a tavern on Wall Street. In time he married the tavern owner's daughter. Shortly after, around 1815, he went into business for himself and opened the Bank Coffee House at the rear of the Bank of New York building at William and Pine Streets in New York's financial district. His patrons consisted of New York's business elite. By the mid-1820s Niblo had made enough money to be able to expand to a new, bigger location. He took a lease on a much larger property located at the northeast corner of Pine Street and Broadway, known at the time as 537 Broadway, which he opened in 1828.

Over the next few years Niblo developed his new property into a fashionable entertainment center for families and business people. It consisted of a major theatre, a hotel, a restaurant and saloon, and a public garden. The garden, with its casual atmosphere, was spacious. It had shrubbery, flowers, illuminated walkways, fountains, caged songbirds, seating, and ice-cream and lemonade stalls and was said to be a delightful place on summer evenings where families could visit and enjoy the music and outdoor social activity. The complex became known as Niblo's Garden.

The theater was reported to have 3,000 seats. Niblo's philosophy of the finest entertainment at the lowest cost resulted in capacity audiences for almost every performance for decades. A seat at Niblo's cost only $.50, compared with $1.50 to $3 elsewhere. Niblo was credited with introducing people to the theater who had never before attended one. In the years that followed, he introduced all sorts of entertainment acts, from musicals, plays, singers, dancers, pantomimes, and circus and acrobatic troupes to Italian and English operatic performances. Leading actors and entertainers, such as Edwin Forrest, Charles Kean, Charles E. Horn, the notorious entertainer Lola Montez, the Ravel family, and Irish playwright and actor Dion Boucicault, performed there. Opera singers Anna Thillon, Henriette Sontag, Marietta Alboni, Adelina Patti, and others all appeared there at one time or another. During the 1850s Michael Balfe's famed opera *The Bohemian Girl,* William Wallace's popular *Maritana,* and other works by these two Irish composers were performed at Niblo's. The New York Philharmonic performed there in its early days. The American Institute, a manufacturer's and agricultural association, held its annual trade fair at Niblo's every year.

Niblo's Garden became one of the most famous and fashionable entertainment centers on New York's Broadway. The Metropolitan Hotel, a part of the complex, also became one of city's best properties for business and family stays. In September 1846 most of the complex was destroyed by fire. Niblo's was rebuilt within three years. In the meantime, Niblo, undaunted, became involved with another theater where he mounted important operatic performances and other forms of entertainment. Niblo's Garden was also the venue for what was probably the premiere of the first American opera, *Rip Van Winkle* by George Frederick Bristow, in September 1855.

Niblo was also a great friend of the famed Irish actor, Tyrone Power, the grandfather of the future movie star of the same name. Niblo retired from the business around 1858. In addition to his entertainment activities Niblo had also developed into an important collector of paintings. His gallery was said to contain one of the finest collections in the city. In his later years Niblo was known for his generosity and kindness. He donated a library of valuable books to the *New York Historical Society.* On his death in 1878, in his will he made a bequest of more than $150,000, an enormous amount for that time, for a library to the charitable Young Men's Christian Association. It was during the second phase at the rebuilt Niblo's Garden that the musical *The Black Crook* premiered. It was to become Broadway's first musical show with dancing girls and other forms of exotic entertainment. The show ran for over 400 performances. Niblo's Garden was closed and sold in 1895, and a new commercial building replaced it. By then Niblo and his wife of many years were long gone. He is buried in the Green-Wood Cemetery in Brooklyn, New York.

Basil Walsh

See also: BALFE, Michael W.; WALLACE, William Vincent

References

Lawrence, Vera Brodsky. *Strong on Music: The New York Music Scene in the Days of George Templeton Strong, 1836–1875.* Vol. 1. New York: Oxford UniversityPress, 1988.

Mason, R. Osgood, *Sketches and Impressions, Musical, Theatrical and Social, 1799–1885.* New York: G. F. Putnam & Sons, 1887.

Ottenberg, June C. *Opera Odyssey: Toward a History of Opera in Nineteenth-Century America.* Westport, CT: Greenwood Press, 1994.

NICARAGUA

The Republic of Nicaragua in Central America was proclaimed in 1821 after gaining its independence from Spain.

Before that, parts of the country had been the target of British pirates, some of whom would have been from Irish families. Sir Peter Parker (1721–1811), who was probably born in Ireland, was involved in an abortive attack on the Spanish on the San Juan River in 1780. However, gradually interest in Nicaragua began to center on the possibility of building a canal through the country. Although the distance was longer than that through Panama, the route through Nicaragua was easier. Curiously, in 1853 when Patrick James Smyth (ca. 1823–1885) effected the release of another Irish nationalist from Australia, he used the code name "Nicaragua."

In 1855 one of the political factions, the Liberals, in the Nicaraguan city of León, decided to ask the American adventurer William Walker to raise an armed band and come to their aid. As a result, Walker, who had made a failed attempt to capture Mexico two years earlier, arrived in Nicaragua with 56 followers, including some Irishmen, and attacked the Conservative faction in the city of Granada. After being elected president of Nicaragua, and establishing a government recognized by the United States of America, Walker was defeated after announcing his intention of taking over the four other Central American republics. One of the armies sent against Walker was from Costa Rica, and among the Americans captured was a 17-year-old Canadian boy from Quebec, who was of Irish ancestry. The lad was taken as a prisoner to San José, the Costa Rican capital; he was later released after the intervention of the Irishman Thomas Meagher.

In the late 1870s, when serious plans were drawn up for building the Panama Canal, the idea of a canal in Nicaragua was abandoned. Although travelers did visit the country over the next forty years, the next major Irish connection with the republic was in 1918 when Dr. Daniel Murrah Molloy (1882–1944) arrived in Managua, Nicaragua's capital, to investigate the yellow fever epidemic that was sweeping through Nicaragua and neighboring Honduras and seek a cure.

During the Nicaraguan rebellion of 1927–1933, organized by Augustino César Sandino (1895–1934), there was some sympathy in a few Irish newspapers, which compared Sandino's exploits with those of earlier Irish nationalists. Indeed in the French-Italian film *Viva Maria!* (1965), a fictional Irish nationalist flees England in 1907 for a Central American republic (possibly Costa Rica, Nicaragua, or Honduras). There he is killed blowing up a bridge, but his daughter, Maria, joins with another girl also called Maria (played by Brigitte Bardot) to stage a revolution.

After the Nicaraguan Revolution of 1978–1979, support in Ireland for the victorious Sandinistas led to criticism by the U.S. government, which set about trying to overthrow the Sandinista government. In the November 1984 elections, in which the Sandinistas won, an interparty parliamentary delegation from Ireland determined that the vote was "free and fair." Three years earlier Ireland's ambassador to the United Nations, Noel Dorr, had tried to broker a peace agreement between the Sandinistas and the Americans. Furthermore, during the late 1980s a number of prominent Irish writers visited Nicaragua. Joseph V. O'Connor (b. 1963) wrote *Desperadoes,* published in 1994; and T. Coraghessan Boyle included a short story set in Nicaragua, which was published in 1998 in an edition of his collected stories.

Other recent books on Nicaragua by Irish observers have included Betty Purcell's

Light After Darkness: An Experience of Nicaragua, published by Attic in Dublin in 1989, and Marcus Arruda's *What Happened to Sandinista Nicaragua?,* which was published by University College Cork in 1992. Purcell, an Irish journalist, spent much time traveling around the country; in her sensitive account she argues that most Western commentators on the country lack an appreciation of Nicaraguan political history.

In recent years Irish aid workers in Agency for Personal Services Overseas and other nongovernment organizations have been prominent in helping people with health and education issues in Nicaragua. For Irish people visiting Managua, the Shannon, owned by Michael Damery from Cork, is billed as the only authentic Irish bar in Nicaragua.

Justin Corfield

See also: MEAGHER, Thomas, Francis

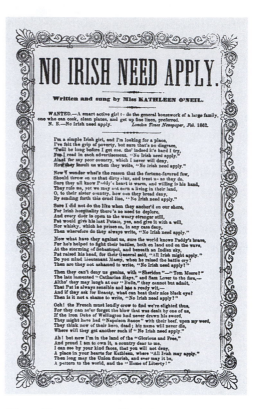

The problems encountered by Irish immigrants are poignantly demonstrated by this song, "No Irish Need Apply," published in the London Times in February 1862. (Library of Congress)

NO IRISH NEED APPLY

Irish Catholics in America have a vibrant memory of humiliating job discrimination against their menfolk, which glared out from omnipresent signs proclaiming "Help Wanted—No Irish Need Apply!" (NINA). These ads called out to non-Irish men: we have a job, and if you are English or German or anything but Irish come in and apply. No historian, archivist, or museum curator has ever been able to find a single genuine NINA sign, nor a photograph of one or a mention in a newspaper report or court case, nor even a recollection of a particular sign in a particular store. (Today anyone can buy fake NINA signs on Ebay.) No Protestant Irishman recalls seeing such a sign; there were no allegations that similar signs ever existed for other Catholic groups or for Jews. Historians using computerized databases have searched through million of pages of newspapers, including the want ads. Since its start in 1851, the daily *New York Times* published exactly one NINA ad for males: a livery stable in Brooklyn in 1854 advertised for a teenage boy who could write, and NINA. What we do have are all the signs of an urban legend: very probably no genuine NINA sign ever existed in America.

The market for female household workers occasionally specified religion or nationality. Newspaper ads for women sometimes did include NINA, because a small proportion of hiring women (less than 10 percent) were reluctant to have a

Catholic inside their home. Irish women in fact dominated the market for domestics in most large cities. They had considerable control over their working conditions because, if dissatisfied with terms, they would quit immediately, knowing their Irish servant network would quickly find them another job and would shun the offending housewife. Middle-class housewives termed the informal but strong Irish control over the market "the servant problem."

The NINA signs did exist in England and Canada. The slogan was commonplace in upper-class London by 1820—referring to English disdain for Irish Protestants (Catholics were beneath contempt). In the London *Times* from 1828 to 1862, NINA appeared in about one want ad a month (fewer than 1 percent) for female servants; it never appeared in the help wanted ads for men. In 1862 in London there was a song, "No Irish Need Apply," purportedly by a maid looking for work who was distressed to see such a sign on a townhouse. The song quickly crossed the ocean where it was modified to depict a man recently arrived in New York who sees a NINA ad and confronts and beats up the miscreant. The song was an immediate hit and is the source of the myth. Hearing the song over and over again, the Irish incorporated it into their folklore, and by 1870, as Mark Twain noted, it had become a bit of stock Irish humor shared by everyone and never used maliciously. But the Irish started to believe some of their relatives had actually seen NINA signs, which proved they were the victims of systematic job discrimination.

The NINA slogan was important because of the way the Irish used it. NINA was an emphatic warning telling fellow Irishmen they must stick together in the face of the enemy. In actual job practice, most Irish worked for other Irishmen, especially in work gangs hired by construction companies, in taverns, or in government jobs controlled by Irish politicians. They were the beneficiaries of strong pro-Irish hiring practices. Job discrimination against Irish men could have occurred without any NINA signs, and it did occur on a major scale in the United Kingdom, but there is no evidence of any systematic discrimination anywhere in America at any time. Statistical data from numerous census sources show no measurable discrimination against the Irish. Although it is of course possible that a particular firm here or there refused to hire Irish, not a single example of that has actually been documented. Outside their community the Irish took jobs with railroads and in textile mills owned by non-Catholics. Hiring for those jobs was bureaucratized and little leeway was allowed to foremen. Railroads—the biggest employers in the nineteenth century—insisted they did not discriminate, and research into payroll records shows the Irish were promoted at the same rate as other ethnics. Most employees of textile mills were Catholics, and no foreman could keep his job if he deliberately alienated a majority of his potential workforce. Labor unions, with their heavy emphasis on group solidarity and collective bargaining rather than individual achievement, were natural media for the Irish. From the 1870s through 2000 about half of all union leaders were Irish. Historians have found no record of a strike over anti-Irish discrimination. By contrast, discrimination against blacks, Chinese, and (in the early twentieth century) Italians, and Poles is readily apparent in the census data, in newspaper files, and in the minutes of labor unions.

Historians can find political hostility that was based on anti-Catholicism and on disgust with the corruption of Irish political machines. That tension does not seem to have affected the job market, however. A loud but small group of Protestants attacked all Catholics, claiming that their "papist" religion diverted them from true religion and made them politically subservient to bishops and especially to a foreign pope. Some reformers complained that the Irish were too drunk and too violent and that corrupt Irish bosses gang-voted ignorant men to subvert local politics and take control of the public payroll. The peak of these attacks came in 1854, when the Know-Nothing movement elected numerous officials, especially in New England. That movement quickly vanished and left no significant legislation and launched no political careers. By the end of the Civil War the old fears had largely subsided. The Irish had proven their patriotism; their many churches, schools, colleges, hospitals, and charitable agencies validated the Catholic commitment to civic betterment. The remarkable success of Irish politicians over the past 150 years afforded proof that they were better than anyone else at winning the votes of non-Irish. Although there were anti-Catholic attacks on Al Smith in 1928 and to a much lesser degree against John F. Kennedy in 1960, these were entirely based on the premise that a Catholic officeholder had to give his highest loyalty to the pope, rather than to the Constitution. (There were no anti-Catholic attacks against John Kerry in 2004, even though he was a devout Catholic whom many people mistakenly thought was Irish.)

Neither Smith nor Kennedy was attacked for being Irish. Indeed no major politicians in America (outside a few in the deep South like Tom Watson) ever made anti-Catholic arguments part of their platform. No American leader ever stood on an anti-Irish platform—in sharp contrast to the United Kingdom or to Canada, where "Orange" Irish Protestants routinely banded together against the "Green" Catholics. Congress never passed or considered legislation to exclude Irish immigrants; they were in fact needed and welcomed. The immigration restriction movement of the 1890–1940 period was led by Irish-controlled labor unions and did not target the Irish in any way.

The Irish were not individualists. They worked in gangs in job sites they could control by force. The NINA slogan told them they had to stick together against the Protestant enemy, in terms of jobs, religion, and politics. The NINA myth justified physical assaults, and it persisted because it aided ethnic solidarity. After 1940 the rapid increase in education made job solidarity a hindrance rather than a help; the city machines disappeared. In 1850 the Irish huddled near the bottom of the socioeconomic scale. By 1900 they were about average. By 1960 they were well above average. Thus, the Irish advanced steadily up the ladder of social success, but they did it as a group standing shoulder to shoulder, with surprisingly few mavericks who tried in individualistic fashion to become successful outside the tight-knit Irish community. After 1960 the labor unions declined in importance and lost most of their Irish members. The sense of being discriminated against faded, except for the old NINA slogan itself, which persisted as a lingering "memory" based on a false stereotype of supposedly hostile Protestants.

Richard Jensen

Reference

Jensen, Richard. "'No Irish Need Apply':
A Myth of Victimization" *Journal of Social
History* 36, no. 2 (2002): 405–429.

NORAID

Noraid is the acronym for Irish Northern Aid, an Irish-American organization supporting Irish republicanism. The group was founded in April 1970 after Joe Cahill and Dáithí Ó Conaill of the new Provisional wing of Sinn Féin and the Irish Republican Army (IRA) asked Michael Flannery, longtime Clan Na Gael activist and veteran of the War of Independence and the Irish Civil War—along with "old" IRA veterans John McGowan and Jack McCarthy—to aid the military campaign in the north of Ireland. Throughout the 1970s and 1980s, Noraid faced allegations that its assistance for the Provisionals found its recipients not among the families of imprisoned IRA members but rather among those buying the weapons to wage the armed struggle.

Under Flannery's leadership, Noraid organized dinner dances, collections in Irish-American bars, and direct-mail appeals for support of dependents of Provisional IRA volunteers jailed by the British. The funds gathered by Noraid went first to the Dublin-based Provisional relief program An Cumann Cabhrach, and then were conveyed to the Belfast organization the Green Cross, which had superseded that city's Northern Aid Committee. However, Noraid did not limit the disbursement of American donations once they had reached Ireland. Therefore, critics from the American, Irish, and British governments all accused Noraid of funding IRA terrorism.

These charges were difficult to prove. Five activists jailed in Fort Worth, Texas, refused to reveal information; a Federal Bureau of Investigation (FBI) crackdown targeting Noraid under the Foreign Agents Registration Act met with opposition from politicians representing Irish-American constituents. Most prominent was Mario Biaggi of New York, and 130 members of Congress at one time joined him on a Northern Ireland action committee. In the 1970s, individual donations to Noraid were often as little as $10 or $20. The lack of easily obtainable financial records from Noraid because of its preferred conveyance of funds to An Cumann Cabhrach by personal courier prevented U.S. inspection along much of the activists' money trail.

The gunrunning network supplying Irish republicans drew bigger funds and existed more parallel to—rather than within—Noraid; the FBI, through informants and surveillance, all but eliminated arms smuggling to republicans. Media coverage and political attacks damaged Noraid's reputation, and the organization suffered from guilt by association. As well as hostility from governmental and press agencies, Noraid met with opposition from within its membership, many of whom identified with an Irish ideology from an earlier era of republicanism. The IRA's advocacy of third world radicalism clashed with an Irish-American stereotype of a more Gaelicized, Catholic defender of an embattled land.

In New York City, the newspaper the *Irish People* reprinted many articles from the Provisional *An Phoblacht/Republican News*. Emphasizing continuity in the physical-force tradition, the *Irish People* promoted an aggressive anti-British position. The paper also publicized Noraid activities throughout the United States. An estimated 10,000 members in 70 branches existed at its height in the early 1970s. As with the earlier Clan Na Gael, East Coast Irish enclaves contributed most to the organization; New York City—with 2,000 members—remained the dominant stronghold. Most members were from middle-class suburban and urban backgrounds.

Each branch numbered between 25 and 50 members; about 10 of these supplied the most committed activists. Noraid supporters comprised a cross-section from Irish America. Although many of its leaders were Irish born, emigrants from the earlier century's IRA campaigns, mixing with more recent arrivals and third- and fourth-generation Irish-Americans, also joined. The question of whether, as in the case of the Fenians a century earlier, members sought social camaraderie more than political commitment has been debated by academics. Often overlooked have been Noraid and other Irish-American republican groups' appeal to activists, sharing diverse political and ideological sympathies, from non–Irish American or mixed national origins.

After the 1980s H-Block protests sparked renewed attention for the IRA, the *Irish People* sponsored solidarity missions, bringing Noraid supporters to the north of Ireland. While the issue of representation for the Marxist Irish National Liberation Army caused friction when families of the hunger strikers were brought by Noraid to raise funds and a media profile in the United States, the necessity for a united front for republicanism between leftists and traditionalists prevailed. The Irish Republican Clubs assisted the radical wing of republicanism, and both competed and cooperated with Noraid in the 1970s and 1980s.

Noraid succumbed to Justice Department pressure and signed (with reservations) the Foreign Agents Registration Act in 1984. Flannery, in 1989, dissatisfied with the mainstream IRA's rejection of abstention from the Dail Eireann, left for the Friends of Irish Freedom, backers of republican Sinn Féin. As the IRA leadership shifted republicans toward the peace process, the end of the armed struggle loomed. In 1994, Friends of Sinn Féin was established in Washington, D.C., as lobbyists for Sinn Féin. Diplomatic efforts to achieve Irish republican aims began to supersede those of physical force. Sinn Féin's office in the national capital signaled a decline in the Fenian-inspired methods of gathering American funds for those associated with Irish militarism. With the peace process, IRA prisoners returned to their families. By the end of the 1990s, Noraid's stated justification appeared increasingly obsolete.

John L. Murphy

See also: IRISH REPUBLICAN ARMY

References

Clark, Dennis. *Irish Blood: Northern Ireland and the American Conscience.* Port Washington, New York: Kennikat Press, 1977.

Holland, Jack. *The American Connection: U.S. Guns, Money, and Influence in Northern Ireland.* Niwot, CO: Roberts Rinehart, 1997.

McCarthy, John P. *Dissent from Irish America.* New York: University Press of America, 1993.

McFerran, Douglass. *IRA Man: Talking with the Rebels.* Westport, CT: Praeger, 1997.

Wilson, Andrew J. *Irish America and the Ulster Conflict, 1968–1995.* Washington, DC: Catholic University of America Press, 1995.

NORTH CAROLINA

North Carolina was one of the original 13 colonies of the United States, and it became the 12th state, founded in 1789. The state of North Carolina covers 52,669 square miles, and its capital, Raleigh, is located in the center of the state. The state owes its name to the English kings Charles I and Charles II (Latin *Carolus*), who granted the first territories. The state earned its slogan, "First in Flight," because the Wright brothers flew the first airplane in Kitty Hawk, North Carolina, in 1903.

Among the first settlers in the colony were the Scots-Irish, known in Ireland as the Ulster Scots. Many of those Scots-Irish, who mainly entered the colonies by the port of Philadelphia, established their settlements in the Appalachian Mountains of southwestern North Carolina. They left their homeland and traveled across the eastern coast of the United States into the present-day counties of Buncombe, Cherokee, Clay, Graham, Haywood, Henderson, Jackson, Macon, Madison, Mitchell, Swain, Transylvania, and Yancey. At a time when religious repression increased and work was precarious in eighteenth-century Ulster, the American colonies offered religious toleration and great opportunities for work. The first stop for the Scots-Irish was Pennsylvania. However, by the end of the eighteenth century, the growth of population, along with the economic problems it brought, led them to sell their lands and look for a better place to live. They traveled southwest into the Valley of Virginia and the mountains of western North Carolina. One of the Ulster families, the Catheys, is considered most representative of this trend. They sold their lands in Maryland and later in Orange County, Virginia. In 1749, they traveled to Rowan County in North Carolina, where they settled in an area known as the "Irish settlement." They emigrated still further into an area known today as Haywood County in North Carolina. In 1746, the Scots-Irish pioneered settlement west of the Yadkin River. The Irish settlement was the largest community of the three established there before 1750. It was located at the head of the Second Creek of the South Yadkin River. By 1750, the Catheys had led some 14 families to the Irish settlement.

Migration into the southern states was accelerated by Virginia's policy of granting land to encourage settlement. Economic motivations likely inspired the Ulster families to sell their land in western Virginia and move into the mountains of North Carolina, where land was cheaper and they could make a fortune. One wealthy Ulster landowner, Arthur Dobbs from Co. Antrim, was granted large extensions of land in Mecklenburg and Cabarrus counties in North Carolina. He was a governor of the royal colony of North Carolina from 1754 to 1765, and he so enthusiastically promoted the colony among his former countrypeople in Ireland that North Carolina became a popular destination for Irish immigrants.

Another leading figure in North Carolina was James Patton, a young weaver from Co. Derry who settled in the town of Asheville. He arrived in Pennsylvania in 1783 and after six years became a merchant who carried dry goods south along the Great Wagon Road. He also drove cattle north from the Carolinas to Philadelphia.

According to H. Tyler Blethen and Curtis W. Wood Jr., those who inhabit the mountains still enjoy a practical and simple lifestyle, which largely stems from the attitudes concerning religion and agriculture introduced by the Scots-Irish. However, nowadays the heritage of the Scots-Irish is also present in the heraldic legacy of the people, the number of Presbyterian churches, and the speech and music of the inhabitants in the Appalachian Mountains. Some places and events also commemorate the historical presence of the Irish, such as the annual Mountain Dance and Folk Festival organized by the town of Asheville. At Montreat, the Presbyterian Historical Society shows the visitor the religious tradition of the Scots-Irish, and Old Fort exhibits how mountain life was from its early inhabitants through today. The northwestern town of Boone, the Firefly Capital of America, was named for Scots-Irish frontiersman Daniel Boone. In 2001, the Town Council in Cary, located in eastern North Carolina, decided to become a sister city with Co. Meath, Ireland.

Marian Pozo Montano

See also: SCOTS-IRISH; SCOTS-IRISH
   PATTERNS OF SETTLEMENT,
   UNITED STATES

References

Blethen, Tyler H., and Curtis W. Wood Jr. *From Ulster to Carolina. The Migration of the Scotch-Irish to Southwestern North Carolina.* Raleigh: North Carolina Division of Archives and History, 1999.
Miller, Kerby. *Emigrants and Exiles: Ireland and the Irish Exodus to North America.* New York: Oxford University Press, 1985.

NOTRE DAME UNIVERSITY

The University of Notre Dame in northwestern Indiana, adjacent to South Bend, is one of the larger independent Catholic universities in the United States; it has an enrollment of approximately 11,500 students—8,300 undergraduates and 3,200 in its Graduate Division, Architecture School and Law School. Coeducational since 1972, Notre Dame's male to female ratio is approaching 50:50. Its famed athletic teams are called the Fighting Irish, reflecting one aspect of the university's ethnic and religious heritage. As one of the preeminent Catholic universities in the United States, Notre Dame has always been highly regarded by Irish Americans as an elite institution that nurtured and represented the ethos of their community.

Notre Dame was founded on November 26, 1842. Its founder was 28-year-old Rev. Edmund Sorin of the Congregation of the Holy Cross, formed a few years earlier in Mans, France, who sought to create a college conducted according to Catholic principles. Sorin was attended by seven other brothers of the Society of St. Joseph, one of the congregation's three societies.

Sorin had recently come to Indiana from France, in response to a call for mission volunteers from the bishop of Vincennes. The bishop provided approximately 500 acres for the university, along with plans for a four-story college building. The site had been purchased from the U.S. government and given to the bishop for a school by Rev. Stephen Badin, a missionary and the first Catholic priest ordained in the United States. It was thought to be less than a mile from the portage route between the Kankakee and St. Joseph rivers, connecting the Mississippi River and Lake Michigan watersheds, which Father Marquette had crossed shortly before his death in 1675.

Despite an extraordinarily cold winter, the northwestern Indiana Catholic community was able to build a 20-foot × 46-foot log church in the clearing and have it open for services on March 19, 1843; A small two-story brick building was built during the summer of 1843, to temporarily hold classes and a bakery, and the university received its first student, Alexis Coquillard of South Bend, Indiana, that fall. The cornerstone for the college building itself was laid on August 28, 1843; the university was chartered by a special act of the Indiana Legislature on January 14, 1844, and that fall the college building opened.

In Notre Dame's early years its college curriculum attracted few students, less than a dozen a year. Most of its students attended its manual labor school, likewise chartered by the Indiana Legislature in 1844, or its elementary and preparatory levels. The first graduate to receive a bachelor's degree, Neal Gillespie, graduated in 1849. He was later to return to Notre Dame as a priest and professor. Gillespie was the first cousin of subsequent U.S. Speaker of the House, secretary of state, and unsuccessful presidential candidate James Gillespie Blaine.

Notre Dame's teacher of mathematics and commercial subjects, Brother Gatain, was lost to the faculty in 1850 after he was sent to California to look for gold. He was left on his own and eventually returned to his family's farm in France. His and Father Sorin's biographies present the earliest views of Notre Dame's first years.

Notre Dame's second catalog, printed in 1850 by Schuyler Colfax, a South Bend newspaperman, shows that Notre Dame had 69 students by that date. Colfax also became U.S. Speaker of the House and later President Grant's first vice president. Notre Dame received its own post office in 1851 through the intervention of U.S. Senator Henry Clay of Kentucky, a friend of Vincennes's former Bishop and a former U.S. Speaker of the House.

Originally reachable only by stage and wagon, or by boat down the St. Joseph River from Lake Michigan, Notre Dame's campus became accessible by rail from the east when the Northern Indiana & Southern Michigan Railroad reached South Bend in 1851, and soon thereafter from the west when it reached Chicago. The availability of rail service essentially opened up Notre Dame to students from the Chicago area and points to the west. Few of Notre Dame's students had come from anywhere west before that time.

Notre Dame's original college curriculum included four years of humanities, poetry, rhetoric, and philosophy. Early on it also offered French, German, Spanish, Italian, music, and drawing. Physics and geology courses were added in 1863, and a College of Science in 1865. Notre Dame opened the first Catholic law school in the United States in 1869, the first Catholic college of engineering in 1873, and the first Catholic program in architecture in 1898.

Wings were added to Notre Dame's college building in 1853, to accommodate increasing enrollment, but it soon proved inadequate and was replaced by a new six-story Main Building, constructed during the summer of 1865. That building and several other structures were destroyed in a three-hour fire during a southwestern gale on April 23, 1879. But enough of a new Main Building had arisen by September 1879 that there was room for fall classes. The new Main Building includes the dome, completed in 1884 and gilded at Father Sorin's insistence, which is Notre Dame's landmark.

Notre Dame's history since Father Sorin's death in 1893 has been one of physical growth and intellectual achievement. Notre Dame faculty members or graduates were among the early pioneers of aerodynamics, discovered the formula for synthetic rubber, and achieved the first wireless transmission in the United States. The law school was significantly expanded in the 1920s and the graduate school in the 1930s. Entrance requirements were raised after World War II, faculty hiring increased, and the number of campus buildings nearly doubled. Father Theodore M. Hesburgh, who served as university president from 1952 to 1987, became an internationally known public figure because of his work in civil rights and education. Secretary of State Condoleezza Rice (MA 1975) is among Notre Dame's many graduates in public service. Its faculty includes both Catholics and non-Catholics, including historian George Marsden, a biographer of Protestant theologian Jonathan Edwards. Approximately 85 percent of its students identify themselves as Catholic. The others do not.

Steven B. Jacobson

References

Ayo, Nicholas, *Signs of Grace: Meditations on the Notre Dame Campus.* Lanham, MD: Rowman & Littlefield, 2001.

Burns, Robert E. *Being Catholic, Being American: The Notre Dame Story, 1842–1934.* South Bend, IN: University of Notre Dame Press, 1999.

Burns, Robert E. *Being Catholic, Being American: The Notre Dame Story, 1934–1952.* South Bend, IN: University of Notre Dame Press, 2000.

Connelly, Joel R., and Howard J. Dooley. *Hesburgh's Notre Dame: Triumph in Transition.* New York: Hawthorne Books, 1972.

Hesburgh, Theodore M., *God, Country, Notre Dame: The Autobiography of Theodore M. Hesburgh.* South Bend, IN: University of Notre Dame Press, 2000.

Klawitter, George. *After Holy Cross, Only Notre Dame: The Life of Brother Gatain.* Lincoln, NE: iUniverse, 2003.

Massa, Mark S., *Catholics and American Culture: Fulton Sheen, Dorothy Day, and the Notre Dame Football Team.* New York: Crossroad, 1999.

Mater, Alma (pseudonym). *A Brief History of the University of Notre Dame du Lac Indiana from 1842 to 1892.* Chicago: Werner, 1895.

O'Connell, Marvin Richard. *Edward Sorin.* South Bend, IN: University of Notre Dame Press, 2001.

Rai, Karanjit Singh. *Four Decades of Vector Biology at Notre Dame.* South Bend, IN: University of Notre Dame Press, 1999.

Robinson, Ray. *Rockne of Notre Dame: The Making of a Football Legend.* New York: Oxford University Press, 2002.

Stritch, Thomas. *My Notre Dame: Memories and Reflections of Sixty Years.* South Bend, IN: University of Notre Dame Press, 1992.

Tucker, Todd. *Notre Dame vs. The Klan: How the Fighting Irish Defeated the Ku Klux Klan.* Chicago: Loyola Press, 2004.

Wallace, Francis. *Notre Dame: Its People and Its Legends.* New York: David McKay, 1969.

O'BRIEN, CHARLOTTE GRACE (1845–1909)

Charlotte Grace O'Brien was born on November 23, 1845, and spent her early years at Cahirmoyle in Co. Limerick. Her father, William Smith O'Brien, was a Protestant landlord who joined the Young Ireland movement and led the 1848 rebellion at Ballingarry, Co. Tipperary. He was convicted of treason and transported to Tasmania when Charlotte was only three years old. Upon his release in 1854, Charlotte moved with her father to Wales, where they remained until his death in 1864. After her father's death, O'Brien returned to Cahirmoyle to help her brother care for his three children over the next several years.

While back at Cahirmoyle, O'Brien turned her attention to studying botany and writing. In 1878 she published *Light and Shade,* a novel about the 1867 Fenian uprising in Ireland. Two years later she published a volume of poetry entitled *Drama and Lyrics.* Her interest in botany led her to produce *Wild Flowers of the Undercliffe,* a study of the flora on the Isle of Wight, in 1881. By that point she had also begun publishing articles in support of the Land League in such journals as *United Ireland,* the *Nation,* and the *Nineteenth Century.* Her writing became increasingly political in the 1880s and 1890s; she wrote in support of Home Rule, political reform, and women's rights. O'Brien joined the Gaelic League shortly after its inception in 1893 and continued to support the Irish language and Irish industries for the remainder of her life.

O'Brien is best remembered for her almost single-handed campaign to improve the conditions of Irish immigrants to America. In an article entitled "Horrors of an Emigrant Ship," published in the *Pall Mall Gazette* in 1881, O'Brien called attention to the appalling conditions Irish emigrants, especially single women, suffered on board "coffin ships" to the United States. Her exposé prompted a public outcry and a Board of Trade investigation into the practices of the White Star shipping line, which grudgingly began to improve its facilities. O'Brien also set up a lodging house— O'Brien Emigrants' Home—in Queenstown (now Cobh) to offer bed, breakfast, and an evening meal to prospective emigrants, especially women and children. In 1882 O'Brien traveled steerage to New York and lived for some time in a tenement to experience firsthand the conditions about which she was writing. Her experience convinced her that a widespread network of support was needed for Irish emigrants and immigrants on both sides of the Atlantic. She prevailed upon the Roman Catholic hierarchy in New York to establish a welcoming center for single female immigrants. The mission of Our Lady of the Rosary, which opened its doors on January 1, 1884, provided shelter and job assistance to 25,000 Irish immigrant women between 1884 and 1890. In a lecture tour of the United States, O'Brien galvanized support for the mission among Irish Americans.

Suffering from poor health and progressive deafness, O'Brien returned to Ireland where she resumed her gardening and writing. She published another volume of poetry, *Lyrics,* in 1886 and a study of the flora of northwest Limerick in 1907. She died suddenly at her home in 1909. She had converted to Roman Catholicism some years earlier.

Kathleen Ruppert

See also: EMIGRATION; IRISH NATIONAL LAND LEAGUE

References

Diner, Hasia R. *Erin's Daughters in America: Irish Immigrant Women in the Nineteenth Century.* Baltimore, MD: Johns Hopkins University Press, 1983.

Ó Céirín, Kit, and Cyril Ó Céirín, eds. *Women of Ireland: A Biographic Dictionary.* Kinvara: Tír Eolas, 1996.

Rappaport, Helen. *Encyclopedia of Women Social Reformers.* Vol. 2. Santa Barbara, CA: ABC-CLIO, 2001

O'BRIEN, JOHN THOMOND (1786–1861)

John Thomond O'Brien was an army general in the independence wars of Argentina, Chile, and Peru. Born in 1786 in Baltinglass, Co. Wicklow, the son of Martin O'Brien and Honoria O'Connor, O'Brien arrived in Buenos Aires in 1812 and opened a merchant house. He enrolled in the army, fought in Uruguay under General Soler, and was promoted to lieutenant. In 1816 he joined José de San Martin's mounted grenadiers regiment in the Andes Army. After the battle of Chacabuco he was promoted to captain and appointed aide-de-camp to San Martin. O'Brien fought in the battles of Cancha Rayada and Maipú, and in the campaign of Peru. In 1821 he was promoted to colonel and was awarded the Orden del Sol and Pizarro's golden canopy, which have been borne by the viceroys of Peru in processions.

In Peru, O'Brien turned his attention to the mining business. The Peruvian government gave him a grant for the famous silver mine of Salcedo, near Puno. O'Brien and his associate, Mr. Page, who represented Rundell and Bridge (London jewelers), embarked on an effort to provide food and supplies to their miners at Lake Chiquito, located at 5,500 meters above sea level, from the port of Arica, located 380 kilometers away in the Pacific coast. They purchased a boat in Arica, stripped it of anchor and rigging, and after two years of hard labor managed to launch her on the lake. This was the first attempt to establish regular communications between the valleys in Bolivia and the Pacific Coast. Unfortunately for O'Brien and Page, a storm destroyed the vessel and with it their hopes of carrying on the mining works. Other remarkable efforts of O'Brien included transporting a steam engine across the Andes, digging a canal 600 meters long and traversed by nine locks through the Laycayota Mountain, and laying a railroad for conveying ore.

In the mid-1820s a group within the Irish elite of Buenos Aires, including doctors

Michael O'Gorman and John Oughagan and the Irish chaplain Father Moran, attracted the interest of the local government to implement an immigration scheme from Ireland to Buenos Aires. They communicated with the archbishop of Dublin and in 1826 commissioned John T. O'Brien, who was back from Peru, to travel to Europe and recruit "moral and industrious" immigrants. He spent two years in Ireland trying to engage emigrants without success. However, he met John Mooney of Streamstown, Co. Westmeath, who went to Argentina in 1828 when O'Brien was returning. This was to be the start of the Irish emigration to Argentina from the Westmeath-Longford-Offaly area. In addition to John Mooney, his sister, Mary and her husband, Patrick Bookey, went with O'Brien. Back in South America in 1835, O'Brien was promoted to general in Peru. He returned to Ireland and died in Lisbon in 1861, on his way back to South America.

Edmundo Murray

See also: ARGENTINA; O'GORMAN, Michael

References

Hammond, Tony. "British Immigrants in South America (Industry, Commerce and Science)." www.hammond.swayne.com/industry.htm#Mining (accessed August 19, 2007).

Nally, Pat. "Los Irlandeses en la Argentina." *Familia* 2, no. 8 (1992).

O'BRIEN, PAT (1899–1983)

Pat O'Brien was born William Joseph Patrick O'Brien in Milwaukee, Wisconsin. All four of his grandparents were born in Ireland: his mother's parents were from Co. Galway and his father's family was from Co. Cork. He attended Marquette Academy in New York, where he met Spencer Tracy, with whom he would remain lifelong friends. After joining the Navy with Tracy during World War I, O'Brien decided against entering a seminary and attended law school at Marquette University. While there, he started acting in college productions. His big break came when he played the character of Walter Burns in the Broadway production of *The Front Page*. For Lewis Milestone's film adaptation of the play, in only O'Brien's second film, he was cast as Hildy Johnson. He married fellow actor Eloise Taylor in 1931. They had four children together, three of whom were adopted: Mavourneen, Brigid, Patrick Sean, and Terence Kevin. The Ancient Order of Hibernians awarded O'Brien the prestigious John F. Kennedy medal, and a testimonial dinner was held in his honor in 1983 by the United Irish Societies of Southern California. He died of a heart attack in Santa Monica in 1983.

O'Brien became famous for playing Irish characters, particularly the roles of priests and policemen. Because of this he came to be known as Hollywood's "Irishman in Residence." He was a member of a group dubbed by Hollywood columnist Sidney Skolsky "the Irish Mafia," which included James Cagney, Spencer Tracy, and Frank McHugh. O'Brien became associated with films starring James Cagney, and the pair appeared in a total of nine films together. In films such as *Here Comes The Navy, Devil Dogs of the Air, Ceiling Zero,* and *Torrid Zone* they played Navy or Air Force buddies forced to rely on each other. *The Irish in Us* told the story of three Irish brothers in New York in which the youngest brother (Cagney) steals the girlfriend of the eldest brother, played by O'Brien. They also appeared in *Boy Meets Girl*. Their most famous film was *Angels with Dirty Faces* in which

Actors Pat O'Brien (right) and James Cagney (left) during a scene in Angels with Dirty Faces *in 1938. (Warner Bros./First National/The Kobal Collection)*

they play two childhood friends in Hell's Kitchen in New York. After a robbery Cagney is sent to reform school while O'Brien escapes arrest. Cagney's character grows up to be a gangster, while O'Brien's becomes a priest, Father Jerry Connolly, who decides to fight against corruption and who ministers to him as he awaits execution. Two years later, the pair starred in *The Fighting 69th,* which told the story of two friends in the 69th Regiment during World War I. The regiment was composed mainly of Irish-American soldiers, and once again O'Brien played the straitlaced priest opposite Cagney's cocky and brash character. Another one of his most celebrated parts at this time was the title character in *Knute Rockne —All American* in which he played

the Notre Dame football coach who makes an inspirational locker-room speech to his players to encourage them to win a game. Like his friend Spencer Tracy in *Boys Town,* in *Fighting Father Dunne* O'Brien played the role of a priest who helps poor newsboys by founding an orphanage. The last film O'Brien and Cagney starred in together was *Ragtime,* the adaptation of the E. L. Doctorow novel in which O'Brien's wife also starred. Throughout the 1950s and 1960s O'Brien mostly worked in television. He also developed a nightclub act in which he combined jokes, stories, and songs. He starred alongside Spencer Tracy in *The Last Hurrah,* in which Tracy played an Irish-American politician, loosely based on Boston Mayor James Michael Curley, who tries to get reelected for the last time. In 1959 he played the Irish-American police-man Mulligan in Prohibition-era Chicago in Billy Wilder's *Some Like It Hot*.

David Doyle

References

Carzo, Eileen Daney. "Pat O'Brien." *The Encyclopedia of the Irish in America,* edited by Michael Glazier. Notre Dame, IN: University of Notre Dame Press, 1999.

Curran, Joseph. *Hibernian Green on the Silver Screen.* New York: Greenwood Press, 1989.

O'Brien, Pat. *The Wind at My Back: The Life and Times of Pat O'Brien by Himself.* New York: Doubleday & Co., 1964.

O'BRIEN, TIM (1954–)

Tim O'Brien is an Irish-American musician who has often said that for him the essence of music is making something new out of something old. At first he worked in American folk forms, as he still does, but as his career has progressed, O'Brien has gone more deeply into his Irish and Irish-American roots.

Musician Tim O'Brien performs on stage at Swallow Hill Music Association in Denver, Colorado in 2005. O'Brien won a Grammy Award for Best Traditional Folk Album for Fiddler's Green *in 2005. (Reggie Barrett Photography)*

Born in Wheeling, West Virginia, in 1954, O'Brien grew up in the heart of bluegrass and mountain music country, at the tail end of the folk music revival. He heard country music from live shows at the WWVA Jamboree and popular music from the Beatles on the radio. With a gift for playing stringed instruments of all sorts and a high clear tenor signing voice, O'Brien found his own way into music, through singing folk and country songs in a duo with his sister Mollie (who also went on to make a career in music), and later, as the pull of bluegrass became stronger, by moving to Colorado and joining in the flourishing newgrass band bluegrass scene in the West. With guitarist Charles Sawtelle, banjo player Pete Wernick, and bass player Nick Forster, O'Brien, playing mandolin and sharing vocals with Foster, started the progressive bluegrass band Hot Rize in 1978. The men also formed a sort of alter ego band, Red Knuckles and the Trailblazers, in which they played country standards and western swing. In whichever form they appeared, the quality of their musicianship and their connection with their audiences was strong. Hot Rize was chosen for the International Bluegrass Music Association's Entertainer of the Year Award in 1990, and O'Brien was named Male Vocalist of the Year by the same group in 1993.

O'Brien wanted to explore even more aspects of his musical heritage. His first solo album, *Hard Year Blues,* found him using folk music and folk ideas as a starting point to connect with and explore country, blues, western music, jazz, and blues, in a wide-ranging and eclectic combination that would set the path for the next years of his career. As a writer, O'Brien connected with rising country star and fellow West Virginian Kathy Mattea, who would take several of his songs to country chart status; recorded several albums with his sister, Mollie; formed a jazz-based group called the O'Boys; cut an album of Bob Dylan covers called *Red On Blonde;* and engaged in a project of Appalachian music inspired by the novel *Cold Mountain.*

O'Brien had been going further back to his roots than Appalachia, though, exploring his family's history in Ireland. His great grandfather came from Kingscourt, Co. Cavan, to West Virginia in 1851 when he was in his early twenties, where he married a fellow Irish immigrant from Donegal. In looking back at his family history, O'Brien was impressed by both the geographical distance his great grandparents had traveled and the courage it took for them to make such changes. He visited Ireland a number of times and saw the landscapes and conditions in which his ancestors had lived.

These experiences began to come out in his music. He composed an original instrumental, "Newgrange," based on his visit to that ancient site, which became the title of an album and the name for the group that recorded it; in addition to O'Brien the group included top acoustic musicians—pianist Philip Aaberg, fiddler Darol Anger, and banjo player Alison Brown. O'Brien went more deeply into the Irish and Irish-American experience of history, emigration, assimilation, and change with his 1999 collection of traditional and

original tunes called *The Crossing,* and followed the idea further in 2001 with *Two Journeys.* In 2005, O'Brien released two recordings: *Cornbread Nation* featured music of the American South and *Fiddler's Green* focused more on the New England/East Coast dynamic. Both include instrumental and lyrical ideas, as well as treatments of traditional songs, influenced by his Irish experience and his Irish-American background. He has described them as a continuation of the events and ideas of *The Crossing* and *Two Journeys* into what happened next.

Kerry Dexter

O'CONNELL, DANIEL (1775–1847)

Nineteenth-century Irish Catholic lawyer and nationalist leader Daniel O'Connell was born on August 6, 1775, near Cahirciveen, Co. Kerry. He once famously declared that he "formed the high resolve to leave my native land better after my death than I found it" (Gwynn 1947, 27). In the course of his career as the greatest advocate of his time, O'Connell firmly believed repeal of the Act of Union of 1800 and Catholic Emancipation were the only measures to improve the dire circumstances of a country without its own parliament and whose Catholic majority was denied fundamental human rights. The certainty with which he pursued these goals was born of the opportunities of an education in France and England, admiration for the liberal and nationalist philosophies that found their fullest expression in the revolutionary activities of the American colonists, and his legal background. O'Connell, a brilliant political strategist, used innovative tactics to achieve his political aims, and succeeded in creating the idea of a link between democracy and the moral force of the people. O'Connell's political life was fraught with disappointments and contradictions as he attempted to win repeal and emancipation for Ireland. His trials and subsequent tribulations received widespread media attention in Europe and to a lesser degree America, and his liberal nationalism subsequently inspired many European causes. In a career founded on unpopular political goals, he was not afraid to champion other unpopular causes, and he was an unflinching supporter of abolition. Indeed, he was deemed an "Atlantic Revolutionary," and his contact with America, Irish Americans, and the American antislavery movement also mirrors the challenges and contradictions that were so much part of his political career. O'Connell took liberal, democratic ideals from the Americans, and he gave to America a group, the Irish Americans, who were skilled in the practice of political and administrative life.

The political causes automatically associated with O'Connell are Catholic Emancipation and repeal of the Act of Union of 1800. Ireland had been under British rule for centuries, but in 1782 Henry Grattan succeeded in obtaining an Irish parliament based in Dublin. However, the minority Protestant ascendency class dominated this parliament and was not subject to the penal code under which the Catholics lived. The statutes of this code, collectively known as the Penal Laws, imposed severe political, economic, religious, and educational restrictions on Irish Catholics. A failed Irish revolution in 1798 and the threat of a French invasion to help Irish Catholics compelled the British government to introduce the Act of Union, thereby uniting the Irish parliament with the British parliament in London. The Irish parliamentarians, and indeed the Irish Catholic hierarchy, who were promised emancipation, supported the Union. O'Connell was singularly unconvinced, and he challenged the political and religious establishments by speaking against the Union in 1800. In the course of time, his fears were realized: Irish manufacturing suffered from the neglect of direct political attention, the cities and towns became dilapidated, Dublin languished as a regional rather than a national capitol, and Emancipation was not granted. This was O'Connell's first speech on a political topic. He took an unpopular stance against a popular cause, and this was to be repeated throughout his long and distinguished career.

In 1823, O'Connell began with a campaign for Catholic Emancipation. First, he organized the Catholic Association, and the following year he established the Catholic Rent to defray the costs he incurred. This rent prompted anti-O'Connellites to label him "King of the Beggermen"; however, it was singularly important as it gave to the masses a proprietary right to the organization and by extension to the democratic process of achieving a constitutional change. In 1829, O'Connell defied the political establishment and in an unprecedented move was elected to Parliament. O'Connell now took his campaign directly to the House of Commons, and by a process of blatant maneuvering in a volatile political climate he paved the way for Catholic Emancipation in 1829. However, Catholic Emancipation was a poisoned chalice, and the Irish electorate was reduced from 200,000 to 26,000 as the forty-shilling freeholders lost their votes. During the 1830s, O'Connell turned his attention to other questions. He "advocated male suffrage, the secret ballot and an elective House of Lords. He championed religious toleration and the abolition of slavery and he condemned discrimination against the Jews. He advocated the abolition of capital punishment and flogging in the army, and he pressed for various reforms of the legal system"(McCartney 1980, 4).

The passage of time convinced O'Connell that union was detrimental to Ireland's political and economic security. In 1840, he founded the Loyal National Repeal Association (LNRA) with the expressed aim of achieving repeal of the Act of Union. O'Connell further refined his administrative system: he launched a rent strike, and he identified the Catholic clergy as his best means of reaching the entire country and helping his local organizers. Through its network, the LNRA was in touch with local grievances and assistance was often given to local problems. As such, the LNRA bore a greater resemblance to a parliament than had heretofore existed. The Temperance movement under the guidance of Father Theobald Mathew was also sweeping the country at this time. Father Mathew tried to distance himself and his organization from political affairs; however, a reduction in alcoholic consumption and the establishment of Temperance reading rooms ensured the spread of the repeal message. The hallmark of this campaign was the enormous meetings held at locations chosen for their symbolic import. The dramatic reduction in the consumption of alcohol facilitated the orderly gathering of huge crowds, and O'Connell's detractors labeled these meetings "monster meetings." The title stuck, but O'Connell was more often identified by his supporters as the Liberator. O'Connell rashly declared 1843 the year of repeal, and huge monster meetings were

held. However, fearing bloodshed after a government ban on a massive rally that was planned to be held at Clontarf, O'Connell canceled the meeting, to the disgust of the younger, rebellious members of his organization, collectively known as the Young Irelanders. O'Connell was then arrested for treason and sentenced before a packed jury. While the House of Lords overturned his conviction, the aged and ill O'Connell was in declining health. In 1847 he traveled to the Vatican, but died en route in Genoa.

Historians have grappled with the difficulties of containing O'Connell's active life, immense workload, and legacy within the confines of a text. Edwards claims he was "reflective of an era" (1975, 11). Gwynn had originally developed this identification of O'Connell with his time and place by pointing out that the economic progress of the O'Connell family paralleled the progress made by an emerging Catholic merchant class that responded to the restrictions of the Penal Laws. Riach, in common with modern American criticism, contends that only by considering the international context of O'Connell's life and work can one fully appreciate O'Connell's legacy to modern democracy and a modern Ireland. O'Connell was endowed with a variety of nicknames, and it is in these that the complexities and contradictions that beset his life's work can best be seen.

McCartney identifies O'Connell as an "Atlantic Revolutionary," and this term identifies key aspects of O'Connell the man and the political activist. The extended O'Connell family was not limited by a parochial viewpoint as they responded to both the Penal Laws and the Macgillicuddy's Reeks, which isolated the Iveagh Peninsula from the rest of the country, by looking seaward. Their physical proximity to continental Europe allowed them to develop trade, military, and educational links, especially with France. Many Kerry families settled there, establishing lucrative trading links with the Kerry coast, and others joined the Irish Brigade, carving out careers in the military. The sons of wealthy merchants were educated in France, and Daniel O'Connell attended English Colleges at St. Omer and Douai. O'Connell and his brother fled the French revolutionaries and escaped to England, where he finished his education and in 1794 entered Lincoln's Inn. As he prepared for the bar, he read widely, and the works of Thomas Paine, the Declaration of Independence, and the Bill of Rights provided the foundation for his liberal nationalist outlook. He was also impressed with the "libertarian and egalitarian principles of American Revolutionaries" (Edwards 1975, 13). The basic premise for the separation of America from England stated that "government exists through a social contract with the people based upon fundamental rights" (Edwards 1975, 81). O'Connell inferred from this that England had broken this contract with Irish Catholics, and this informed the principles and actions of his political career. America did not merely offer a philosophical backdrop to O'Connell. He commended the American abolitionists and subsequently had a disagreement with them and was also compelled to address the Irish Americans on their ambivalence about slavery.

O'Connell was a revolutionary who sowed the seeds for a dramatic and far-reaching change in the attitudes, democratic system, and conditions of Ireland. His personal experience of the French Revolutionaries forever colored his attitude to violence, and Gwynn points out that O'Connell maintained that a democracy built on bloodshed could never be stable. O'Connell was conscious that human nature placed limits on the scope of democracy, and he warned against "the profligation of corruption and violence of unreasonable patriotism" (Gwynn 1947, 55). This nonviolent revolutionary won the faith of the people by his inexhaustible capacity for hard work, his legal expertise, his innovative and dramatic victories in court, and his unshakable love for Ireland and the Irish. Within the confines of the courthouse, he defied the establishment and "he forced [them] to rule in accordance with law and the constitution" (Edwards 1975, 38). O'Connell became known as "the Counsellor," and his name and exploits passed into folklore. His brand of liberal nationalism, his intimate knowledge of the people and the law brought him to identify constitutional agitation as the means to his ends. Indeed, constitutional agitation using the moral force of the disenfranchised provided the template for future democratic mobilizations.

On a practical level, contact with America mirrors the difficulties and contradictions that accompanied his political work. The Irish masses were not directly involved in the antislavery movement. This was the preserve of a small group of liberal Protestants, Quakers, and nonconformists. The Irish, however, welcomed any black slaves or freedmen. Frederick Douglass, the then fugitive slave, arrived in Ireland in September 1845. He spoke highly of his visit and his cordial reception. Douglass and O'Connell met in Dublin, and Douglass, like O'Connell, was a renowned orator. They shared a platform in the Conciliation Hall at a meeting to promote repeal of the

Act of Union. At this meeting O'Connell acknowledged Douglass and called him the "Black O'Connell of the United States" (Jenkins 1999, 82). Lee Jenkins gives an account of the "common vocabulary between the abolitionist rhetoric of Douglass and the liberation rhetoric of mid-nineteenth-century Ireland" (Jenkins 1999, 82). At the end of this trip to the British Isles, Douglass's final address contained an adaptation of O'Connell's interpretation of the course of Irish history "which may be traced, like the track of a wounded man through a crowd" (Jenkins 1999, 83), and he applied it to American slavery.

This was not O'Connell's introduction to antislavery. In his article "O'Connell and Slavery," Riach details O'Connell's introduction to the antislavery movement by James Cropper, an English abolitionist who visited Ireland in 1824. Cropper hoped to ease the plight of the West Indian slave by revitalizing the textile industry in Ireland and simultaneously easing the plight of the Irish. It was not only the Irish dimension that attracted O'Connell; he was antislavery because as a humanitarian he considered slavery a sin, and as a utilitarian he recognized that slavery harmed both slave and master and was not a productive use of resources. In 1833 the British government voted to abolish slavery in the British colonies and replace it with a system of "negro apprenticeship." O'Connell quickly identified this scheme as slavery under another guise and spoke against it. O'Connell became one of the British abolitionists' best speakers, and when the Negro Apprenticeship scheme was abolished in 1838 he was invited to Birmingham to celebrate the event. While this event could have marked the conclusion of British abolitionist activities, O'Connell wrote to the organizers and advised them to tackle

slavery and the slave trade in general and American slavery in particular. They followed his advice and from this moment, antislavery truly became a transatlantic reform movement.

O'Connell was renowned for his theatrical performances and his shocking comments. Although he loved America and had learnt from her great institutions, he was not blind to her hypocrisy. "Of all men living," he observed in 1829, "an American citizen who is the owner of slaves, is the most despicable" (Temperley 1962, 219). At the Birmingham celebrations, he identified George Washington as "a hypocrite par excellence for he had waited until his death before permitting his slaves to be emancipated" and declared the American ambassador to the Court of St. James, Andrew Stevenson, a slave breeder (Temperley 1962, 221). Stevenson challenged O'Connell to a duel, but O'Connell abhorred the practice having killed a Dublin man, D'Esterre, in a 1815 duel. While this was in effect a minor incident, it demonstrated how O'Connell, the political opportunist, managed to embarrass Stevenson during the affair, and the coverage it received in the American press hinted that Southern slavery was losing support amongst the public.

O'Connell's view of nationalism emphasized the emancipation of Irish Catholics, and one of his principal maneuvers was to locate the source of Ireland's difficulties with England and not the Irish Protestant ascendancy. O'Connell was also very loyal to the British monarchy. However, when the Potato Famine of 1845 led to starvation followed by mass emigration to America, the impoverished Irish emigrants found themselves in an Anglo-American society antagonistic to them, and they had to compete with free blacks for work and status.

The successful Irish Americans on the other hand, "worked for an Irish nation-state to improve their relative position in America" (McCaffrey 1980, 101). Regardless, both groups carried with them a hatred of England as the source of their grief, and they could not understand O'Connell's commitment to constitutional agitation and his aversion to revolutionary tactics. They identified with the youthful, revolutionary wing of the repeal movement, the Young Irelanders. The Irish Americans did not align with the American abolitionists as they saw the abolitionists as a radical group with ulterior motives for befriending the Irish Americans.

The abolitionists recognized that the Irish in America were capable of influencing the election of the president and various members of the state legislatures. However, on the vexed question of slavery the Irish were at best indifferent and at worst supportive of slavery. At different times in 1838 and again in 1840 first Elizur Wright and then James Haughton, the English and Irish abolitionists, respectively, discussed this with O'Connell. Finally, after the World Anti-Slavery Convention held in London, in June 1840, O'Connell was again asked to address the Irish in America. He replied that he had an address in mind; however, this was superseded by an address drawn up by a group of the abolitionists who visited Ireland after the World Convention. Charles Lenox Remond and John A. Collins, along with the Irishmen James Haughton, Richard Allen, and Richard Davis Webb, formulated the *Address from the People of Ireland to Their Countrymen and Countrywomen in America*. Up to 60,000 Irish people signed the Address. O'Connell was among the last to sign, as apparently he was unaware of its existence.

Father Theobald Mathew also signed it, and possibly to their dismay, their names carried more weight than the 60,000 others. The Address called attention to the vexed subject of slavery in America, and it advised the Irish Americans that neutrality was not an option in this subject: they either supported slavery or they did not. It proclaimed "America is cursed by slavery! WE CALL UPON YOU TO UNITE WITH THE ABOLITIONISTS," as they "*are the only consistent advocates of liberty*," and with a final flourish it advised the Irish men and women: "*Treat the colored people as your equals, as brethren*. By your memories of Ireland, continue to love liberty—hate slavery—CLING BY THE ABOLITIONISTS—and *in America you will do honor to the name of Ireland*" (Ignatiev 1995, 10).

Charles Lenox Remond brought the Address back to America and presented it to an American audience on January 28, 1842, in Faneuil Hall, Boston. The abolitionists, spearheaded by William Lloyd Garrison, genuinely believed this would have a positive effect on the Irish Americans. During that meeting, the abolitionist Frederick Douglass complimented the Irish on their support; however, one Irish American informed the meeting that "the Irish-Americans were ruled neither from Home nor Rome" (Riach 1980, 180). The nation's press took up the issue, and the Irish press in America, led by the *Boston Pilot*, began by questioning the Address, its authenticity, and its provenance and finally by declaring its annoyance at the audacity of a foreign, albeit Irish source under the signatures of the Liberator, Daniel O'Connell, and the Apostle of Temperance, Father Mathew, for daring to dictate policy to the Irish Americans. Ignatiev gives a detailed account of this event. The Irish Americans were sensitive about the subject of slavery: antislavery advocates were considered radicals, and O'Connell's directions to support the abolitionists were seen as undermining the efforts of the Irish Americans to be accepted into American society. In an effort to appease abolitionists, O'Connell promised to return any repeal money sent from slave-holding states. While some repeal money was returned, it appears that this money had been accompanied with requests for violent agitation to achieve repeal. These requests contradicted O'Connell's beliefs. O'Connell's contribution to Irish-American ideology is limited; however, his legacy to America resides in the training the Irish received in the practice of democracy as they campaigned for Catholic Emancipation and repeal. The Irish Americans embraced political and administrative life in America and were considered the most productive political activists in nineteenth- and twentieth-century America.

Ann Coughlan

References

Edwards, R. Dudley. *Daniel O'Connell and His World*. London: Thames and Hudson, 1975.

Gwynn, Denis. *Daniel O'Connell*. Cork: Cork University Press, 1947.

Ignatiev, Noel. *How the Irish Became White*. New York: Routledge, 1995

Jenkins, Lee. "Beyond the Pale: Frederick Douglass and Cork." *The Irish Review* 24 (Autumn 1999): 80–95

McCaffrey, Lawrence J. "O'Connell and the Irish American Nationalist and Political Profiles." In *The World of Daniel O'Connell*, edited by Donal McCartney, 100–111. Dublin: Mercier, 1980.

McCartney, Donal. "The World of Daniel O'Connell." In *The World of Daniel O'Connell*, edited by Donal McCartney, 1–18. Dublin: Mercier, 1980.

Riach, Douglas C. "O'Connell and Slavery." In *The World of Daniel O'Connell*, edited by Donal McCartney, 175–185. Dublin: Mercier, 1980.

Temperley, Howard. "The O'Connell-Stevenson Contretemps: A Reflection of the Anglo-American Slavery Issue. *The Journal of Negro History* 47, no. 4 (October 1962): 217–233.

O'CONNOR, EDWIN (1918–1968)

Born in Woonsocket, Rhode Island, on July 29, 1918, Edwin Greene O'Connor was the eldest son in a second-generation Irish-American family, the son of a local physician and a teacher. He graduated from the University of Notre Dame (1939) and worked at radio stations in Providence, Rhode Island; West Palm Beach, Florida; Buffalo, New York; and Hartford, Connecticut. After serving in the U.S. Coast Guard's public relations office (1942–1945), he was a radio announcer in Boston. In 1946, the tall, robust O'Connor began his literary career in Boston with stories published in the *Atlantic Monthly*. When freelance writing proved unprofitable, he eked out a living as a television critic for the *Boston Herald* newspaper (1950–1952). His friend Edward Weeks, the *Atlantic Monthly* editor, hired O'Connor in 1953 to edit *Treadmill to Oblivion* (1954), a humorous memoir by the Boston Irish comedian Fred Allen. O'Connor, who became a close friend of Fred Allen, also edited Allen's autobiography, *Much Ado About Me* (1956). Another *Atlantic Monthly* editor, Robert Manning, recalled that the Boston magazine office was O'Connor's club, which he visited daily from his monastic apartment in the once genteel Back Bay and later on Beacon Hill.

O'Connor's first novel, *The Oracle* (1951), a satire on radio broadcasters, was not a success. He then earned a living as a *Boston Post* (1953–1956) newspaper columnist while writing his masterpiece, the best-selling novel *The Last Hurrah* (1956). Loosely based on the tumultuous political career of Massachusetts Governor James Michael Curley, this insightful book was adapted for director John Ford's film (1958) by the same title. Although the talented Irish-American actor Spencer Tracy played the lead as Governor Frank Skeffington, O'Connor was bitterly disappointed by the movie. However, the public enjoyed this sentimental film so much that Carroll O'Connor remade it as a television film in 1977.

The Last Hurrah reveals O'Connor's fascination with rough-and-tumble ward politics so far removed from his own upper-middle-class origins. Most critics were quite favorable, *The New York Times* book reviewer hailed it the "first successful Irish-American novel," and the Book-of-the Month Club quickly selected the novel. *The Last Hurrah* remains a subtle, sophisticated, and humorous account of American municipal politics in the twentieth century. House Speaker Tip O'Neill recalled in his memoirs how he discovered that many politicians across the country were fascinated by the novel and by Curley's (or Frank Skeffington's) colorful career.

O'Connor also wrote an unsuccessful children's book, *Benjy: A Ferocious Fairy Tale* (1957), but then won the Pulitzer Prize for his best novel, *The Edge of Sadness* (1961), which describes three generations of Irish-Americans through the eyes of a troubled alcoholic priest, Father Hugh Kennedy. Many critics admired the dark and witty best seller's convincing portrait of daily life in a Catholic rectory and its astute exploration of Irish-American middle-class family mores. O'Connor's next novel, *I Was Dancing* (1964), reflects his love for vaudeville

in the main character, the aged Waltzing Daniel Considine. He wrote the play first, but it was not produced on Broadway until 1966. Both the novel and play met with limited success.

Central to O'Connor's writing are the Catholic Church and Massachusetts politics, both dominated by Irish Americans and essential to their cultural identity. However, O'Connor's image of Boston is one of profound defeat for the Irish and is best seen in his rogue hero, Frank Skeffington, an aged clan chieftain in political exile. Although Curley was initially critical of the novel and film, and threatened a lawsuit against O'Connor and Columbia Pictures, he came to embrace Frank Skeffington as his alter ego.

With his last novel, *All in the Family* (1966), O'Connor returned to Massachusetts politics with some inspiration from the Kennedy clan. This book was only modestly successful in sales and reviews. O'Connor's finest writing, in *The Last Hurrah* and *The Edge of Sadness,* represents a poignant account of the Irish-American journey from suffering, exile, survival, and the struggle to success. In *The New Yorker,* his friend John Kenneth Galbraith dubbed O'Connor "the leading prophet of the acculturation of the Irish."

Ed O'Connor, the witty, shy, and abstemious Beacon Hill bachelor, married Veniette Caswell Weil in 1962. He spent summers in Wellfleet on Cape Cod, a popular but reserved friend to the writers and scholars who vacationed there. He made frequent visits to Ireland, although he urged the Irish in America to assimilate more fully. Pointedly, he never joined Irish-American organizations or accepted their awards, and he avoided all Saint Patrick's Day celebrations.

Edwin O'Connor, a devout Catholic who never smoked or drank, died in a Boston hospital on March 23, 1968, and was buried at Holyhood Cemetery in Brookline. Recognized as the foremost Irish-American writer, he worked steadily at his craft without grants, fellowships, or academic appointments. In 1970, his friend Arthur Schlesinger, Jr., edited an anthology of his work, *The Best and Last of Edwin O'Connor*. The O'Connor papers are preserved at the Boston Public Library.

Peter C. Holloran

See also: ALLEN, Fred; CURLEY, James Michael; FORD, John

References

Duffy, Charles F. *A Family of His Own: A Life of Edwin O'Connor*. Washington, DC: Catholic University of America Press, 2003.

O'Connell, Shaun. *Imagining Boston: A Literary Landscape*. Boston: Beacon Press, 1990.

Schlesinger, Arthur, Jr. ed. *The Best and Last of Edwin O'Connor*. Boston: Little, Brown, 1970.

Portrait of Flannery O'Connor, author of Wise Blood *and* The Violent Bear It Away, *as well as many short stories. (Library of Congress)*

O'CONNOR, "MARY" FLANNERY (1925–1964)

In spite of her short career, modest output, and tragically young death, Flannery O'Connor's literary reputation as one of the preeminent short story writers and novelists in the United States is firmly established. Despite her Irish-American background, however, she never appeared to reflect directly on the hyphenated significance that Irish-American identity might have held, either in her life or in her work. Perhaps there was complexity enough in those other definitions that were, and are still, commonly applied to her: southern writer, woman writer, Catholic writer, grotesque writer, and the many permutations and combinations thereof. O'Connor's work is characterized by an absolute and unflinching belief in Catholicism, though the workings of her God's grace are presented paradoxically through the violence and desperation of "poor white" lives and attitudes that are typically Protestant, as befits the Bible Belt of O'Connor's home region. Any apparent anomaly she addresses in one of her occasional essays, "The Catholic Novelist in the Protestant South," collected in her only nonfiction publication, *Mystery and Manners* (1969). That title provides an apt synopsis of O'Connor's work in general—the manners of those good country people who populate her stories and novels are used, frequently satirically, to reveal religious mysteries of redemption and grace.

O'Connor was born in Savannah, Georgia, only child of Edward F. O'Connor, a realtor by profession, and his wife Regina Cline O'Connor. In 1937 the family moved to Milledgeville, Georgia, where Regina's father had been mayor for many years, apparently in search of greater job opportunities during the Depression, but also to seek family support when Flannery's father died in 1938 of systemic lupus erythematosus, the disease that would in turn claim her own life at the early age of 39. She attended Georgia State College for Women and the University of Iowa Writers' Workshop, where she earned an MFA in creative writing in 1945. At Iowa, O'Connor met such luminaries of the southern literary tradition as Allen Tate and Robert Penn Warren and impressed them with her emerging talent. In 1947, she won the Rinehart-Iowa Fiction Award for her thesis story collection, *The Geranium.* The following year she gained a place at Yaddo, the prestigious writers' colony, where she worked on her first novel, *Wise Blood,* a task that continued when she moved first to New York City and then to the Connecticut home of friends, Robert and Sally Fitzgerald. Up to this point in her life, O'Connor seemed set on a successful literary career that would have taken her outside the South, but in 1950 she developed the first symptoms of lupus, which forced her to return to the care of her mother in Milledgeville. With the exception of a few short trips away from home, she remained on the family farm, Andalusia, for the rest of her life.

Though Haze Motes, the protagonist of *Wise Blood,* appears thoroughly "down home" in his bearing and expression, the fundamentalist Protestantism that enrages him so—to the extent that he determines to found "the Church Without Christ"—is not dissimilar to that of the Scots-Irish settlers whose descendants continue to form a significant population group in the South. Indeed, John Huston's 1979 film adaptation opens with a montage of tin signs bearing fundamentalist Christian slogans tacked to trees, an image not unfamiliar in many parts of Ulster even today. Despite the resistance of this "Christian *malgré lui,*" as O'Connor describes Haze, he is subject to the type of redemption that her muscularly beneficent Catholicism allows, and the paradox of his fate illustrates that God will not be gainsaid when He, not man, decides salvation is due. The humor with which O'Connor details Haze's resistance, however, and the devious, dishonest, or downright sinful behavior of the novel's minor characters explain why certain critics, notably John Hawkes, have suggested that O'Connor has at least a passing regard for transgression, a charge she strenuously denied.

O'Connor's first story collection, *A Good Man is Hard to Find,* was published in 1955. Her concerns with the grotesque, the religious, and the southern come together more successfully here than in *Wise Blood,* which had been greeted with fairly hostile reviews. The title story is perhaps O'Connor's most anthologized piece, and a perfect example of her method. A sanctimonious, dominant grandmother, who displays all the negative "old South" traits of snobbishness and complacent racism, insists on detouring during a family motoring holiday and, leaving the highway, encounters The Misfit, a homicidal maniac, and his gang, who promptly massacre all the family members, ending with the old woman herself. Facing death, she discovers a moment's revelation as her former narrow-mindedness falls away, and she finds human kinship with her executioner who, transformed thus into an agent of God's grace, delivers her to her Heavenly Father with the savagely redemptive statement: "She would of been a good woman if it had been somebody there to shoot her every minute of her life."

The short story form suited O'Connor's talents, and the influence of the ideas of New Criticism is apparent, both in the finely crafted stories themselves and in her self-interpretations in *Mystery and Manners.* A second novel, *The Violent Bear It Away,* appeared in 1960, but did not receive the acclaim that was given to the posthumously published story collection, *Everything That Rises Must Converge* (1965), which completed her modest output of work and consolidated her position as one of America's leading short story writers. In this respect, her allusions in letters to the two major Irish figures who dominated the short story form through the twentieth century, Frank O'Connor and Seán O'Faoláin, are worth noting. Though she does not refer directly to their respective treatises on the genre, *The Short Story* and *The Lonely Voice,* her own short fiction bears all the hallmarks that the Irish masters praised as essential. Of O'Faoláin she announced with an uncharacteristic lack of reserve: "I like all that he writes"; while, more characteristically, and more humorously, she confessed of Frank O'Connor: "I keep waiting for some club lady to ask me if I am kin to [him]. At which I hope to reply, 'I am his mother'" (*The Habit of Being* 1979, 121).

By nature a private person, O'Connor directly revealed little about her own life. We can assume that she carried her Irish ancestry fairly lightly, but her deep concern for religious values in a relatively secular age, and a wicked wit that could be simultaneously mocking yet indulgent of her characters, are features that link her to an Irish tradition of writing, every bit as much as an American one.

Bill Lazenbatt

See also: HUSTON, John; SCOTS-IRISH

References
O'Connor, Flannery. *A Good Man is Hard to Find.* New York: Harcourt Brace and Co., 1955.
O'Connor, Flannery. *The Habit of Being: Letters / Flannery O'Connor,* edited by Sally Fitzgerald. New York: Farrar, Straus, Giroux, 1979.

O'CONNOR, FRANCISCO "FRANK" BURDETT (1791–1871)

Franciso ("Frank") Burdett O'Connor was a colonel in the Irish Legion of Simón Bolívar's army in Venezuela and later became chief of staff to Antonio José de Sucre and minister of war in Bolivia. Born on June 12, 1791, in the city of Cork, from a landowning Protestant family from England (originally named Conner), Frank O'Connor was the son of Roger O'Connor and Wilhamena Bowen, brother of the member of Parliament and Chartist leader Feargus O'Connor (1794–1855), and nephew of Arthur O'Connor (1763–1852), member of Parliament and hard-line leader of the United Irishmen. Frank O'Connor's godfather was Sir Francis Burdett, a baronet and radical member of the English parliament.

In July 1919, the lieutenant-colonel of the 10th Lancers Francisco Burdett O'Connor boarded the *Hannah* in Dublin together with 100 officers and 101 men of the Irish Legion in Simón Bolívar's army of independence. The commanding officer of the 10th Lancers, Col. William Aylmer, was also second in command of the Irish Legion. They arrived in September 1819 in the island of Margarita near Venezuela. No preparations had been made to receive them, and the men of the Irish Legion suffered under the combined effects of the officers' lack of experience, scarce victuals, and deficiency of buildings. Many of the officers died and others refused to remain and returned to Ireland.

In December 1819 the Irish Legion was reorganized, and O'Connor was appointed commandant of a regiment formed by mixed forces. In March 1820 the regiment sailed for the mainland to attack the city of Rio Hacha together with other units. O'Connor's lancers hauled down the Spanish royal ensign and raised in its place their own standard, displaying the harp of Ireland in the center. When on March 20, 1820, the enemy attacked the patriots near Laguna Salada, O'Connor's lancers were the only ones to rush out of their barracks and to storm the royalist forces, forcing them to withdraw in flight. One hundred seventy Irishmen, supported by a company of sharpshooters and one small field gun, defeated 1,700 royalists.

When the division was marching out of Rio Hacha the advance guard walked into an ambuscade. O'Connor was slightly wounded in the right shoulder when he and his lancers were charging the enemy with a terrible "hurrah." After a mutiny, the Irish Legion was dispatched to Jamaica, but some hundred of the lancers O'Connor had managed to keep loyal disembarked again in the mainland and took an important part in the siege of Cartagena and the campaign against Santa Marta.

Bolívar had quickly gained a high regard for the young Irish colonel, whom he appointed chief of staff of the United Army of Liberation in Peru within six months of his joining it from Panama early in 1824. It was O'Connor who kept the patriot forces coordinated and supplied as they maneuvered under Sucre's command in distinctly hostile territory to bring the last Spanish viceroy in mainland America to battle and defeat. At the battle of Junín in August 1824, O'Connor was chief of staff of the patriot army with 1,500 men against the viceroy's 7,000 troops and nine artillery pieces. The engagement was confined to cavalry charges and ended within an hour with not a single shot fired.

Once established in the area that is present-day Bolivia, almost 15 years later O'Connor rejoined forces with Otto Braun, ex-commander of the grenadiers at the battle of Junín, to aid the Peruvian-Bolivian army. On June 24, 1838, they defeated the invading Argentine army at the battle of Montenegro (known as Cuyambuyo by the Argentines). The battle of Montenegro consolidated the present southwest border of Bolivia and allowed O'Connor to retire from military service and dedicate himself to his farms.

Since 1825 O'Connor had contributed to *El Condor* of Chuquisaca. In June 1827, he published a proclamation encouraging Irish people to settle in the "New Erin" of Tarija, "where the poor of my flesh and blood will be received with open arms." O'Connor's memoirs were published in 1895 by his grandson Tomás O'Connor d'Arlach with the title *Independencia Americana: Recuerdos de Francisco Burdett O'Connor*. They are an essential contemporary account of the South American wars of independence.

In 1826, O'Connor was appointed military governor of Tarija. The congress of Bolivia awarded him 5,000 pesos as a "liberator," but he himself never used that title despite the rare honor it bestowed. In 1827, he married Francisca Ruyloba, the 17-year-old daughter of a family of clerks and priests. O'Connor died in Tarija on October 5, 1871, at 81 years of age. An atheist while in Ireland, he became a devout Catholic in South America and died with the last rites. Although only one of his children survived—a daughter, Hercilia—O'Connor d'Arlach is still a recognized family name in southern Bolivia, and one of the provinces of the department of Tarija carries the name of O'Connor.

Edmundo Murray

See also: O'LEARY, Daniel Florence

References

Dunkerley, James. *The Third Man: Francisco Burdett O'Connor and the Emancipation of the Americas.* Occasional Papers No. 20. London: University of London, Institute of Latin American Studies, 1999.

Hasbrouck, Alfred. *Foreign Legionaries in the Liberation of Spanish South America.* New York: Columbia University Press, 1928.

McGinn, Brian. "St. Patrick's Day in Peru, 1824." *Irish Roots* 1 (1995): 26–27.

O'CONNOR, PAT (1943–)

Since the 1980s Pat O'Connor has established a strong reputation on both sides of the Atlantic through a series of films that explore the reality of lives lived in twentieth-century Ireland. Many of his films have a literary orientation recognizable to both Irish and American audiences; the screenplays for *The Ballroom of Romance, Cal, Circle of Friends,* and *Dancing at Lughnasa* are based on short stories, novels, and plays, all with the same titles, by William Trevor, Bernard MacLaverty, Maeve Binchy, and Brian Friel, respectively. Since his earliest work, O'Connor has proved himself more interested in the effects that a particular set of circumstances have upon characters and character interactions than in analyzing the political and social circumstances themselves. Many of his films have been categorized as examples of heritage filmmaking, a genre known for its nostalgic and often literary look at the conservative values and social world of the seemingly idyllic past. O'Connor films with more contemporary settings often portray social and familial circumstances as inescapable; characters cannot change events, but they can choose their response to them.

O'Connor was born in Ardmore, Co. Waterford, into a family of six children. He left the Christian Brothers' school at age 17 and held a series of menial jobs, such as road paver and wine corker. O'Connor moved to the United States to earn a BA in liberal arts at University of California at Los Angeles, but had to return to Ireland for familial reasons. He later took a degree in film and television at Ryerson Institute in Toronto, Canada, and again returned to Ireland after his graduation in 1969. In 1970, O'Connor accepted a position at Radio Telefís Éireann in the documentary and drama departments, where he spent the 1970s directing and producing more than 45 documentaries and dramas, including *The Four Roads, The Shankhill, Kittyclogher, One of Ourselves, Night in Ginitia, Mobile Homes,* and *Miracles and Miss Langan,* and also wrote episodes of RTÉ's successful and long-running series *The Riordans. The Ballroom of Romance* (1981) was his breakout piece. The television movie depicted the repressive sexuality of rural Ireland in the 1950s and earned him a BAFTA and the New York Festival's Silver Drama Award. Following this success, O'Connor commenced freelance work on a Neil Jordan script called *Night in Tunisia* and another project, *One of Ourselves,* both of which appeared in 1982. His first cinematic film, *Cal,* debuted in 1984 and depicts a reluctant Irish Republican Army driver in a relationship with a woman widowed by his unit. Helen Mirren won the Best Actress Award at the Cannes Film Festival for her work in the film.

Other O'Connor film credits include a film version of J. R. Carr's novel *A Month in The Country* (1987), a heritage film set in Yorkshire that helped launch the careers of Kenneth Branagh and Colin Firth. *Stars and Bars* (1988) and *The January Man* (1989) reveal O'Connor unsuccessfully trying his hand at black comedy and thriller, respectively, after O'Connor's move back to the United States. He returned to the heritage film genre with *Fools of Fortune* (1990), a drama portraying an Anglo-Irish family during the Irish War of Independence that was honored with a Best Picture nod at the Barcelona Film Festival. O'Connor then went back to television in the first half of the 1990s, yielding *Zelda* (1993), a portrayal of the life of Zelda Fitzgerald, wife of author F. Scott Fitzgerald. He returned to the big screen with *Circle of Friends* (1995), which introduced actress Minnie Driver to American audiences and also stars Chris O'Donnell and Colin Firth. The story of three Irish girls coming of age in the 1950s was the highest grossing independent film in the United States that year. O'Connor's next film, *Inventing the Abbots* (1997), is also set in the United States during that same period and features performances by Liv Tyler, Joaquin Phoenix, and Jennifer Connelly. In *Dancing at Lughnasa* (1998), starring Meryl Streep, Brid Brennan, and Michael Gambon, O'Connor returns to an Irish setting and continues his focus on family dynamics, this time by presenting five sisters in the 1930s. His most recent film, *Sweet November* (2001), featuring Charlize Theron and Keanu Reeves, presents a terminally-ill woman who temporarily escapes from her family to live and love before returning home.

O'Connor is married to American actress Mary Elizabeth Mastrantonio, who played the lead female role in *The January Man*. The couple has two sons, Jack and Declan.

Kelly J. S. McGovern

See also: FITZGERALD, F. SCOTT; JORDAN, Neil; SHERIDAN, Jim

References

Aloon, Yoram, Del Cullen, and Hannah Patterson, eds. *Contemporary British and Irish Film Directors*. London: Wallflower, 2001.

Lennon, E. "Inventing the Director." *Film Ireland* 58 (April–May 1997): 12–17.

MacKillop, James, ed. *Contemporary Irish Cinema: From the Quiet Man to Dancing at Lughnasa*. Syracuse, NY: Syracuse University Press, 1999.

Pettitt, Lance. *Screening Ireland: Film and Television Representation*. Manchester, UK: Manchester University Press, 2000.

O'FAOLAIN, NUALA (1942–)

A columnist and author made famous by her "accidental" memoir of life as a young woman from a large family in mid-twentieth-century Ireland, Nuala O'Faolain's *Are You Somebody: The Accidental Memoir of a Dublin Woman* (1998) began as an introduction to a collection of her *Irish Times* columns but became a popularly acclaimed and critically accepted description of her path toward journalism and adult womanhood. The memoir's success encouraged her to commence her next project, a novel entitled *My Dream of You* (2001), which ties together the story of an affair between an Anglo-Irish wife and servant in the decade of the Potato Famine and the experiences of a modern middle-aged female journalist who recently returned to Ireland from London to research the historic affair. O'Faolain returned to the memoir form in *Almost There: The Onward Journey of a Dublin Woman* (2003), in which she documents how the publication of her memoir affected her outlook, relationships, and identity as an aging Irish woman. O'Faolain not only carves out an identity for older Irish women but also allows women past middle age a sexual identity.

Are You Somebody records the trials of growing up in the 1950s as the second of nine children born to a philandering father and an alcoholic mother who had a penchant for escaping into novels. Her father's occupation as a social columnist emphasized the discrepancy between his extravagant lifestyle and the family's poverty and neglect. O'Faolain was sent to boarding school at age 14. She later attended both University College Dublin and Oxford on scholarships. She received a PhD in medieval literature from the University of Hull and returned to lecture at University College Dublin before becoming a television producer for the BBC. Her presentations on the progressive television series *Women Talking* caught the attention of the *Irish Times* and led it to offer her the columnist position. Though unmarried, O'Faolain has had a series of long-term relationships, including one with prominent Irish feminist Nell McCafferty. She has no children. She resides both in Ireland and in Brooklyn, New York with her boyfriend and his daughter.

Kelly J. S. McGovern

See also: GREAT FAMINE, The

Reference
Merkin, Daphne. "A Thorny Irish Rose." *New York Times Magazine,* February 18, 2001, 22–25.

O'GORMAN, CAMILA (1828–1848),

Camila O'Gorman, who was executed in 1848 after eloping with the Catholic priest Uladislao Gutierrez, was born in 1828, the daughter of Adolfo O'Gorman and Joaquina Ximénez Pinto. She was a granddaughter of Thomas O'Gorman, a merchant born in Ennis, Co. Clare, who settled in Buenos Aires in 1797. Thomas O'Gorman's brother was the distinguished physician Dr. Michael O'Gorman (b. 1749), founder of the first school of medicine in Buenos Aires.

Educated in the rigid rules of the Hispano-Creole elite of postindependence times, Camila O'Gorman belonged to a renowned family of Buenos Aires. At 19 years old she was a beautiful and intelligent young lady. She had good relations with the family of Juan Manuel de Rosas, the traditionalist and pro-Catholic governor of Buenos Aires, and his daughter Manuelita. Father Uladislao Gutierrez (1823–1848), nephew of the governor of northwestern province of Tucumán, entered the local theological school when he was a teenager. He was sent to the city of Buenos Aires, and, although he was only 24 years old, in August 1846 he was appointed as deputy parish priest of Nuestra Señora del Socorro church. Father Gutierrez, a friend of Camila's brother Father Eduardo O'Gorman, was among those frequently invited to gatherings at the O'Gorman's residence.

On December 12, 1847, Camila O'Gorman and Father Gutierrez eloped, and using false names they left Buenos Aires on horseback with the idea to reach Rio de Janeiro some months later. However, when they arrived at Goya, Corrientes province (800 kilometers north of Buenos Aires) they decided to settle there. The couple worked as teachers and opened a school, but the parish priest, Irish-born Father Michael Gannon (who was Admiral William Brown's uncle) informed the provincial authorities of Corrientes against them. On June 19, 1848, Governor Virasoro ordered them to be brought back to Buenos Aires province.

Camila's father Adolfo O'Gorman; the bishop of Buenos Aires, Dr. Medrano; the Irish chaplain Father Anthony Fahy; lawyer Dalmacio Vélez Sarsfield; and journalist Santiago Kiernan were some of those who demanded an exemplary punishment of the wayward daughter who was giving a bad name to the industrious and well-regarded Irish community. In a highly politicized case, after receiving the scorn of the opposition and signs of lack of allegiance from his followers, Governor Rosas condemned the couple to death. They were executed by firing squad on August 18, 1848, in Santos Lugares, near Buenos Aires. Camila was 20 old and eight months pregnant. This drama inspired many fictional books, poems, and other works of art, most notably the film *Camila* by Maria Luisa Bemberg (Buenos Aires, 1984), which was nominated for an Academy Award for Best Foreign Film in 1985.

Edmundo Murray

See also: ARGENTINA; FAHY, Father Anthony; O'GORMAN, Michael

References

Julianello, Maria Teresa. *The Scarlet Trinity: The Doomed Struggle of Camila O'Gorman against Family, Church and State in Nineteenth-Century Buenos Aires.* Cork: Irish Centre for Migration Studies, 2000.

Luna, Félix, ed. *Camila O'Gorman.* Buenos Aires: Planeta, 1999.

Molina, Enrique. *Una Sombra Donde Sueña Camila O'Gorman.* Buenos Aires: Losada, 1973.

O'GORMAN, EDMUNDO (1906–1995) AND JUAN (1905–1982)

Sons of the painter and engineer Cecil Crawford O'Gorman (1874–1943), who arrived in Mexico from Ireland in 1895, Edmundo, who became a historian, and Juan O'Gorman, who became an artist and architect, were the great-grandchildren of Charles O'Gorman, who in the 1820s was the first British consul to Mexico City. Charles O'Gorman and his Mexican wife returned to the British Isles with their son John, who attended Eton and returned to Mexico.

Edmundo O'Gorman was born in Mexico City on December 24, 1906. He graduated from the school of law in 1928 but later decided to research and teach history. He obtained a PhD in philosophy in 1948 and a PhD in history in 1951. From 1932 to 1952, Edmundo worked in the Mexican public records office and contributed to the *Boletín del Archivo General de la Nación*. He was appointed member of the Mexican academies of literature (1969) and of history (1972). For his outstanding research Edmundo was awarded the Mexican national literature award (1964), the Rafael Heliodoro Valle history award (1983), the Humanities Teaching award of the Universidad Autónoma (1986), and the *honoris causa* doctorate of that university (1978).

Among his works are "Historia de las Divisiones Territoriales de México" (1937), "Fundamentos de la Historia de América" (1951), "La Supervivencia Política Novohispana" (1961), "México: El Trauma de su Historia" (1977), "La Incógnita de la Llamada 'Historia de los Indios de la Nueva España,' Atribuida a Fray Toribio Molinia" (1982), and "Destierro de Sombras" (1986). However, his most popular book is *La Invención de América* (1958), in which Edmundo opposed the traditional concept of America's "discovery" with an innovative reading of the primary sources from original perspectives. For his work with contemporary sources of Columbus and other conquistadors, Edmundo O'Gorman is often singled out as one of the pioneers of postcolonial studies in Latin America.

Juan O'Gorman, the famous painter, muralist, and architect, was born in Coyoacán on July 6, 1905, and graduated from the school of architecture at Academia San Carlos in 1927. He entered the studio of Obregón, Tarditi, and Villagrán García and later Obregón Santacilia. Juan was one of the architects who worked on the reconstruction of Banco de México. In 1931 he frescoed the library of Azcapotzalco, and in 1937 he decorated and painted the murals of Mexico City's first airport. In 1940, he was engaged in the great mural of Gertrudis Bocanegra library, including scenes of Michoacán conquest, and the struggle for independence from Spanish rule. Juan's most important work was the painting of the Central Library in the campus of Universidad Autónoma. The works there lasted from 1949 to 1953 and covered 4,000 square meters of historical scenes. Other important works include the Social Security Center and the International Bank in Reforma Avenue, but he also created works for parks, theaters, museums, and private houses, most notably the painter Diego Rivera's "functional house."

Juan strove to incorporate Mexican culture, history, and environment in his works. He studied the styles of Le Corbusier and Villagrán, and as a muralist he was a member of the group formed by Diego Rivera, Clemente Orozco, Pablo O'Higgins, and Rufino Tamayo.

Edmundo Murray

References

Johnston, Henry McKenzie. *Missions to Mexico. A Tale of British Diplomacy in the 1820s.* London: British Academic Press, 1992.

Musacchio, Humberto. *Gran Diccionario Enciclopédico de México Visual.* México, 1989.

O'GORMAN, MICHAEL (1749–1819)

Michael O'Gorman, a physician and founder of the first school of medicine in Argentina, was born in Ennis, Co. Clare, son of Thomas O'Gorman and Mary Baria, who came from a well-known family in the west of Ireland. O'Gorman studied medicine in London, Paris, and Reims, where he graduated in 1773.

The following year General Alejandro O'Reilly invited O'Gorman to join the Spanish academy of medicine. O'Gorman accompanied O'Reilly to Algeria as surgeon in the Hibernia Regiment and played an important role in establishing hospitals during the military campaigns at Orán and Alicante. In recognition of his medical experience and military merit, O'Gorman was appointed medical head of Viceroy Pedro de Cevallos's expedition to the River Plate in 1776.

Once in the River Plate area, O'Gorman practiced both in Buenos Aires and Montevideo. To improve the public health of the colony and to counter quack doctors who swarmed around the region, O'Gorman founded the first school of medicine in the country, which opened officially on August 17, 1780, under the rule of Viceroy Vértiz. The first authorities of the "Protomedicato" were O'Gorman, Cosme Argerich, and Capdevilla, and the school was installed in San Carlos College. On July 19, 1798, King Charles III of Spain formally approved the school of medicine and authorized its operations. On April 8, 1799, O'Gorman was appointed professor of medicine. All doctors were obliged to pass a test to qualify as able professionals and to demonstrate that they were not quacks, and a quarantine was established for arriving passengers to the port of Buenos Aires. Public works were undertaken to improve public health in the city. In 1799, the school of medicine was upgraded to university institute and the curricula were adapted to graduate studies. The new plan was extended to six years. In 1801 there were 13 students.

O'Gorman was responsible for introducing in Spain and later in the River Plate the inoculation method he had learned in London. Since 1785 he had also tested many preventive treatments against smallpox, and wrote a guideline for cattle inoculation at the request of Viceroy Sobremonte. In 1804, to guarantee the health on board the arriving ships, O'Gorman was appointed member of the Health Committee together with Cosme Argerich. During the British campaigns in the River Plate in 1806–1807, O'Gorman was not able to help the wounded soldiers because of his own precarious health. When Mariano Moreno opened the national library in 1810, O'Gorman donated his own collection of books and three ounces of gold.

In 1815 O'Gorman was blind and poor. In April of the following year the government awarded him a pension equivalent to two-thirds of his salary. He died in Buenos Aires on January 20, 1819, supported by his friends and disciples. A street in the the Buenos Aires district of Almirante Brown was named after him in 1904.

Edmundo Murray

See also: ARGENTINA; O'GORMAN, Camilla

Reference

Cutolo, Vicente Osvaldo. *Buenos Aires: Historia de las Calles y Sus Nombres*. Buenos Aires: Editorial Elche, 1994.

"Número del Centenario." Special issue, *The Southern Cross* (1975).

O'HARA, FRANK (1926–1966)

Francis Russell O'Hara was born in Baltimore, Maryland, on March 27, 1926, and raised in the small farming town of Grafton, Massachusetts. His parents, Russell and Katherine Broderick O'Hara, both came from strict Irish-Catholic families. Russell O'Hara managed the family's three farms and a farm machinery dealership. The eldest of three children, Frank O'Hara attended parochial schools throughout his childhood. He rejected Catholicism at a young age, however, perhaps in part because of his homosexuality, which the Catholic Church would not countenance. He began studying piano at the age of seven and aspired to become a great pianist and composer.

After graduating from St. John's High School in Worcester, Massachusetts, in 1944, O'Hara enlisted in the U.S. Navy. He served on the USS *Nicholas* in the South Pacific during World War II but was not involved in actual combat. O'Hara was honorably discharged from the Navy in 1946 and enrolled at Harvard on the GI Bill. After majoring in music for his first year, he changed his major to English literature. O'Hara wrote several short stories, poems, and plays while at Harvard, some of which were published in the *Harvard Advocate*. He also read widely and sat in on as many art history classes as possible. His exposure to Dada and French surrealism would influence his writing for years to come. Following his graduation in 1950, O'Hara spent a year at the University of Michigan, where he earned an MA in comparative literature and won the coveted Hopwood Award for poetry.

O'Hara moved to New York City in the autumn of 1951 and accepted a job as a desk clerk at the Museum of Modern Art. After working at the museum in a nonprofessional capacity for two years, O'Hara resigned to work instead as an editorial associate with *Art News* magazine. He quickly established a reputation as a talented art critic and was accepted as an insider in artistic circles. Before long, O'Hara occupied a central place in the avant-garde art scene of the 1950s. He returned to the Museum of Modern Art in 1955 as the assistant to the director of the museum's international program. O'Hara advanced steadily in his career with the museum: he was made an assistant curator in 1960 and promoted to associate curator five years later. His work brought him into close contact with the painters of the New York School of abstract expressionism, and he collaborated on poem-paintings (paintings with word texts) with a number of painters, including Larry Rivers and Norman Bluhm.

In addition to pursuing a successful career with the Museum of Modern Art, O'Hara continued to concentrate on his poetry. He published his first volume of poems, *A City in Winter,* in 1952. He followed this up with several other volumes, including *Meditations in an Emergency* (1957), *Second Avenue* (1960), and *Lunch Poems* (1964). Together with fellow poets John Ashbery and Kenneth Koch, O'Hara was at the core of a group loosely known as the New York School of poets. O'Hara's work first received national attention when Donald Allen selected 15 of his poems for inclusion in an anthology, *The New American Poetry, 1945–1960* (1960). Much of O'Hara's work falls under the heading of what he called "I do this I do that" poetry because his poems read like diary entries, capturing in a casual style but with great specificity the details of his daily life in the city. In O'Hara's opinion, the purpose of poetry and art was not to convey timeless values or moral lessons but rather to capture the colors and textures of life's ephemeral moments.

O'Hara was struck by a beach buggy on Fire Island just before dawn on July 24, 1966; he died from his injuries the following day. Several more volumes of O'Hara's poetry were published after his death, including *The Collected Poems of Frank O'Hara* (1971), *The Selected Poems of Frank O'Hara* (1974), and *Poems Retrieved: 1950–1966* (1977).

Kathleen Ruppert

References

Berkson, Bill, and Joe LeSueur, eds. *Homage to Frank O'Hara.* Bolinas: Big Sky, 1988.

Feldman, Alan. *Frank O'Hara.* Boston: Twayne Publishers, 1979.

Gooch, Brad. *City Poet: The Life and Times of Frank O'Hara.* New York: Knopf, 1993.

Perloff, Marjorie. *Frank O'Hara: Poet Among Painters.* Chicago: University of Chicago Press, 1997.

O'HARA, MAUREEN (1920–)

Born Maureen FitzSimmons in Milltown, Ireland, near Dublin, O'Hara began acting as a child. While a member of the famed Abbey players, she was discovered by Charles Laughton, who chose her for the lead in *Jamaica Inn* (1939). She went on to star in almost 60 motion pictures throughout her career. She is best known for her roles in films directed by John Ford, such as *How Green Was My Valley* (1941), and opposite John Wayne in Ford's *Rio Grande* (1950) and *The Quiet Man* (1952). Other memorable films include *The Black Swan* (1942), *Miracle on 34th Street* (1947), and *The Parent Trap* (1961). O'Hara retired in 1973, but she continues to appear occasionally in films and on television.

O'Hara was born on August 17, 1920, the second of six children in a talented family. Her mother, a Dublin stage actress and singer, and her father, a retail clothing businessman and founding officer of Dublin's Shamrock Rovers, encouraged her to pursue her love of acting at an early age. O'Hara attended the Abbey Theatre School, the Guildhall School of Music, and Trinity College. By age 17, she had won numerous awards, including the All-Ireland Cup for her performance as Portia in *The Merchant of Venice*. In addition, she performed on radio shows and had roles in several movies, including her first leading role in a British film, *My Irish Molly,* in 1938.

In 1938, prominent actor and director Charles Laughton discovered O'Hara while she was performing with the Abbey Players. After giving her a screen test, Laughton chose her to play the female lead in *Jamaica Inn,* a period piece about the Caribbean. Realizing O'Hara's potential, Laughton persuaded her to change her name (FitzSimmons was too long for a billboard) and leave the Abbey to pursue a career in Hollywood. She made her first U.S. film the next year, starring as Esmeralda to Laughton's Quasimodo in *The Hunchback of Notre Dame* (1939). She made several other films in the next few years, including *Bill of Divorcement* (1940), *Dance, Girl, Dance!* (1940), and *They Met in Argentina* (1941), all of which brought her greater attention and success. O'Hara filmed well in Technicolor action adventures and became one of the most sought-after actresses in Hollywood, particularly for prominent director John Ford.

While many directors often underutilized her talents, Ford showcased her dramatic, singing, and comedic abilities to their best advantage in such films as *How Green Was My Valley* (1941). Her portrayal of Angharad in Ford's Oscar-winning film about a Welsh coal-mining family won her critical acclaim for the first time, and

proved her range as an actress. Linked by their Irish backgrounds, Ford developed a lasting professional and personal relationship with O'Hara, using her in some of his best films, and pairing her with another of his favorites, John Wayne. The five-foot eight-inch, athletic O'Hara was a good match for the Duke's six-foot four-inch frame. Her quick wit mixed with his dry humor created a legendary onscreen partnership in such films as *Fort Apache* (1948), *Rio Grande* (1950), *The Wings of Eagles* (1957), and *McLintock!* (1963).

The most famous film that Ford, O'Hara, and Wayne made was *The Quiet Man* (1952), adapted from Maurice Walsh's short story. Ford first approached O'Hara and Wayne in the mid-1940s about his labor-of-love project, and he even worked on the script with O'Hara for several years, but Republic Pictures made him complete other projects first, hoping to recoup their losses with moneymaking Westerns. Filmed on location in Cong, Co. Mayo, *The Quiet Man* won Oscars for its lush Technicolor filming of the Irish landscape and for Best Director. The film contained an almost all-Irish cast, including family members of Ford, O'Hara, and Wayne. The chemistry created by Wayne's portrayal of the ex-boxer Sean Thornton who has returned home to Ireland and O'Hara's depiction of the fiery colleen Mary Kate Danaher whom Thornton falls in love with made the film an overwhelming success. They were supported with memorable performances by John Victor McLaglen, as Mary Kate's bullheaded brother Squire "Red" Will Danaher, and Barry Fitzgerald, as the irrepressible matchmaker Michaeleen Flynn. While some critics have panned the film as a stereotypical, stage-Irish view of a nonexistent Ireland, others view it as a provocative, postmodern look at a romanticized Ireland as seen through the eyes of the "returned Yank," consciously playing on subjects like the role of the church, political violence, gender, and tradition in modern Ireland. Regardless, *The Quiet Man* remains the most lasting filmic representation of Ireland to date and a classic romantic comedy.

Between 1952 and 1973, O'Hara starred in more than 20 films, mainly period action adventures, with such legends as Tyrone Power, Errol Flynn, James Stewart, and of course, John Wayne. Some notable films from the period include *The Long Grey Line* (1955), *Spencer's Mountain* (1963), and a television adaptation of Steinbeck's novel, *The Red Pony* (1973). By the 1960s O'Hara had graduated to playing mother roles, including memorable performances in Disney's *The Parent Trap* (1961), with Brian Keith and Hayley Mills, and *Mr. Hobbs Takes a Vacation* (1962), with James Stewart.

O'Hara retired from acting in 1973 to enjoy time with her husband, aviator General Charles Blair, whom she had married in 1968. They moved to the Caribbean to manage a commuter seaplane service, made various trips around the world, and had a daughter Bronwyn. O'Hara also published a monthly magazine, *The Virgin Islander,* in which she wrote a column, "Maureen O'Hara Says." She was also elected chief executive officer and president of her airlines, making her the first woman to gain that distinction in the United States. Since Blair's death in 1978, she has returned to the screen periodically, most recently appearing as John Candy's obstinate mother in *Only the Lonely* (1991) and several television movies, including *The Christmas Box* (1995) and *The Last Dance* (2000). O'Hara continues to live in semiretirement

in St. Croix, although she maintains homes in New York, Los Angeles, and Ireland.

Although O'Hara became a U.S. citizen in 1940, she retains close ties to her family and her roots in Ireland. She is a member of several Irish and Irish-American organizations, and has received various Irish-American awards, including the prestigious John F. Kennedy Memorial Award for an "outstanding American of Irish descent for service to God and country." In 1999, she became only the third woman ever to lead the New York City Saint Patrick's Day Parade as Grand Marshall. O'Hara remains one of the most enduring leading ladies of the screen, and certainly the most memorable Irish "colleen" of movie history.

Meaghan Dwyer

See also: FITZGERALD, Barry; FORD, John; SAINT PATRICK'S DAY PARADES; WAYNE, John

References

Curran, Joseph M. *Hibernian Green on the Silver Screen: The Irish and American Movies.* New York: Greenwood Press, 1989.
English, Thomas. "America's Colleen: Maureen O'Hara." *Irish America Magazine* (February 1987): 30–36.
Gibbons, Luke. *The Quiet Man.* Cork: Cork University Press, 2002.

O'HERLIHY, DAN (1919–2005)

Born in Wexford, Ireland on May 1, 1919, Dan O'Herlihy was educated at Blackrock College. Following in the footsteps of his father, he studied architecture at the National University of Ireland, later graduating. He soon gravitated toward the theater, however, and he began acting with the Abbey Players. Later, he moved to Dublin's Gate Theatre, where he ended up appearing in more than 50 plays. He played the lead role in the first production of Sean O'Casey's *Red Roses For Me* in 1943. His breakthrough role as a film actor came in Carol Reed's *Odd Man Out* in 1947, in which he played an Irish Republican Army (IRA) gunman. The following year he made his first film in America, appearing with Orson Welles in *Macbeth*. Then he appeared in an adaptation of Robert Louis Stevenson's *Kidnapped* (1948) opposite Roddy McDowall. After this he played a number of supporting roles in films such as *At Sword's Point,* in which he played the son of one of the Three Musketeers, and *The Black Shield of Falworth.* In 1952 he starred in Luis Buñuel's *The Adventures of Robinson Crusoe.* He was nominated for an Academy Award for Best Actor for this role, in which he was alone on the screen for 60 minutes out of the film's 90 minutes running time and was only required to utter a few lines. It was said at the time that he hired a cinema to show the film to members of the Academy to persuade them to vote for him. Still, he lost out to Marlon Brando in *On The Waterfront.*

O'Herlihy appeared in the Cold War–era B movie, *Invasion USA,* as well as adventure films such as *Soldier's Three* and *Bengal Brigade.* The melodramatic *Imitation of Life* was followed by a reprise of his role as an IRA man in *A Terrible Beauty* as well as a remake of *The Cabinet of Caligari* in 1962. In 1964 he played Brigadier General Black opposite Henry Fonda in Sidney Lumet's *Fail Safe,* in which he is ordered to drop a nuclear bomb on New York City. He played Franklin Delano Roosevelt in *MacArthur* in 1977. He continued his love of theater after his move to America. He appeared alongside Orson Welles (another actor who had trained at Dublin's Gate Theatre) in *Macbeth* at the Mercury Theatre

as well as in John Houseman's *Measure for Measure* in Los Angeles. He also appeared in *The Life of Charles Dickens* on Broadway, in *King Lear* at the Houston Shakespeare Festival, and in *Mass Appeal* at the Drury Lane Theatre. He starred as Mr. Brown in John Huston's final film, *The Dead,* which was an adaptation of James Joyce's short story in *Dubliners.* He also appeared in both *Robocop* and *Robocop 2,* playing the part of a ruthless executive. He has appeared in numerous television series, including *The Travels of Jamie McPheeters, The Long Hot Summer, A Man Called Sloane, Whiz Kids,* and *Twin Peaks.* He married Elsa Bennett in 1945, and they remained together for 50 years until his death. They had five children together, two daughters and three sons. Two of his sons, Gavan and Cormac, and one of his daughters, Patricia, followed their father by becoming actors. His son Cormac appeared alongside his father in *The Dead.* Dan's brother Michael O'Herlihy was also involved in films as a director. Dan O'Herlihy died of natural causes at his home in Malibu, California, on February 17, 2005.

David Doyle

O'HIGGINS, AMBROSE (AMBROSIO) (CA. 1721–1801)

As governor and captain-general of Chile, and later viceroy of Peru, Ambrose O'Higgins was probably the eighteenth-century Irish emigrant who attained the highest position in the Spanish empire. The son of Charles O'Higgins and Margaret O'Higgins of Ballinary, Co. Sligo, and later of Summerhill, Co. Meath, Ambrose O'Higgins was educated in Ireland. His early instruction was in mathematics, and later he was trained to become a surveyor or draughtsman.

O'Higgins went to Spain in about 1751 and worked for the Irish merchant firm of Butler in Cadiz. On the company's behalf, he undertook a commercial journey to South America in 1756, where he visited his younger brother William, who was living in Asunción with a wife and two children. In 1761 Ambrose O'Higgins was back in Spain, where he joined the army as "ingeniero delineador" (engineer draughtsman, with the rank of lieutenant). Three years later he was sent again to South America as assistant to the military governor of Valdivia, the Irish John Garland. On his first journey across the Andes, O'Higgins conceived the idea of improving the route by constructing a chain of brick shelters, and by 1766 an all-year postal service was operating between the Atlantic Coast and Chile. He returned to Spain and wrote the *Description of the Realm of Chile,* a memorandum containing recommendations about the Indian population, agriculture, trade, and administration.

Again in Chile in 1770, O'Higgins was named captain, lieutenant colonel, and field marshall. In the 1770s his troops were engaged in wars with the Llanos and Pehuenches, and he was twice wounded. In 1780 he was appointed commandant general of the Spanish army in Chile, defending the town of Concepción against the attacks of the British army. O'Higgins attained his highest titles in 1787 as governor and captain general of Chile, and in September 1795 as viceroy of Peru. In addition, the king of Spain granted him the titles of Baron of Ballenary and Marquis of Osorno. Among his most important achievements was the abolition in 1789 of the cruel *encomienda* system, whereby landowners kept Indian laborers in conditions close to slavery. He also pushed reforms with the Catholic Church to benefit the poor, exciting the antagonism of the reactionary Creole elite. He likewise performed his duties as viceroy most ably for nearly five years.

O'Higgins never married, and his titles died with him. In his late fifties he had a romantic and illegitimate liaison with María Isabel Riquelme de la Barrera, an attractive 18-year-old Chilean woman from a well-known local family. Their son, Bernardo O'Higgins, was born in Chile, but he was never on intimate terms with him. Bernardo was a leading figure in the Chilean War of Independence and is remembered as the emancipator of Chile. Ambrose O'Higgins died on March 19, 1801, in Lima, Peru, where he was buried in the church of San Pedro.

Edmundo Murray

See also: MACKENNA, John

References
De Breffny. "Ambrose O'Higgins: An Enquiry into his Origins and Ancestry." *The Irish Ancestor* 2, no. 2 (1970): 81–89.
Donoso, Ricardo. *El Marqués de Osorno Don Ambrosio Higgins, 1720–1801.* Santiago: Publicaciones de la Universidad de Chile, 1941.

OHIO

The Native American population of the Ohio region changed significantly as a result of various epidemics, war, migration, and forced movement from the first contact with Europeans onward. The French claimed large amounts of the region in 1671, and in the eighteenth century the French established trade relations, particularly in fur.

As a result of the Seven Years' War (1756–1763), France ceded control of Ohio and the old Northwest to Great Britain. In the same year, the British issued the Proclamation of 1763, restricting white westward expansion beyond the Appalachian Mountains into Ohio country. Colonists' resentment against the perceived restriction of westward expansion was one of many factors contributing to the list of grievances culminating in Revolution.

In the new Republic, much Indian resistance was quelled in the 1794 Battle of Fallen Timbers and in campaigns against Tecumseh and his brother the Prophet, who led an uprising covering the Ohio Valley down to the Creek nation in the south.

Cincinnati was established in 1788 and Cleveland in 1796. There was a marked influence of Scots-Irish as soon as the territory was opened to settlement: large numbers arrived from Pennsylvania. Ohio was admitted as a state in 1803, and from the earliest days to 1842 the vast majority of immigrants were German. From 1842 to 1860, the population grew very rapidly; the numbers of German immigrants continued to grow, although the new majority was Irish. In the last decades of the century immigrants from eastern and southern Europe became predominant.

The digging of the Ohio Canal began in the same year work on the Erie Canal ended, and many of the laborers transferred from one job to the other while others signed up after disembarking from transatlantic crossings. More than 3,000 Irish "diggers" commenced work on July 4, 1825. By the late 1820s as many as 1,200 Irish immigrants were arriving in Northwest Ohio each month, most looking to work on the canals.

The canal brought new strategic and economic importance to Cleveland and provided many Irish with new job opportunities on the myriad of canal boats now using the waterway, as well as the riverfront warehouses, storehouses, and dockyards.

The Irish population spread along waterfront towns, and the city's Irish population doubled in the 1830s. The gender imbalance began to level out as more women arrived, and the population would continue to grow rapidly in the Famine years as many escaped the overcrowded cities in the east. Ghettos emerged, however, often backing onto the water. Frequently unskilled, poor, illiterate, and discriminated against, many of these areas became large and distinct, such as Whiskey Island and Irishtown Bend. The dock settlements soon encompassed Saint Patrick Parish (1853) and the steel mills in the Parish of the Holy Name (1854). Work was secured for many through the emergence of the iron and steel and shipbuilding industries, a mainstay for Irish laborers for decades. Frustration about the poverty in some areas was vented through an 1863 riot in the Irish and black neighborhoods of Cincinnati, working-class communities detrimentally affected by the wartime loss in river traffic, trade, and work.

The nineteenth century was often a turbulent time for the Irish communities for a variety of reasons. Largely urban (around 70 percent of Irish lived in Cleveland and Cincinnati), their large, visible communities and strongly perceived Catholicism drew a significant amount of discrimination that affected employment and residential area among other things. This underlying tension came to the surface in the 1850s with the popularity of the Know-Nothing Party, which was opposed to immigration and Catholicism and resented the competition for jobs, as Irish workers were seen to undercut wages. A number of city newspapers in Ohio ran notably anti-Irish propaganda, stirring up popular fears of overcrowding and crime while Know-Nothings rioted in German neighborhoods in 1855.

Further turbulence was intra-racial/intra-ethnic. Cincinnati, and indeed the state of Ohio, was a center of abolitionism, owing in part to being across the river from slaveholding Kentucky. It was also a common stop on the Underground Railroad. However, many Irish were fearful of competition over unskilled manual labor with blacks, whether slave or free, and this simmering tension occasionally flared up into confrontations. Irish immigrants were involved in riots in Cincinnati in 1829 over a growing black population and job competition, and in 1841 Irish immigrant dockworkers rioted against black dockworkers, an episode that involved a six-pound cannon.

In 1853, intra-ethnic tension manifested itself in the Christmas riot. A group of radical Germans who had left Europe to escape religious persecution in the tumult of the late 1840s objected to the visit of a papal emissary. The mayor called in the police, who were mostly Irish, and a riot ensued.

Most residents of Ohio fought for the Union during the Civil War but significant numbers left to support the Confederacy. Ohio experienced a notable level of support for the Copperheads, Unionists who opposed the war and any move to emancipate blacks, and the Irish figured strongly in their support base.

Turbulence would continue to flare up. The 1884 Courthouse Riot was the state's worst rioting over the sentence given to a German-American resident in Cincinnati. Later, in 1967, blacks rioted during the "long hot summers" that affected the nation from 1965 to 1968 and in the aftermath of Martin Luther King's assassination in the spring of 1968. More recently, Cincinnati experienced race riots in April 2001 after police shot a 19-year-old black man, Timothy

Thomas, highlighting tensions that had been strained for a number of years. Today the state is often regarded as a microcosm of the nation in terms of its politics and its demographics, which offer insights into the cross-section of America. Ohio is also considered a swing state. Most recently it supported both of Bill Clinton's terms and both of George W. Bush's terms in office, although the close finish between Bush and John Kerry in the 2004 election brought a national spotlight.

Of the state's 2000 population of 11,353,140, those reporting German ancestry made up 25.2 percent, while the second largest ancestry group was the Irish at 12.7 percent of the population.

Sam Hitchmough

References

Doyle, David Noel, and Owen Dudley, eds. *America and Ireland, 1776–1976: The American Identity and the Irish Connection,* Westport, CT: Greenwood Press, 1980.

Havighurst, Walter. *Ohio: A History.* Champaign: University of Illinois Press, 2001.

Miller, Kerby A. *Emigrants and Exiles: Ireland and the Irish Exodus to North America.* 1985. Reprint, Oxford: Oxford University Press, 1988.

Kenny, Kevin. *The American Irish,* Longman, 2000.

O'KEEFFE, GEORGIA (1887–1986)

Georgia Totto O'Keeffe was born in Wisconsin in 1887. By 1903, the O'Keeffe family had moved to Virginia. O'Keeffe attended private art lessons at a number of private schools in both Wisconsin and Virginia. In 1905, she moved to Chicago to attend the school of the Art Institute of Chicago; however, typhoid fever prevented her from returning in 1906. Instead, she

Artist Georgia O'Keeffe poses for a portrait at Ghost Ranch in New Mexico in 1968. (Getty Images)

enrolled at the Art Student League in New York City in 1907. She began to work as a commercial artist in Chicago in 1908. She enrolled in a teacher training course at Columbia Teaching College in 1914 and taught drawing in a number of schools in Virginia, Texas, and South Carolina.

In 1916, a number of her drawings were featured in an exhibition at the 291 Gallery, run by respected art critic Alfred Stieglitz. In 1916, she accepted a teaching job at the West Texas State College. During this period, she painted at least 50 watercolors inspired by the plants she found at the nearby Palo Duro Canyon. Her first solo exhibition opened in 1917. Most of the exhibits were watercolors from Texas. In 1918, she returned to New York with Stieglitz. They were married in 1924. During that same year, she also began to paint the large flowers with which she is primarily

associated today. The giant flower paintings were first exhibited in 1925. With her paintings selling for about $25,000 in 1928, O'Keeffe became the focus of media attention. In 1925, she and Stieglitz moved to the Shelton Hotel in New York, taking an apartment on the 30th floor of the new building. They would live here for 12 years. Inspired by the views, O'Keeffe began to paint the city.

In 1929, O'Keeffe began to make yearly visits to New Mexico, drawn to the open spaces and the light. The dried animal bones she found during her walks in the desert began to feature in her paintings. When Stieglitz died in 1946, she made New Mexico her permanent home. The Art Institute of Chicago held a retrospective of her work in 1943. However, her work went out of fashion, and she held only three solo shows during the 1950s.

In 1962, O'Keeffe was elected to the 50-member American Academy of Arts and Letters, the nation's highest honor society for people in the arts. By the 1970s, interest in her work began to grow again. She was invited to show at the Whitney Museum, and her retrospective exhibit traveled to the Art Institute of Chicago and the San Francisco Museum of Art. Her eyesight began to fail in 1971, and she stopped painting the following year. She became increasingly frail in her late 90s and moved to Santa Fe, where she would die in 1986, at the age of 98.

Aoileann Ní Eigeartaigh

Reference

Osborne, Harold, ed. *The Oxford Companion to Twentieth-Century Art.* Oxford: Oxford University Press, 1981.

O'KELLY, ALOYSIUS C. (1853–CA. 1941)

Born in Dublin, Aloysius Kelly immigrated to London in 1861, where he adopted the prefix "O." He was the youngest of an extended political family, the most notable being James J. Kelly. O'Kelly, who saw active service in the French Foreign Legion, played a leading role in building up the Irish Republican Brotherhood in Britain, was a much respected journalist in America, was elected member of Parliament for Roscommon in 1880, and was active in the Land League. His other brothers, Stephen and Charles, were sculptors, and his sister, Julia, married Charles Hopper, brother-in-law of James Stephens, the founder or the Irish Republican Brotherhood.

In 1874, O'Kelly was one of the first Irish artists to study at the École des Beaux-Arts in Paris, in the prestigious studio of the Orientalist, Jean-Léon Gérôme. Around the same time, he studied portraiture with Léon Bonnat. As well as working in Paris and Fontainbleau, he spent extended periods painting in Brittany. Here, under the influence of Jules Bastien-Lepage, he blended a form of rural realism and naturalism. In his interiors, he often reverted to a traditional genre style, but his landscapes displayed an understanding of the more avant-garde trends of the time. O'Kelly had a clear understanding of Breton separatism, and perceived underlying similarities with Ireland.

Somewhat eclectic, O'Kelly adapted himself to local styles and conditions: realist in Ireland, naturalist in France, and Orientalist in North Africa. As a republican realist, he challenged the conventional relationship between high art and popular culture. And in multiple colonial circumstances, he explored the underlying connections between art and nationalism. He projected the west of Ireland as the repository of the spiritual, cultural, and social values of the imagined nation, thereby giving visual form to an emerging national identity. By 1881, he was appointed special artist to the *Illustrated London News,* for which he produced a remarkable suite of illustrations highlighting the Land League in Connemara. Here he painted the recently rediscovered masterpiece, *Mass in a Connemara Cabin,* the first painting of an Irish subject ever exhibited in the Paris Salon.

O'Kelly's interest in North Africa led to a dangerous adventure in which he allied himself with the anti-imperialist forces of the Mahdi, which he visually documented for the *Pictorial World.* In Cairo, O'Kelly painted many Orientalist scenes—games of draughts, street and bazaar scenes, desert scenes, and mosque paintings—but avoided the emblems of Orientalism that appeared to justify colonial domination. O'Kelly is unusual in that although he worked in the Orientalist style, he was not ideologically so himself.

In 1895, his adoption of a *nom de pinceau* points to ongoing political activism, culminating in his return to Ireland, even after his immigration to the United States in 1895, to unsuccessfully offer himself for election as an MP for South Roscommon in 1897, the matching Roscommon constituency to his brother, James J. Kelly.

In New York, he executed a series of political portraits of prominent Irish men. Some of his most captivating paintings are of a quintessential American subject, Huckleberry Finn, at least one of which is said to have been commissioned by Mark Twain himself. O'Kelly moved around the art colonies of America, as well as returning frequently to France to paint. It would appear that he returned to France, living in Paris until he died, probably during the World War II.

Although described in the House of Commons as a "young painter of genius" and admired by Vincent van Gogh, O'Kelly remained a shadowy figure who effaced his much-traveled footsteps. Nevertheless, he exhibited in the important exhibition venues in Ireland, Britain, France, and the United States, including the Royal Academy, the Royal Society of British Artists, the Royal Institute of Painters in Watercolours, the Royal Hibernian Academy, the National Academy of Design, the New York Water Color Club (of which he was a member), the American Water Color Society and the Society of American Artists in New York, the Art Institute of Chicago, the Corcoran Gallery in Washington, the Boston Art Club, and the Paris Salon. A major retrospective exhibition of his work took place in the Hugh Lane Municipal Gallery of Modern Art in Dublin in 1999–2000.

Niamh O'Sullivan

See also: IRISH REPUBLICAN BROTHERHOOD; LAND LEAGUE

References
Campbell, Julian. "Aloysius O'Kelly in Brittany." *Irish Arts Review.* 1996.
O'Sullivan, Niamh. "Lines of Resistance: the O'Kelly Brothers in the Sudan." *Éire-Ireland.* Fall 1999.
O'Sullivan, Niamh. *Re-orientations. Aloysius O'Kelly: Painting Politics and Popular Culture.* Dublin: Hugh Lane Municipal Gallery of Modern Art, 1999.
Potterton, Homan. "Aloysius O'Kelly in America." *Irish Arts Review.* 1996.

OKLAHOMA

The history of the Irish in Oklahoma precedes Oklahoma statehood (1907) by more than 100 years. Don Alexandro O'Reilly, born in Dublin of Spanish/Irish descent, was the last governor of the Spanish territory, which included the future state of Oklahoma. His reign as governor began in 1769 and ended in 1800. Irish trappers were already in the area because of the bountiful fur-bearing animals. Fort Gibson, a major military base, was established in Oklahoma Territory in 1824, and many Irish enlisted in the military to earn more money. However, the building of railroads, coupled with mass Irish immigration in the 1840s, brought in vast numbers of Irish who were eager to move west for prosperous farmland and economic opportunity. The Potato Famine pushed Irish to move farther west than many other ethnic groups because they were desperate to forge new lives for themselves and to become economically sound in an area of the country where land was plentiful and cheap.

After the Civil War, more Irish laborers began to move in. Track layers ended up staying in what was then known as Indian Territory. Many Irish married American Indians and lay claim to land in Oklahoma as Indian citizens. One such Irishman started a controversy that would become known as Shanahan's War. Patrick Shanahan, a railroad worker, had been fired by the railroad. Believing his dismissal to be unfair, he bought up land he believed the railroad would later need. Because he was married to a Cherokee woman, he claimed Indian citizenship and built his barn right in line with the tracks the railroad was laying. He refused to tear down his barn and negotiations continued for several months. He later sold his land to the railroad for a very high price and became a very wealthy man.

Many Irish communities were created in Oklahoma Territory. The town of Edgewood was renamed Erin Springs by Frank Murray, an early settler to the area. The towns of Hennessey and Deer Creek also had large Irish populations. Oil boomtowns, such as Shamrock, Oklahoma, appeared almost overnight in the 1910s. In fact, Shamrock's town color was green, and the newspapers were *The Brogue* and *The Blarney*.

Oklahoma Territory also attracted skilled Irish miners from Pennsylvania to work in the southeastern Oklahoma coal mines. Many Irish became victims of mining disasters. In the 1890s, Irish union activists were deported by the U.S. Army for leading mining strikes. In 1877, a railroad strike was led by Mary Harris Jones, known as "Mother Jones," a fearless rally crier from Co. Cork. She led rallies for almost 50 years. Her speeches packed union halls in the territory, and when she died in 1930, her death marked the end of an era for the Irish labor movement. The song "The Death of Mother Jones" became a popular song in the United States shortly after her death.

Although many Irish were of the Catholic faith, they attended Protestant services, as there were few priests in the territory. It was not unusual for many to convert to Protestant sects. Saint Patrick's Church, established by brothers Father Laurence Smyth and Michael Smyth in Atoka, Oklahoma, in 1868, became the center for Catholic life. Later, Sacred Heart Mission was founded as a Benedictine Abbey. In 1929, it was moved to St. Gregory's in Shawnee, Oklahoma, where St. Gregory's College stands today.

As for Irish in early Oklahoma politics, Dennis T. Flynn stands out as one of the most influential. In 1889, Flynn was appointed postmaster of Guthrie, Oklahoma; he arrived on April 22, the day of the Oklahoma Land Run. In that same year, he became a Republican delegate from Oklahoma Territory. He was one of the most effective political campaigners in Oklahoma history, for although he was a Republican Catholic and distrusted for being so, he won over the public with his knowledge of homesteading and prairie life. He worked tirelessly for homesteaders and sponsored the "piecemeal absorption" plan that paved the way for Oklahoma statehood. This plan initially failed but it served to start the ball rolling for Oklahoma's eventual statehood in 1907.

During the Oklahoma Land Run on April 22, 1889, many Irish participated in the rush to obtain land in Indian Territory. Together with those of British descent, the Irish formed the largest of any European group in Oklahoma Territory. In 1992, the film *Far and Away*, starring Tom Cruise and Nicole Kidman, was filmed in Oklahoma. Even though it is a fictional account of Irish involved with the Oklahoma Land Run, it nevertheless brought attention to Irish presence during the pre-statehood period.

The Depression hit Oklahoma hard, and the Irish were not immune to its effects. Many Irish departed for California in a mass exodus during the Dust Bowl, having lost all of their crops to the incessant wind and terrible drought. In 1930, Governor William "Alfalfa Bill" Murray, who was of Irish descent, opposed New Deal legislation that would have helped out many citizens of the state. The number of immigrants from Ireland to Oklahoma and Irish birthrates dropped significantly, and the state never recovered from this loss. After World War II, some Irish immigrated into Oklahoma as war brides. In the 1950s, Bishop McGuiness urged Irish priests to immigrate to Oklahoma to establish Catholic churches. Most of these priests are now deceased, and the Irish Catholic presence in Oklahoma has declined tremendously.

Today, the Irish-born presence in Oklahoma is certainly not what it was before statehood. However, because of earlier Irish political involvement, union activism, and business leadership, the contribution of the Irish in Oklahoma cannot be denied, for it was not only an integral factor in Oklahoma's statehood, but it was also very central to the founding of industrial, business, and educational entities in present-day Oklahoma.

Cynthia A. Klima

See also: AMERICAN CIVIL WAR; GREAT FAMINE, The

References

Blessing, Patrick. *The British and Irish in Oklahoma*. Norman: University of Oklahoma Press, 1980.

Byron, Reginald. *Irish America*. Oxford: Clarendon Press, 1999.

Fitzpatrick, Marie-Louise. *The Long March: The Choctaw's Gift to the Irish Famine Relief*. Hillsboro, OR: Beyond Words Publishing, 1998.

OLCOTT, CHAUNCEY (JOHN CHANCELLOR) (1858–1932)

The grandson of Irish immigrants who settled in Buffalo, New York, Chauncey Olcott was the reigning Irish-American tenor from 1898 into the early 1920s. He starred in numerous "Irish" musicals, out of which came many of the best-known Irish-American popular songs, some of which Olcott helped to write.

Starting in minstrelsy, Olcott established a reputation as a singer and a leading man on both sides of the Atlantic, once playing opposite Lillian Russell. In 1891, the New York impresario Augustus Pitou asked Olcott to replace the ailing William Scanlan as the star for Pitou's series of popular musicals set in Ireland. Olcott fit perfectly into the mold of the new type of romantic Irish tenor that Pitou and Scanlan had helped to create. Olcott moved easily into shows in which Ireland was a fantasized backdrop for historical romances and idealized love stories, perfect vehicles for some of the best songs Tin Pan Alley could produce.

While the musicals were forgettable, the songs delivered by Olcott's fine lyric tenor voice captured the hearts of American audiences. One did not have to be Irish to enjoy "My Wild Irish Rose" (*A Romance of Athlone*, 1899), "Mother Machree" (*Macushla*, 1911), "When Irish Eyes Are Smiling" (*Isle O' Dreams*, 1912), "Too-ra-loo-ra-loo-ra (That's An Irish Lullaby)" (*Shameen Dhu*, 1912), and "A Little Bit of Heaven (Sure, They Call It Ireland)" (*Heart of Paddy Wack*, 1914). Although Olcott wrote "My Wild Irish Rose," and collaborated on other songs, Pitou was careful to hire some of the best Tin Pan Alley talents to guarantee his star first-rate material: lyricists, such as George Graff, Jr., Rida Johnson Young, and J. K. Brennan, along with composers of the stature of Ernest Ball. The resulting songs, many of which Olcott recorded himself, virtually defined Irish-American musical themes for much of the twentieth century. Although John McCormack (to whose voice Olcott's was once compared) is today remembered as the popularizer of these songs, it was Olcott for whom they were written and who introduced them to the American public.

Although Olcott occasionally sang a traditional Irish song, such as "The Wearing of the Green," his songs, like the musicals in which he appeared, were American confections. They presented a storybook Ireland scrubbed of poverty and political violence. Irish nationalism was limited to swashbuckling historical romances, set far enough back in the past so that failure did not hurt. The musicals also helped to foster that peculiar Irish love triangle: the lad, his colleen, and his mother. Moreover, there was none of vaudeville's rough-and-tumble Paddy comedy that had entertained Irish immigrants in the post–Civil War years. Olcott's musicals were made for the upwardly mobile American-born Irish who wanted an identity that did not shame them, one that they could embrace, even if it had little to do with reality.

William H. Murphy

See also: BALL, Ernest R.; DAY, Dennis; MCCORMACK, John; SCANLAN, William J.

References

Fiedler, Mari Kathleen. "Chauncey Olcott: Irish-American Mother-Love, Romance, and Nationalism." *Éire-Ireland* 22, no. 2 (1987): 4–26.

Olcott, Rita. *Song in My Heart,* New York: Fields, 1939.

O'LEARY, DANIEL FLORENCE (1801–1854)

Born in Cork, Daniel Florence O'Leary became a compatriot and chronicler of Simón Bolívar's campaign for South American independence. Not much is known of O'Leary's childhood apart from the supposition that he must have received a good education, owing to his mature ability to read, write, and speak English and Spanish. At 16, he enlisted as an ensign in the First Division of the Red Hussars of Venezuela, a cavalry regiment being raised in support of the war in northern South America. The regiment sailed from Portsmouth on December 3, 1817, and reached Angostura (now called Ciudad Bolívar), over 250 miles above the delta of the Orinoco, sometime in April 1818. This was the temporary capital of Simón Bolívar's Venezuelan republic.

Unimpressed with his new English colleagues—not only had many deserted but the commander, Colonel Wilson, had been implicated in a plot to replace Bolívar as captain general of the army—Daniel applied and obtained a transfer to a native unit, the Guard of Honor of General José Antonio Anzoátegui. Also, at this time, he was introduced to Bolívar, a meeting to which he ascribes the esteem and friendship that Bolívar ever afterwards showed him. O'Leary went to Anzoátegui as a second lieutenant, not yet 18, but just a year later he was a captain and one of Anzoátegui's aides-de-camp.

As such, O'Leary took part in Bolívar's famous invasion of New Granada, where soldiers had not only to cross the flooded plains of Casanare, often waist deep in water, but also had to scale the Andes by climbing 13,000 feet over the Páramo de Pisba. After accomplishing this seemingly impossible feat, this young army then managed to fight and defeat the professional and well-equipped Spanish Army in battles at Pántano de Vargas (July 25, 1819)—where O'Leary suffered a severe head wound but continued to fight on—and Boyacá (August 7), freeing New Granada from Spanish rule. O'Leary also participated in the culmination of the Venezuelan campaign, in the second battle of Carabobo in 1821, and the battle of Pichincha in 1822, effectively ending Spanish rule in Ecuador. By this time he had risen to the rank of lieutenant colonel and had become an aide-de-camp to Bolívar himself. By the time Bolívar had succeeded in liberating Peru, at the battle of Ayacucho in 1824 (a battle O'Leary missed as he had been sent on a mission to Chile), O'Leary had become Bolívar's principal aide-de-camp.

In 1825, with the creation of the new state of Bolivia, Bolívar reached the height of his power and fame. However, his attempts to create a Spanish League of Nations with constitutions modeled on the one he drafted for Bolivia resulted in dissension, mutinies, and failure. Bolívar died on December 17, 1830, his last moments recorded by O'Leary as, "the last embers of an expiring volcano, the dust of the Andes still on his garments" (Humphreys 1969, 14). By this time, O'Leary had married Soledad Soublette, a sister to General Soublette (who would later become president of Venezuela). After the death of Bolívar, O'Leary immigrated with his family to Jamaica—to avoid the backlash against Bolívar's former allies—finally returning to Venezuela in 1883, after General Soublette advised him that all was now safe. In 1834, O'Leary acted as secretary to a Venezuelan mission to London, Paris, and Madrid and, in 1837, was appointed chargé d'affaires to the Vatican. On June 1, 1841, he became acting consul for Caracas for the British Foreign Service and, later in the year, consul at Puerto Cabello. Finally, on November 28, 1843, he was appointed Her Majesty's chargé d'affaires and consul-general at Bogotá. He died there, 10 years later, on February 24, 1854.

O'Leary had been collecting all the information he could on the wars of independence in northern South America since he first arrived in Venezuela in 1818. After Bolívar's death O'Leary renewed his interest in writing a history of the wars and a biography of Bolívar. Though a draft of O'Leary's memoirs, written partly in English and partly in Spanish, seems to have been completed by 1840, they remained in this state for 40 years, until the *Memorias del General O'Leary publicados por su hijo Simon B. O'Leary, por orden del Gobierno de Venezuela* were printed in 32 volumes between 1879 and 1888. These memoirs added greatly to the legacy of Simon Bolívar and to Daniel O'Leary's legacy as compatriot and chronicler of the northern states' struggle for South American independence.

James P. Byrne

See also: PANAMA

References

Humphreys, R. A., ed. *The Detached Recollections of General D. F. O'Leary.* The Athlone Press: London, 1969.

O'Leary, Peter. "Celebrating Venezuela's General Daniel Florence O'Leary." March 16, 2003. www.vheadline.com/readnews.asp?id=4464 (accessed August 21, 2007).

O'LEARY JANE (1946–)

Born in Hartford, Connecticut, on October 13, 1946, Jane (Strong) O'Leary is an American composer who has lived in Ireland since 1972. She is one of the best-known and most often performed contemporary composers in Ireland today.

O'Leary studied at Vassar College (BA 1968) and at Princeton University (MA 1971, PhD 1978) where her composition teachers included Milton Babbitt and J. K. Randall. Before she moved to Ireland with her Irish husband she taught at Swarthmore College in Pennsylvania (1971–1972). In Ireland, O'Leary taught at the College of Music in Dublin (1974–1977) and lectured in music at University College Galway (1978–1983). She is the founder (1976), pianist, and artistic director of the chamber ensemble Concorde, which specializes in contemporary music. The group has given many first performances of music by contemporary Irish composers and frequently tours the country and abroad and performs on radio. O'Leary has spoken at many gatherings of women composers around the world and has had her music performed there. She has also been a member of the executive committee of the International League of Women Composers (1986–1994).

Besides her work as a composer and performer O'Leary has taken an active part in the administration and organization of music in Ireland. She was a founder of *Music for Galway* in 1981 (chairperson 1984–1992), a member of the Board of Directors of the National Concert Hall in Dublin (1986–1996), a member of the Irish Arts Council (1998–2003), chairperson of the Contemporary Music Centre in Dublin, and a member of the Cultural Relations Committee at the Irish Department of Foreign Affairs. She has been a member of Aosdána, the Irish academy of creative artists, since 1981 and received the prestigious Marten Toonder Award for composition in 1994.

Before 1983, O'Leary's music was oriented toward dodecaphonic and serial techniques. Most of these pieces were short movements for chamber music combinations such as a *Quartet* (1969) for clarinet, bass clarinet, violin, and violoncello, and some piano and vocal music. This early opus was published by Mobart Music (today APNM, New Jersey).

Her membership in Aosdána brought about a change of style in her music from strict 12-tone procedures of a fragmentary character to a more personal music characterized by long and fluid melodic lines and rich harmonic textures. Sometimes modal elements in harmony and folk-song-like melodies tend to reflect her adopted home country. Extramusical influences can be found in the landscape of the Irish west coast and in poetry, especially of the Irish poet Brendan Kennelly. Important orchestral works along these lines are *from the flatirons* (1985), *sky of revelation* (1989), *Islands of Discovery* (1991), and *From Sea-Grey Shores* (1999).

Axel Klein

Reference

Klein, Axel. *Die Musik Irlands im 20. Jahrhundert.* New York: Georg Olms, 1996.

O'LEARY, JUAN EMILIANO (1879–1969)

Juan Emiliano O'Leary, a Paraguayan historian, poet, and journalist born in Asunción on June 1, 1879, is considered to be one of the most important intellectuals in modern Paraguay. His key contribution was the historical studies of Paraguayan revisionism, as well as his support of the Guaraní-language poetry revival. He was the son of John O'Leary, who was probably born in 1841 in Salto, Uruguay, and María Dolores Urdapilleta. John O'Leary arrived in Paraguay during the War of the Triple Alliance working as a peddler. He had a relation with Natividad Mercedes Moreno, and from this illegitimate union was born Fulgencio Ricardo Moreno, writer, historian, and minister of foreign affairs. On February 3, 1870, John O'Leary married María Dolores Urdapilleta. He died in Pergamino, Buenos Aires (Argentina).

Juan O'Leary studied in the school of law in Asunción. He actively participated in public life, following General Bernardino Caballero of the National Republican Association ("Partido Colorado"), which dominated political life of Paraguay. O'Leary occupied key posts in the party, as head of the National Archive and later as diplomat. For a short time, he was foreign affairs minister during Alfredo Stroessner's administration.

O'Leary's major contribution to Paraguay's historiography was the reappraisal of Francisco Solano López and his role in the War of the Triple Alliance against Brazil, Argentina, and Uruguay (1864–1870). In the beginning, surely under family influence, O'Leary was bitterly critical of Solano López, and was distinguished for his poem against the dictator written while he was a student at the Colegio Nacional. However, at age 25, O'Leary considered that López's régime, though tyrannical and authoritarian, was beneficial to the country in the context of the aggressive foreign policies of its neighboring countries. O'Leary painted the *Mariscal* as a great hero, a great patriot, and a great promoter of nationalism. One of his close personal friends was Enrique Solano, son of the *Mariscal*.

O'Leary distinguished himself as the pioneer of historical revisionism in Paraguay. His nationalist—sometimes overly racist—views expressed in his narrative of Paraguayan history were effectively used by politicians to raise the awareness of native identity among the population that was emerging after the catastrophic results of the war. Among his books of history are *Páginas de Historia* (1916), *Nuestra Epopeya* (1919), *El Mariscal Solano López* (1920), *El Paraguay en la Unificación Argentina* (1924), *El Héroe del Paraguay* (1930), *Los Legionarios* (1930), *Apostolado Patriótico* (1933), *Historia de la Guerra de la Triple Alianza* (1912), and *Prosa Polémica* (published posthumously in 1982).

By the beginning of the twentieth century O'Leary was a member of the group of poets who began writing to reaffirm national identity, and his name is linked with the Guaraní renaissance of Rosicrán (Narciso R. Colman). In the magazine *Ocara Poty Cue-mi* he encouraged readers "to preserve our language; we must develop Guaraní and protect it from the corrupt and intruding effects of Spanish." Several of his poems are epic ballads about the Paraguayan War of Independence and against the Triple Alliance. He also researched oral legends and narrated them in the form of short stories or epic poems. O'Leary published the following books of poetry: *El Alma de la Raza* (1899), *A la Memoria de Mi Hija Rosita* (1918), *Salvaje* (1902), *Los Conquistadores* (1921), and several anthologies in Guaraní language. O'Leary died on October 31, 1969 in Asunción. A street in this city and a district of Alto Paraná department bear O'Leary's name.

Edmundo Murray

See also: PARAGUAY

References

Bareiro Saguier, Rubén, and Carlos Villagra Marsal, eds. *Poésie Paraguayenne duXX^e Siècle: Édition Trilingue en Espagnol, Français et Guarani.* Geneva: Patiño, 2003.

Wolf, Lustig. *Chácore Purahéi—Canciones de Guerra: Literatura Popular en Guaraní Eidentidad Nacional en el Paraguay.* Mainz, Germany: Author's Edition, 2005.

O'MAHONY, JOHN (1816–1877)

John O'Mahony was born in Mitchelstown, Co. Cork, in 1816 and attended Trinity College Dublin from 1833 to 1835. The O'Mahony family was well known for their support of Irish Catholic nationalism and had played a part in the abortive 1798 Rising. As a member of the Young Ireland movement, which had broken away from the cautious policies of Daniel O'Connell, O'Mahony took part in the abortive 1848 uprising; at its conclusion, he fled to France to avoid prosecution. While there, he supported himself by working as a tutor while imbibing the radical republican rhetoric of a Parisian community fresh off its own revolt.

O'Mahony immigrated to New York City in 1853, where he became involved in diasporic nationalism. O'Mahony recognized that the United States, with its large population of Irish immigrants, would be an important recruiting ground for the cause of Irish independence, and that Irish Americans were an important constituency for anti-British activism. To this effect, O'Mahony was a founding member of the Emmet Monument Association, a military organization that had as its expressed aim the liberation of Ireland. It was hoped that Britain's difficulties in the Crimean War could become Ireland's opportunity, but the speedy resolution of that crisis prevented

Portrait of John O'Mahony, founder of the Fenian Brotherhood. (Library of Congress)

the realization of O'Mahony's plans. A skilled Gaelic scholar, O'Mahony supported himself by editing a translation of Geoffrey Keating's *History of Ireland.* Appearing in 1857, it received good reviews and gave much attention to the Fianna, a band of Celtic warriors who further inspired in O'Mahony a desire to liberate his homeland.

O'Mahony was a founding member of the Fenian Brotherhood. Organized in 1858, the Fenians were the American branch of a transatlantic organization that had as its aim the forced removal of Great Britain from Ireland. Serving as head centre of the Fenians, O'Mahony sought to funnel money, war materiel, and trained soldiers to his revolutionary brethren—the Irish Republican Brotherhood, headed by James Stephens— in Ireland. These plans were interrupted by the American Civil War, a conflict in which O'Mahony took part—he raised and served as colonel of the 99th New York

Regiment—though he feared the divisive impact the war had on Irish nationalism.

Although his relationship with Stephens was often bitter, O'Mahony was an effective organizer, who oversaw the coalescence of disparate bands of embittered Irishmen into a cohesive organization. Despite a slow start, by 1865 the Fenians had some 40,000 members and were contributing several hundred thousand dollars per year to the cause. But there was dissension in the ranks.

Many within the movement chafed at O'Mahony's autocratic style; at their annual convention (1865) he was stripped of his title as head centre; though he was retained as president, he was now restrained by a senate. A few months later a quarrel over finances split the Fenians, and the anti-O'Mahony forces lined up behind dry goods magnate W. R. Roberts. The Roberts wing made plans for an invasion of Canada, hoping to use that territory as ransom for Irish independence. O'Mahony, for his part, was opposed to action anywhere but in Ireland. In April 1866, against his better judgment, O'Mahony reluctantly backed a plan to stage military raids in Canada against the British; the results were farcical, and O'Mahony was forced to resign from his position of leadership.

Despite their considerable financial and political influence, the Fenians soon fell into disunion and disarray. They were superseded in later years by such organizations as the Clan na Gael and the Friends of Irish Freedom. Seeking to revive the movement in 1872, O'Mahony was coaxed out of retirement and reinstated as head centre, but he was unable to restore the movement to its former prestige and prosperity. O'Mahony died in relative obscurity and poverty in New York on February 6, 1877.

His remains were sent to Dublin's Glasnevin Cemetery, where a massive funeral took place on March 4, 1877. Ironically, in his death he achieved the one thing that had escaped him in life: a union of Irish and Irish American nationalists. O'Mahony was never married.

Tim Lynch

See also: FENIANS; IRISH REPUBLICAN BROTHERHOOD

References

Denieffe, Joseph. *A Personal History of the Irish Revolutionary Brotherhood*. Shannon: Irish University Press, 1969.

O'Leary, John. *Recollections of Fenians and Fenianism*. London: Downey and Company, 1896.

O'MALLEY, WALTER (1903–1979)

Walter O'Malley owned the Brooklyn Dodgers and moved them to Los Angeles; thus, he may be regarded as the father of baseball's expansion to the West Coast. O'Malley was born in New York City, the son of Edwin J. O'Malley and Alma Feltner. O'Malley's grandfather came to the United States from Co. Mayo. Edwin O'Malley was a prominent local politician, who once served as commissioner of public markets. Walter O'Malley earned an engineering degree from the University of Pennsylvania in 1926 and a law degree from Fordham University in 1930. His drive and personal political connections soon put him near the top of New York's business world. He sat on the board of the Brooklyn Borough Gas Company and the Long Island Railroad, among other companies. He represented many more companies as an attorney. In 1941 he replaced Wendell Willkie as corporate attorney for the Brooklyn Dodgers.

O'Malley now had a springboard to control of the club. In 1944, O'Malley, Dodgers president Branch Rickey, and Charles Pfizer Chemical Company president John Smith purchased 25 percent of the team from the Brooklyn Trust Company. In 1945, they expanded their holdings to 75 percent of the team. Smith played little or no role, leaving O'Malley and Rickey to battle for control of the team. In 1950, Rickey's contract as president expired. O'Malley bought his shares for $1.05 million and all other outstanding shares for $1 million. Soon O'Malley began to put his stamp on the Dodgers. He considered Rickey's construction of the farm system and establishment of a training camp at Vero Beach, Florida, as wastes of money. After the 1953 season O'Malley fired manager Charlie Dressen, despite a 105-win season, and replaced him with Walter Alston. Alston remained the manager until the end of the 1976 season, although O'Malley twice considered replacing him with Leo Durocher. The Dodgers were a laughingstock in the 1930s, but they became a powerhouse in the O'Malley years, winning pennants in 1947, 1949, 1952, 1953, 1955, and 1956. Brooklyn won its only world championship in 1955, defeating their most frequent postseason opponents, the Yankees. The Dodgers also had the most devoted fan base in the game.

O'Malley believed the main obstacle to the future success of the Brooklyn Dodgers was their stadium, Ebbets Field. State of the art when it opened in 1913, Ebbets Field was a typical urban stadium with limited facilities and almost no parking. O'Malley saw that the demographic shifts of the postwar era, particularly the move to the suburbs, made a new stadium necessary. As early as 1947, O'Malley had plans for a domed stadium, at the time considered a fantasy. O'Malley also saw that baseball would move west. In 1953, O'Malley and Giants owner Horace Stoneham asked the National League to approve relocating the Boston Braves to Milwaukee. O'Malley noted that the Braves' revenue doubled, and he feared they would soon dominate the league. O'Malley's first choice was to remain in Brooklyn. In 1955 he asked for the city's help in purchasing a lot in the Flatbush/Atlantic area. City officials balked at the request, and O'Malley talked of playing in Jersey City. Preparing an alternative plan, O'Malley met with Los Angeles officials in October 1956. In February 1957 O'Malley purchased the Los Angeles Angels of the Pacific Coast League from Cubs owner Philip K. Wrigley. That April, Robert Moses offered a site at Flushing Meadows in Queens. O'Malley concluded that Los Angeles was the better option. He convinced Giants owner Horace Stoneham to abandon plans for Minneapolis and embark for San Francisco instead. The two longtime National League rivals moved to the West Coast for the 1958 season.

On June 3, 1958, the citizens of Los Angeles approved the contract giving O'Malley 300 unused acres at Chavez Ravine. Initially, the Dodgers played in cavernous Los Angeles Coliseum. In May 1959 the Dodgers set a single-game attendance record when 93,103 fans paid tribute to Roy Campanella, the former Dodgers catcher who was paralyzed in an automobile accident after the 1957 season. The Los Angeles Dodgers won their first world championship in 1959. The team moved into Dodger Stadium in 1962. It was privately financed, seated 56,000, and had parking space for 16,000 cars. Throughout the O'Malley years the Dodgers drew 2 million fans per year, reaching 3 million in 1979. The Dodgers won the National League pennant in 1963, 1965, 1966, 1974, 1977, and 1978 and the World Series in 1963 and 1965. O'Malley was a hands-on owner who handled the business end while leaving player personnel to the field manager and general manager. O'Malley ceded day-to-day control of the team to his son Peter in 1970.

Robert W. Smith

See also: BASEBALL

References

Kowet, Don. *The Rich Who Own Sports.* New York: Random House, 1977.

Parrott, Harold. *The Lords of Baseball.* New York: Praeger, 1976.

Sullivan, Neil J. *The Dodgers Move West.* New York: Oxford University Press, 1987.

O'NEILL, EUGENE (1888–1953)

Eugene O'Neill is generally recognized as the founding father of modern American drama. In a theatrical career spanning four decades, O'Neill won four Pulitzer prizes—for *Beyond the Horizon* (1920), *Anna Christie* (1921), *Strange Interlude* (1928), and *Long Day's Journey into Night* (1956). In 1936, he was awarded the Nobel Prize for Literature. Son of the celebrated Irish-American actor James O'Neill, Eugene repudiated in early naturalistic works the theater of Victorian melodrama that had provided a lucrative, if artistically unchallenging, livelihood for his father, an ex-Shakespearean actor and long-term leading man in a vaudevillean dramatization of *The Count of Monte Cristo.* He also rejected the unquestioning Irish Catholicism of his father, replacing it with a Nietzschean concept of man's tragic destiny, though his struggle with what he termed the relation between man and God would pursue him throughout his dramatic career.

O'Neill's young manhood was colorful, providing him with many of the experiences that later found their way into his plays. Suspended from Princeton, he married, and promptly abandoned his pregnant wife; tried gold prospecting; then worked as a seaman, spending drunken times between trips living at Jimmy the Priest's, a notorious waterfront saloon-hotel in New York. In 1912, recovering from a suicide attempt and a bout of tuberculosis that placed him in a sanatorium for six months, O'Neill wrote his first one-act plays, one of which, *Bound East for Cardiff,* would be produced by the Provincetown Players in 1916, appropriately in a converted fish warehouse at the tip of Cape Cod. O'Neill later claimed as a formative influence the work of the Irish Players who had successfully toured in the United States in 1911, awakening him to the possibilities of "real theatre as opposed to the unreal—and to me then hateful—theatre of my father." While there is little to rival the poetic naturalism of a J. M. Synge in these early plays, there are characters such as Driscoll, a stereotyped Irish seaman who demonstrates both O'Neill's fondness for the type and his inability to render a "brogue" convincingly. Indeed, it is on the question of language that much of O'Neill's definition of Irishness seems to rest. The characteristic he identifies in his first three-act Broadway play, *Beyond the Horizon,* when he describes Robert Mayo as having "a touch of the poet" is one that he associated with both an Irish propensity for artistic vision and a flair for poetic expression. Evidence of Mayo's language skills is slight, but the concept was one that O'Neill pursued through his career, achieving greater success with characters in the dark plays of his maturity whose eloquence is truly poetic and emotionally moving.

The plays of O'Neill's middle period contain his greatest experimentation and possibly his greatest legacy to future American dramatists. While he demonstrated new uses to which the naturalistic stage could be put, he also addressed contemporary social themes such as race, in both *The Emperor Jones* (1920) and *All God's Chillun Got Wings* (1924). In the context of a burgeoning Harlem Renaissance, O'Neill's treatment of African-American experience probes the psychology of racism, though of the former play the celebrated black actor Charles Gilpin boasted that he had created the role of the Emperor, dismissing O'Neill as "that Irishman" who just wrote the play. In the latter, more Freudian drama, Ella Downey, whose name clearly denotes Irish origins, makes a disastrous mixed-race marriage with Jim Harris, a "new negro" of the era; though it is to be hoped that her decline into a delusional racism is not intended as representative of relations between African-American and Irish-American ethnic groups.

The protagonists' Irish origins are again evident in those plays of O'Neill's late period that secure his greatness in terms of world drama. In *The Iceman Cometh* it is not the corrosive truth of death, which the "iceman" Hickey brings, that prevails at the end of the play, but the protective dreaming of Larry Slade, whose "gaunt Irish face" and melancholy touch of the poet make him the most sympathetic character: "I'll be a weak fool looking with pity at the two sides of everything till the day I die."

A similar sympathy informs the speeches of Edmond Tyrone in the harrowingly autobiographical *Long Day's Journey into Night*, a play "written in tears and blood" according to O'Neill, but one that nevertheless manages, amid so much family angst, to trace the Irish origins and milieu of the Tyrones: servant girls named Bridget and Cathleen, one with a singing voice like a "wild Irish lark"; Shaughnessy, the troublesome tenant farmer, described as a "wily Shanty Mick" by James Tyrone; the family physiognomy likened frequently to the map of Ireland; James Tyrone's parsimony, attributed to his boyhood experience as a penniless Irish immigrant, abandoned by a homesick father who returned to Ireland to die. Within such a context, the crippling burden of family guilt suggests that the intellectual acceptance of Nietzsche did not altogether compensate for the emotional loss of Irish Catholic faith, either by the Tyrone brothers, or O'Neill himself.

Certainly, Irishness remained important to O'Neill, not just emotionally, but creatively, too; in fact, he wished to hire a cast exclusively of Irish actors for *A Moon for the Misbegotten* (1943), the last of the plays to be produced in his lifetime, and an unfortunately anticlimactic coda to *Long Day's Journey*. While the rambunctious Phil Hogan delights in a stage-Irish display of drinking, cursing the English, and singing Famine songs like "Oh the praties they grow small," his daughter Josie is given the touch of the poet that allows her to console the despairing James Tyrone in phrases that confirm O'Neill's abiding dramatic kinship with the peasant drama of Synge.

After a lifetime as America's leading dramatist, O'Neill's health began to decline. The stress of work and his haunted family history, added to years of alcohol abuse earlier in his life, weakened him and in his later years he suffered from a hereditary motor neuron condition, for which he was nursed by his third wife, Carlotta Monterey.

O'Neill died in a Boston hotel on November 27, 1953. His work remains the most important contribution to modern American drama; indeed, without O'Neill, modern American drama would not exist in its present form.

William Lazenbatt

References

Bogard, Travis, *Contour in Time: The Plays of Eugene O'Neill.* Oxford: Oxford University Press, 1988.

Manheim, Michael, ed. *The Cambridge Companion to Eugene O'Neill.* Cambridge: Cambridge University Press, 1998.

O'Neill, Eugene. *Complete Plays.* 3 vols. New York: The Library of America, 1988.

Shaughnessy, Edward L. *Eugene O'Neill in Ireland: The Critical Reception.* New York: Greenwood Press, 1988.

Shaughnessy, Edward L. *Down the Nights and Down the Days: Eugene O'Neill's Catholic Sensibility.* Notre Dame, IN: University of Notre Dame Press, 1996.

O'NEILL, FRANCIS (1848–1936)

Born in Tralibane, Co. Cork, near Bantry, Francis O'Neill established himself in Chicago, where he eventually became the superintendent of police and the collector and publisher of several of the most important collections of traditional Irish music. *The Music of Ireland* (1903) and *The Dance Music of Ireland: 1001 Gems* (1907) provided musically literate musicians on both sides of the Atlantic with a treasure trove of tunes. It remains a major resource for anyone interested in the music.

O'Neill first left Ireland and went to sea in 1865. After a series of adventures, including shipwreck, he eventually found his way to the United States. Arriving in Chicago in 1870, he tried several jobs before entering the city's police force in 1873. He was promoted through the ranks, becoming superintendent in 1901, a position he held until 1905. By the time he left the force O'Neill had already published the first of his two great tune collections.

O'Neill was born into a musical family, and his love of Irish music accompanied him to America. He was an accomplished musician and was able to play the fiddle, various types of bagpipes, and the flute, his main instrument. He had a natural inclination to pick up tunes in his travels. However, when he arrived in Chicago he found himself at a sort of crossroads of Irish traditional music. The rapidly growing city attracted many traditional musicians among the Irish immigrants who passed through or settled there. Who better to pick out Irish music flowing through the city than a policeman circulating through the streets and neighborhoods?

There were certainly times when music and policing were quite compatible. For example, when he met young James O'Neill, a skilled fiddler from Co. Down, who could note down music as he heard it (a skill the Corkman lacked), the older O'Neill managed to find his fellow musician a place in the ranks of Chicago's police force. Working with James, O'Neill began by getting onto paper the tunes he recollected from his family and neighbors in Cork. Then the two men began collecting tunes from numerous Irish musicians around the city.

By around 1900 the two O'Neills had around 2,000 tunes in manuscript. Deciding to publish the collection, the Chief formed a committee of traditional musicians to help him collate his material. When it appeared in 1903, *O'Neill's Music of Ireland,* financed entirely by the compiler himself, contained 1,850 airs and dance pieces. It was the largest collection of Irish music ever published, until the two-volume *Sources of Irish Traditional Music,* edited by Aloys Fleischmann and containing some 7,000 tunes, appeared in 1998.

Published in a limited edition, O'Neill's first collection was too expensive for most musicians, who were primarily interested only in dance music. So in 1907, O'Neill brought out *The Dance Music of Ireland,* containing 1,001 tunes, most drawn from the larger compendium. Known generally as "The Book," it was used by musicians in Ireland and the United States. By this time, Irish music was being played in "respectable" halls and in households that could afford pianos. *O'Neill's Irish Music,* offering 250 pieces with piano accompaniment, was published in 1908. With several decades of active collecting behind him, O'Neill began writing up his experiences and his ideas about Irish music. *Irish Folk Music: A Fascinating Hobby* came out in 1910, and *Irish Minstrels and Musicians* followed in 1913. O'Neill continued to publish new editions of his tune collections, and in 1922 he brought out *Waifs and Strays of Gaelic Melody,* a collection of 335 Irish and Scottish tunes, drawn from a variety of manuscript sources.

O'Neill was a dedicated musician and collector, not an academic folklorist. He sometimes corrected James O'Neill's generally accurate transcriptions, relying on his own sense of the music. He filled in notes when his informants forgot parts of a tune. He supplied titles when they were missing. Tunes in "odd" modes were transposed into the more popular keys.

Like the recordings of skilled musicians such as Michael Coleman in the 1920s and 1930s, O'Neill's collections were not an unmitigated blessing for the Irish musical tradition. On the one hand, tunes that might have disappeared were preserved. Moreover, the collections helped to valorize the music, providing it with some authority and respectability. Yet in cases where his versions of tunes took precedence and eclipsed local variants, too much authority may have occasionally been granted to O'Neill's work.

Nevertheless, O'Neill's collections could not have appeared at a more important time. During the first half of the twentieth century traditional Irish music was under great pressure in both Ireland and America. O'Neill's works provided invaluable support in preserving it for later generations.

William H. A. Williams

See also: COLEMAN, Michael

Reference
Carolan, Nicholas. *A Harvest Saved: Francis O'Neill and Irish Music in Chicago.* Cork: Ossian, 1997.

O'NEILL, ROSE CECIL (1874–1944)

Rose Cecil O'Neill, a writer, illustrator, and doll designer who created the Kewpies, was born on June 25, 1874, to bookseller William Patrick O'Neill and former schoolteacher Alice Smith O'Neill in Wilkes-Barre, Pennsylvania. The O'Neills lived in a home with ornamental cupids on the living room ceiling. It is likely that this early childhood memory prompted O'Neill to create the Kewpies, plump infants with tiny wings, who also reflect the influences of Irish mythology. In 1878, the family moved to Omaha, Nebraska. By 1879, O'Neill had begun selling drawings to magazines and newspapers.

With the hope of finding a publisher for her novel, O'Neill moved to New York City in 1893. She had no luck marketing the book, but New York magazines began

Illustration by Rose Cecil O'Neill. O'Neill was a writer, illustrator, and doll designer who created the Kewpies, plump infants with tiny wings. (Library of Congress)

Already the best-known female commercial illustrator in the United States, O'Neill began drawing her famous Kewpie characters after the end of her marriage. The characters would become the most widely known cartoons in American popular culture until the advent of Mickey Mouse. The Kewpies first appeared in *Ladies' Home Journal* in 1909. Instantly popular, the Kewpie illustrations accompanied stories in *Woman's Home Companion, Good Housekeeping,* and the *Delineator.* By 1913 the chubby, winged infants, with their impish faces and rakish tufts of hair, had become a commercial phenomenon decorating soap, fabric, and stationery. Generations of Americans would read about the exploits of the Kewpies in comic strips, play with Kewpie dolls, and purchase Kewpie inkwells, napkin rings, tableware, and other spin-offs. O'Neill became a millionaire.

Perhaps in reaction to the sweetness and innocence of the Kewpies, O'Neill produced a series of Titans, or monster drawings, that depicted the tragic tensions between the physical and spiritual aspects of life. O'Neill's writings took on the same dark qualities as the monster drawings. *Master-Mistress* focused on the sadness of lost love. Her novel *Garda* (1929) told a strange story, drawn from her Irish heritage, of unbearable love between a twin brother and sister. O'Neill lost much of her money in the Great Depression. In 1936, she retreated to the family homestead, now in Branson, Missouri. Living with her mother and younger sister, she continued to sell illustrations to magazines and publish poems. O'Neill died on April 6, 1944.

Caryn E. Neumann

purchasing her illustrations. In 1896, she embarked on a brief marriage to Virginia aristocrat Gray Latham; the relationship ended in divorce in 1901. O'Neill then married writer Harry Leon Wilson in 1902. Neither marriage produced children, but life with Wilson proved creatively fulfilling for O'Neill. She published *The Loves of Edwy: Tale and Drawings* in 1904 and illustrated Wilson's *Lions of the Lord* (1903), *The Seeker* (1904), and *The Boss of Little Arcady* (1905). Unfortunately, the solemn Wilson clashed with the gregarious, free-spirited O'Neill to the point that the couple separated in 1907. One of O'Neill's best poems, "Established," published in her only book of poetry, the *Master-Mistress* in 1922, apparently refers to her sadness at parting from Wilson.

References

Brunell-Formanek, Miriam. *Made to Play House: Dolls and the Commercialization of*

American Girlhood, 1830–1930. New Haven, CT: Yale University Press, 1993.

Brunell-Formanek, Miriam, ed. *The Story of Rose O'Neill: An Autobiography.* Columbia: University of Missouri Press, 1997.

O'NEILL, JR., THOMAS "TIP" (1912–1994)

Born in Cambridge, Massachusetts, on December 9, 1912, Thomas Phillip "Tip" O'Neill, Jr., was the grandson of immigrants from Ireland, and the son of Thomas P. O'Neill, a bricklayer and Cambridge city councilman. After graduating from Boston College in 1936, Tip O'Neill worked as a real estate agent and insurance broker in Cambridge and served in the state legislature (1936–1952). He was also a member of the Cambridge school committee (1946–1947). O'Neill became the first Democratic Speaker of the Massachusetts House of Representatives (1949–1952). In 1953 he succeeded John F. Kennedy in the House of Representatives (1953–1987), rising rapidly in the national Democratic Party leadership.

Under the mentorship of House Speakers Sam Rayburn and John W. McCormack, O'Neill became House majority whip (1971–1973), House majority leader (1973–1977), and Speaker of the House (1977–1987). O'Neill became an inside man who mastered the internal processes of Congress and its political nuances. His good humor and intimate knowledge of the Congress made him both influential and respected by Democrats and Republicans. Always loyal to the New Deal Democratic tradition, like many urban Irish-American Catholic politicians, O'Neill was liberal on economic issues and more conservative on social issues. His congressional district included the elite Harvard University campus, where he had mowed the lawns as an adolescent, but the motto his father taught him, "all politics are local," became his byword. O'Neill prided himself on serving his constituents and protecting the poor, sick and helpless. When John McCormack arranged his appointment to the powerful Rules Committee in 1955, O'Neil became a source of information and influence for hundreds of House members and steered important federal funds to Massachusetts.

Although a loyal ally of President Kennedy, by 1967 O'Neill openly opposed President Lyndon B. Johnson's Vietnam War policies. He was the most prominent Democrat calling for the impeachment of President Richard M. Nixon in 1974. Primarily focused on domestic issues, O'Neill was frustrated by President Jimmy Carter's preference for foreign policy rather than practical legislation. During the administration of President Ronald W. Reagan, O'Neill defended the liberal Democratic House against relentless neoconservative Republican criticism. The tall, stout, cigar-smoking O'Neill, who opposed Reagan's frugal economic and aggressive foreign policies, became the target of vicious partisan attacks as a big spending old-fashioned liberal in cartoons and television commercials. In the wake of Watergate and other Washington scandals, O'Neill worked tirelessly to restore the tarnished image of Congress, and he supported a rigorous code of ethics.

O'Neill retired from politics in 1987, wrote his autobiography with William Novak, *Man of the House: The Life and Political Memoirs of Speaker Tip O'Neill* (1987), and retired to his summer home on Cape Cod. A beloved figure among bread-and-butter liberal Democrats everywhere, he bridged the eras of Governor James

Michael Curley and Senator Edward M. Kennedy in Massachusetts politics. Unlike Curley, the roguish Irish-American chieftain, O'Neill rose from the narrow world of ward politics to play a major role in the national government. In 1979, he was a key member of the congressional delegation visiting Northern Ireland to support peace negotiations. The eighth Speaker from Massachusetts, and the person with the longest tenure in that office, O'Neill's represents the impressive contributions the Bay State has made to national government. The library at Boston College (1984) and a federal office building (1987) in Boston bear his name. O'Neill died in Boston on January 5, 1994, and was buried at Mt. Pleasant Cemetery in Harwichport, Massachusetts.

Peter C. Holloran

See also: CURLEY, James Michael; KENNEDY FAMILY; KENNEDY, John Fitzgerald; MASSACHUSETTS; REAGAN, Ronald Wilson

References

Clancy, Paul, and Shirley Elder. *Tip, A Biography of Thomas P. O'Neill, Speaker of the House.* New York: Macmillan Publishing, 1980.

Farrell, John. *Tip O'Neill and the Democratic Century.* Boston: Little, Brown, 2001.

O'Neill, Tip, and Gary Hymel. *All Politics is Local, and Other Rules of the Game.* New York: Times Books, 1994.

Savage, Neil J. *Extraordinary Tenure: Massachusetts and the Making of a Nation, from President Adams to Speaker O'Neill.* Worcester, MA: Ambassador Books, 2004.

ONTARIO

From the times of early European settlement in the seventeenth and eighteenth centuries, Irish people have immigrated to what is now Ontario. A small number of Irish served New France as missionaries, soldiers, geographers, and fur trappers. After the creation of British North America in 1763, the migration of Irish-born Anglicans and Presbyterians increased as settlement schemes began to appear offering land for suitable farm families. By contrast, early Irish Catholic immigrants in Upper Canada coped with severe disabilities, being a small minority of the population and marked by their religious persuasion. After the war of 1812, a growing number of Catholics joined the flow of immigration, enticed by employment opportunities with infrastructure projects, including canals, roads, and railroads. Faced with high levels of distrust and suspicion from their Protestant counterparts, many Catholic Irish in Canada remained torn between loyalty to their new home and memories of harsh British rule in Ireland.

In 1847, as the Potato Famine devastated Ireland, boatloads of desperate migrants arrived in Ontario, and quarantine facilities were hastily constructed to accommodate them. Nurses, doctors, priests, nuns, compatriots, politicians, and ordinary citizens provided aid according to their abilities, and yet thousands died that summer alone, mainly from typhus. As the survivors began to establish themselves, the animosities from the Old World spilled over into the streets of Upper Canadian cities, and militant Irish Catholics fell back on their traditional peasant prerogative to defend themselves and thereby compensate for the failure of the authorities to protect their rights. Religion functioned as a unifying force in each community, but so did ingrained attitudes toward the Orange Order. While British Protestants tended to celebrate Orangeism, from the outset Catholics viewed the Order as the main enemy in their new environment. Furthermore, the emergence of distinct class differences created acute divisions within the Irish community.

In general, the Irish community in Ontario tended to demonstrate a greater concern for Catholic, as opposed to Irish, issues than their counterparts in the United States. This is partly because the clergy functioned as spokesmen for Ontario's Irish Catholics. The laity became prominent in journalism, in politics, and in the churches, where they agitated for religious toleration and responsible government. In particular, they aggressively demanded that separate schools be established. This inadvertently stoked paranoia concerning an impending coalition between French Canadian and Irish Catholics. Such an alliance would not occur. Although the potential voting power of the French was considered a last line of defense for Catholic rights in Ontario, the Irish resisted being linked with a group viewed as an implacable barrier to Canadian nationalism. Irish Catholics instead strove to establish themselves as a part of the linguistic mainstream, emphasizing their new identity as English-speaking Catholics.

The Canadian confederation was a political innovation that would be emulated by many British colonies, including Ireland itself. Irishman Thomas D'Arcy McGee espoused the vision of a new nation in North America and inspired colonists scattered across the northern colonies. Without his oratory it may have been possible to distill confederation down to a matter of railway dividends, freight rate, and tariffs. At the time of confederation, people of Irish origin were the second-largest group in Canada after the French Canadians. McGee first tried to ally himself with George Brown's Reformers, but his dream of an all-powerful Irish-Reform alliance proved untenable, and McGee was forced to acknowledge the preference of the Catholic clergy, who favored the paternalistic, sympathetic ethos of the Conservatives and who believed John A. Macdonald's more conciliatory attitude was reliable because of his dependence on French Canadian votes. After Confederation and McGee's mysterious assassination (1864), Irish Catholics continued to face difficult conditions and widespread oppression. Bishop John Joseph Lynch and his colleagues assumed the role of mediators between the Irish and the political establishment. The bonds of ethnicity endured for decades, and spiritually sensitive issues never failed to rally the Irish vote. At the end of the nineteenth century, under the leadership of Charley Murphy, the majority of Irish Catholics transferred their support to Wilfred Laurier's Liberal party. By this point, sectarian struggles were already beginning to abate.

In 1877 Nicholas Flood Davin had published *The Irishman in Canada,* in which he declared that his objective was to "sweep aside misconceptions, to explode cherished fallacies, to point out the truth and to raise the self-respect of every person of Irish blood in Canada." The same year, the Irish Benevolent Society, a brotherhood of Irish men and women of both Catholic and Protestant faiths, was established in London. The society promoted Irish Canadian culture, but it forbade members to speak of Irish politics when meeting. This companionship between Irish people of all faiths had a considerable impact, and branches of the Society are still operating.

During the twentieth century, the majority of Irish in Ontario, and in Canada generally, came to reconcile Catholic and

Protestant Irish identities. The gradual dissipation of Orange-Green friction accelerated as the two groups cooperated and participated in the world wars as Irish Canadians. This measured amelioration can also be viewed as an index of assimilation and political adjustment to Canadian society. However, to some extent it also reflected the experience of the Irish Republic, where the Catholic majority has sought to reassure their fellow countrypeople about their continued place in the community. Today it is common for Canadians of Protestant Irish descent to participate in Saint Patrick's Day celebrations, and for those of Irish Gaelic descent to take as much pride in the great Irish figures of Protestant tradition, including Edmund Burke, Jonathan Swift, and William Butler Yeats, as they do to the heroes of their own faith, such as Daniel O'Connell and the fathers of the Irish republic.

Mike Cottrell

See also: DAVIN, Nicholas Flood; GREAT FAMINE, The; LYNCH, Archbishop John Joseph; McGEE, Thomas D'Arcy; ORANGE ORDER

References

Akenson, Donald Harman. *The Irish in Ontario: A Study in Rural History*. 2nd ed. Montreal: McGill-Queen's University Press, 1999.

Burns, Robin B. "McGee, Thomas Darcy." In *Dictionary of Canadian Biography Online*. Library and Archives Canada. Available online at www.biographi.ca/EN/ShowBio.asp?BioId=38705 (accessed August 21, 2007).

Cottrell, Michael. "St. Patrick's Day Parades in Nineteenth-Century Toronto: A Study of Immigrant Adjustment and Elite Control." In *A Nation of Immigrants: Women, Workers, and Communities in Canadian History, 1840s–1960s*, edited by Franca Iacovetta with Paula Draper and Robert Ventrescan, 35–55. Toronto: University of Toronto Press, 1998.

Davin, Nicholas Flood. *The Irishman in Canada*. London: S. Low; Toronto: Marston, 1877.

Elliot, Bruce. *Irish Migrants in the Canadas: A New Approach*. Kingston: McGill-Queen's University Press, 1988.

Reynolds, Lorna and Robert O'Driscoll, eds. *The Untold Story: The Irish in Canada*. Vols. I and II. Toronto: Celtic Arts of Canada, 1988.

ORANGE ORDER

The Orange Order was founded in 1795 after the Battle of the Diamond near Loughall, Co. Armagh, at which the Protestant Peep O' Day Boys killed 48 Catholic defenders. The organization that was formed took its name from King William of Orange who had defeated the Catholic King James II at the Battle of the Boyne in 1690. Members of the Orange Order were required to be Protestant and had to swear allegiance to the British monarch. Each year on July 12 they paraded to commemorate King William's victory, which they viewed as establishing the civil and religious liberties associated with the Glorious Revolution. Within a few years of its founding, the Order had spread rapidly, and it soon established lodges throughout Ireland. However, the majority of its lodges were in Ulster, where there was the greatest concentration of Protestants. Lodges were also established in Scotland, England, Canada, West Africa, Australia, and New Zealand. With increased emigration from Ireland to America, Protestant immigrants founded the first Orange lodges in New York in the 1820s. The Loyal Orange Institution in America, as it was called, was affiliated with the Grand Orange Lodge of Ireland. As most of the immigration at that time was to the East Coast of America, the majority of the Order's lodges were located in eastern states such as Pennsylvania, Delaware, Massachusetts, and Connecticut, and most Orange activity was concentrated in New York where the majority of immigrants had settled. However, there were even lodges as far away as Michigan, Illinois, and California. In short, wherever large numbers of Protestant immigrants from Ulster congregated, there could be found an Orange lodge. By 1872, the Order claimed to have 42 lodges, and this figure increased to a total of 120 lodges with 10,000 members in 1875. As well as acting as a forum for Ulster Protestant immigrants to assert the common ties they shared, the Order also warned against the dangers of Catholic immigration to America.

With the growth of the Orange Order in America there were frequent clashes with Irish Catholics. In 1824 there were battles in Greenwich Village, and in 1831 Irish Catholics rioted against the Orangemen in Philadelphia. The most significant episodes in American history involving the Orange Order were in 1870 and 1871, when there were fierce riots at the Orange parades in New York City. In both years on July 12 Irish Catholics tried to prevent Orangemen from parading through the streets of New York. In 1870, when it was claimed that Orangemen had fired a gun at a Catholic church, armed Irish Catholic immigrants left their jobs and confronted the Orangemen, who were also armed. A battle between the two sides ensued, and the police arrived too late to quell the disturbance. In total, eight people were killed, fifteen injured, and six arrested. The following year the violence was much worse: at least 62 dead, more than 100 injured, and another 100 arrested. With the memory of the preceding year's events, there were rumors that elements on each side were planning to orchestrate trouble for their own ends. While the Ancient Order of Hibernians and the Knights of St. Patrick demanded that the authorities ban the Orangemen's parade, the Order called for the police to ensure that the parade went ahead. When violence followed, the National Guard opened fire on the Irish Catholics who were trying to prevent the parade from proceeding. In both years the Orange parades and the riots that accompanied them were used as an excuse to undermine the political administration in New York City. Orangemen alleged that the Tammany Hall leader William Marcy "Boss" Tweed had pandered to the Irish Catholic masses who voted for him and his Democratic Party. Irish Catholics, on the other hand, viewed the violent crackdown against them as evidence that the Orangemen were attempting to suppress them in the United States as they had done in Ireland. After these riots the Orangemen did not parade again until 1890.

David Doyle

References

Gordon, Michael A. *Orange Riots: Irish Political Violence in New York City 1870, 1871.* Ithaca, NY: Cornell University Press, 1993.

Long, Samuel E. *A Brief History of the Loyal Orange Institution in the United States of America.* Orange Institution, 1979.

OREGON

The clear, cool, rainy climate of Oregon seems familiar to those who have spent time in Ireland, and so it cannot come as a surprise to learn that many Irish found themselves among the earliest settlers of the temperate western territory. Many came to help build the railroads, others came across on the Oregon Trail, still others came with the Army, and at least one came as part of the Lewis and Clark expedition in 1804–1806. Some came to flee the Famine in Ireland, and some came in response to the western gold rush. All of them came in hopes of at last owning land, educating their children, and escaping religious persecution, dreams that seemed possible to achieve in Oregon.

On August 14, 1848, the Oregon Territory was established; in 1859, part of that territory became the 33rd state in the United States. Although some say the name came from a wandering Celt named Michael Patrick O'Regan, who arrived even before the Native Americans did, none have been able to prove it, and most believe the first Irish settlers appeared as part of the group coming over the Oregon Trail. Of the 780 who made it across in that group, 14 were originally from Ireland. The trek across country was difficult and expensive, and most of the Irish who made it to Oregon had spent a considerable amount of time on the East Coast first, saving money for the journey; most of those who had recently emigrated from Ireland lacked the resources for such a journey. For those who had some resources, however, and considerable pluck, one of the most obvious draws to Oregon was the promise of virtually free land. The Donation Act of 1850 promised a husband and wife 640 acres if they could live on that land for five years; the later Homestead Act of 1862 revised that amount to 160 acres and required a nominal fee to file the paperwork.

Many of the arriving Irish initially settled in St. Paul, south of Portland near the Willamette River, where there was a Catholic mission, but many others built up an Irish community in Portland itself, establishing churches, schools, and fraternal organizations such as the Ancient Order of Hibernians (AOH). From 1877 to 1933, the AOH remained one of the key social and philanthropic organizations in Oregon for the Irish in the Pacific Northwest, especially after the opening of Hibernian Hall in 1914. The Clan na Gael (also known as the United Brotherhood or the Robert Emmet Literary Society) was active in the area as well between 1910 and 1922. John McLoughlin, a Canadian of Irish descent and the head of the Hudson's Bay Company in Portland, brought in a group of French-Canadian nuns to start up St. Mary's Academy, a Catholic school for the young girls of Portland; they also opened St. Joseph's, for boys, but had to close it when many of the nuns died. Although non-Catholic students were also attracted by the discipline and quality of education provided, these schools were free to teach about Catholicism without the same social and political stigma that had long been troublesome in Ireland, and many of the Irish families sacrificed to send their children there. In 1870, the *Catholic Sentinel* began publication, a newspaper that is still being published today, providing the voice for Catholics to speak out about their own concerns; in the early days, the newspaper was criticized for being more Irish than Catholic.

The Irish population in Portland, however, was never very constant. Many unskilled laborers came and went, and although some became professionals and stayed (as Irish Catholics were not barred from holding public office in Oregon), and although the churches and schools were built largely by volunteers among the Irish community, there was never a strong sense of community bound by long history together. By the early 1920s, many of the Irish who had helped settle Portland had gone. Other immigrant groups began to populate Portland; the Germans established their own Catholic church within the city, and the Chinese began to take many of the jobs that had hitherto been given to the Irish. Tension between the groups increased as the economy declined. By the time Eamon de Valera, president of the Dail and soon-to-be president of Ireland, came to Portland in November 1919, the dissension between the Irish immigrants and other ethnic groups had reached a peak: the American Legion attacked de Valera while the Irish acclaimed him.

Many of those who made it to Oregon did not settle in Portland, choosing instead the more rural areas of Oregon. The potential for sheepherding was evident, as much open land remained, and the climate and terrain were favorable. It was a lucrative business, though difficult and challenging. Much of the land, especially east of the Cascade Mountains, remained part of the public domain, and initially there were no restrictions about grazing those lands. Tension with cattle ranchers, coyotes, and bears made the job of sheep herding dangerous, and weather that could sometimes be unpredictably treacherous could result in a total loss of fortune, but banks were, by and large, willing to bail out destitute sheepherders, knowing that another fortune could easily be made. In time, however, sheepherding became impracticable. The Taylor Grazing Act of 1934 stipulated that an itinerant sheepherder must be able to prove land ownership; presumably land ownership would guarantee that a herd of sheep would have access to at least two months' supply of hay in the winter, hay that did not have to be purchased from a second party, thus ensuring a better survival rate for the sheep in winter. The requirement, however, could not be met by many sheepherders, whose only capital was the sheep. (Most of the profits from successful sheepherding were sent back to Ireland.) With the onset of the Great Depression and World War II, the influx of Irish immigrants who could help herd the sheep also decreased, and profits were hurt. By about 1934, sheepherding in Oregon was basically over, and cattle herding was on the rise.

World War II affected the city populations as well, and many Irish men went off to war. By the mid-1930s, the AOH in Portland was down to thirty members, and the group disbanded completely with the onset of World War II. It was, however, reestablished with 27 new members in 1998. Portland today remains an active, vibrant scene for the Irish, featuring many cultural events and organizations that celebrate all things Irish. The All-Ireland Cultural Society has been active for 65 years, bringing music, dance, sports, and language to the area. Other towns in the state, settled long ago by the Irish, continue to hold large Irish celebrations, especially on Saint Patrick's Day; Heppner, Irish Bend, Bandon, St. Paul, and other towns continue to align themselves with Irish culture. As the 1990 census lists 19.8 percent of Oregonians claiming Irish descent, Irish influence in Oregon does not appear to be waning any time soon.

Kathleen Heininge

See also: ANCIENT ORDER OF HIBERNIANS; DE VALERA, Eamon

References

The Irish in Early Oregon History. Portland, OR: Irish Interest Group Genealogical Forum of Oregon, 1993.

Kazin, Michael. "Irish Families in Portland, Oregon: 1850–1880: An Immigrant

Culture in the Far West." Master's thesis. Portland State University, Portland, OR, 1975.

Kelleher, Marie. *Duhollow to Oregon: 1880–1960*. Lakeview, OR: Duhallow Development Association, 1985.

Kilkenny, John F. *Shamrocks and Shepherds: The Irish of Morrow County*. Portland: Oregon Historical Society, 1969.

Ó Longaigh, David, ed. *We Irish in Oregon*. Portland, OR: 1998.

O'REILLY, JOHN BOYLE (1844–1890)

On June 28, 1844, John Boyle O'Reilly, the son of a schoolteacher, was born in Co. Meath. In 1863, he enlisted with the British Army's Tenth Hussars, then stationed in Dublin. Arrested in 1866 as a Fenian, he was court-martialed and condemned to 20 years of hard labor. In 1868, O'Reilly was sent to Western Australia on the last convict ship ever sent to the penal colonies, *The Hougoumont*. With the assistance of a parish priest and local settlers and funded by overseas Fenian sympathizers, O'Reilly managed to escape in February 1869. He was smuggled aboard an American whaling ship, *The Gazelle,* and eventually, in November 1869, he arrived in the United States. Settling in Boston, O'Reilly was taken under the wing of the Irish-American community. Within a couple of months he established himself as a reporter for *The Pilot,* then an eight-page weekly newspaper covering Irish and Irish-American affairs. He quickly made a name for himself covering events such as a disastrous 1870 invasion of Canada by a group of Irish-American Fenians and bloody Orangemen's riots in New York City between Catholic and Protestant Irish immigrants in 1870 and 1871. His balanced and critical assessment of such events reflected his increasing detachment from

Portrait of John Boyle O'Reilly, revolutionary, newspaper editor, and poet. (Library of Congress)

his revolutionary past. By the time he died in 1890, O'Reilly was one of the best-known American poets and undoubtedly one of the best-known Irish immigrants in the United States.

O'Reilly was rapidly promoted at *The Pilot* and soon felt established enough to wed Mary Murphy, a daughter of Irish immigrants. By 1876, he had become part owner and editor-in-chief of *The Pilot.* From then until his death in 1890, O'Reilly controlled what was probably the second most powerful media outlet in Massachusetts short of the *Boston Globe.* He wrote editorials, hired writers, and built *The Pilot* up from a minor Catholic news weekly to a major newspaper with an international reputation. O'Reilly was elected president of the Boston Press Club in 1879, and his status ensured that the "ethnic" papers in Massachusetts would get a serious hearing. As befitted his position as an interpreter of all things Irish, rival newspapers would regularly run to O'Reilly for his analysis of both Irish, and increasingly, Irish-American, issues. O'Reilly's ascendancy through Boston society was rapid. Within a short number of years he was not only considered a spokesman for the Irish immigrants of Boston, but he was also a well-known poet, public speaker, sportsman, and activist for political causes ranging from labor reform to Civil Rights. He counted among his good friends not only the stalwarts of what was rapidly becoming the Irish political machine, but also literati such as Oliver Wendell Holmes and Julia Ward Howe and activists such as Wendell Phillips. He became friendly with President Grover Cleveland and with Cardinal Gibbons, the head of the Catholic Church in America. O'Reilly was president of both the literary Papyrus Club and the Boston Press Club. A member of numerous Catholic charities and radical reform movements, within a few years of his arrival, O'Reilly became a recognizable figure of Boston's social elite. Bridging the gap between the affluent area of Beacon Hill and what was rapidly becoming a city dominated by Irish-American immigrants, O'Reilly was hailed as a cross-cultural ambassador. O'Reilly had begun writing poetry as a child, which he continued to do during his long stints in prison and aboard ships. With *The Pilot* as a ready outlet, O'Reilly was prolific with his verse. His specialty was ballad stanza political couplets that would call out for freedom and against tyranny. These immensely popular poems, written in a romantic and sentimental tradition, promoted a genteel bourgeois sensibility. Nostalgic, often didactic, and essentially propagandistic, these poems

appealed to the Irish immigrants who sought assimilation and to well-established Bostonians alike. Through works such as his most famous poem, "In Bohemia," written in 1888 and later included in an important anthology of the same name, O'Reilly attracted a broad readership. He had a fervent belief that the arts could provide a vehicle to bridge the gap between the powerful and the powerless, although his incongruous mixture of political radicalism and sentimental themes does not appeal to modern audiences. Other notable works include *Ethics of Boxing and Manly Sport* (1888); *The King's Men* (1884); *The Moondyne* (1878), which is set in Australia and draws on many of his own experiences as a prisoner and escapee; and poetry collections such as *Songs from the Southern Sea* (1873), *Songs, Legends, and Ballads* (1878), and *The Statues in the Block and Other Poems* (1881).

O'Reilly's poetry attracted important commissions throughout the 1870s and 1880s. He also wrote hundreds of occasional poems to mark significant events. Some of his most important poems include ones written about the African-American patriot Crispus Attucks, whaling adventures, the American Civil War, and western Australia. In 1889, O'Reilly was commissioned to write the dedicatory poem for the Pilgrim monument at Plymouth Rock; it was a remarkable achievement for a foreign-born writer to be chosen to help define a founding symbol of American national identity.

O'Reilly died suddenly in 1890 as a result of an accidental overdose of his wife's sleeping medicine. He had suffered terribly from exhaustion and insomnia for the months before his death, which many scholars have ascribed to the unrelenting pressure he felt to constantly appease, explain, and negotiate among Boston's various groups. Whatever the cause, his sudden death at a comparatively young age—leaving a wife and four daughters—shocked Boston and the world. Tributes poured in from memorial services that were held in cities and townships around the world. The New York Metropolitan Opera House was filled to capacity for a civic ceremony of remembrance. Reading groups and social clubs were founded in O'Reilly's name, scholarships were endowed, statues were put up, and honorary poems were written.

Susanna Ashton

See also: BOSTON; FENIANS; MASSACHUSSETS

References

Betts, John R. "John Boyle O'Reilly and the American Paideia." *Éire Ireland* 2 (1967): 36–37.

Brady, Veronica. "The Innocent Gaze: John Boyle O'Reilly's 'The King of the Vasse.'" *Kunapipi* 16, no. 2 (1994): 1–6.

Doyle, David. "John Boyle O'Reilly and Irish Adjustment in America." *Journal of the Old Drogheda Society* (1996): 7–25.

Evans, A. G. *Fanatic Heart: A Life of John Boyle O'Reilly, 1844–1890.* Boston: Northeastern University Press, 1997.

Goldie, Terry. "Emancipating the Equal Aborigine: J. B. O'Reilly and A. J. Vogan." *SPAN* 20 (April 1985): 44–66.

O'Reilly, John Boyle, Robert Grant, Frederic Jesup Stimson, and John T. Wheelwright. *The King's Men: a Tale of Tomorrow.* New York: Charles Scribner's Sons, 1884.

O'ROARKE, JULIÁN "HUBERTO" (1852–1913)

Julián O'Roarke was born in 1852 in Baradero, the oldest city of Buenos Aires province, the son of Michael O'Roarke (1822–1867) and Mary Maguire (1819–1890). During his public life he supported the organization of Argentine institutions in the province of Buenos Aires during the last decades of the nineteenth century. In 1881 O'Roarke was appointed proxy and later president of Baradero's city council, and he served additional terms in 1882 and 1883. He was elected mayor of Baradero in 1890, 1894, 1904, 1905, and 1910. Sarmiento Park in Baradero (previously named *Parque del Bajo*) was created by O'Roarke in 1905. This park was designed by the French architect Charles Thays, and in 1906 it housed the celebrations for the 50th anniversary of Baradero's Swiss colony. In 1902 O'Roarke was elected member of Parliament in the provincial parliament of Buenos Aires, representing Baradero department. O'Roarke was a member of the Conservative Party of Buenos Aires province, which became a major political force representing provincial, and later national, landed elite.

In March 1879 a group of 300 influential Irish and Irish-Argentine businessmen and *estancieros* (ranchers) led by the Catholic priest Patrick J. Dillon founded the General Brown Club. Among the members were O'Roarke and other representatives of Baradero and San Pedro departments. The club, structured in the fashion of the political organizations of the Argentine ruling elite, was determined to secure representation in Parliament, protect and encourage immigrants from the British Isles, and improve the moral and material life of native rural workers, "making the voices of the English-speaking *Porteños* [people from Buenos Aires] heard in the Senate." A political alliance was shaped with the hegemonic Autonomist Party, and the following year Father Dillon and Eduardo Murphy were elected members of Parliament to Buenos Aires in the provincial lower house. The General Brown Club lasted less than 10 years, but its members pioneered the political participation of many Irish Argentines within the social circles of the landed class in Buenos Aires. In 1910 Julián O'Roarke, Alfredo Butty, Eduardo Doyle, Jack Kelly, Ricardo C. Kennedy, Benito E. Lynch, Enrique Lynch, Guillermo Mooney, Miguel Murphy, Antonino O'Gorman, and others with Irish names who had participated in the General Brown Club were members of the powerful provincial Conservative Party. O'Roarke contributed to the celebrations of the 100th anniversary of Argentine independence, which the ruling elite in Argentina viewed as an opportunity to create a series of nationalist symbols for the country.

Julián O'Roarke died on June 28, 1913, in Buenos Aires. The municipal authorities of Baradero changed the name of Sauces street to Julián O'Roarke (the street is near the railway station).

Edmundo Murray

> *See also:* DILLON, Patrick Joseph, LYNCH, Benito Eduardo

References
Barbich, Alejandro. *Historia de Santiago del Baradero*. Buenos Aires: Author's Edition, 1989.

Cané, Gonzalo, "Don Julián O'Roarque," *The Southern Cross*, April 2001.

Coghlan, Eduardo A. *Los Irlandeses en la Argentina: Su Actuación y Descendencia*. Buenos Aires: Author's Edition, 1987.

O'SULLIVAN, DENIS (1868–1906)

The Denis O'Sullivan Medal honoring this American-born singer is one of the principal awards at Ireland's national musical competition, the Feis Ceoil, which is held annually. Initially, O'Sullivan studied with Karl Formes in San Francisco, Giovanni Sbriglia in Paris, and then Charles Santley in London, where he made his concert debut in 1895.

Later he joined the touring Carl Rosa Opera Company in Dublin making his operatic debut in Giuseppe Verdi's *Il Trovatore* in August 1895. He continued to sing various roles with the Carl Rosa Company. In 1896, he sang the title role in the first performance of Irish composer C. V. Stamford's opera, *Shamus O'Brien* in London, a role he later also sang in Dublin and at the Broadway Theatre in New York in 1897. In America he was also successful in the one-act opera *The Post Bag* by composer Michele Esposito of the Royal Irish Academy of Music in Dublin. In 1900 the Dublin Academy invited O'Sullivan to sing at their concerts, where he was quite successful. He continued his involvement with the Academy over the next three years, after which he returned to America. In addition to his musical activity he found time to perform in the plays of the Dublin-born playwright Dion Boucicault while in America. After O'Sullivan's death in 1908 his widow donated an initial fund to the Academy to create a Denis O'Sullivan Medal award in his honor. The award still exists to this day and most years at the Feis Ceoil, the Denis O'Sullivan Medal is awarded to one of the participating competitors.

Basil Walsh

References
Baker's Biographical Dictionary of Musicians, 4th ed. New York: G. Schirmer, 1940.

Pine, Richard, and Charles Acton, *To Talent Alone, The Royal Irish Academy of Music 1848–1998*. Dublin: Gill & Macmillan, 1998.

O'SULLIVAN, TIMOTHY H. (1840–1882)

Timothy H. O'Sullivan had a remarkable career as a documentary photographer. His subjects extended from the battlefields of the Civil War to the exploration of the Southwestern frontier. Although few details about his life are known, the apparently adventurous Irishman was the first to photograph the Great Salt Lake, the Mojave Desert, and the Grand Canyon. These, along with images of underground mining in Nevada and Native American culture in New Mexico, resulted in an evocative yet realistic body of work.

Reports of O'Sullivan's birthplace differ. Some say he was born in Ireland and came to the United States with his parents after the Great Famine; others contend he was born in Staten Island, New York. In any event, by the time he was 16, O'Sullivan began an apprenticeship in photography, first with Mathew Brady in his New York gallery and later in Brady's Washington, D.C., studio under the tutelage of Scottish photographer Alexander Gardner. When the Civil War broke out, O'Sullivan signed on to photograph the field operations of the Army of the Potomac. In that capacity he copied maps for immediate distribution to field commanders. He also captured battle scenes, war strategy sessions, group and individual portraits of officers and enlisted men, and the general devastation of war. Known as a master technician, O'Sullivan often put his own life in jeopardy to capture a particular image, at one point coming so close to the action that his camera was destroyed by a stray shell. He was present at Gettysburg, Antietam, the Wilderness, Fredericksburg, and Appomatox. As was the custom at the time, many of his photographs were printed in *Photographic Incidents of the War from the Gallery of Alexander Gardner* while others appeared in *Harper's Weekly,* credited to Brady. In his best known picture, "Harvest of Death," the fallen soldiers of the Iron Brigade, the

24th Michigan Infantry, are strewn across the landscape at Gettysburg. After the war, Brady offered O'Sullivan the position of manager of his Washington, D.C., photographic studio, but O'Sullivan chose instead the life of a traveling documentarian.

In 1867 he accompanied Clarence King's exploration of the 40th Parallel, charting the expansive territory between the Rocky Mountains and the Sierra Nevada. Except for a journey in 1869 to the Isthmus of Darien in Panama (then part of Colombia) to explore possible routes for a canal, O'Sullivan spent the next seven years crisscrossing the American frontier, including portions of present-day Nevada, Utah, Arizona, New Mexico, Colorado, and Wyoming, to document the wilderness for civilian and military commissions. Using a converted horse-drawn ambulance as a portable dark room and withstanding rough terrain and extreme climatic conditions, O'Sullivan made hundreds of glass plates of geological formations and natural landscapes, such as the lime tufa formations and volcanic islands on Pyramid Lake in Nevada. While in Virginia City, Nevada, he also produced the first photographs of subterranean mining ever made in America, descending several hundred feet into extremely cramped shafts and using magnesium flares for light. O'Sullivan's 1869 views of the Devil's Slide and Witches Rocks in Utah were among the first to capture the immense and barren landscape west of the Mississippi. In 1871 he joined the George Wheeler–led expedition surveying the territory west of the 100th meridian and traveled up the Colorado River from Nevada, a particularly arduous trek, to record the isolation and majesty of both the Black Canyon in Arizona and the Shoshone Falls in Snake River, Idaho.

In 1873 and 1874, not satisfied to record only geological features for internal distribution to the scientific and educational communities, O'Sullivan returned to the Southwest to document what remained of the pueblo and rock-dwelling tribes in the Canyon de Chelly region in New Mexico, the San Miguel Church in Santa Fe, and Apache culture in Arizona.

O'Sullivan was married in 1873 to Laura Virginia Pywell, the sister of fellow photographer William Reddish Pywell, an event that perhaps influenced him to end his expeditionary work around 1875. The couple had no children. O'Sullivan was a working photographer in the nation's capitol for several years, accepting an appointment to the U.S. Geological Survey Office in 1879. In November 1880, he became photographer to the U.S. Department of the Treasury but was forced to resign a few months later because of ill health. Laura O'Sullivan died of tuberculosis in October 1881 and three months later, at the age of 42, O'Sullivan succumbed to the same disease while at his parents' home on Staten Island.

Patricia Fanning

See also: AMERICAN CIVIL WAR

References

Dingus, Rick. *The Photographic Artifacts of Timothy O'Sullivan*. Albuquerque, NM: The University of New Mexico Press, 1982.

Horan, James D. *Timothy H. O'Sullivan: American's Forgotten Photographer*. New York: Bonanza Press, 1966.

Snyder, Joel. *American Frontiers, The Photographs of Timothy H. O'Sullivan, 1867–1874*. New York: Aperture, 1981.

P

PANAMA

The part of Central America that became Panama was occupied by the Spanish from the early sixteenth century until Colombia (which included Panama) gained its independence, as Gran Colombia, in 1821. During the seventeenth century, the region was attacked by ships belonging to British buccaneers—which no doubt included Irishmen in their crew—culminating in Henry Morgan's attack on Panama City in 1671.

When the rebellions against Spanish rule broke out in the late 1810s, one of the men who rallied the independence forces around Panama City was Daniel Florence O'Leary (1801–1854), who had been born in Cork. His father was a friend of the Irish nationalist Daniel O'Connell. Despite his young age, Simón Bolívar sent O'Leary to Panama to hold it against the Spanish Royalist troops. He later moved to Bogota where he died, but his body was later exhumed and buried close to that of Bolívar in Caracas, Venezuela.

Europeans had long realized that Panama included the narrowest part of Central America, and the possibility of building a canal had been raised as early as 1524. However, it was not until the 1849 gold rush in California that the idea was raised as a serious engineering proposition. With so many people anxious to get to California while avoiding the dangerous trail across the United States or the long and hazardous journey around Cape Horn, plans were quickly hatched to push a railway across Panama, if a canal proved too difficult. Planning was helped by an Irish physician and a member of the Royal Geographical Society, Dr. Edward Cullen, who had, in 1850, walked from the Atlantic coast of Panama to the Pacific across Darien, apparently several times. His book, *The Isthmus of Darien,* was published in London in 1852, by which time a railway line was being built, and much of the work was undertaken by Irish navvies. Cullen's later book, *Over Darien by a Ship Canal,* published in 1854, started raising the idea of a canal, a year before the railway was finally completed, at the cost of many Irish and local lives.

The idea of a canal continued, and, when the man behind the Suez Canal, Frenchman Ferdinand de Lesseps, became interested, so did other Frenchmen, including Lt. Lucien Napoleon-Bonaparte Wyse, the illegitimate son of Napoleon I's niece Princess Laetitia. Although she had long since separated from her husband, the Irish diplomat Sir Thomas Wyse, the boy took his surname. Wyse was to help de Lesseps with the futile attempt to build the Panama Canal in the 1870s.

The plans for a Panama Canal were welcomed by many in Panama, including the *Star & Herald* newspaper, which had been established in Panama City in 1852 by Archibald Boyd, a migrant from Clemenstown, Co. Fermanagh. In the early years of the twentieth century, with renewed interest in the Panama Canal from the United States, a breakaway movement in Panama led the province to independence from Colombia in 1903. Archibald Boyd's eldest son, Federico Boyd, was a member of the junta that seized power in the newly proclaimed Republic of Panama. He was acting president of Panama in 1910 and foreign minister from 1911 to 1912.

Federico Boyd, born on November 3, 1851, in Panama City, was a member of the Panama City Municipal Council from 1888, and became the acting president from October 1 to 5, 1910. He subsequently served as minister for foreign relations, and then ambassador to Germany, Netherlands, and Belgium, before becoming Panama's business representative in Honduras and El Salvador. Boyd died on May 25, 1924, in New York City. His son, Augusto Samuel Boyd (1879–1957) was the 18th president of Panama, serving from December 18, 1939, until October 1, 1940.

The Missouri-born botanist Paul Carpenter Standley (1884–1963), author of *Flora of the Panama Canal Zone,* which was published in 1928, was also of Irish descent through his mother. Another important Panamanian of Irish descent was Marcos Gregorio McGrath (1924–2000), archbishop of Panama from 1969 until 1994.

Justin Corfield

See also: O'LEARY, Daniel Florence

Reference

McCullough, David. *The Path Between the Seas: The Creation of the Panama Canal, 1870–1914.* New York: Simon & Schuster, 1977.

PARAGUAY

Under the old Spanish regime, Paraguay included the Argentine provinces of Tucumán, Córdoba, and Buenos Aires, all of which were subject to the Adelantado of Asunción. Toward the end of the sixteenth century, Governor Fernando Arias introduced the Jesuits to check the cruelties of the Spanish conquistadors. For nearly 200 years the Jesuit missions were the admiration of travelers, and, as Voltaire confessed, they were a triumph of humanity. The missions included 30 self-governing cities of native Guaraní people strung along both sides of Paraná River, which today forms the border between eastern Paraguay and northern Argentina. Raids of the white slave traders from southern Brazil convinced the Jesuits of the need to establish these missions. In the late sixteenth century, three priests, one of them the Irishman Thomas Field (1547–1626) of Limerick, ventured into the area to work with the Guaraní. Father Field had entered the Jesuits in Rome in 1574 and landed in Brazil on December 31, 1577, where he spent 10 years as a scholastic at Piratininga (today's São Paulo). In 1857, he moved to Paraguay, and he eventually arrived in Asunción with Father Ortega from Portugal and Father Saloni from Italy. Father Field got to know the Guaraní people through his missionary travels, and his recommendations about their evangelization were to have a major influence on how the Jesuit missions were set up. Father Field attended the key synod of 1603 where decisions were made to set up the missions (or *Reductions* as they were called). Father Field died in Asunción in 1626 and is credited by the Irish Jesuit historian, Father Aubrey Gwynn, with being the first Irish priest to celebrate the Roman Catholic Mass in the Americas.

Other Irish Jesuits followed Father Field and worked in the Paraguayan missions: Father Thomas Browne of Waterford (1656–1717), Brother William Leny of Dublin (1692–ca. 1760), and Father Thaddeus Enis who was working in the Reductions at the time of the Jesuit expulsion. Brother Andrew Stritch arrived in Paraguay as the Jesuits were being expelled and was deported to Italy, where he died in 1773. The governor of Paraguay from 1766 to 1772, Lt. Col. Carlos Morphi, was a Spanish officer related to the Murphy family of southern Ireland. Morphi founded the city of Caacupé in April 1770. When he received the order to expel the Jesuits, Morphi helped them to conceal and destroy documents and to escape from Paraguay. He was prosecuted for this reason and sent back to Spain.

Science, culture, and music flourished in the missions; they had some of the earliest printing presses in the Americas and published books in Guaraní. Angered by the Jesuits' defense of the native people, the colonial authorities finally persuaded King Charles III of Spain to expel the order from his territories in 1767. This opened the way for the breakup of the Jesuit missions in Paraguay. However, the legacy lived on, as the absence of a landholding class in this part of South America made Paraguay the most progressive state in the Americas after its independence in 1811, and today Guaraní is the only native vernacular language of any American state.

Undoubtedly the most colorful Irish person to enter Paraguayan history was Cork-born Elisa Lynch (1835–1886), who met Dictator Francisco Solano López when he was visiting Paris in 1853. She returned with him to Asunción, and in 1862 López became president and Eliza Lynch the first lady. She played an active role in the War of the Triple Alliance (1864–1870), and some historians argue that many of the cruelties that marked López's rule were attributed to his mistress. The second Paraguayan president after López, Juan B. Gill (1840–1877) also had Irish origins. His term was 1874–1877. Gill was murdered on April 2, 1877.

Edmundo Murray

See also: LYNCH, Elisa (Eliza); O'LEARY, Juan Emiliano; RE-EMIGRANTS WITHIN THE AMERICAS

References

Cawthorne, Nigel. *The Empress of South America*. London: Heinemann, 2003.

Kirby, Peadar. *Ireland and Latin America: Links and Lessons*. Dublin: Trócaire, 1992.

Williams, John Hoyt. *The Rise and Fall of the Paraguayan Republic, 1800–1870*. Austin, TX: Institute of Latin American Studies, 1979.

PASSENGER ACTS

Laws regarding immigration were first enacted in Massachusetts in 1701 to prevent the diseased, infirm, and impoverished from entering port and becoming a burden to society. People who could not support themselves were returned to their port of origin. During the next several years other states would follow the Massachusetts example and enact statutes of their own regarding immigrants into the colonies. These statutes in the colonies were actually the precursors to the Passenger Acts, which were adopted in the United States in 1847.

The Passenger Acts of 1847 were created to limit the immigration of large numbers of aliens. They were to prevent shipping companies from taking advantage of Irish immigrants at this time by stopping greedy companies from overloading ships and underproviding passengers. The number of Irish immigrants into the United States had grown exponentially because of the Potato Famine, which left many Irish starving and desperate to leave Ireland. The population of Ireland had also grown greatly as a result of the devastation by the Napoleonic Wars in 1803; thus, the Passenger Acts served to restrict the number of European immigrants, particularly the Irish and the Germans; to relieve the country of any fiscal burden; and to reduce crime committed by those of amoral character. There was also fear of disease resulting from the great numbers of immigrants who were entering the ports. Many were sick with typhus, dysentery, and severe abdominal illnesses.

Before these laws were created, ships from Ireland and England were loaded with passengers headed for the New World. However, the ships were often unsafe, overloaded, and lacked provisions. British ships were worse than the American ones, as they often had temporary toilets, usually two for 250–300 immigrants on board; were poorly ventilated; and had captains of questionable talent for steering ships. It was not uncommon for a ship to take up to eight weeks to reach Canada or America because of the incompetence of a British sea captain, a situation that resulted in the death of fully 20–30 percent of immigrants on board because of a lack of fresh water and food. Rats passed diseases to passengers, and, because many immigrants had lived in squalor before coming aboard ship, they carried blankets and clothing infested with lice, which spread typhus.

Although Great Britain had previously enacted regulations in 1842 similar to the U.S. Passenger Acts of 1847, these regulations were ignored and ship employees were bribed to turn a blind eye to lawbreakers. The U.S. ordinances were very strict compared with the British ones. Each passenger was to be allotted a certain amount of space to avoid overcrowding, and a doctor was required to be on board ship, contrary to the British regulations. American boats were usually in better shape, contained more toilets, and were managed by well-trained sailors. There had to be a certain amount of provisions for passengers aboard American ships. However, American ship passage was more than double the price of passage aboard a British ship bound for Canada. To make matters even worse, many Irish decided to depart out of lesser-kempt ports of Ireland, where it was impossible to maintain regulations. In many cases, there was almost no food on board, water was stagnant, and the ships were not very seaworthy. It is not known how many Irish died on British ships or drowned when ships sank because there was no enforcement of laws regarding the number of passengers. All that is known is that ships simply vanished and all on board were assumed drowned on their way to the "promised land" of the United States. In addition, those who died as a result of illness were quickly dumped into the sea without services or record of their deaths. Thus, such vessels were known as "coffin ships."

Ships that did make their way to Canada were, in fact, quite lucky to make port. Those who survived the sea journey found that they could make their way to America by simply walking across the border. Many Irish did so, and thus, they became one of the largest groups of immigrants to come to America. Although the Passenger Acts of 1847 were later repealed and replaced with the Passenger Acts of 1852, which were much more stringent, they did not slow the flow of immigrants into the New World. The price for a ticket to America, even at double the price of British passage, was small compared with the number of deaths on unregulated and unhealthy British ships.

Cynthia A. Klima

References

Gallagher, Thomas. *Paddy's Lament*. New York: Harcourt Brace & Co., 1982.

Scally, Robert James. *The End of Hidden Ireland: Rebellion, Famine and Emigration*. New York: Oxford University Press, 1995.

Woodham-Smith, Cecil. *The Great Hunger: Ireland 1845–1849*. London: Penguin Books, 1991.

PATTERSON, FRANK (1938–2000)

The singer Frank Patterson was born in Clonmel, Co. Tipperary, on October 5, 1938, and died in New York City on June 10, 2000. He began performing as a child, but received formal training from 1962 in Dublin with Hans Waldemar Rosen, the German-born conductor of the RTÉ Singers. By the mid-1960s he had collected several prizes for his tenor voice at the Dublin Feis Ceoil, and he was in constant demand in classical recitals and oratorio. As a member of the Irish Festival Singers (Feis Éireann) he toured the United States in 1966 and a year later married the ensemble's director, the pianist Eily O'Grady.

The couple lived in Paris (1968–1972) while Patterson continued his studies with Janine Micheau. During this time he received a recording contract from the Philips company and has since recorded more than 40 albums of both classical and Irish repertory. Although he was classically trained, Patterson's popularity stemmed from his recordings of Irish ballads, similar to John McCormack who had a similar repertory 50 years previously. As "Ireland's Golden Tenor," and with an increasing mix of musical styles, including broadway songs and other favorites, Patterson won the heart of Irish-American audiences, while also being in demand for his renderings of Bach cantatas, Handel arias, and the songs of Beethoven, Schubert, Berlioz, and Wolf. In the latter capacity he performed with major European orchestras in London, Paris, Rome, Rotterdam, and Basel. In the United States, he performed with the National Symphony Orchestra in Washington, D.C., as well as with the Colorado, St. Louis, Hartford, Syracuse, Rochester, Utah, and Seattle symphonies. He has sung to sold-out audiences at Carnegie Hall in New York, the Kennedy Center in Washington, D.C., the Boston Symphony Hall, and the Ray Thompson Hall in Toronto.

From 1974 to 1984 Patterson hosted his own show on RTÉ television, *Frank Patterson: For Your Pleasure,* entertaining his audiences with light classics and humorous commentary. In the United States he had a number of engagements with commercial television and three famous specials on public television: *Ireland's Golden Tenor—Ireland in Song, Frank Patterson: Songs of Inspiration,* and *God Bless America.* For the movie screen he had two short stints in *The Dead* (1987), directed by John Huston, and *Michael Collins* (1996), directed by Neil Jordan. He was invited to perform before President Ronald Reagan in 1982 and President Bill Clinton in 1995, and he was honored by being asked to perform on the occasion of the pope's visit to Ireland in 1979 with 1.3 million people present.

Frank Patterson received numerous awards for his art and for his commitment to social causes. In 1984, the pope conferred upon him the Knighthood of St. Gregory. He also became a Knight of Malta and a Knight Commander of the Holy Sepulcher of Jerusalem. He was awarded honorary doctorates by Salve Regina University in Newport, Rhode Island (1990) and Manhattan College in New York City (1996). In 1998 both Patterson and his wife were awarded the Gold Medal of the Éire Society of Boston.

Axel Klein

See also: CLINTON, William Jefferson; HUSTON, John; JORDAN, Neil; McCORMACK, John; REAGAN, Ronald Wilson

PEARSON, NOEL (1941–)

Noel Pearson was born in Dublin on January 5, 1941. Pearson has been a well-known and much respected figure in the Irish theatrical and entertainment industry. His early career included both the serious and the comical theatrical worlds. Indeed, Pearson is credited with discovering such Irish entertainment artists as "Twink" and Eileen Reid. He was later employed as director of the Gaiety Theater in Dublin and as chairman and artistic director of the world-renowned and historical Abbey Theatre. However, it was for his role as producer in the Tony award–winning Broadway version of *Dancing at Lughnasa* and as producer of the two-time Oscar-winning film *My Left Foot* that Pearson became an internationally recognized figure.

Pearson will be forever connected with Brian Friel's *Dancing at Lughnasa.* The play originally opened in Dublin's Abbey Theatre in 1990. On October 11, 1991, Pearson took the play to Broadway. By the time it closed just over a year later, after 436 performances, the play had won a Tony for Bríd Brennan in her role as Agnes, a Best Direction award for Patrick Mason, and a Best Play Award for Pearson. In 1998 Pearson brought *Dancing at Lughnasa* to the big screen in a version that starred Meryl Streep.

Pearson's 1989 production, *My Left Foot,* starring Daniel Day-Lewis as disabled artist Christy Brown, received five Academy Award nominations, including one for Best Picture. It won two Oscars—Best Actor for Day-Lewis and Best Actress for Brenda Fricker. The film also earned Pearson top European film awards, including a Donatello and a BAFTA.

Pearson's film success continued in 1990 when Richard Harris was nominated for an Academy Award for his role in the Pearson-produced *The Field.* Other less successful Pearson film productions have included *Frankie Starlight* (1995) and Maeve Binchy's *Tara Road* (2005). The most current production is *How About You,* based on a another story by Maeve Binchy.

Pearson's production company, Ferndale Films, has also been involved in successful documentary work for television. Among his works here are *Luke,* an account of the life and death of Luke Kelly of the Dubliners folk group, and *Brian Friel,* which provides an insight into the work and life of the elusive author of *Dancing at Lughnasa, Translations,* and *Wonderful Tennessee.* Friel unusually makes an appearance for a brief interview at the end of each documentary.

In 1992, Pearson, along with Gregory Peck, set up a film school in University College Dublin, where he often guest lectures. In 1994, the National University of Ireland, recognizing his artistic work and his delight at passing on opportunities to younger Irish filmmakers, awarded him an honorary doctorate. Pearson is known to seriously guard his privacy; he does not give interviews and prefers not to comment on any aspect of his work or career.

Brid Nicholson

See also: GLEESON, Brendan; HARRIS, Richard; DAY-LEWIS, Daniel; PECK, Gregory; SHERIDAN, Jim.

References

McLoone, Martin. *Irish Film: The Emergence of a Contemporary Cinema.* London: University of California Press, 2001.

Pettitt, Lance. *Screening Ireland.* Manchester, UK: Manchester University Press, 2000.

PECK, GREGORY (1916–2003)

Eldred Gregory Peck was born in La Jolla, California, in 1916 to a father of Irish descent and a Missourian mother. Peck was related to Thomas Ashe, who took part in the 1916 Easter Rising and died on a hunger strike in 1917. Peck's parents divorced when he was five, and he was raised by his grandmother. She took him to the cinema once a week, and his earliest film memory was of being terrified by *The Phantom of the Opera*. He attended a Roman Catholic military academy in Los Angeles that was run by Irish nuns. Peck planned to become a doctor and studied medicine at the University of California at Berkeley. During his senior year the director of the campus theater invited him to audition for a part in a play. He was so taken by the stage that he switched his major to English, performing in five plays that year.

Eager to pursue an acting career, he headed for New York without graduating. There, as Gregory Peck, he enrolled at the Neighborhood Playhouse. It was while studying movement under Martha Graham that he sustained the back injury that kept him out of World War II. His Broadway debut in Emlyn Williams's *The Morning Star* (1942) impressed the New York Times theater critic. A year later he was in Hollywood to appear in his first film, playing a Russian partisan fighting the Nazis in *Days of Glory* (1944). His second film, *Keys of the Kingdom* (1944), based on the A. J. Cronin novel, in which he played a Roman Catholic priest, earned him the first of five Academy Award nominations. Leading roles in *Spellbound* (1945), *The Yearling* (1946), and *Duel in the Sun* (1946) followed. In *Gentleman's Agreement* (1947), he played a journalist posing as a Jew to investigate anti-Semitism. That year also, with Dorothy McGuire and Mel Ferrer, he founded the La Jolla Playhouse where he acted in such plays as Patrick Hamilton's *Angel Street,* Elliot Nugent's *The Male Animal,* and Moss Hart's *Light Up The Sky.* He returned to screen acting as the lawyer in love with his dangerous client in *The Paradine Case* (1948), which he followed with *Twelve O'Clock High* (1949), in which he took the role of a stressed-out air force officer.

One of his best performances was as Johnny Ringo, a hired gun at the end of his tether, in *The Gunfighter* (1950). He acted in two Hemingway adaptations, *The Macomber Affair* (1947) and *The Snows of Kilimanjaro* (1952), and in between he played the leader of a gang of bank robbers in the fine western, *Yellow Sky* (1948). He switched to romantic comedy in *Roman Holiday* (1953) with Audrey Hepburn, and starred in the *Man in the Gray Flannel Suit* (1956), a tale of adultery, angst, and disaffection in the advertising industry. As Captain Ahab he struggled with his demons in *Moby Dick* (1956), which was largely filmed in Youghal, Co. Cork, and featured many Irish actors. He returned to comedy in *Designing Woman* (1957) with Lauren Bacall. He showed his tough side in an epic fistfight with Charlton Heston in *The Big Country* (1958). Another western, *The Bravados* (1958), was followed by *Pork Chop Hill* (1959), a story of the Korean War that he also produced. As the producer of *Cape Fear* (1962), in which he also acted, he cast Robert Mitchum in the meatier, more memorable role; he took a cameo role in Martin Scorsese's 1991 remake of the film. In 1962 he also produced and starred in his most celebrated film, *To Kill a Mockingbird,* playing a southern lawyer who incurs the wrath of his fellow townspeople when he defends a black man accused of raping a white woman. He won an Oscar for his portrayal of Atticus Finch, the hero of Harper Lee's best-selling novel. In May 2003, the American Film Institute voted the character of Finch the greatest screen hero of all time.

Subsequent films included *How the West Was Won* (1962), *Captain Newman, M.D.* (1963), *Behold a Pale Horse* (1964), and two Hitchcockian thrillers, *Mirage* (1965) and *Arabesque* (1966). He played the mission controller in *Marooned* (1969), an excellent film about a NASA accident, which was withdrawn when its release coincided with a real-life space mishap. He was ill at ease in the hit horror film *The Omen* (1976), in command as *MacArthur* (1977), and miscast as the Nazi scientist Josef Mengele in *The Boys from Brazil* (1978). Often described as Lincolnesque, he played the Great Emancipator in the TV miniseries *The Blue and the Gray* (1982). There followed *The Scarlet and the Black* (1983), another TV series, in which he portrayed Monsignor Hugh O'Flaherty, an Irish-born Vatican priest who helped Allied soldiers and civilians to escape from the Nazis during World War II. And he made the most of the dramatic opportunities presented by the role of Ambrose Bierce in *Old Gringo* (1989), playing opposite Jane Fonda.

In 1993 he produced a TV adaptation of an off-Broadway play, *The Portrait,* which provided ideal parts for himself, Lauren Bacall, and his daughter Cecilia Peck. His last film role was as Father Mapple in a remake of *Moby Dick* (1998); in all he acted in 52 films. For seven years, from 1995 on, he toured in an entertaining one-man show in which he reminisced about his career.

Peck never hid his liberal sympathies. In 1947 he risked being blacklisted when he signed a letter of protest against a House Un-American Activities Committee investigation of alleged communists in the film industry. A lifelong Democrat, he seriously considered challenging then California Governor Ronald Reagan's reelection campaign in 1970, making a last-minute decision not to do so despite pressure from the Democratic Party leadership. He was an outspoken critic of the Vietnam War, although he supported his son Jonathan, who served there. In 1972 he produced the film version of Philip Berrigan's play, *The Trial of the Catonsville Nine,* about the prosecution of Vietnam protestors for civil disobedience. The Nixon White House feared him.

In 1992 Peck was one of the driving forces behind the initiative to set up the

Centre for Film Studies at University College Dublin. In 1997, *Irish America* magazine named him Irish-American of the Year. In an interview with the magazine he revealed that President Lyndon Johnson had told him that he would have nominated him as ambassador to Ireland in a second term. A patron of the Ireland Funds, in 2000 he was made a doctor of letters of the National University of Ireland.

Patrick Gillan

See also: PEARSON, Noel; REAGAN, Ronald Wilson; WALSH, Raoul

References
Fishgall, Gary. *Gregory Peck: A Biography*. New York: Scribner 2002.
Munn, Michael. *Gregory Peck*. London: Hale, 1998.

PENNSYLVANIA

Pennsylvania, the host state of the 1787 Constitutional Convention, was the second state to ratify the U.S. Constitution (after Delaware). From the late eighteenth century onward, Pennsylvania grew into an industrially powerful state, synonymous with steel and coal. Irish Americans were prominent in its growth, and in supplying much of the industrial labor they were involved in several significant events in the history of state and national labor relations. Pennsylvania's population of 28,522 in 1790 made it the second largest state, and it continues to be one of the largest states in the nation with a 2000 population of 12,281,054.

After early disputes among the English, Dutch, and Swedish, the first permanent settlement was established in 1643, but in the space of 20 years the area moved from Swedish to Dutch (1655) to British control (1664). William Penn, a devout Quaker, was given proprietary rights to most of modern-day Pennsylvania in 1681 and set about creating a visionary City of Brotherly Love (Philadelphia). Penn's "Frame of Government" provided liberal governance, and he signed a peace treaty with the Delaware tribe.

Quakers, English, and Welsh were concentrated in the city, which would quickly become a large and influential city, and in the eastern counties. Ongoing immigration diversified the area, and several religiously persecuted groups were drawn there, notably the Mennonites (including the Amish), Moravians, Lutherans, and Germans (Pennsylvania Dutch). Penn's colony also attracted Irish immigrants. Several travelers on the first ship, the *Welcome* (1682), were from Wexford and Cashel in Ireland, and James Logan, from Lurgan, was colony administrator from 1701 to 1751. In 1719, George Taylor, who later signed the Declaration of Independence, also arrived.

In the 1710s, settlement patterns began to push into western Pennsylvania, and very significant numbers of Scots-Irish continued to arrive in the decades leading up to the Revolution. Many settled in Pennsylvania, while others moved on to Virginia and the Carolinas. Large numbers of eighteenth-century Scots-Irish were from Ulster, relatively educated, better off, and able to assimilate fairly quickly. By the late 1720s the number of new Irish arrivals in Philadelphia was estimated to be in the region of 6,000 per year.

Tension between settlers and native tribes continued for a number of decades and included the alliance between Native Americans and the French in the Seven Years' War against the British. Parts of Pennsylvania also became embroiled in Pontiac's Rebellion in 1763.

The history of the state is intimately entwined with the American Revolution and the birth of the Republic: the Commonwealth of Pennsylvania was declared in 1776; the state provided some of the most influential leaders, including Benjamin Franklin; and the state witnessed some significant military engagements, such as Germantown and Valley Forge. The city of Philadelphia hosted the First and Second Continental Congresses (1774, 1775–1781), as well as the Constitutional Convention of 1787. Philadelphia was also where the Declaration of Independence was signed, and it was the seat of the new federal government from 1790 to 1800.

Canal and railroad work, docks, and coal mines all attracted more settlers, and there was more movement into the west of the state, resulting in the emergence of Pittsburgh. Philadelphia and Pittsburgh grew rapidly, numbers bolstered by the Irish famine. By 1850, the Irish population was 18 percent of the total population of Philadelphia, and there were more than 72,000 Irish-born residents in the region. At the same time, areas such as "Little Ireland" had emerged in Pittsburgh. The overcrowding led to waves of anti-Irish and anti-Catholic anxiety and propaganda, manifested through organizations such as the Know-Nothings. In 1844, the Philadelphia Nativist Riots, sometimes known as the Bible Riots, took place between recent Irish Catholic immigrants and city Protestants, including Irish, ostensibly over the issue of religion in schools.

One of the defining moments of the Civil War occurred in Pennsylvania when Confederate forces were defeated in 1863 at the Battle of Gettysburg, where, in the aftermath, President Abraham Lincoln made his famous Gettysburg Address. The Philadelphia Brigade's 69th Pennsylvania Infantry was predominantly Irish, marched with a green regimental flag, and was involved in the heart of the battle.

Oil, coal, and steel would make the state immensely successful, all industries buoyed by immigrant labor. Pittsburgh's role as a steel center began in the 1870s, when Andrew Carnegie started steel-making operations on a huge scale. The city's industrial progress was reflected when Alexander Graham Bell's telephone was first demonstrated publicly at the Philadelphia Centennial Exhibition in 1876.

In such an industrial state, the potential for friction between the working classes and union representation with the factory owners was realized on several occasions in the late nineteenth century and rumbled on into the twentieth century. This was famously manifested with the emergence of the Molly Maguires in the anthracite minefields of east Pennsylvania in the 1860s–1870s; the group protested against a raft of issues. A secretive society that had evolved in Ireland in the 1840s–1850s, the Molly Maguires used intimidatory tactics in confronting mine officials, leading Pinkerton agents to infiltrate the group, notably James McParlan, himself Irish. This resulted in a series of sensationalist and clearly biased trials, which saw 20 men hanged for 16 murders, of mostly mine officials; a further 19 men were imprisoned. Uncertainties surrounding the group have led to many interpretations since: some consider them working-class revolutionaries, and others regard them as terrorists.

Friction flared up again in the Railroad Strike of 1877 and the Homestead strike of 1892, when steel workers protested against wage cuts, which led to running battles between strikers and Pinkerton agents. There was steel-based unrest in 1919, and the area was instrumental in forming the unions that became the United Steelworkers of America in 1942.

Pennsylvania flourished in the immediate period after World War II. From the mid-1960s, however, the state began to experience a gradual erosion of its industrial strength. The term "rust belt" came to be applied to it and other old industrial states, as the steel, auto, and rubber companies found themselves increasingly uncompetitive with overseas factories. In 1940, David Lawrence, an Irish politician, was elected mayor of Pittsburgh and ushered in a sequence of high-profile Irish officeholders, including mayor and governor, but today the state is considered an electoral swing state.

Today, those of Irish ancestry make up 16.1 percent of the total state population, the third largest population in the country, and they form the largest ancestry group in the Philadelphia region. The state also claims to have the town with the highest percentage of Irish surnames in the country—Havertown.

Sam Hitchmough

See also: AMERICAN CIVIL WAR;
    AMERICAN WAR OF
    INDEPENDENCE

References
Doyle, David Noel, and Owen Dudley
    Edwards, eds. *America and Ireland,*
    1776–1976: The American Identity and the
    Irish Connection, Westport, CT: Greenwood
    Press, 1980.
Ignatiev, Noel. *How the Irish Became White,*
    London: Routledge, 1995.
Kenny, Kevin. *The American Irish,* London:
    Longman, 2000.
Kenny, Kevin. *Making Sense of the Molly*
    Maguires, Oxford: Oxford University Press,
    1998.
Miller, Kerby A. *Emigrants and Exiles: Ireland*
    and the Irish Exodus to North America,
    Oxford: Oxford University Press, 1988.

POLITICAL PARTIES, IRISH

Of perennial interest to political scholars and commentators on Irish-American relations, the Irish party system defies traditional party system analysis and is regularly classified as sui generis. This derives from a combination of issues, such as the electoral system in use and the divergent make up of Irish society, but the primary factor determining Ireland's unique party system is the legacy of British rule and specifically the split that rended the country apart during the civil war in 1922.

Throughout the nineteenth century Ireland was part of the Union of Great Britain and Ireland. Party political activity, therefore, was channeled through the Westminster parliament in London. Irish political parties during this era agitated for greater, or outright, independence from Britain. Those minority groups committed to complete separation aligned themselves with violent organizations, such as the Irish Republican Brotherhood, who carried out unsuccessful campaigns for Irish freedom. The parliamentary route to autonomy proved only marginally more successful, but majority opinion in Ireland consistently supported parties committed to exclusively peaceful politics such as the Irish Parliamentary Party led for a time by Charles Stewart Parnell, who was regarded as one of Ireland's greatest parliamentarians.

When World War I began, political opinion in Ireland was divided over how to react. The Irish Parliamentary Party, then led by John Redmond, supported the British forces in the war, while Sinn Féin and other militant groups viewed the war as an opportunity to strike at a distracted Britain. The 1916 rebellion, a complete failure in military terms, changed the Irish political landscape, and thereafter public support shifted toward the radical separatists, as evidenced by Sinn Féin's triumph in the 1918 elections. Sinn Féin's elected representatives refused to take their seats in Westminster and in 1919 established the Dáil (parliament) in Dublin. A two-year war of independence with Britain followed, which ended with the signing of the Anglo-Irish Treaty in 1921. The provisions of the treaty established a 26-county independent Ireland while a six-county region in the North remained under British dominion.

The treaty bitterly divided Ireland, and Sinn Féin split into pro-treaty and anti-treaty factions. Soon after the 1922 elections, which demonstrated a majority in favor of the treaty, the country was plunged into civil war, the legacy of which is still the most obvious cleavage within the Irish party system. Those who had been committed to subverting the British State in 1916 now turned against each other in a bloody war that saw friends and family fight to the death. The civil war ended in 1923 when Eamon de Valera, leader of the anti-treaty faction, issued a proclamation stating that the war was over. The treaty, however, remained a major issue in Irish politics, both overtly and covertly. The bitterness created by the treaty was so great that it precluded opponents from seeking reconciliation, even when they agreed on virtually ever other issue. A person's stance on the treaty became that person's, and hence the party's, most defining feature, regardless of policy platforms in other areas. The continued existence of both Fianna Fail and Fine Gael, who differ on little else other than the treaty, attests to the ongoing salience of the treaty's legacy.

Sinn Féin Standing Committee on March 9, 1922. (Bettmann/Corbis)

Given that the central issue upon which Irish political parties divided was constitutional and nationalistic, it followed that future debates within the Irish political system centered on these issues more than economic and social issues. The differing positions taken with respect to the treaty transcended left and right, urban and rural, and social classes, thereby dividing the electorate into two camps diametrically opposed on this one issue; however, each group lacked any unifying bond outside of its perspective on the treaty.

The effect of the treaty split remains the primary reason the Irish system is so unique in the European context. Comparative studies of European democracy have struggled to situate Ireland within the prevailing party classifications. Essentially, the Irish party system has three unusual features. First, Ireland lacks any clear social cleavage that manifests in the party structure. Irish voters do not divide politically along class, religion, or regional lines. The three major political parties in Ireland—Fianna Fail, Fine Gael, and Labour—compete for votes in the same areas and among broadly similar voters. The supporters of each party have no obvious social characteristics, and this is particularly evident in the supporters of Fianna Fail and Fine Gael.

The second feature that adds to the Irish system's uniqueness is the electoral weakness of the Left. In European democracies it is typical for one of the two major parties to have a conservative or Christian democrat nature and the other major party to have a social democratic persuasion; however, in Ireland the Labour Party has never progressed beyond its position as the third most popular party in the country. Its support base has often fluctuated widely,

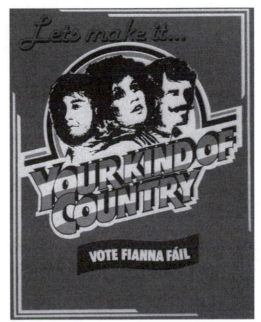

Fianna Fáil, the Republican Party of Ireland— traditionally translated as Soldiers of Destiny—*is the largest political party in Ireland. From its establishment in the early twentieth century, the party moved from being a radical, slightly left of center party, to become the establishment, its influence dominating government and Irish political life from the 1930s onward. (Library of Congress)*

and although it has been in coalition government with both Fianna Fail and Fine Gael, it has never been able to break the monopoly of the big two. The Labour Party has averaged around 11–14 percent of the vote in elections since 1945. A number of smaller communist and socialist parties are active in Ireland, but when they have occasionally enjoyed electoral success, as the Workers Party did in the 1980s, it has tended to be at the expense of the Labour party or independent left wingers. Combined electoral support for parties of the Left in Ireland has consistently averaged at most 16 percent, while the average in the rest of Europe is 45 percent. Even in countries where there has been traditionally less support for the Left, such as Iceland and Switzerland, the overall figures far exceed those evident in Ireland.

The third unique feature of the Irish party system, as identified by analysts of comparative European politics, is the extent to which the two major parties have similar policies and support bases. In the post–cold war era it is evident that major political parties across Europe have moved toward the center and away from clear left-right divides, thus leading to a blurring of distinctions between prospective governmental parties. However, the fight for dominance of the center has long been a feature of Irish politics, and Fianna Fail and Fine Gael have often struggled to define what makes them different, apart of course from their positions on the Anglo-Irish Treaty. Ideologically and socially the parties are almost identical, and both have strong ties to the business community and the Catholic Church. Yet, although it is unique to have two dominant parties that are so similar in a democracy, the situation is further complicated by the fact that it is very difficult to locate either Fianna Fail or Fine Gael in the broader European party spectrum. Neither party fits readily within existing European party families, and the constitutions of both make it difficult to draw accurate parallels with other parties in Europe.

The party system in Ireland has proved remarkably stable, and while most European countries experienced increased volatility in party alignments after the 1960s, Ireland maintained its traditional formation, arguably until 1987 when a new party, the Progressive Democrats, polled 12 percent of the vote. Support for the Progressive Democrats has fallen since then, however, and apart from the rise of Sinn Féin since the Belfast Agreement was signed in 1998, the party structure has remained dominated by Fianna Fail and Fine Gael, with the Labour party and the Progressive Democrats acting as minor coalition partners.

The parliament in Ireland is elected by a proportional representation system. The state is divided into 42 constituencies, which return between three and five Teachtaí Dála (TDs—members of Parliament) depending on the population of each constituency. This system enables smaller parties to achieve electoral success by concentrating their resources in a small number of areas. As a result of this system Ireland has tended to have many parties represented in Parliament and coalition governments. This means that relatively small parties, such as the Progressive Democrats and the Democratic Left (now defunct), have at times formed part of the government and had some of their representatives appointed to cabinet positions. In this respect Ireland differs significantly from countries like Great Britain, where a traditionally two-party system has precluded people from "'wasting" their votes on the smaller parties, as they have very little chance of getting elected and even less chance of forming part of the government. In Ireland, independent Teachtaí Dála are quite common and are usually elected on a left-wing or single-issue agenda. After the 1997 election, four independent Teachtaí Dála held the balance of power in Parliament and propped up a minority government coalition of Fianna Fail and the Progressive Democrats.

The lineage of most major parties in Ireland, and the majority of smaller parties, can be traced along two family trees—the nationalist and the socialist. As already mentioned the political parties of the nineteenth century were preoccupied with the national question, and by 1919 the less radical Irish Parliamentary Party had all but disappeared, leaving Sinn Féin dominant. Following the split within Sinn Féin in 1922, Cumann na Gaedheal came to represent the pro-treaty faction, and it formed the first Irish government in 1922. In 1926, the anti-treaty faction itself split when Eamon DeValera recognized the 26-county state and formed Fianna Fail (meaning Soldiers of Destiny). Fianna Fail is a classic catch-all party and has attracted support from a very wide and varied constituency. It is ideologically indistinct but has sought to portray itself as a center left party, though its recent coalition governments with the center right Progressive Democrats has undermined this claim. In 1933 Cumann na Gaedheal merged with the Centre Party and the fascistic Blueshirts to form Fine Gael (meaning the Family of Ireland). Fine Gael has been accused as defining itself as whatever Fianna Fail is not. Like Fianna Fail it is difficult to situate it on the ideological spectrum, and it has gone through phases of being left and right of center. Sinn Féin, originally established in 1905, lost much support in the 1920s as people tended toward either Fianna Fail or Fine Gael, both of whom, unlike Sinn Féin, took part in the administration of the 26-county state. The party, along with its armed wing, the Irish Republican Army (IRA), has endured numerous splits, and the recent centenary celebration of the party's formation was observed by a number of groups purporting to be the true heirs to the original party, such as Republican Sinn Féin. Sinn Féin endured a very significant split in 1970 over the issue of recognizing both the Dublin and British parliament. The majority group,

which had a more socialist inclination, became known as Official Sinn Féin, while the more republican minority was termed Provisional Sinn Féin. In 1974, the Irish Republican Socialist Party split from the Officials. In 1977, Official Sinn Féin became Sinn Féin the Workers Party. In 1992, all but one of the Workers Party's elected representatives left the party to form the Democratic Left, which formed part of the "Rainbow coalition" with Fine Gael and the Labour Party in 1994. In 1999, the Democratic Left merged with the Labour party. Provisional Sinn Féin itself split in 1984 when Republican Sinn Féin was formed to reflect those who again refused to recognise the Dáil. Provisional Sinn Féin, which maintained close ties to the provisional IRA, the largest and most active Irish terrorist organisation, has achieved great electoral success since the peace process was initiated in the 1990s. Sinn Féin is now the fastest-growing party in Ireland—north and south—and, provided the IRA maintains its cease-fire, is likely to be part of a governing coalition in the coming years.

In 1985, a number of prominent members of Fianna Fail left the party to form the Progressive Democrats, which have formed coalition governments with Fianna Fail on three occasions since. To the right of center, the Progressive Democrats, despite their narrower electoral appeal, have exercised great influence on Irish politics, and their representatives have held many of the more important ministerial positions.

Parties of the Left in Ireland have emerged from a different political lineage that owes its origins to the emergence of trade unions in the late nineteenth century. In 1912, the Irish Trade Unions Congress proposed that "the independent representation of labour upon all public boards be and is hereby included among the objectives of this congress." While the Labour party cites this as its starting point, the party existed only in the vaguest form until 1922, and even then local trade unions were largely responsible for determining the policies of their candidates. In 1917, most of the congress leaders were members of the Socialist Party of Ireland (SPI), although they left in 1921 when the SPI became the Communist Party. The Labour party, more conservative than most social democrat parties in Europe, has enjoyed limited success and has had to rely on coalitions with Fine Gael and Fianna Fail to achieve governmental office. In 1996, the Socialist Party was formed by Trotskyites who had left the Labour party in the late 1980s. The Communist Party has gone through many incarnations and endured many ideological splits, the largest occurring after the breakdown of Soviet-Sino relations, when members sided with either the USSR or China. The radical left in Ireland has attracted negligible support, and since the 1980s the Labour Party itself has moved toward the center in a bid to increase its support.

Parties that have evolved outside these nationalist and socialist family trees include the Green Party, which has seen its support increase rapidly in the past 20 years. The Greens emerged from the ecology movements of the 1970s and 1980s and, though their more radical policies have been abandoned, today constitute a potential coalition partner for the major parties. Various religious conservative parties have come and gone, and the Christian Solidarity Party remains the sole voice of the Christian right. The far right, like the far left, has never achieved popular support in Ireland since the National Guard, more commonly known as the Blueshirts, were active for a time in the late 1920s and early 1930s.

The Irish party system is therefore both difficult to explain and unique in the European context. The electoral system encourages voters to support smaller parties, and coalition governments are therefore common. Given that there is no major ideological difference between the major political parties, governments have been formed from many different party combinations. Despite the numerous splits that have occurred among Irish parties, the system remains very stable and is dominated by Fianna Fail and Fine Gael, although Fianna Fail has maintained a traditional dominance. Emerging trends, such as the rise of Sinn Féin and the Green Party, may threaten the predictability of the system, but it is unlikely that the dominance of the two major parties will be challenged for many years to come.

Aidan Hehir

See also: DE VALERA, Eamon; IRISH REPUBLICAN ARMY

References

Coakley, John, and Michael Gallagher. *Politics in the Republic of Ireland.* Limerick: Folens and PSAI Press, 1993.

Collins, Stephen. *The Power Game: Ireland Under Fianna Fáil.* Dublin: O'Brien, 2001.

Laver, Michael. *A New Electoral System for Ireland?* Dublin: The Policy Institute in association with The All-Party Oireachtas Committee on the Constitution, 1998.

Mair, Peter. *The Changing Irish Party System: Organisation, Ideology and Electoral Competition.* London: Pinter, 1988.

Manning, Maurice. *Irish Political Parties: An Introduction.* London: Macmillan, 1972.

Moss, Warner. *Political Parties in the Irish Free State.* New York: AMS Press, 1968.

POWDERLY, TERENCE VINCENT (1849–1924)

The son of Irish immigrants, Terence Powderly was born in Carbondale, in northeastern Pennsylvania's anthracite coal region, on January 22, 1849. He left school when he was 13 to become a railway worker. By the time he was 24 he had gone on to complete an apprenticeship, become a machinist, join the Machinists' and Blacksmiths' International Union, become that union's president, and lose his machinist's job after the Panic of 1873.

Powderly joined the "great brotherhood" of the Noble and Holy Order of Knights of Labor in 1874, as it was expanding outward from its founding local in the Philadelphia area. The order had been organized as a secret society by six Philadelphia garment cutters on Thanksgiving Day in 1869. At first membership was limited to its founders' craft, but the vision of at least one founder, Uriah Stephens, was to create a new type of labor organization uniting wage earners of all crafts and skill levels, and after a year the founding local's members had voted to include nonvoting skilled workers from other crafts. They thought that the nonvoting sojourners—so named using Masonic terminology—would eventually be able to create locals in their own crafts. The Knights were able to gradually expand their membership among the skilled workers of Philadelphia and adjacent southern New Jersey, to survive the corporate bankruptcies and unemployment after the Panic of 1873, and to expand to include both skilled and unskilled workers in Pennsylvania's anthracite mines and railways.

Powderly's organizing and political skills led to his being elected mayor of Scranton on the Greenback-Labor Party

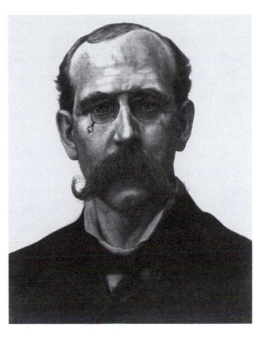

Portrait of Terence Powderly, leader of the Knights of Labor (1879–1893). (Library of Congress)

ticket in 1877, to his becoming active in the order's national affairs—helping to resolve an internal dispute over ritual—in 1878, and to his succeeding Stephens as the Knight's grand master workman (the order's president) in 1879. He served as mayor of Scranton from 1878 to 1884 and as grand master workman from 1879 until he resigned in 1893 at the age of 44.

Powderly's 14 years as the Knights' grand master workman remain controversial to this day. The order had approximately 9,300 members when Powderly took office in 1879. Its small numbers declined in 1881, but then grew to around 50,000 in 1883 and exploded to between 700,000 and 1,000,000 members following railway strikes in the mid-1880s, only to decline precipitously in the aftermath of the Haymarket Riot in 1886. Instead of one big brotherhood, America's workers increasingly chose to follow the path of individual craft or industry unions after 1886. When the Industrial Workers of the World attempted to create One Big Union in the early twentieth century, it was less successful than the Knights had been.

Some of Powderly's difficulties resulted from one of the Knight's strengths. The order excluded from membership only lawyers, bankers, stockbrokers, gamblers, liquor dealers, scabs, and spies, so it included skilled and unskilled workers, blacks, women, owner-proprietors of small businesses, shop foremen, and other business people who chose to join. Powderly was successful in bringing workers of all ideological stripes—anarchists, socialists, middle-class reformers—into the order. But that very mixture was certain to engender substantial internal conflict and to exacerbate conflicts with business and local communities, as it did. The order faced many issues, any response to which was, necessarily, not going to please everyone. For example, the order had to decide how to respond to local strikes and the Haymarket Riot (Powderly chose to denounce rioters) and whether to support a third party in the 1892 elections.

Needing to support himself and his family after resigning as grand master workman, Powderly studied for the Pennsylvania bar and was admitted in 1894, resulting in his expulsion from the Knights. The Knights' new leaders simultaneously expelled miners and glassblowers, who had been Powderly supporters and were seen as the order's backbone. The expelled miners promptly joined the rival United Mine Workers. A year later the Knights' new leaders denied the credentials of socialist Daniel DeLeon at the order's national assembly, resulting in the irritated socialists forming the Socialist Trade and Labor Alliance and taking with them an estimated 13,000 of the order's 30,000 remaining members. Comparative unity had been achieved, but at the cost of reducing the order's membership to an unsustainable level.

The later years of Powderly's life were mostly spent as a federal official in Washington, D.C. He was appointed commissioner-general of the Bureau of Immigration by President William McKinley in 1897, where he served until he was removed by President Theodore Roosevelt in 1902. After a few years in small business ventures, Powderly was appointed chief of the Bureau of Immigration's Division of Information, a position he held until 1921. He then became a Department of Labor employee. He died in Washington on June 24, 1924.

Steven B. Jacobson

References

Buhle, Paul M. *From the Knights of Labor to the New World Order: Essays on Labor and Culture*. London: Taylor and Francis, 1997.

Dubofsky, Melvyn. *We Shall Be All: A History of the Industrial Workers of the World*. Chicago: Quadrangle Books, 1969.

Falzone, Vincent J. *Terence V. Powderly, Middle Class Reformer*. Lanham, MD: University Press of America, 1978.

Fink, Leon. *Workingmen's Democracy: The Knights of Labor and American Politics*. Urbana: University of Illinois Press, 1985.

Fitch, Robert. *Solidarity for Sale*. New York: Public Affairs, 2006.

Phelan, Craig. *Grand Master Workman: Terence Powderly and the Knights of Labor*. Westport, CT: Greenwood Press, 2000.

Powderly, Terence V. "The Army of Unemployed." In *The Labor Movement: The Problem of Today*, edited by George E. McNeill. Boston: A. M. Bridgeman & Co., 1887.

Powderly, Terence V. *Thirty Years of Labor, 1859–1889*. New York: Augustus M. Kelly, 1967.

Voss, Kim. *The Making of American Exceptionalism: The Knights of Labor and Class Formation in the Nineteenth Century.* Ithaca, NY: Cornell University Press, 1993.

Weir, Robert E. *Beyond Labor's Veil: The Culture of the Knights of Labor.* University Park: Pennsylvania State University Press, 1996.

Weir, Robert E. *Knights Unhorsed: Internal Conflict in a Gilded Age Social Movement.* Detroit, MI: Wayne State University Press, 2000.

POWER, FREDERICK TYRONE, SR. (1869–1931)

Although born and raised in London, Frederick Tyrone Power had many ancestors from Co. Waterford, including his grandfather, Tyrone Power (1795–1841), who was considered to be one of the greatest Irish actors of the nineteenth century. Frederick's father, Harold Power, and his mother, Ethel Levenu, were both entertainers who, as "Mr. and Mrs. Power at Home," performed satirical lectures and short sketches. However, when young Frederick expressed an interest in acting, his education at Dulwich College in London was abruptly terminated, and at the age of 16 he was sent to a plantation in Florida to learn how to grow oranges.

Frequently punished and tormented by the plantation foreman, Power ran away to nearby St. Augustine, where in 1886 he pursued his ambitions and made his acting debut as Gibson in *The Private Secretary.* Following the lead of his famous grandfather, who had performed frequently in the United States, Frederick dropped his first name, and became known as Tyrone Power the Younger.

For the next ten years, Power appeared in a variety of roles in a variety of places—Philadelphia, Montreal, New York, London, and many other places on tour—slowly building his reputation. In 1898 he married Edith Crane, an Australian actress, but they separated several years later. By the first years of the twentieth century, Power had entered the top ranks of acting, playing Caliban in *The Tempest,* Bassanio in *The Merchant of Venice,* Judas Iscariot in *Mary of Magdala,* the Marquis of Steyne in *Becky Sharp,* Ulysses in *Ulysses,* and many more roles in which he was able to portray everything from evil to elegance. As described by one of his contemporaries, Power appeared "massive and imposing. His face is large, with strongly marked features, and is expressive of acute sensibility. His eyes, dark and brilliant, are communicative equally of tenderness and fire. . . . His voice is deep, strong, copious, and of a rarely melodious, resonant tone" (Winter, p. 172).

Shortly after Edith Crane died in 1912, Power married Patia Réaume, a former actress who taught the dramatic arts in Cincinnati. In 1914, their first child, Tyrone Edmund Power, was born; he would later achieve great fame in Hollywood, the third in the line of actors known as Tyrone Power. A second child, Anne, was born in 1915. However, the marriage became strained when Power became infatuated with Bertha Knight, one of the dancers in a Broadway production. The couple separated in 1917, and then divorced in 1920. The following year, Power married Knight, who died 1927.

Although Power continued to enjoy success on stage—most notably as Brutus in *Julius Caesar*—he also found work as an actor in the new medium of the movies. From his film debut in 1914 to his final role as a wagon driver in the epic western, *The Big Trail* (1930), Power appeared in 41 films: dramas, mysteries, westerns, comedies, and adventures. He was hired to play the role of the Patriarch in *The Miracle Man,* but suffered a massive heart attack shortly after the filming had started. He died in the arms of his son, Tyrone.

James I. Deutsch

References

Arce, Hector. *The Secret Life of Tyrone Power.* New York: William Morrow and Co., 1979.

Guiles, Fred Lawrence. *Tyrone Power: The Last Idol.* Garden City, NY: Doubleday & Co., 1979.

Power, Tyrone. "The Actor as a Gambler." *Green Book Album,* 2 (December 1909): 1214–1218.

"Tyrone Power Dies Suddenly on Coast." *New York Times,* December 31, 1931: 12.

Winter, William. *Tyrone Power.* New York: Moffat, Yard, and Co., 1913.

PRESBYTERIANISM

The term "presbyterian" refers to a form of church government based on the rule of elders. It is, in a sense, a republican or representative system, which is distinct from a simple monarchy (e.g., rule by the pope), an oligarchy (e.g., rule by bishops), and a pure democracy where individuals in a particular congregation make important decisions for the life of their church. Ruling and teaching elders constitute a session. Their duty is to teach, train, and, if need be, discipline church members. The elders are distinct from another important office: deacons, whose job it is to provide for the material needs of congregants. The local session is part of a broader regional presbytery, composed of a few churches within a particular area, and a general assembly, where representatives from various presbyteries discuss matters related to the national church.

Beyond the mere defining characteristics, Presbyterianism has a rich history. Its more immediate and institutional origins, though many believe the New Testament church was presbyterian in orientation, can be traced back to the Scottish Reformation, a branch of the much larger reforming impulse sweeping Europe in the sixteenth century. The Protestant Reformation began in 1517 with a German monk, Martin Luther, who protested (hence the word "Protestant") the wayward practices of the reigning Roman Catholic Church. Protestants sought a return to the essence of Christianity in both faith and practice as delineated in the scriptures of the Old and New Testament alone. Galvanized by the flames of Protestantism, John Knox (1514–1572), a former bodyguard who became the father of Scottish Presbyterianism, regularly interacted with and imbibed the works of Geneva's John Calvin (1509–1564), the Reformation's leading intellectual next to Martin Luther. Calvinism, a term many believed encapsulated the fundamental doctrines of the Bible, highlighted the centrality of God's sovereignty in the works of creation and salvation. Knox virulently criticized Catholicism in England and Scotland, denouncing it as idolatrous and false. He worked to incorporate Calvinism, recognized broadly as Reformed theology, into the culture of Scottish Presbyterianism.

Beginning in the seventeenth century, the Scottish church underwent significant social and geographic changes. James VI of Scotland inherited the English and Irish thrones in 1603, eventually consolidating each and changing his title to James I. To persuade the recently conquered Irish to accept the union, James orchestrated the resettlement of English-speaking Protestants (mainly Scottish Presbyterians) in Ulster after confiscating the acreage from two Ulster chieftains. The Scots flooded the area. The north Ireland settlement marked the beginning of the history of Presbyterianism among the Irish. A presbytery at Ulster was formed in the early 1640s.

In the late seventeenth and early eighteen centuries, Presbyterianism gained a foothold in North America. Francis Makemie (1658–1708) is commonly recognized as the father of American Presbyterianism. He was born in Northern Ireland, attended the University of Glasgow, and ministered in Ireland, Barbados, and on the east coast of North America, particularly New York, Maryland, Virginia, and North Carolina. He organized the first Presbyterian Church in Maryland in 1684. Many religious leaders at the time, including New England's Mathers, appreciated Makemie's work.

In 1706, Makemie helped bring together English, Welsh, and Scots-Irish to form the first presbytery in Philadelphia and the first synod in 1716. Beginning in 1717, Ulster Presbyterians, for both economic and political reasons, initiated a series of mass migrations to North America. Increased land rent, drought, poverty, famine, and political oppression posed a challenge for future survival in Ulster. The majority of Scots-Irish Presbyterians found solace in North America. In 1788, the Philadelphia synod formed the General Assembly of the Presbyterian Church and formally adopted the seventeenth-century *Westminster Confession of Faith* and its *Catechisms,* each a summation of Protestant Calvinism as they related to the doctrines of revelation, creation, salvation, and the church.

Presbyterianism has left an indelible mark on America's founding institutions and traditions. Hostility to British authority laid the groundwork for the American Revolution. In 1707, for example, the governor of New York, Lord Cornbury, arrested Makemie for preaching without a license. Makemie appealed to the English Toleration Act of 1689, which granted tolerance to religious dissenters not part of traditional Protestantism. Likewise, Presbyterians in England were barred from government offices and were forced to pay tithes to the established Anglican Church. Ministers preached against what they viewed as English tyranny and encouraged their parishioners to migrate. The majority of newcomers who settled in Pennsylvania, Virginia, and the Carolinas found stable jobs, acquired cheap land, and participated in colonial administration, an opportunity largely unavailable to them in their mother country. Makemie's trial and the experience of the Scots-Irish presented a picture of the Presbyterians as a group that would oppose dictatorial governments.

Aside from politics, Presbyterians played a key role in America's religious life. In both Scotland and Northern Ireland they would gather annually to celebrate the Lord's Supper. After a marathon of sermons emphasizing the importance of spiritual renewal through Christ's atoning work, the multitude participated in communion. These "communion seasons" fit well with America's religious awakenings, which corresponded with farming seasons, especially along the frontier. The Reverend James McGready, with a few other ministers, organized a camp meeting at Cane Ridge, Kentucky, in 1800, inaugurating America's Second Great Awakening.

Yet such evangelical fervor created internal divisions. Revivalism tended to accentuate the importance of the emotions over theological rationality, which relegated confessionalism, elevated impulsive spirituality above institutional religion, and thus emphasized the role of the individual's ability to choose salvation, threatening doctrines related to God's sovereignty. The first American Presbyterian split occurred in 1741. Ministers, divided between "Old Side" and "New Side," argued over revivalism, requirements for ordained teaching elders, and the interpretation of confessional standards. The church reunited in 1758. The second division in 1837 revolved around the 1801 Plan of Union, which combined the efforts of Congregationalists and Presbyterians ("Presbygationalists") to evangelize the western frontier. Issues of church discipline, revivalism once again, and slavery were the dividing factors. When the Civil War broke out in 1861, the church was divided regionally. Southern churches of the "Old School" variety, as they were known, formed the Presbyterian Church of the Confederate States of America, weakening the Old School churches in the North. The "New School" also divided during the war, forming the United Synod, which later merged with the Confederate branch. The newly consolidated Confederate church reorganized into the Presbyterian Church in the United States. The regional denominations finally reunited in 1869.

Presbyterians were also at the forefront of higher education, laying the foundation for America's intellectual infrastructure. During the time of the first schism, New Side Presbyterians established the College of Jersey, which later became Princeton. John Witherspoon—a signatory of the Declaration of Independence and mentor to James Madison, the "Father of the Constitution"—became the college's first president. By the 1850s, the church had been instrumental in organizing two-thirds of America's educational institutions for higher learning, and by 1861 49 permanent schools were associated with—if not directly founded by—Presbyterians.

Yet the Americanization of Presbyterianism included religious intolerance. With the massive wave of Irish and German immigration to the United States in the 1840s, the Irish became inextricably linked to Catholicism. American nativists forgot that many of the Irish who came in the early eighteenth century were Presbyterian. Protestant nativists viewed Catholicism and therefore the Irish as a detriment to the American Republic. The Irish fought to secure a foothold in antebellum America. Irish Catholics flourished after the Civil War.

Ryan McIlhenny

See also: AMERICAN CIVIL WAR; AMERICAN WAR OF INDEPENDENCE; SCOTS-IRISH; SCOTS-IRISH CULTURE

References

Brooke, Peter. *Ulster Presbyterianism, 1610–1970: The Historical Perspective.* New York: St. Martin's Press, 1987.

Griffin, Patrick. *The People with No Name: Ireland's Ulster Scots, America's Scots Irish, and the Creation of a British Atlantic World, 1689–1764.* Princeton, NJ: Princeton University Press, 2001.

Leyburn, James G. *The Scotch-Irish: A Social History.* Chapel Hill: University of North Carolina, 1962.

PRESS, THE ETHNIC IRISH

Mainstream newspapers, and now the electronic media, have long played an important role in Irish America, with a presence that has included Irish Americans as reporters, commentators, and managers. Today, as in the early nineteenth century, when the first Irish-American newspapers

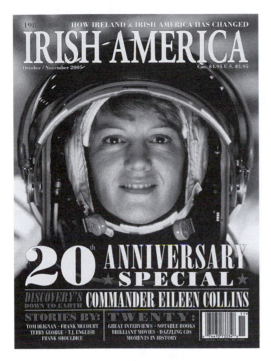

October/November 2005 edition of Irish America *magazine. (Courtesy of* Irish America *magazine)*

were published, the Irish ethnic media continue to play a key role in chronicling and in interpreting the Irish American experience throughout the United States.

With the significant Irish exodus to America in the 1820s, a number of Irish publications appeared to inform, entertain, and guide Irish immigrants in their new land. In cities such as Boston, Chicago, New York, and Philadelphia, the new immigrants experienced situations that often resulted in violent clashes and heavy prejudice (such as "No Irish Need Apply"). To counter this, the Irish-American press played an important part in working out misunderstandings and easing fears, instructing the Irish about the United States, and emphasizing that Catholicism and Irishness were not threats to the liberty and independence of the United States and that they could exist harmoniously with

American institutions. Most important, ethnic newspapers provided Irish Americans with an outlet to criticize their new country on their own terms and to compare their own lifestyles with the Irish struggle on both sides of the Atlantic Ocean.

The Irish-American press had two distinct types of papers: those that addressed their readers as a national group in the United States, with their own unique political, economic, and social interests connected with both America and Ireland, and those that dealt chiefly with religious issues and with the Irish as Catholics. During this period Catholic publications, such as *The Boston Pilot* and the *New York Freeman's Journal,* which took their names from newspapers in Ireland, enjoyed much success, because nationalist opinion was not yet fully formed and articulated in the United States. *The Boston Pilot,* which continues today as the archdiocesan paper, contained news from Ireland and the United States. *Donahoe's Magazine* printed fiction for its Irish immigrant readers and advice columns to help them negotiate American customs while declaring that Irish Catholics would deliver Protestant America back to the Catholic faith. Other popular Catholic magazines were the *Columbiad* and the *Republic.*

In the early 1840s, the *Freeman's Journal* was organized to promote the Catholic cause in the New York school controversy, in which Catholic children were required to read the Protestant Bible for religious instruction, and textbooks often made disparaging remarks about Catholicism. *Freeman's Journal* defended Catholic parents and Archbishop John Hughes of New York and supported the Maclay Law of 1842, which broke up the Protestant monopoly over education and forbade state aid to religious schools. Like the *Boston Pilot,* the journal encouraged Catholics to vote for supporters of their cause. Aggressiveness of this sort further inflamed nativist fears and hatred of the Catholic presence in America.

The success of the Irish-American press was largely the result of the editors, who were influential in shaping Irish nationalist opinion and in helping the Irish transform themselves from foreigners and immigrants to American citizens. Outstanding editors included Patrick Donahoe, who published *The Boston Pilot* for more than 60 years; James A. McMaster, who edited the *New York Freeman's Journal* (1848–1885); John Mitchell, an Ulster Protestant and Young Irelander, who wrote for the *Irish Nation* and founded the *United Irishman* to inspire others toward revolutionary nationalism; Patrick Lynch, who worked for several American newspapers, including the *New York Herald,* and edited *The Boston Pilot* and the *Irish American,* as he attempted to reconcile nationalism with Catholicism; Patrick Ford, editor of the *Irish World* (1870–1913), whose newspaper became the voice of the politically conscious Irish-American working class; and John Devoy, who directed the Clan na Gael as the dominant revolutionary nationalist organization in Irish America and edited the *Irish Nation* (1881–1885) and the *Gaelic American,* founded in 1903, in his pursuit of an Irish party in the United States.

The mid-nineteenth century marked the height of Irish-American journalism, but gradually Irish-American assimilation into mainstream American society reduced the need for ethnic newspapers. Since the mid-1960s, there has been a growing interest in Irish and Irish-American history, and several scholarly journals have emerged to cater to this interest, among them *Eire-Ireland, James Joyce Quarterly, New Hibernia Review,* and *Irish Literary Supplement.* Other newspapers, such as the monthly *Boston Irish Reporter,* the *Irish Edition* (Philadelphia), the San Francisco *Gael, Desert Shamrock* (Arizona), and the *Irish American Post* (Chicago), benefited from the late twentieth century interest in all things Irish, and another publication, the quarterly *World of Hibernia,* was launched in the mid-1990s to promote the affluence and the accomplishments of Irish America.

Today, the premier publication is probably *Irish America,* a magazine established in 1985 to inform Irish-Americans of the latest happenings in Ireland, especially Northern Ireland, and to spotlight the rich and varied history of the Irish in the United States. In an editorial in October 1986, founding publisher Niall O'Dowd expressed his hope that the publication would be "a powerful vehicle of expression for Irish Americans." The first issue contained a listing of the top 100 Irish Americans, and Senator Edward Kennedy, tennis star John McEnroe, and then-U.S. president Ronald Reagan were featured on the front cover alongside the proud boast of "Irish America's finest."

The Irish-American press served its constituents in many ways, from helping them understand, adjust to, and eventually assimilate into American society to arousing and formulating Irish nationalist opinion, but the Irish were not as dependent on ethnic newspapers as other immigrant groups because they spoke English and were to an extent culturally Anglicized. The general American press was often sufficient for their needs.

Other Media

Another source of Irish identity has been through radio and television and, now, the Internet. Irish radio programs in markets across the country have taken on many of the former functions of newspapers. They offer a forum for ideas and news of interest to Irish Americans, including events in Ireland as well as in local neighborhoods. Since 1970, Irish Radio Network USA, headquartered in New York, has provided a unique platform for airing all crucial political, social, and economic issues affecting the Irish in America as it continues to offer fast-paced magazine shows that aim to entertain and inform its listenership. It has developed an intimate relationship with its core audience in the American Irish community. Promotion of benefit concerts, dances, fund-raising, and not-for-profit support groups and provision of current immigrant informational matters are an integral part of each radio broadcast and webcast.

Locally, there are programs that address their local communities, such as WROL 950 AM, the Irish channel in Boston, which broadcasts hours of music every Saturday. A Brockton, Massachusetts, station also hosts an Irish music program with Jim Larkin *(Sounds of the Emerald Isle),* a local program since 1982 on WBET Radio 1460 AM. Other cities with large Irish populations, such as Chicago and Philadelphia, also have radio programs with music and current events of special interest to Irish Americans in that area.

In the mid-1990s, ethnic media expanded to the national airwaves with the debut of *Out of Ireland,* hosted by Patricia O'Reilly; it now appears weekly on public television stations across the country. Another source of Irish television has been programs imported for viewing from Ireland's RTÉ (Radio Telefis Eireann), from the BBC, or from other television outlets, instead of those created directly for the medium in the United States. This includes popular Irish sports programs, such as rugby and Gaelic football, and the serial drama, *Ballykissangel,* filmed in Ireland and shown on BBC America, and now available on DVD. The series title was a play on Baile Coisc Aingil, in Co. Kerry. With its popularity in the United States, the actual locations in Avoca, where the show was filmed, became a popular tourist attraction for many Americans when visiting Ireland. Finally, there is the Internet, which seems to bring the earlier forms of communication together; it has made it possible to view Irish-American newspapers online and check out websites.

Journalism continues to be a signature profession for Irish-Americans: Jimmy Breslin (*New York Daily News*), Anna Quindlen (*New York Times*), Jim Dwyer (now-defunct *New York Newsday*), and Eileen McNamara (*Boston Globe*) have won Pulitzer Prizes. Major Irish-American television news commentators include Patrick Buchanan (CNN), John King (CNN), and Tim Russert (NBC), while Maureen Dowd (*New York Times*), Michael Kelly (*National Journal*), and William F. Buckley (*National Review*) have entertained readers with their opinions.

Martin J. Manning

See also: BUCKLEY, William F., Jr.;
DEVOY, John; FORD, Patrick;
HUGHES, Archbishop John; NEW
HIBERNIA REVIEW; NO IRISH
NEED APPLY

References
Blessing, Patrick J. *Irish in America.*
Washington, DC: Catholic University Press of America, 1992.

Clark, Dennis. *Hibernia America: The Irish and Regional Cultures.* Westport, CT: Greenwood Press, 1986.

Coffey, Michael, ed. *The Irish in America.* New York: Hyperion, 1997.

Glazier, Michael, ed. *Encyclopedia of the Irish in America.* Notre Dame, IN: University of Notre Dame, 1999.

Eleuterio-Comer, Susan K. *Irish American Material Culture: A Directory of Collections, Sites, and Festivals in the United States and Canada.* Westport, CT: Greenwood Press, 1988.

McMahon, Eileen. "The Irish-American Press." In *The Ethnic Press in the United States: A Historical Analysis and Handbook,* edited by Sally M. Miller, 177–189. Westport, CT: Greenwood Press, 1987.

Weaver, Jack W., and DeeGee Lester. *Immigrants from Great Britain and Ireland: A Guide to Archival and Manuscript Sources in North America.* Westport, CT: Greenwood Press, 1986.

PRESS, THE IRISH IN LATIN AMERICA

Since the beginning of the nineteenth century, the Irish presence in the Latin American press has been representative of the diversity of opinion and influence of Irish communities in the region and has served to convey the culture, ideas, and business strategies of professional journalists, entrepreneurs, and community leaders. Compared with traditional literary production and publishing, Irish-linked newspapers have always been relatively more important and have channeled the production of poets and writers of fiction.

Argentina is undoubtedly the Latin American country where most Irish-owned newspapers were published. The settlement of significant numbers of English-speaking immigrants in rural and urban areas of this country during the nineteenth and early twentieth centuries provided the core readership for these newspapers, only some of which were aimed specifically at the Irish community.

Stephen Hallet, an Irish-born printer who arrived in Buenos Aires in the early 1820s, established and edited *Cosmopolite, The American, The North Star,* and *Prices Current and Statistical Register* between 1826 and 1836. Hallet was also an editor of *La Gaceta Mercantil,* which published a section in English. James Kiernan (1806–1857), who arrived from Ireland in 1823, assisted Halley and later became editor and owner of *La Gaceta Mercantil.*

Published in Buenos Aires from 1861 to 1959, the *Standard* was long considered one of the most important (and the first daily) English-language newspapers in South America. The *Standard* was founded by Dublin-born brothers Edward Thomas Mulhall (1832–1899) and Michael George Mulhall (1836–1900) with the aim of forging "the bond of fellowship between the various members of our Anglo-Celtic race [and to be] interesting to all who read our language: offensive to none. Liberty without anarchy, religion without sectarianism, fusion without confusion is our motto" (from the first editorial, May 1, 1861). Although the Mulhall brothers were Irish, they usually referred to themselves as English, championing the commercial and political interests of the British community in Argentina. For this reason, especially from the late 1880s, the Mulhalls were often castigated by Irish nationalists, among them historian Thomas Murray and journalist Padraig MacManus, who dismissed them as representing the *shoneen* (anglophile) sector of the Irish community. The *Standard* was published in three editions: the daily for Buenos Aires and Montevideo, the weekly for the provinces, and the fortnightly for Europe.

The latter accompanied thousands of emigrants' letters sent home to Ireland and to family members scattered throughout the English-speaking world. The circulation in 1869 was 3,000 (by comparison, *Tribuna*, the largest newspaper in Buenos Aires at that time, had a circulation of 5,000). Contents included European and North American news (with particular attention paid to Irish events), local church news, and advertising, especially by shipping companies. Argentine news often focused on sensationalistic stories, such as murders and Indian raids. The *Standard* ceased publication in 1959 because of financial troubles, in particular as a consequence of competition from the *Buenos Aires Herald*.

The *Southern Cross* was founded in 1875 by Father Patrick Joseph Dillon; it is still produced, now as a monthly tabloid, claiming to be the oldest Irish newspaper published outside Ireland. When launched, the *Southern Cross* was aimed at the traditional Irish Catholic audience living in rural areas. However, during the first years, the editorial content of the *Southern Cross* appeared very similar to that of the *Standard*. The first issues of the *Southern Cross* were produced at the office of the *Standard*, and one of the first editors, Francis Healy Mulhall (1845–1898), was a brother of the *Standard*'s owners. But in the 1880s the *Southern Cross* succeeded in increasing its circulation, thanks to the inclusion of news of Irish events, such as the Land Wars and the nationalist movement in Ireland, clearly linking such stories with the Catholic Church. In 1882 Father Dillon was succeeded by Michael Dineen (1839–1896), a Corkborn university professor. Dineen had arrived in South America after being hired by the Chilean government to develop educational policy, and he later moved to Buenos Aires. A fluent Irish, French, Italian, and of course English speaker, Dineen inspired the nationalist content of the *Southern Cross*. After Dineen's death in 1896, the journalist and writer William Bulfin (1862–1910) was appointed editor, and he later purchased the paper. Bulfin was a skilled and intelligent editor, who through his short stories and articles merged the identity aspirations of the Irish in Argentina with an empathy toward the vanishing gauchos, the cowboys of the pampas. In 1906, Bulfin was succeeded by Gerald Foley (1868–1927), who, together with his brother Frank, covered the period of World War I and the Irish independence and civil war. From then on, the Roman Catholic Church has owned the *Southern Cross*, either directly or through its lay institutions. In the early 1960s, the *Southern Cross* began to feature articles in Spanish; today only a small proportion of its articles are in English.

The most difficult period of the *Southern Cross* was during the 1976–1983 military dictatorship. The editor, Father Fred Richards, condemned human rights abuses, alienating much of the paper's readership—who tended to be extremely conservative—and Argentina's reactionary Catholic Church. The *Southern Cross*, the *Buenos Aires Herald*, and *La Opinión* were among the few journalistic voices in Argentina to clearly criticize the regime's human rights record. For instance, the account of the Massacre at Saint Patrick's Church in 1976 and an interview with liberation theologian Dom Helder Camera of Brazil were perceived by both supporters and critics of the *Southern Cross* as acts of defiance.

There were other Irish newspapers in Argentina with less significance than the *Standard* and the *Southern Cross*. The *Irish Argentine* (1888–1889) was founded by Pallotine Father Bernard Feeney (1844–1919) in Azcuénaga, a village in an area with a significant Irish farming community. Father Feeney started an industrial school in nearby San Antonio de Areco to provide orphaned boys with opportunities to learn a trade. As a training exercise he edited 12 issues of a monthly magazine, *Flowers and Fruit.* The school was moved to Azcuénaga, and Father Feeney created a more professional journal, the *Irish Argentine,* which published articles of William Bulfin under the pen name "Bullfinch." In 1906, John Nelson (1859–1931), businessman and founder of the Nelson shipping company and a cold-storage plant, Las Palmas, in Entre Ríos province, launched the *Hibernian-Argentine Review,* a weekly that continued publication until 1927. The *Review* was moderately nationalistic in politics and strongly clerical, although there was less coverage of Catholic Church affairs than appeared in the *Southern Cross.* During World War I the *Review* rallied in defense of the British cause. *Fianna,* a nationalist review published from 1910 to 1912, was edited by Padraig MacManus (b. 1852) and supported by the Irish chaplain of San Pedro, Father Edmund Flannery, and farmer James Hennesy. MacManus led a republican group and sought to be appointed as diplomatic representative of Ireland in Argentina. The content of *Fianna* included sensationalistic stories of the British in Ireland, and the newspaper never missed an opportunity to attack Britain's occupation of the Falkland/Malvinas Islands.

Thomas J. Hutchinson (1820–1888?) and Nicholas Lowe (1827–1902) were individual entrepreneurs who among other businesses launched diverse journalistic undertakings. While both Hutchinson and Lowe came from Ireland, their newspapers did not display strong Irish influences. Hutchinson was a physician who traveled widely in Africa in the 1850s and 1860s, and he published several books recounting his adventures. In 1864 he was appointed British consul in Montevideo and later in Rosario. Hutchinson began the *Argentine Citizen,* which was primarily concerned with encouraging immigration and industrial progress, in 1865; the paper ceased publication after just one year. Nicholas Lowe, of Co. Cork, settled in Mercedes in 1855. He was a successful sheep farmer, banker, and educator. Lowe founded a number of short-lived newspapers: the *Daily News* (1874), addressed to Protestant readers, and the *Buenos Ayres News and River Plate Advertiser* (1873–1874).

In 1865, Irish-born William Scully started the *Anglo-Brazilian Times,* "to develop and foster British enterprises; [. . .] to point out, and seek remedies for grievances and defects in the commercial and political intercourse of England and Brazil." Scully remained the editor for almost 20 years. Even though the *Times* received a subsidy from the Brazilian authorities, the paper was capable of criticism. For example, Scully—a founder of the Sociedade Internacional de Imigração—opposed restrictions on Protestants, seeing this as impeding the attraction of immigrants.

In 1988 in Uruguay, the Argentine businessman Eduardo Casey financed the *Independent,* a weekly paper edited by W. H. Denstone. In 1889, Casey also purchased the *River Plate Times* (established in 1877), merging it with the *Independent* to form one larger paper, retaining the title the *River Plate Times.* As Uruguay's Irish population was small, for commercial reasons the papers set out to appeal to the country's wider English-speaking community.

Edmundo Murray

See also: BULFIN, William; CASEY, Eduardo; DILLON, Patrick Joseph; MASSACRE AT SAINT PATRICK CHURCH, The; MULHALL, Michael George; MURRAY, Thomas; SCULLY, William

References

Graham-Yooll, Andrew. *The Forgotten Colony: A History of the English-Speaking Communities in Argentina.* 1981. Reprint, Buenos Aires: Literature of Latin America, 1999.

Marshall, Oliver. *The English-Language Press in Latin America.* London: Institute of Latin American Studies, 1996.

QUEBEC CITY

From its foundation in 1608 to 1763, Quebec City was the most important town in what was known as *Nouvelle France*, which included most of Canada down into the Mississipi Valley and Louisiana. The first waves of Irish immigration in Quebec City came after the British invasion of 1759, and culminated in the mid-nineteenth century.

In the mid-nineteenth century, Quebec City was the second most important town in Canada, and in 1867 it became the capital of the francophone province of Quebec. From 1815, many Irish immigrants arrived in the (by then) colonial town, the nearest from the very active immigration center located at Grosse Ile, on the St. Laurent River. In 1847, the population of Quebec City doubled, going from 40,000 to almost 100,000 persons, because of the massive arrivals of Irish families. The trip across the Atlantic was not expensive per se, but it took six weeks, in terrible, unhealthy conditions. Quebec City suffered from two epidemics of cholera in 1832 and 1834 because of the massive European immigration.

Hundreds of orphan children whose parents died in the ships coming from Ireland were adopted by francophone and Irish families living in Quebec City. The working-class Irish community living in Quebec City was often rejected by the local English elite and found hospitality from the francophone population who were also of the Roman Catholic faith. Quebec City's Notre-Dame-des-Victoires Church in Place Royale, was designated by the bishop of Quebec City as the church of the Irish in 1824, until the Irish population built their own Saint Patrick's church uptown, on McMahon Street, in 1833.

According to various census numbers cited by Robert Grace, the Irish represented almost one-third of Quebec City's population in 1861. Their number was around 12,000 in 1871, but they had declined to 4,170 or 3.2% of the population in 1931. Most of these Irish came from Munster, Ulster, and Leinster. As many Canadians became affected by the lack of jobs, many Irish newcomers migrated toward Montreal and the United States. Those who stayed in Quebec City were mostly integrated, and later generations became francophone (or bilingual): nowadays, many French-speaking Quebecois are named Johnson, Ryan, O'Neil, McGoldrick, among many other names. Among those who stayed were Charles Joseph Alleyn (1817–1890), who arrived in Quebec City in 1837 from Co.

Cork; he learned French and became mayor of Quebec City (1854–1855), deputy at the Assemblée législative (Provincial Parliament) (1854–1867), and district sheriff (1866–1890). Similarly, James McInenly was the mayor of the city of Sillery (now part of Quebec City) between 1878 and 1880.

Today, Quebec City is completely francophone, but it still has a population of about 30,000 persons of Irish descent who have their own English-speaking schools. St. Patrick's High School, which teaches exclusively in English, and street names such as Maguire are further proof of the tolerance and diversity that still exists in this French part of Canada. There are still Irish communities living in rural villages located 25 kilometers north of Quebec City, in Tewksberry, Stoneham, Shannon, Saint-Gabriel de Valcartier, and Ste-Catherine de la Jacques-Cartier, most speaking English rather than Gaelic.

On the south shore of the St-Laurent River, there are also many villages founded by Irish newcomers, not far from Quebec City: Armagh, Coleraine, Saint-Jacques-de-Leeds, St-Adrien d'Irlande. Today, there is an association called Irish Heritage that promotes the history, traditions, and contributions of the Irish in the region of Quebec City. In 2000, a memorial cross was offered by Ireland to the population of Quebec City for its hospitality; it can be seen near the Parc de l'Artillerie, in the old part of the capital, where the Irish population was at its highest during nineteenth century.

Yves Laberge

See also: ETHNIC AND RACE RELATIONS, IRISH AND FRENCH CANADIANS

References

Grace, Robert G. "The Irish in Quebec City in 1861: A Portrait of an Immigrant Community." Mémoire de maîtrise, Université Laval, 1988.

Tessier, Yves. *An Historical Tourist Guide to Québec City.* Quebec: Sociétéhistorique de Québec, 2005.

QUILL, MICHAEL JOSEPH (1905–1966)

Michael Quill was a U.S. labor leader and one of the founding members of the Transport Workers Union of America (TWU). Influenced by his experiences in the Irish republican movement, Quill was one of a group of Irish subway workers in New York who aligned with the Communist Party in 1934 to found the TWU, which eventually become a national body whose members include bus, subway, railway, and airline workers. Serving as the union's president for three decades, Quill was a colorful, dynamic speaker who was popular among workers for spearheading successful union efforts to raise the qualities of workers' lives.

Quill was born into a republican family in Gortloughera, Kilgarvin, Co. Kerry in 1905. As a youth he became involved in Irish Republican Army activities and fought against the Black and Tans in the War of Independence, although his accounts of his activities sometimes varied. After he immigrated to New York in 1926, Quill took a series of labor jobs, but he settled into a job as a ticket agent for the Interboro Rapid Transit Company, a poorly paid job featuring 12-hour shifts, seven days a week. Quill also became involved with fellow republican activists through Clan na Gael, a revolutionary group active in the United States. He and his fellow Clan na Gael members were influenced by the works of James Connolly, the socialist labor leader executed in Dublin for his part in the 1916 Rising; Connolly had cofounded the Irish Transport and Workers General Union of Ireland, and the new union would be named in tribute to the Irish union.

The Communist Party, which recognized the potential power of an organized body of transit workers, was instrumental in the founding of the new union. The official date of the TWU's founding was April 12, 1934, when party organizers met with Quill and fellow Clan na Gael members in a cafeteria at Columbus Circle in New York. John O'Shea was the first union president, but he was quickly replaced by Quill, whose militant dynamism, strength of conviction, and wit combined to make him a charismatic leader.

At first, to foil company spies, the union recruited members mainly through clandestine meetings of trusted associates. Quill became one of the first public faces of the union, reaching his fellow workers through speeches from the soapbox and on the radio. At the time of the union's founding, the Depression's effects were resulting in layoffs, pay cuts, and longer hours for transit workers. The union grew in strength throughout the 1930s, gaining members from throughout the transit system as it succeeded in winning better pay and conditions and shorter work weeks. A decisive strike in 1937 supporting TWU members fired from the BMT subway line demonstrated the union's power and increased membership dramatically. By the middle of that year, the union had more than 40,000 members among the city's bus and subway companies, as well as streetcar and taxicab companies, and had joined the Congress of International Organizations. Also that year, Quill was elected to the city council of New York, where he would serve from 1937 to 1939 and from 1943 to 1949.

The Communist Party would maintain strong control over the union leadership, until Quill led a backlash against the party in the late 1940s. After his split with the communists, Quill stayed in power and continued to play an often controversial role in ensuring that city politicians met the union's demands. He remained a leftist throughout his career, taking strong stances against racism and anti-Semitism, and he was also an early opponent of the Vietnam War.

Quill's final union activity, and the one for which he is arguably best remembered, was leading New York City's bus and subway workers in a major strike that began on January 1, 1966; it would cripple the city for 12 days. In a public act of defiance early in the strike, Quill tore up an injunction to halt it, and declared famously, and with characteristic provocation, "The judge can drop dead in his black robes." He was arrested on January 4, along with several other union leaders, but his stay in jail was short: he collapsed from a heart attack and was hospitalized. Although Quill recovered enough to address a union event celebrating the win of a substantial wage increase and greater pension benefits, he died only days later on January 28. His funeral was held at Saint Patrick's Cathedral and was attended by many of the workers whose lives he had helped improve.

Noreen Bowden

See also: IRISH REPUBLICAN ARMY

References

Freeman, Joshua B. *In Transit: The Transport Workers Union in New York City, 1933–1966.* New York: Oxford University Press, 1989.

Whittemore, L. H. *The Man Who Ran the Subways: The Story of Mike Quill.* New York: Holt, Rinehart and Winston, 1968.

QUINN, DECLAN (1957–)

Part of a cinematic family that includes actors Aidan and Marian Quinn and director Paul Quinn, Declan Quinn was born in Chicago in 1957 to Irish parents. After a childhood divided between Co. Offaly and Chicago, he attended Columbia College in Chicago, where he studied filmmaking. After graduating in 1979 he worked as a news cameraman for an NBC affiliate in Illinois; he also worked as a cinematographer (director of photography) of commercials and industrial films. In 1980 he headed back to Ireland and got a job at Windmill Lane studios in Dublin. There he worked as a cinematographer/codirector (with Barry Devlin) on a number of music videos, including "Pride" for U2 and the documentary, *The Unforgettable Fire*. He also found work on Irish television as a cinematographer on *Clash of the Ash* and *Last Catholics*.

In 1985 he returned to New York and made music videos for a range of artists that included Debbie Harry and Whitney Houston. He also won a Clio Award in 1991 for his work as a cinematographer on an MTV short film on the subject of AIDS.

In 1989 Quinn branched into films and made his debut as a feature cinematographer on *The Kill Off*, a gritty film noir based on the novel by cult writer Jim Thompson and directed by Maggie Greenwald. More features and television work followed, including *Freddy's Dead: The Final Nightmare* (1991), yet another entry in the *Nightmare on Elm Street* series. He teamed up again with Greenwald for *The Ballad of Little Jo* (1993), an unusual western shot in Montana that told the story of a middle-class woman who reinvents herself as a male rancher on the American frontier of the late nineteenth century. The evocative, expressive cinematography of the film effectively conveyed the harsh nature of life on the frontier and won Quinn much critical praise. In 1994 he returned to Ireland to shoot *All Things Bright and Beautiful*, directed by his former collaborator, Barry Devlin, which told the story of a young boy whose claims that he has witnessed a miracle throw his small town into chaos. The film featured Gabriel Byrne in a small role.

Upon his return to America in 1994 he teamed up with legendary French director Louis Malle to make the acclaimed film *Vanya on 42nd Street*. His work on that film attracted the attention of a number of directors, including Mike Figgis and Mira Nair. Figgis employed him as cinematographer on his Academy Award–winning film, *Leaving Last Vegas*, a poignant love story that told the story of a suicidal alcoholic (Nicolas Cage) who travels to Las Vegas to kill himself and there meets a lonely prostitute (Elisabeth Shue) with whom he begins a pitiful affair. Quinn's innovative work on the film won much critical praise and was a key element of the film's success; he went on to work with Figgis on two later features, *One Night Stand* (1997) and *Cold Creek Manor* (2003). Quinn's work on *Vanya on 42nd Street* also inspired Nair, the Indian-born director of the hit film *Salaam Bombay* (1998), to approach him to work on her latest feature, *Kama Sutra* (1996), which was shot in India and was notable for its sumptuous visual design. Quinn worked again with Nair on *Monsoon Wedding* (2001), a comic story of an elaborate Indian wedding.

In the past decade Quinn has made a number of Irish and Irish-American films. He served as a cinematographer on *2 By 4* (1998), written and directed by Dublin-born Jimmy Smallhorne and set in the Irish community in New York. He has also worked with Irish directors such as

Neil Jordan (for whom he shot *Breakfast on Pluto,* released in 2005) and Jim Sheridan. His work with Sheridan was particularly productive: he shot Sheridan's semibiographical *In America,* which told the story of an Irish family trying to survive in New York in the 1980s, and *Get Rich or Die Tryin'* (2005), which marked the acting debut of rapper 50 Cent.

In 1998 Quinn took on a film that was very close to his family: *This Is My Father.* It gave him the opportunity to work with his brothers, Aidan and Paul (who directed), and his sister Marian; it was shot around Dublin, Kildare, and Wicklow. Although the film received mixed reviews, it was an important personal project for his family.

Most recently, Quinn has been working on a range of U.S. and European films, including *Vanity Fair* (2004) and *Pride and Glory,* scheduled for release in 2007. He has received many nominations and awards, including an Emmy nomination for his work on *Hysterical Blindness,* a television film directed by Nair in 2002, and Independent Spirit Awards for his work on *In America, Kama Sutra,* and *Leaving Las Vegas.* Quinn and his wife, Etta, have four children and live in New York State.

Gwenda Young

References

Davenport, Richard. "One Drink Minimum: Interview with Mike Figgis and Declan Quinn." *American Cinematographer,* February 1996, 28–33.

Thompson, Andrew O. "The Look of Love: Director Mira Nair and cinematographer Declan Quinn on *Kama Sutra.*" *American Cinematographer,* February 1997, 96–102.

QUINN, GLENN (1970–2002)

Born in Dublin, Glenn Martin Christopher Francis Quinn grew up in Cabinteely, Co. Dublin, and attended Clonkeen College in Blackrock. As a teen, he played drums and guitar in local bands, influenced by his father, Murty Quinn, an Irish musician and singer. However, in 1988, Quinn moved to southern California with his mother and two sisters, finding work as a housepainter, factory worker, construction worker, and waiter.

Discovered by a Hollywood casting director, Quinn first appeared in a 1989 music video, playing a pool shark, and quickly moved into minor roles on several television programs, including *Beverly Hills, 90210* in 1990. His big break came that same year when he was cast as Mark Healy, the boyfriend of Becky Connor on the popular television series *Roseanne.* Quinn's character was a biker and mechanic, who after several years of dating Becky eventually elopes with her, thereby becoming the onscreen son-in-law of the show's star, Roseanne.

Quinn played Mark Healy on 76 episodes of *Roseanne* from 1990 until the show ended in 1997. During this time, he made his feature-film debut as a drummer in *Shout* (1991), starring John Travolta, and played the sensitive son, Cedric Grey, in the short-lived television series, *Covington Cross* (1992), which was set in fourteenth-century England.

Quinn had no difficulty shifting accents in these roles—American as Mark Healy, English as Cedric Grey—but he was especially pleased to use his natural voice for his next starring role, playing Allen Francis Doyle, an Irish half-demon (on his father's side), in the popular television series, *Angel.* As Quinn explained, "I've been hiding it [his native accent] for so long that it's amazing to have some freedom. It was like putting on an old pair of shoes—it's bringing my soul back to life"

(Hayward 2002, 18). Quinn reportedly proclaimed his Irish heritage with two tattoos: "Erin Go Bragh" (Ireland Forever) on his left shoulder, and a harp on his right shoulder.

Unfortunately for Quinn, his role in *Angel* was terminated abruptly in the ninth episode of the first season when Doyle sacrificed himself to save dozens of other half-demons from an evil horde of pure-demons. Many fans (known as "Doyle's Loyals" and "Quinn-T-Essentialists") protested. "I think it's a crime that Doyle was killed off so early in the first season," wrote one fan in an Internet forum. "He was a character that had been developed, he was multidimensional, and now he's gone, just like that?" (Mitchell 1999, 3).

The character Doyle died in the episode aired on November 30, 1999. Glenn Quinn died almost exactly three years later, on December 3, 2002, apparently from an overdose of heroin, in a friend's apartment in North Hollywood, California. His final role was as a professor of criminal psychology, Dr. Hal Evans, in the film *R.S.V.P.* (2002).

James I. Deutsch

References

Fretts, Bruce. "Parrying the Luke Perry Factor." *Entertainment Weekly,* September 18, 1992: 62.

Hayward, Anthony. "Obituary: Glenn Quinn." *The Independent,* December 18, 2002: 18.

Martindale, David. "His Irish Returns." *Houston Chronicle,* October 10, 1999: 5.

Masson, Charles. "Fighting Irish: Glenn Quinn." *New Orleans Times-Picayune,* September 27, 1992: T4.

Mitchell, Pamela. "Doyle's Doom: *Angel* Fans Not Happy with Sidekick's Demise." *Houston Chronicle,* December 9, 1999: 3.

Reed, Christopher. "Obituary: Glenn Quinn." *The Guardian,* December 21, 2002: 18.

R

REAGAN, RONALD WILSON (1911–2004)

Ronald Reagan was born on February 6, 1911, in Tampico, Illinois. The son of a shoe salesman, Reagan spent most of his youth in Dixon, Illinois, and was thus firmly rooted in the midwestern middle-class; for this region and social group he felt a lasting affinity and from them he drew his most firm political support. Even in his youth and adolescence Reagan was distinguished by his geniality, optimism, and physical vigor. In his teens he became a certified lifeguard and is credited with saving dozens of people in peril of drowning. Although not an outstanding student, he performed credibly in academic pursuits. He attended Eureka College. Upon graduation he began his professional career as a sports broadcaster for radio stations in Davenport and Des Moines, Iowa.

In 1937 a radio colleague with contacts in California helped him obtain a screen test. When this was successful Reagan began his film career, eventually making 50 movies. Despite later political gibes that depicted him as an untalented hack, his work in Hollywood contained several accomplished performances. His role as George "the Gipper" Gipp in *Knute Rockne—All American* was probably his best role, and it gave him one of his more enduring nicknames. He is said to have considered *King's Row* of 1942 as his best film. Although he never attained absolute stardom, Reagan earned numerous desirable roles, and he appeared in films with such stars as Humphrey Bogart and Bette Davis (and, memorably, Bonzo, a chimpanzee). Reagan was also active in the Screen Actors Guild, holding its presidency for several terms.

In 1964 Reagan gave a televised speech in support of Republican presidential candidate Barry Goldwater. Goldwater was crushed in the election, but Reagan's political career was born. He was a natural politician, for he was able to intermix persuasive optimism, suspicion of government, and personable geniality without appearing insincere. Within two years Reagan had won the governorship of California. He served as governor until 1975, during which time he became one of the most nationally prominent Republicans. In 1980, he ran for the presidency, eventually defeating the incumbent, Jimmy Carter. He assumed office in January 1981.

Economics dominated Reagan's first term. His initial campaign promises emphasized lowering taxes, showing greater strength in the world, confronting communism directly, and lessening governmental regulation of citizens' lives. Despite inheriting a significant economic depression, Reagan lowered taxes, believing that the government spends money rashly, people spend it wisely, and the economy would therefore accelerate if people retained more of their own money. Moreover, he believed it was possible to promote his political policies and attack economic stagnation simultaneously; therefore, he instituted a massive increase in military and other defense spending (e.g., research and development of advanced weapons technologies). These increases succeeded in reviving the economy, but came at the cost of accumulating enormous governmental debts. It has also been claimed that this spending was an undeclared attempt to force the Soviet Union to match American defense spending, eventually driving the Soviets into economic collapse.

Shortly after taking office, on March 30, 1981, Reagan was shot by an attempted assassin. Although the severity of his wound was minimized at the time, it has since emerged that the bullet came closer to killing him than was originally acknowledged. Several of his colleagues standing nearby were grievously wounded, his press secretary James Brady being the most severely harmed. Reagan's good humor when speaking with the emergency room surgeons ("I hope you're all Republicans") and during his recuperation ("Honey, I forgot to duck") endeared him to the American people. Even those politically opposed to him began to acknowledge his personal charm for the magnificent political advantage it was.

Reagan ran for reelection in 1984, on a platform that emphasized strength, optimism, and economic recovery. He crushed his opponent Walter Mondale in one of the most lopsided victories in modern U.S. political history.

Reagan's international policies in both his first and second terms were largely based on confronting and discrediting the Soviet Union. When, however, his friend British Prime Minister Margaret Thatcher met the new Soviet leader, Mikhail Gorbachev, Thatcher's willingness to work with Gorbachev led Reagan to begin his own negotiations. The Reagan-Gorbachev summits were among the major diplomatic events of the 1980s and served, on the whole, to lessen tensions between the superpowers. Other major international events in which Reagan had a leading role were the deployment and withdrawal of U.S. Marines as peacekeepers in Beirut (1983), the invasion of Grenada (1983), and repeated air strikes against targets in Libya. He also covertly supported the Afghan rebels in their war against the invading Soviet armies, and he supported the Nicaraguan contra rebels in their fight against the ruling Sandinista regime.

Reagan's support for the contra rebels led to the greatest crisis in Reagan's presidency. In late 1986, rumors began to circulate that there was an intricate, covert, and illegal scheme to fund the Nicaraguan rebels by selling weapons technology to Iran and funneling the proceeds to the contras. Despite initial denials, it emerged that such a plot did indeed exist, and seemed to reach near, and possibly into, the Oval Office itself. Reagan unquestionably authorized arms shipments, although his remaining involvement, if any, is still debated. Aside from the outright illegality of the scheme, the entire Iran-Contra scandal left Reagan looking like a man either too inattentive or too exhausted by the presidency to be effective. His reputation never fully recovered. It was the nadir of his presidency. By the time his successor, George H. W. Bush, took the White House in January 1989, Reagan appeared almost relieved to relinquish his presidential responsibilities.

Reagan's political legacy remains a source of intense partisan disagreement. To his supporters he was one of the great U.S. presidents, embodying American conservatism's post-Vietnam and post-Watergate resurgence. They view his most significant accomplishments as being the destruction of European bolshevism; the global reassertion of U.S. military might; the diminishment of governmental intrusion into American civil life; a reduction of the tax burden on citizens; and a general renewal of patriotism and optimism in the United States. Opponents sharply dispute this interpretation of Reagan's legacy. To his detractors, Reagan was recklessly provocative of an already stagnating Soviet Union; concealed regressive social policies behind populist antigovernment banalities; ignored the crucial early years of the AIDS/HIV epidemic; spent wildly with no plan to pay the concomitant debts; and directly broke the law in the Iran-Contra scandal, then lied about his actions. The two sides continue to differ, yet the intensity and durability of the debate signifies the undoubted consequentiality of Reagan's administrations.

After leaving the White House Reagan lived quietly in California. Although he gave occasional speeches in support of Republican political candidates or conservative social causes, he largely left politics to his successors. In 1994, however, he reentered American public life in an unexpected and pitiable way. After being diagnosed with the beginning stages of Alzheimer's disease, he immediately disclosed his condition to the American people, who responded with sorrow and support. For reasons of health and personal dignity Reagan spent most of the rest of his life in privacy. During this period his wife Nancy became widely admired for her constancy in supporting him through his illness. He died on June 5, 2004, at his family home in Los Angeles, California. He was accorded a state funeral in Washington, D.C., after which his body was interred on the grounds of his presidential library in California.

Reagan's connections with Ireland have been largely overemphasized. Although he unquestionably took pride in his Irish heritage, he does not appear to have had a distinctive or unusually informed interest in the country or its culture. The elements of his personality that were often described as being peculiarly Irish—his "Irish humor" or "the Irish twinkle of his eye"—have a greater relevance to American popular sentiment than to any reality in Ireland.

Reagan nonetheless holds an important place in the history of Irish-American relations. He attained the significant distinction of being an Irish American who rose to the highest position of power in the world. Despite the undoubtedly American qualities of his life and outlook, he represented to the United States, and to the world, the social and political achievements of the Irish in America. Reagan was himself highly popular in Ireland, despite the misgivings many Irish felt about his policy of deploying advanced missile systems in Europe. His 1984 visit to his ancestral home of Ballyporeen, Co. Kerry, was accorded a warm welcome. Whatever Reagan's personal interest in Ireland may have been, his numerous achievements and enormous political legacy will continue to be regarded as yet another enduring accomplishment of the Irish peoples in America.

Andrew Goodspeed

See also: MULRONEY, Brian; O'NEILL, Thomas P. "Tip"; PATTERSON, Frank; PECK, Gregory

References
Noonan, Peggy. *When Character Was King.* New York: Viking, 2001.
Reagan, Ronald. *An American Life.* New York: Simon and Schuster, 1990.
Reagan, Ronald. *Speaking My Mind: Selected Speeches.* New York: Simon and Schuster, 1989.
Reagan, Ronald. *Where's the Rest of Me?* New York: Duell, Sloan & Pearce, 1965.
Stockman, David A. *The Triumph of Politics: Why the Reagan Revolution Failed.* New York: Harper and Row, 1986.

REDSHAW, THOMAS DILLON (1944–)

Born in Salem, Massachusetts, and raised in nearby Marblehead, Thomas Dillon Redshaw was educated at the Mt. Hermon School and at Tufts University, where he edited the literary magazine before graduating in 1966. Redshaw attended University College Dublin in 1966–1967, earning an MA in Anglo-Irish Literature under the direction of Roger McHugh. During his years in Ireland, and later in the Twin Cities, Redshaw published poetry and frequently gave readings from *Such a Heart Dances Out* (1971), *Heimaey* (1974), and *The Floating World* (1979). In Dublin, he established lifelong literary friendships, most notably with the poet John Montague, the subject of his 1980 dissertation at New York University, which was directed by M. L. Rosenthal.

In 1971, Redshaw moved to Minnesota to take a position with the College (now University) of St. Thomas. His association with the quarterly journal *Éire-Ireland,* the journal of the Irish American Cultural Institute, lasted from 1974 to 1985. Redshaw spent a year as a senior fellow in Irish studies at Queen's University Belfast in 1986–1987 and returned to *Éire-Ireland* as editor from 1989 to 1995. In 1997, Redshaw and others launched *New Hibernia Review/Iris Éireannach Nua,* published by St. Thomas's Center for Irish Studies. In both publications that he has edited, Redshaw has expanded the journals' creative writing, coverage of the visual arts, and Irish-language materials. He has spent several summers studying Irish in Carraroe, Co. Galway.

Redshaw's critical writings tend toward historicism and focus on twentieth-century Irish poetry, particularly the work of Thomas Kinsella, Austin Clarke, George Reavey, Thomas McCarthy, and John Montague. In 1989, he compiled *Hill Field: Poems and Memoirs for John Montague on His Sixtieth Birthday,* and in 2004, Redshaw edited a collection of 21 critical articles, *Well Dreams: Essays on John Montague,* including his own survey of Montague criticism, a study of Montague's fiction, and an annotated checklist of Montague's publications. Since the mid-1990s, Redshaw has published articles through Liam Miller's Dolmen Press. He has edited a series of acclaimed broadsides and limited editions of Irish poets for Traffic Street Press in Minnesota.

James Silas Rogers

See also: MONTAGUE, John

References
Redshaw, Thomas Dillon. *Collected Poems of Thomas MacGreevy.* Dublin: New Writers' Press, 1971.

RE-EMIGRANTS WITHIN THE AMERICAS

Traditionally, historians have understood the migration process as a linear phenomenon in which the emigrants depart from one place and settle in another. However, most of the Irish emigrants to Latin America had an opportunistic mind and their migration pattern can be seen more as circular than linear. When they were not successful in attaining their goals in one place, they swiftly re-emigrated to another destination with better prospects.

In the 1820s, Irishmen who had served in the British Army were applying for assistance from the British Colonial Office to settle in the New World, mostly Canada. They looked for free passages and the possibility of free land. Once in the New World, they often moved on to the United States and possibly to Latin America. In the same period there was a flux of Irish immigrants in Brazil, Uruguay, and Argentina from the United States and Canada. On the one hand the North Atlantic seaway was safer than the South Atlantic route, as most of the new republics in South America were still fighting for their independence against Spain. On the other hand, positive news circulated among Irish circles in the United States through private family letters, newspapers, and travel guides. This particular migration resulted in what was known in Argentina as the "Irish Yankees." In the same period, hundreds of members of the Irish Colony in Brazil traveled to Argentina, while Irish and Irish-American rural settlers in California and Texas crossed the southern frontier and settled in Mexican land or farther south in Panama and Central America.

During and after the U.S. Civil War a new flow of Irish immigrants traveled from North America to Rio de Janeiro, Montevideo, and Buenos Aires. Most were experienced soldiers and enlisted for some time in the Triple Alliance army against Paraguay. Among these soldiers were John Stephen Dillon and Peter Garland, who successfully managed to gain positions in the Argentine government as immigration agents in Ireland.

In 1890–1920, following thousands of European settlers in Argentina and Brazil who re-emigrated to the United States, numbers of poor Irish emigrants and their families who would not find an opportunity in South America decided to try their luck in the United States. The records of the Ellis Island Database also include some families who were victims of the Dresden Affair and would later be transferred to the United States.

Edmundo Murray

See also: DRESDEN AFFAIR; PARAGUAY

References
Murray, Thomas. *The Story of the Irish in Argentina.* New York: P. J. Kenedy & Sons, 1919.

REPEAL MOVEMENT

From the granting of Catholic Emancipation in 1829 until the onset of the Irish Famine in 1845, Daniel O'Connell—known as "the Liberator" for his successful leadership of the emancipation movement—led a campaign for the repeal of the Act of Union. The Act, passed in 1800, had dissolved the Irish parliament and transferred legislative power to Westminster. Repeal, according to O'Connell's plan, would restore an Irish parliament to Dublin. O'Connell was convinced that only an Irish parliament could properly address the political, social, religious, and economic problems unique to Ireland. The relationship that an independent Irish parliament would have to Britain and the Empire was not made explicit, though O'Connell consistently emphasized loyalty to the British crown.

Despite his large following during the emancipation campaign, initially O'Connell had a difficult time garnering support for repeal. The Anglo-Irish ascendancy feared that an end to the Union would mean an end to their privileged position within Irish society. Many Irish people in the middle classes, Catholics and non-Catholics alike, were reluctant to risk the social upheaval that might accompany such a constitutional change. At the same time, rural discontent was largely focused on the question of tithes (imposts levied by the Church of Ireland) and could not easily be channeled to support the repeal movement. Meanwhile, regional variations in the economy led many people in the north of Ireland to oppose repeal, as the textile and linen industries depended on British capital and technology. Nor did O'Connell find support for repeal among British politicians, whose backing would be crucial for the repeal movement to succeed. When, in April 1834, O'Connell introduced a motion for repeal before the House of Commons, the motion was overwhelmingly defeated by a vote of 523 to 38.

Unable to gain widespread support for repeal in the early 1830s, O'Connell sought an alliance with the governing Whig party. A Benthamite Utilitarian, O'Connell hoped to gain concessions for Ireland, even if those concessions fell short of his ultimate goal of repeal. The government, in return, believed that by granting concessions it could more fully reconcile Irish Catholic

opinion to the Union. An informal agreement was reached in March 1835; according to the Lichfield House Compact, O'Connell agreed to suspend his repeal agitation in exchange for a number of legislative reforms. While those reforms, which included a new tithe bill and an Irish poor law, ultimately fell short of O'Connell's expectations, they—together with a new willingness on the part of the Irish administration in Dublin Castle to open large areas of patronage and employment to Catholics—were enough to keep the repeal movement fairly quiescent for several years.

Pessimistic about the Whigs' chances for success in the next British election, O'Connell took steps to revive the campaign for repeal in 1840. In April he launched the National Association of Ireland, which was soon renamed the Loyal National Repeal Association. Hoping to gain mass support, as he had for Catholic Emancipation, O'Connell modeled the Repeal Association on the enormously successful Catholic Association. Members paid £1 in annual dues; those who could not afford the annual membership dues were invited to become associate members for a shilling per year. As part of the effort to popularize the repeal movement, reading rooms were established throughout the country where anyone interested in the movement could read nationalist newspapers and pamphlets. Foremost among the literature was the *Nation,* first published in October 1842 by Thomas Davis, John Dillon, and Charles Gavan Duffy. These three men, along with John Mitchel and William Smith O'Brien, formed the core of the Young Ireland movement. As cultural nationalists, Davis and his associates believed an Irish parliament would help protect Ireland from the contaminating influence of British culture. When repeal activity tapered off temporarily in 1842 while O'Connell served as lord mayor of Dublin, the *Nation* newspaper helped to keep the movement alive.

During the spring of 1843, the Repeal Association grew in strength, numbers, and financial stability. The upsurge of support can be partly explained by widespread discontent over the new poor law, which O'Connell wisely channeled to his cause. The public meetings held on Sunday afternoons in different parts of the country also contributed greatly to the movement's popularity. Hundreds of thousands came to hear O'Connell speak. In addressing the vast outdoor meetings, O'Connell promised his audiences that they would have a parliament in Dublin before the year was out. He emphasized, however, that theirs would be a moral victory and that the audiences at his "monster meetings" should disperse and go home peacefully. O'Connell's commitment to nonviolence was put to the test in October 1843 when the government proscribed a massive meeting scheduled to be held at Clontarf. Rather than risk a potentially violent confrontation with the authorities, O'Connell canceled the meeting, much to the dismay of his followers. A week later, O'Connell was arrested and charged with sedition. He was sentenced to a year in prison, but after seven months the Law Lords reversed the decision and ordered O'Connell's release from Richmond Gaol.

The repeal movement never again regained the momentum that it had enjoyed in the spring and summer of 1843. For one thing, the Conservative government under Sir Robert Peel adopted a policy of conciliation that seemed to undermine the case for repeal. In addition, the Young Irelanders became increasingly critical of O'Connell's pragmatic utilitarianism and what they considered his sectarian rhetoric. Tensions ran especially high over the question of university education; whereas Davis supported Peel's 1845 proposal to establish nondenominational colleges in Galway, Cork, and Belfast, O'Connell joined Archbishop MacHale of Tuam in opposing the "godless" colleges. The conflict initiated a feud that eventually ended in a split between O'Connell and Young Ireland, ostensibly over Young Ireland's unwillingness to abjure violence unconditionally. Finally, the onset of the Famine hastened the collapse of the repeal movement, as the struggle for basic survival temporarily eclipsed political concerns. By the time O'Connell died in Genoa in May 1847, the movement had already run its course.

Kathleen Ruppert

See also: O'CONNELL, Daniel

References

Boyce, D. George. *Nineteenth-Century Ireland: The Search for Stability.* Savage, MD: Barnes and Noble Books, 1991.

Hoppen, K. Theodore. *Ireland Since 1800: Conflict and Conformity.* London: Longman, 1989.

MacDonagh, Oliver. *The Emancipist: Daniel O'Connell, 1830–47.* New York: St. Martin's Press, 1989.

RESEARCH COLLECTIONS, IRISH, IN CANADA

Libraries and archives in Canada that contain major collections in Irish history, language, and literature vary greatly in their holdings. Large Irish collections that are suitable for serious research are often held in major universities or in research organizations. Interest in Irish research in

Canada, as in the United States, has coincided with the development of Irish studies programs in academic institutions and research organizations. The other positive sign is the number of active Irish cultural and historical societies, many of which work closely with the local academic community, that serve specialists and those whose interests are more broadly based. Although only a sampling of these collections, mainly the largest and most important, are described here, there are many other Irish collections, smaller in scale, many with only a few holdings useful to Irish research, in Canada. Researchers should examine their online catalogs and websites to get an overview of their collections. Most require special permission for visitors to use and are open by appointment only.

Government Archives, Private Organizations, and Public Libraries

At the federal level, the best source is still Library and Archives Canada in Ottawa, which is the national repository for Canadian history and records. Library and Archives Canada combines the collections, services, and staff expertise of the former National Library of Canada and the National Archives of Canada, as an easy, one-stop access to the texts, photographs, and other documents that reflect Canadian cultural, social, and political development. It includes the National Photography Collection, among other units, and eleven provincial archives scattered throughout Canada. The archives have the papers of many Irish Catholic politicians and correspondence between government departments and Irish Catholic leaders.

Genealogical collections include city/county/provincial directories, family histories, census records, birth/marriage/death records, church/parish records, land records/claims, and estate records. A number of Record Groups (RGs) are of special interest to Irish research. In Military/Naval Records, RG-8 includes materials relating to the War of 1812, medal registers, Fenian Raids, Red River and North West Rebellions, and the South African (Boer) War. Registers from 1866 to 1902 are available on microfilm. RG-9 covers Fenian Raids and bounty claims of militia veterans (on microfilm), although the information included is scanty and incomplete. RG-38 includes information on veterans' applications for land grants under the Volunteer Bounty Act for those who served in the Boer War. Among the Immigration Records there are few lists before 1865, however, passenger manifests since 1865 are included for major Canadian ports and some U.S. ports. Loyalist Sources includes muster rolls for Loyalist regiments.

In the National Photography Collection, collections of special interest to Irish research are the following: Robert F. H. Bruce Collection (black and white photographs, 1880–1900); Canada, Department of Manpower and Immigration Collection (black and white, 1958–1960); Canada, Immigration Branch Collection (black and white, 1894–1934); W. Worth Davis Collection (black and white, 1917–1919), with scenes in Ireland; Eva McKitrick Collection (black and white, 1898–1914); Irish Canadian Society; Edward Plunkett Taylor Collection (black and white, 1956–1970), which includes brewing operations in Ireland; Frank Curry Collection; Arnold Heeney Collection; W. J. Topley Collection; and Robert Magill

Collection. The Other Countries (Ireland) Collection includes World War I military photos of the Duchess of Connaught's Own and Irish Canadian Rangers.

The major research organization is the Canadian Association for Irish Studies (CAIS), which has been serving students of Irish culture for more than 30 years, seeking to foster and encourage the study of Irish culture in Canada. It also works to encourage young scholars, develop the next generation of Irish studies enthusiasts, and support discussion of current issues in Irish studies and culture through conferences, publications, and online resources. CAIS brings together all those who are committed to promoting Irish culture in Canada. Members of CAIS can be found in every province and territory of Canada. Members also come from Ireland, Northern Ireland, Britain, the United States, Europe, Asia, and Australasia. Every year, the Association convenes at one of Canada's universities for a celebration of Irish culture and heritage. CAIS publishes a semiannual scholarly journal, *Canadian Journal of Irish Studies*, a semiannual newsletter for members; information about CAIS's annual conference; and a Web site for discussion of matters relevant to CAIS members.

The Canadian Catholic Historical Association (CCHA), which calls itself "A National Society for the Promotion of Interest in the History of the Canadian Catholic Church," was founded in 1933 by James F. Kenney, a descendant of pre-famine immigrants, who was motivated by a love of his Canadian and Irish roots; he hoped CCHA would "bring to light the silent and neglected records of her [Canadian Catholic Church's] adventurous and spacious past." It has now become one of the primary agencies for researching and publishing Irish Catholic Canadian history, primarily through its journal, *Historical Studies* (started in 1984). Members belong either to the English Section of the CCHA, or to the French Section of La Société Canadienne D'Histoire de L'Eglise Catholique. Each section is autonomous and holds its own annual conference. The French section usually holds its conference in French-speaking cities in the autumn.

Across the Atlantic, in Dublin, there is the Association for Canadian Studies in Ireland (ACSI), established in May 1982 to support and encourage the study and understanding of Canada; its culture, history, and institutions; and the connections and parallels between the two countries. It sponsors an international conference every two years. ACSI strives to initiate and support courses on Canadian topics in universities and third-level colleges, facilitate the exchange of scholars and scholarship between Canada and Ireland, and encourage research and publication on Canada.

An interesting resource in Toronto is the United Empire Loyalists' Association of Canada, which preserves the history and traditions of the families who, as a result of the American Revolution, sacrificed their homes to retain their loyalty to the British. There is a specialized library on Loyalists of Canada, including materials relating to those Irish who were United Empire Loyalists and left the United States during and after the American Revolution (1776–1783). *The Loyalist Gazette* is published semiannually.

Colleges and Universities

Besides research organizations, several academic institutions have established research collections to support programs of Irish studies, but these archives and special collections are also invaluable to researchers interested in Irish history and literature. A major repository is in Vancouver, at the University of British Columbia. The library's Norman Colbeck Collection contains Irish materials that make up a relevant part of the collection of 1,508 volumes. The Anglo-Irish portion of this Collection includes writers from the Irish Literary Revival (Austin Clarke, Padraic Colum, Daniel Corkery, Thomas Crofton Croker, Lord Dunsany, Darrell Figgis, Robin Flower, Monk Gibbon, Oliver St. John Gogarty, Eva Gore-Booth, Robert Graves, Lady Gregory, Stephen Lucius Gwynn, Nesta Higginson [Moira O'Neill], Katharine Tynan Hinkson, Douglas Hyde, James Joyce, Emily Lawless, Sir Shane Leslie, Thomas MacDonagh, Anna Johnston MacManus [Ethna Carbery], Edward Martyn, George Moore, Sean O'Casey, Standish O'Grady, Seumas O'Kelly, Padraic Pearse, Joseph Mary Plunkett, Forrest Reid, Lennox Robinson, George Russell (Æ), George Bernard Shaw, James Stephens, John Millington Synge, Oscar Wilde, Jack Yeats, and W. B. Yeats. There is also a miscellaneous collection of 81 titles, including memoirs and biographies of prominent Irish figures, anthologies and histories of Irish literature, and sets of *Irish Statesman* (1923–1929) and *Dublin Magazine* (1923–1958), among other items. Also in British Columbia, there is the University of Victoria's McPherson Library, which contains the Dolmen Press Archive, with its Anglo-Irish literature material on John Yeats, Jack Yeats, W. B. Yeats, Padraic Colum, Philip Hobsbaum, Frank O'Connor, and Sir William Orpen.

Another important research collection is the Thomas Fisher Rare Book Library,

University of Toronto. Among its extensive holdings are books and material relating to Anglo-Irish revival. The Alfred Tennyson De Lury Collection of Anglo-Irish Literature contains his 1890–1941 papers (12 boxes and items), including his extensive correspondence with Anglo-Irish writers, his diaries, a bound volume of DeLury's memoranda, and Yeats's works. However, much of DeLury's correspondence received from Irish writers is in Trent University, Peterborough. The books in the Delury Collection include more than 5,000 volumes centered on works of W. B. Yeats and his contemporaries (Thomas Davis, J.C. Mangan, and Samuel Ferguson), plus a small sampling of William Carlton, strong holdings (about 30 volumes) of William Allingham, and nearly complete runs of Emily Lawless and Jane Barlow. There are materials on Yeats's contemporaries, including Lady Gregory, Katharine Tynan Hinkson, George Russell (Æ), George Moore, Standish O'Grady, Oliver St. John Gogarty, Douglas Hyde, Frank O'Connor, Austin Clark, Padraic Colum, Lord Dunsany, James Stephens, Sean O'Faolain, Liam O'Flaherty, and James Joyce, and records relating to the Abbey Theatre (Yeats, Lady Gregory, J. M. Synge, Lennox Robinson, St. John Ervine, Sean O'Casey, Edward Martyn, Seumas O'Kelly, among others), plus a collection of Abbey Theatre programs and ads (1903–1925). Also important are materials relating to Arthur Symons and Michael Field and a fine collection relating to Cuala Press. Periodicals include *The Yellow Book, The Hobby Horse, The Savoy, Samhain,* and *Beltaine.* Fisher also has the personal library of an Irish gentleman, Quentin Dick, which represents the country house library of the late eighteenth and early nineteenth century. The entire collection was acquired by William Henry Barrett, who donated it to the university.

In Hamilton, Ontario, McMaster University's Mills Memorial Library, in its William Ready Division of Archives and Research Collections, maintains material on the Anglo-Irish renaissance (1890–1939), which houses the holdings of several major writers, including W. B. Yeats, James Joyce, Samuel Beckett, Oscar Wilde, Lady Gregory, and J. M. Synge. There is also a small amount of manuscript material, including the holograph manuscript of Liam O'Flaherty's *The Informer*, letters and manuscripts of Samuel Beckett, letters of Jack Yeats, and Anglo-Irish literary periodicals. A copy of *Rules and Orders to be Observed in the Upper House[of Lords] of [the Irish] Parliament [between 1750 to 1760]* is also found.

Another set of material at McMasters University pertains to C. F. McLoughlin (1886–1967), a member of the United Arts Club in Dublin and an acquaintance of Jack Butler Yeats and other Irish writers. The collection consists of 37 letters from Jack Butler Yeats (1871–1957) to McLoughlin, a Christmas card signed by Yeats, and an unsigned, unaddressed post card, possibly from Yeats. Other items belonging to McLoughlin are a poem by Padraic Colum (1881–1972), "The Sea Bird to the Wave," which, McLoughlin notes, Colum wrote down for him one night at the Arts Club in 1958, and two manuscripts, one about the Irish troubles in 1916–1921 and the other a collection of Irish proverbs from a social evening at the Club in 1967. The first manuscript is the result of McLoughlin contacting veterans of the troubles and getting them to write down their memoirs in 1966. There are

also several items that do not appear to have a direct tie to McLoughlin, including a poem, "Sleep Song," by Frederick Robert Higgins (1896–1941), editor, poet, and playwright; a signed Christmas card from James Sullivan Starkey and E. F. Starkey to J. J. Chichester containing a printed poem, "1939," by Seumas O'Sullivan (1879–1958) and signed by O'Sullivan (O'Sullivan was the pseudonym of James Sullivan Starkey); a letter from Katharine Tynan (1861–1931), poet and novelist, to Mr. O'Leary; two letters from W. B. Yeats (1865–1939), one to Sara Allgood and the other to Mr. Farrell; poems on Christmas cards by Donagh MacDonagh (1912–1968), barrister, editor, poet, and playwright; a sermon by the Right Reverend Robert Wyse Jackson, bishop of Limerick; and an Irish National Theatre Society program.

For the music researcher, there is the Irish and Scottish Song Collection, collected by Harry S. Higginson [ca. 188–], a bound, 621-page manuscript of lyrics, with song lyrics by Thomas Moore, Robert Burns, Sir Walter Scott, Lever, Christie, and others. There is also a collection on English, Irish, Scottish and German composers, conductors, musicians, writers and publishers (1827–1957). Irish musicians include Michael William Balfe (1808–1870, a singer and the most successful composer of English operas in the nineteenth century; Thomas Moore (1779–1852), a poet, musician and composer of songs; and Vincent Wallace (1812–1865), a composer of operas and piano pieces.

In Halifax, the Patrick Power Library at St. Mary's University is a resource center for the study of the Irish, supplemented by the Thomas D'Arcy McGee Chair in Irish Studies. Stauffer Library at Queen's

University, Kingston, focuses on Anglo-Irish literature of the late nineteenth and early twentieth centuries and features 200 works by or about W.B. Yeats; 250 works by or about James Joyce; 270 works by or about George Bernard Shaw; works of Æ (George Russell), Maria Edgeworth, Thomas Croker, Katherine Tynan Hinkson, and Monk Gibbon; and a complete set of the Cuala Press publications. The University Archives has regional collections (House of Industry registers, Kingston General Hospital registers, and manuscript census microfilm, including Irish immigrants). Two collections include materials for Irish immigrant workers (Calvin Company and Tett Family). Literary papers include those of Katharine Tynan (1861–1931) and Æ (pseudonymn for George Russell). The Monk Gibbon Papers, the largest collection (almost 30 linear feet), with more than 300 items, include lectures, proofs, reviews, typescripts and galleys, illustrations, journals for travel books, manuscripts, news cuttings, correspondence, revisions, essays, radio scripts, letters from publishers, photocopy of AE diary, BBC debate, TV appearances, essays on K. Tynan, D. Hyde, etc., film/ballet essays, unpublished play by Gibbon, World War I materials, two Army journals, jotting for poems, copies of poems, and so on. Douglas Library also has materials on the Roger Casement controversy, ballet, an outline for a film on Jenny Lind, education, religion, Dublin Rebellion, miscellaneous notes on war and rebellion, historical diaries and letters regarding the Easter Rising of 1916, and Gibbon's poetry publications.

The holdings in the libraries at the University of New Brunswick in Fredericton include material from the Royal Irish Academy; Ordinance Survey Memoirs; immigrant lists to New Brunswick from the counties of Antrim and Londonderry (1834–1835); extracts from the Douglas Hyde manuscript diary in the National Library of Ireland, January-May 1891 (microfilm); and *Sources for the History of Irish Civilisation: Articles in Irish Periodicals,* ed. by Richard J. Hayes. 9 vols. Boston: G.K. Hall, 1970.

Killam Library, at Dalhousie University in Halifax, Nova Scotia, includes several items in the areas of general literature and history, as does the Queen Elizabeth II Library, Memorial University of Newfoundland, St. John's, which also keeps material on Gaelic literature, Anglo-Irish literature, Irish history, geography, politics, linguistics, and folklore, along with approximately 14,000 monograph titles and several hundred back runs of nineteenth- and early twentieth-century Irish newspapers and a number of statistical publications relating to population and land use.

The Rare Books and Special Collections at McLennan Library, McGill University, Montreal, has the William Butler Yeats collection, composed of first, early, and variant editions of most of his writings, some 86 volumes in all. There is some criticism and a few books by his brother Jack Butler Yeats. The Yeats material is complemented by a selection of material in the Colgate History of Printing Collection, published by the Cuala Press. This includes a complete run of *A Broadside* (1908–1915), early works by Yeats and others, and some of their more recent works dealing with the Celtic Twilight.

The University of Alberta in Edmonton has strong holdings in Anglo-Irish literature in its University Library, including a complete run of Cuala Press publications and the works of Liam O'Flaherty in original editions. The University of Ottawa's Morisset Library has a facsimile reprint of the James Joyce Archive and Irish Texts Society.

Religious Archives

Church archives remain one of the best sources of information on the Irish immigrant populations that settled in various communities throughout Canada. The richest unpublished material on the history of Irish Catholics in the country can be found in the major archdiocesan and diocesan archives in Canada. Particularly useful are the archives of the archdioceses of Toronto, Quebec, and St. John's, Newfoundland. Much of the correspondence from the Archives of the Archdiocese of Halifax is on microfilm at the Provincial Archives of Nova Scotia.

Collections of Irish Catholic newspapers are rare, but the Archives of the Archdiocese of Kingston has an excellent collection of originals of twentieth-century journals, as does St. Paul's College (University of Manitoba) and St. Michael's College (University of Toronto). Both Memorial University in St. John's and St. Mary's University in Halifax contain research centers for the study of Irish culture and folklore. Overseas, Irish Catholic materials for Canada can be found in the Secret Vatican Archives and in the Archives of the Propaganda Fide (Rome), the Public Record Office (London), and the Archives of the Archdiocese of Dublin.

For the Irish in the Anglican Church, a good source is at McMaster University, Hamilton, Ontario. In 1975, the university reached an agreement with the Anglican Diocese of Niagara to collect, describe, and preserve the records of the churches in the diocese as well as the nonactive diocesan records. Since that time the records of almost all of the churches in the diocese have been deposited at McMaster, accounting for more than 100 parishes. The diocese covers approximately 3,320 square miles in the province of Ontario. The most northerly towns are Harriston and Mount Forest, the western boundary is Nanticoke, the eastern perimeter is marked by Oakville, and the diocese extends southwards to Fort Erie. These records, which have been described by type of record and date, but are not indexed by personal name, are of particular value for genealogical research. They supply information concerning baptisms, confirmations, marriages, burials, and church membership. They also provide a unique perspective on the social history of the area. The earliest records date from the 1780s. In the early nineteenth century the Niagara region was part of the Diocese of Quebec and it belonged to the Diocese of Toronto from the 1830s until 1875. The Diocese of Niagara was established in 1875. For further information concerning Anglican Records in Ontario, see *Guide to the Holdings of the Archives of the Ecclesiatical Province of Ontario* (Agincourt, ON: Generation Press, 1990). Researchers should also be aware of the Gladys McAndrew collections, which relate to missionary work and residential schools undertaken by the Anglican Church in Canada from 1943 to 1954.

Martin J. Manning

See also: AMERICAN CONFERENCE FOR IRISH STUDIES; ANCIENT ORDER OF HIBERNIANS; PRESS, The IRISH ETHNIC; RESEARCH COLLECTIONS, IRISH, IN THE UNITED STATES

References

Clark, Dennis. *Hibernia America: The Irish and Regional Cultures*. Westport, CT: Greenwood, 1986.

Eleuterio-Comer, Susan K. *Irish American Material Culture: A Directory of Collections, Sites, and Festivals in the United States and Canada.* Westport, CT: Greenwood Press, 1988.

Glazier, Michael, ed. *Encyclopedia of the Irish in America.* Notre Dame, IN: University of Notre Dame, 1999.

Lester, DeeGee. *Irish Research: A Guide to Collections in North America, Ireland, and Great Britain.* Westport, CT: Greenwood Press, 1987.

Magocsi, Paul R., ed. *Encyclopedia of Canada's Peoples.* Toronto, ON: University of Toronto; published for the Multicultural History Society of Ontario, 1999.

Weaver, Jack W., and DeeGee Lester. *Immigrants from Great Britain and Ireland: A Guide to Archival and Manuscript Sources in North America.* Westport, CT: Greenwood Press, 1986.

RESEARCH COLLECTIONS, IRISH, IN THE UNITED STATES

Libraries and archives in the United States that contain major collections in Irish history, language, and literature vary greatly in their holdings. Some focus on contemporary material while others have older material that highlights specific areas. Large Irish collections that are suitable for serious research are often held in major universities or in research organizations. Interest in Irish research in the United States and around the world has coincided with the development of Irish studies programs in academic institutions and research organizations. Scholars and teachers with Irish research interests have been well served by an Irish studies organization, the American Conference for Irish Studies (formerly the American Committee for Irish Studies) that not only supports their work but also brings together academicians and others interested in Irish studies. The other positive sign is the number of active Irish cultural and historical societies, many of which work closely with the local academic community, that serve specialists and those whose interests are more broadly based. Although only a sampling of these collections, mainly the largest and most important, are described here, there are many other Irish collections, smaller in scale, many with only a few holdings useful to Irish research, in the United States and Canada.

Government Archives, Private Organizations, and Public Libraries

The oldest of these private organizations is the American Irish Historical Society, founded in Boston in 1897 to document the contributions of the Irish in the United States. It moved to its present New York City location in 1940. The society's library and archives hold an unparalleled collection of newspapers and periodicals chronicling the American Irish experience, including copies of the *Northern Star* and *Belfast Newsletter,* dating back to the late eighteenth century, and several early and mid-nineteenth century newspapers, such as *The Nation, The United Irishman,* and *The Dublin Penny Journal.* The library also has a unique collection of letters from Patrick Pearse and Charles Stewart Parnell, along with the archives of other societies and organizations and the personal papers of leading Irish Americans like Daniel F. Cohalan. The collection is complemented by works of art from such noted Irish artists as Nathaniel Hone, John Faulkner, George Russel (Æ), John Butler Yeats, Aloysius O'Kelly, and Augustus St. Gaudens; an extensive collection of Irish music and theater, including a taped interview with Brendan Behan that became his *Confessions of an Irish Rebel;* and documents and papers of Friends of Irish Freedom, the Land League, the Society of the Friendly Sons of St. Patrick, the Catholic Club, and the Guild of Catholic Lawyers. The library's journal, *The Recorder,* is usually published twice a year.

The wide range of programs created by the Irish American Cultural Institute (IACI) has developed an appreciation of Irish heritage among young and old. Founded in 1992 by Eoin McKiernan, professor of English at the College (now University) of St. Thomas in St. Paul, Minnesota, and supported by local philanthropist Patrick Butler, the IACI and its local branches sponsored the Irish Fortnight lecture series while the society's library houses more than 10,000 volumes, the most complete private collection of Irish and American Irish history and literature in the United States. There is also a small genealogical collection and appropriate reference volumes. In addition, the institute publishes the quarterly *Eire-Ireland,* an internationally acclaimed interdisciplinary journal; *Ducas,* a newsletter that offers members insight into the world of Irish culture, history, and the latest happenings at the IACI; and *IACI Bulletin,* a monthly e-mail newsletter that provides the latest news and events related to Irish and Irish-American culture and heritage.

The American Conference for Irish Studies (ACIS), established in 1962, is an interdisciplinary organization whose purpose is to encourage research and writing in Irish studies and to promote Irish studies as a distinct course of study in American colleges and universities. Beginning in 1963, ACIS has held an annual spring conference. In 1976, ACIS began to sponsor fall regional conferences in New England, the Middle Atlantic States, the South, the Midwest, and the West. A number of ACIS publications and affiliated publications, *The ACIS Newsletter,* the *Reprint Series,* and the *Irish Literary Supplement,* further encourage the development of Irish studies by providing news, reviews, bibliographies, and research reports and queries.

The Ward Irish Music Archives in Wauwatosa, Wisconsin, is a private collection that developed from one person's background in the field of Irish music. It has several major collections, most notably the Michael and Mary Comer Collection, which has more than 5,000 reel-to-reel, CD, cassette, LP, 45 rpm, and 78 rpm records on Irish labels, with material dating from the 1940s through 1980s, and the Ed and Cathy Ward Collection of more than 400 LPs, CDs, and cassettes collected since the 1970s, when Ward ran Irish Music Ltd., which distributed for numerous Irish recording labels. The collection also has more than 1,000 pieces of Irish sheet music, several thousand Irish and Irish-American 45 rpm and 78 rpm records, hundreds of songbooks and music periodicals, and a number of authentic antique phonographs and juke boxes. The Ward Irish Music Archives also houses the Irish Fest Collection, which has more than 6,000 items, including many of the LPs, tapes, and CDs collected from bands sending material to Irish Fest for possible booking, as well as the Irish Fest John McCormack Collection, one of the world's largest public collections of the great Irish tenor's recordings. This collection features 11 very rare cylinders from 1903 and 1904 and rare McCormack recordings on such labels as Odeon, Columbia, Regal, Okeh, Gramophone G & T, HMV, and Victor; advertisements; books; postcards; more than 40 photographs; and LPs. Finally, the Bing Crosby Collection is the largest public collection of his recordings and memorabilia outside Gonzaga University.

Washington, D.C., houses two national archival repositories. The Library of Congress has very strong holdings of Irish materials. Irish children's books are well represented in the general collection, and the library recently has begun purchasing titles in Gaelic. Many of the leading illustrators of children's books are represented in the collections. The library's microform collections include Irish biographies (1840–1940), with biographical entries for more than 180,000 persons. Proceedings of the Irish parliament are contained in *Printed Records of the Parliament of Ireland, 1613–1800.* The Local History and Genealogy Reading Room contains British and Irish parish registers, family histories, record society publications, and county histories of interest to genealogists, historians, and social historians. The numerous American, Irish, and English editions of *Blackstone's Commentaries on the Laws of England,* a primary text on the development of the English common law, form the core of the William Blackstone Collection.

In College Park, Maryland, outside Washington, D.C., the National Archives and Records Administration has substantial Irish materials throughout its invaluable holdings, including military records and ship and passenger records. For U.S. diplomatic relations with Ireland, the National Archives has the records of the U.S. Department of State relating to internal affairs in both the Irish Free State (1910–1929) and Ireland (1930–1944), on microfilm and in the hard copy texts. There are also records for U.S. consular posts in Ireland and material on U.S. postwar economic aid to that country.

The New York Public Library contains papers relating to the history of Ireland from the beginning of the Fenian movement to the proclamation of the Irish Republic. The papers include Sir Roger Casement's correspondence from 1904 to 1916, reflecting his activities in the United States as a spokesman for Irish independence and in Germany as a fund-raiser for the Irish Volunteers and organizer of the Irish Brigade. Also included are the papers of Jeremiah O'Donovan Rossa (1857–1904), relating to the history of the Irish Revolutionary Brotherhood and the Fenian Brotherhood; papers of Joseph McGarrity (1911–1937), relating to the Irish Republican Movement in the United States; papers of Patrick McCartan (1915–1949), including reports on conditions in Ireland after the Easter Rising in 1916 and copies of his reports as envoy of the Provisional Government of Ireland to the Soviet Union; letters to James O'Donoghue (1888–1912), chiefly regarding his 1912 book *Poets of Ireland* and other writings; papers of James McGurrin from his time as secretary of the Joint Committee on the Immigration Act of 1924; correspondence of Darmuid Lynch (1919–1922), relating to the Irish bond certificate campaign; and papers of William J. Maloney relating to Sir Roger Casement, the Irish Volunteer Movement, and Irish-American relations.

The library's Berg Collection contains some 30,000 printed volumes, pamphlets, and broadsides, and 2,000 linear feet of literary archives and manuscripts, representing the work of more than 400 authors. This collection has extensive manuscript holdings from the period 1820–1970. For the Irish, a short list would include W. B. Yeats, Lady Gregory, and Sean O'Casey (comprising the remnants of his fire-ravaged papers). Institutional papers found in the Berg include those of the Abbey Theatre.

Public libraries in cities with large Irish immigrant population, such as the Boston Public Library and the Chicago Public Library, have the collections of important Irish officials and organizations from their regions along with passenger and ship records and microfilmed copies of Irish newspapers and other publications that were created by those cities' ethnic presses. Also useful are state archives and diocesan church archives in cities with large Irish immigrant populations (e.g., Boston, Chicago, St. Louis, New York); the Embassy of Ireland in Washington, D.C., and the Irish consulate-generals in Boston, New York, Chicago, and San Francisco; the Ancient Order of Hibernians in America; Gaelic League–Irish American Clubs in the Detroit area; and local historical societies, such as the Irish American Heritage Center in Chicago and the Irish Family Historical Society Library in Newton, Massachusetts.

Colleges and Universities

Besides research organizations, several academic institutions have established research collections to support programs of Irish studies, but these archives and special collections are also invaluable to researchers interested in Irish history and literature.

The University of St. Thomas created the Center for Irish Studies (Larionad an Leinn Eireannaigh) in March 1996 to provide academic, scholarly, and cultural programs on Irish topics. The center's quarterly, *New Hibernia Review* (Iris Eireannach Nua), publishes articles of Irish and Irish-American interest. The center advances teaching and scholarship in Irish studies through an extensive publications and education program that provides a regional focus for the scholarly consideration of Irish culture. The university's significant library holdings in Irish literature complement its work. The rarest of the materials are held in the substantial Celtic Collection in O'Shaughnessy-Frey Library Center.

A collection that has grown to national renown as a guardian of Irish research is at Boston College, in Chestnut Hill, Massachusetts. It is presently considered the largest of its kind in North America and represents nearly every aspect of Irish history and literature in its Irish Collection. The foundation of the renowned Irish rare book collection at the Burns Library consists of books, pamphlets, manuscripts, newspapers, periodicals, and landholding records documenting Irish history and society from the late 1700s to the present. In recent years the collection has expanded into the areas of literature, art (especially the book arts), music, agricultural history, and economic history. Boston College also maintains very fine literary collections of Samuel Beckett, William Butler Yeats, and Seamus Heaney. To promote greater awareness and use of the impressive holdings, in 1991 the University established the Burns Library Visiting Scholar in Irish Studies Chair, which is open on an annual basis to scholars who have distinguished themselves in the areas of Irish history, culture, and life.

Part of the Irish Collection, although housed in a separate building, is the Irish Music Center, which provides access to the Irish Music Archives. These archives include traditional music recordings, sheet music, videotapes, and special collections of note, such as the Frederick M. Manning Collection of John McCormack and the Gaelic Roots Festival Collection. The Irish Music Archives include commercial and field recordings, video recordings, sheet music, manuscripts, photographs, memorabilia, and books about music.

DePaul University in Chicago has its Irish Collection, which began in 1927, when the Irish American Association's Chicago chapter donated books to the university library. The portion of the collection housed in Special Collections includes resources relating to key figures of the Irish literary renaissance, such as William Butler Yeats, Edward Martyn, and Lady Gregory, and the plays and poetry of those associated with the Abbey Theatre. The collection also contains numerous contemporary nineteenth-century histories of Ireland, travel accounts of the customs of the Irish as seen by British observers, various histories of Ireland printed in the United States during the late nineteenth and early twentieth centuries, and facsimilies and studies of *The Book of Kells.*

Harvard University has enormous, diverse Irish collections that cover Irish history, literature, drama, and language, including a Celtic Collection of nearly 400 rolls of microfilm copies of medieval Celtic manuscripts and some 40 volumes of more modern Irish and Welsh manuscripts.

The Archives of Irish America at New York University are a repository of primary research materials that aim to transform an understanding of the Irish migration experience and the distillation of American Irish ethnicity over the past century. The archives have been building on a pilot project started in 1997 to survey and collect materials related to the New York Irish community. The archives are housed in a climate-controlled building close to Glucksman Ireland House and are a part of New York University's Elmer Holmes Bobst Library.

Another repository of major Irish literary figures is at Kenneth Spencer Research Library at the University of Kansas. In 1953, the Library acquired Chicago attorney and book collector James F. Spoerri's collection of James Joyce; it contains nearly all the books and pamphlets devoted entirely to the author and his works and more than 200 books and periodicals containing critical and biographical material. Particularly rare items in the Joyce collection are copies of two broadsides, *The Holy Office* (1904 or 1905) and *Gas from a Burner* (1912), the latter bearing in holograph the author's story of the destruction of the first (Dublin) edition of *The Dubliners.* Also present is a copy of the first edition of *Ulysses* in French, signed by Stuart Gilbert, who oversaw the translation, and inscribed by Joyce to Gilbert's daughter Lucia on the date of issue; this copy has the novelty of bearing the strange post-mortem bookplate of the author. There is also a copy of the elusive *Pomes Penyeach* (Cleveland, 1931).

The William Butler Yeats collection has all of Yeats's works in first edition except the very scarce *Mosada* (1886) and *The Hour-Glass* (1903) as well as many later and variant editions and printings; books edited or containing contributions by Yeats; several score of books from Yeats's personal library (including copies of his own works with his annotations) or books that have close association in one way or another with the Yeats family; runs of periodicals with which Yeats was associated, such as *Samhain, The Arrow, Shanachie,* and *Dana;* and many single issues of periodicals in which material by or about Yeats appeared, including particularly elusive journals such as the *Kilkenny Monitor* and the *Irish Home Reading Magazine*.

The Irish literary renaissance figures other than Yeats are here in profusion: the Abbey Theatre plays; an extensive group of Abbey Theatre programs, more than 160 of them ranging from 1904 to 1922; the plays of Lady Gregory and John Synge; the complete output of the Dun Emer and Cuala presses, including broadsides and other ephemera; books and periodicals reflecting this national literary movement. Also, Irish history, from the seventeenth century to the revolutionary movements of the twentieth century, is extraordinarily well represented by newspapers, propaganda pamphlets, broadsheets, local history publications, songs, and scholarly works. Indeed, the Irish holdings of the O'Hegarty Library, taken together with the Joyce collection; the Sean O'Casey publications given to the library by Franklin D. Murphy, former Chancellor of the University; and the earlier Irish writers already in the collections, give Kansas outstandingly strong Hibernian resources.

At Notre Dame, which was founded as an educational institution for the Irish, several collections document that ethnic group's experiences. The O'Neill Collection of Traditional Irish Music is made up of over 1,000 volumes relating to Irish studies. While most relate in some way to Irish music, only about 150 of the volumes are exclusively devoted to music. The collection includes first editions of O'Neill's own works, notably *The Music of Ireland*. The majority of imprints are late nineteenth and early twentieth century, but the collection also includes some rare eighteenth century titles. With selected recent additions, this collection was Captain O'Neill's personal library, which he donated to Notre Dame in 1931.

The Monsignor Arthur T. Connolly Irish Collection at the Catholic University of America honors a man who was a major donor to the library. A child of Irish immigrants, Connolly amassed a considerable collection of material relating to Ireland and the Irish in America. These books, periodicals, and pamphlets, some 2,292 volumes, were among the first of his gifts to arrive at Catholic University in March 1916. In 1925, the University announcements described this material as "possibly the most complete collection of Irish history and literature in the United States." Of particular importance is the collection of more than 1,000 Irish pamphlets from about 1700 to 1850, which contains "a wide range of the popular literature of the early stages of Ireland's campaign for parliamentary reform and the first appearance of the Catholic Question. The content of these series and monographs depicts the mutually influential currents of agrarian, economic, social and cultural change which affected the national political process."

Chestnut Hill College in Philadelphia has an extensive collection of books, cassettes, and videos related to Ireland. These materials are housed on the second floor of the Logue Library in its Special Collections. The holdings concentrate on Irish literature, language, history, and culture.

In Atlanta, Emory University's Irish Rare Book Collection is an exceptional collection of rare books and periodicals that bolsters the university's Irish literary renaissance and contemporary poetry manuscript collections. The library holds numerous first editions and other rare volumes by Yeats, including many presentation copies to Lady Gregory that retain corrections in the poet's hand. A diverse and extensive collection of Samuel Beckett's volumes includes French, English, and American editions, along with early published work, significant variant editions, first serial publications, and various fine press editions. Emory also maintains a complete run of the *Honest Ulsterman* and holds large collections of works published by the Cuala Press, Dolmen Press, Peppercanister Press, Gallery Press, and other Irish literary presses. Among the contemporary poets, the Seamus Heaney collection of rare and special edition books stands out.

There are also other libraries, archives, and research organizations that maintain Irish materials. Researchers should examine their online catalogs and Web sites to get an overview of their collections. Most require special permission for visitors to use and most are open by appointment only. For a more complete listing, see *Subject Collections: A Guide to Special Book Collections and Subject Emphases as Reported by University, College, Public, and Special Libraries and Museums in the United States and Canada,* compiled by Lee Ash and William G. Miller, with the collaboration of Barry Scott, Kathleen Vickery, and Beverley McDonough, published in two volumes in 1993. To date, this is the latest edition but many of the institutions described in this encyclopedic work maintain websites that can be reviewed for more current information on their collections.

Martin J. Manning

See also: AMERICAN CONFERENCE FOR IRISH STUDIES; ANCIENT ORDER OF HIBERNIANS; PRESS, The IRISH ETHNIC; RESEARCH COLLECTIONS, IRISH, IN CANADA

References

Clark, Dennis. *Hibernia America: The Irish and Regional Cultures.* Westport, CT: Greenwood Press, 1986.

Glazier, Michael, ed. *Encyclopedia of the Irish in America.* Notre Dame, IN: University of Notre Dame, 1999.

Eleuterio-Comer, Susan K. *Irish American Material Culture: A Directory of Collections, Sites, and Festivals in the United States and Canada.* Westport, CT: Greenwood Press, 1988.

Hamer, Philip M., ed. *A Guide to Archives and Manuscripts in the United States.* New Haven, CT: Yale University; for the National Historical Publications Commission, 1961.

Lester, DeeGee. *Irish Research: A Guide to Collections in North America, Ireland, and Great Britain.* Westport, CT: Greenwood Press, 1987.

Malone, Russ. *Hippocrene U.S.A. Guide to Irish America.* New York: Hippocrene Books, 1994.

Weaver, Jack W., and DeeGee Lester. *Immigrants from Great Britain and Ireland: A Guide to Archival and Manuscript Sources in North America.* Westport, CT: Greenwood Press, 1986.

REYNOLDS, DEBBIE (1932–)

Born Mary Frances Reynolds on April 1, 1932, in El Paso, Texas, to parents of Irish ancestry (Raymond F. and Maxene Reynolds), Debbie Reynolds, the quintessential all-American girl-next-door bundle of energy, has entertained generations around the world. Seven years after she was born, the family moved to Burbank, California, when her father, a carpenter for Southern Pacific Railroad, was transferred. She attended John Burroughs High School in Burbank, and in 1948, at age 16, she was chosen Miss Burbank, lip-synching to a Betty Hutton recording. A Warner Brothers talent scout soon contacted her parents, and, after a screen test, Debbie was offered a $65-a-week contract. Jack L. Warner, the studio head, changed her name to "Debbie."

That same year, 1948, she made her film debut in *June Bride,* and in 1950, she played one of June Haver's sisters in *The*

Daughters of Rosie O'Grady. When Warner Brothers dropped her option, Debbie signed with MGM, and that studio determined to make her a success. She was cast in *Three Little Words* (1950), playing Helen Kane. In the musical *Two Weeks with Love,* that same year, she sang "Aba Daba Honeymoon" with Carleton Carpenter. The two recorded the song for MGM, and it became her first million-selling record.

Following other supporting roles in several other movies, MGM, seeing her star potential, cast her, at age 19, as the ingenue in *Singin' in the Rain* (1952). Though Gene Kelly was a strict taskmaster, the part made her a star. That stardom was solidified when she was teamed with her *Singin' in the Rain* costar Donald O'Connor in *I Love Melvin* (1953). She appeared in comedies and musicals throughout the 1950s, working with such stars as Frank Sinatra in *The Tender Trap* (1955) and husband Eddie Fisher in *Bundle of Joy* (1956). She and Fisher married September 26, 1955, and divorced in 1959, after Fisher's highly publicized affair with Elizabeth Taylor. Reynolds and Fisher had two children, the actress and writer Carrie Fisher and Todd Emmanuel Fisher.

In 1957, Debbie played the title role in *Tammy and the Bachelor,* and the movie produced her second million-selling recording "Tammy." In 1964, Debbie was cast in the lead of MGM's *The Unsinkable Molly Brown,* for which she was nominated for an Oscar. In 1969, she turned to television, starring in the short-lived *The Debbie Reynolds Show,* for which she received a Golden Globe nomination. In 1974, she divorced her second husband, Harry Karl, a wealthy shoe magnate and producer whom she had married in 1960; after the divorce, she discovered that she owed millions of dollars, and her determination to pay off the debt led to her Broadway debut in 1973 in the musical *Irene;* for that role she received a Tony nomination.

After her record-breaking performances in *Irene,* Debbie began working in Las Vegas and other resorts with her nightclub act. She also began collecting movie memorabilia for the Hollywood Movie Museum at the Debbie Reynolds Hotel and Casino, which opened in April 1995 but had to close in July 1997, the same year she received her star on the Hollywood Walk of Fame. Throughout the 1970s Debbie continued her one-woman act in nightclubs and on the stage, including the London Palladium. Another short-lived television show, *Aloha Paradise,* came in 1981, following a cameo appearance in ABC-TV's *The Love Boat.* She married for the third time to Richard Hamlett in 1985; the couple divorced in 1996. Reynolds appeared as a guest star in numerous television series and talk shows, and in the spring of 1989 she made a popular videocassette exercise tape, *Do It Debbie's Way.*

Throughout the 1990s and into the present, Reynolds has continued to work, appearing regularly in a variety of feature films, television specials, and animated movies, including *In and Out* (1997); *These Old Broads* (2001), where she appeared with Elizabeth Taylor and Shirley MacLaine; and in a recurring role in the television series *Will & Grace,* for which she received an Emmy nomination.

An indefatigable performer, Reynolds has said, "I'm going to perform till I drop. Then they can stuff me like Trigger and you'll find me in my own museum. Put a quarter in my mouth and I'll sing 'Tammy'."

Gary Kerley

See also: KELLY, Gene

References

Parrish, John Robert, and Michael R. Pitts. *Hollywood Songsters: Singers Who Act and Actors Who Sing: A Biographical Dictionary.* New York: Routledge, 2003.

Purciello, Maria. "Reynolds, Debbie." In *Women and Music in America Since 1900: An Encyclopedia.* Westport, CT: Greenwood Press, 2002.

Reynolds, Debbie, with Bob Thomas. *If I Knew Then.* Bernard Geis Associates/Random House, 1962.

Reynolds, Debbie, and David Patrick Columbia. *Debbie: My Life.* New York: William Morrow, 1988.

Riggs, Thomas, ed. "Reynolds, Debbie." *Contemporary Theater, Film and Television.* Vol. 31. Detroit: Gale Group, 2000.

RHODE ISLAND

The smallest state in the Union, the State of Rhode Island and Providence Plantations was the first of the 13 colonies to declare independence from Britain, but it was the last to ratify the Constitution and achieve statehood (May 29, 1790). Rhode Island, also known by its original Indian name Aquidneck Island, is the largest island in Narragansett Bay, and Providence became the sole capital in 1900 (Newport had been the joint capital since 1854).

Giovanni da Verrazano was the first explorer to visit the area during a voyage that started off the coast of the Carolinas and ended up in Nova Scotia. Subsequent visits of note included those of the English explorer John Smith and the Dutchman Adriaen Block, and then in 1620 settlers from the Plymouth Colony and Massachusetts Bay ventured into the region to trade with local Indian tribes. The Narragansett was the largest of a number of tribes in the area, and the first permanent white settlement in Rhode Island, Providence, was founded in 1636 on land Roger Williams purchased from the tribe.

Williams had left the Massachusetts Bay Colony wishing to establish a community that was markedly freer in political and religious outlook. Enough fellow nonconformists followed suit in settling in the bay area that King Charles II of England granted a charter in 1663 that provided the most liberal form of self-government to be granted during the colonial era. Other nonconformists included Anne and William Hutchinson and William Coddington, all of whom founded Portsmouth in 1638 as a haven for Antinomians; thus, Portsmouth became the first town in America founded by a woman.

After surviving King Philip's War (1675–1676), in which Providence was burned by Indian forces, the colony had, by the late seventeenth and early eighteenth century consolidated itself as a prosperous region, and Newport and Providence had become two of the busiest ports in the New World. Despite a strong agricultural character, the colony had a sophisticated and expansive involvement in the slave trade, was engaged in smuggling, and evaded the British Navigation Acts. As the British government tightened economic and navigational controls in the aftermath of the Seven Years' War, Rhode Island was prominent in the evolving resistance movement and most famously scuttled and burned the British customs ship *Liberty* (1769) and burned the British ship *Gaspee* (1772). The first to select delegates to attend the Continental Congress, Rhode Island was also the first colony to declare independence from the British on May 4, 1776.

The aftermath of the American Revolution witnessed reforms that aimed to reduce anti-Catholicism (1783) and emancipate slaves (1784). The antislavery of the Quakers and a widespread anti-federalism contributed to its being the last of the original 13 states to ratify the U.S. Constitution, on May 29, 1790, by two votes.

In the same year, America's first successful water-powered cotton mill, owned by Samuel Slater, ensured Rhode Island's involvement in the Industrial Revolution, and industry in the state expanded into jewelry, textiles, and silverware. From the mid-1820s onward, large numbers of Irish Catholics settled in Rhode Island, and the numbers continued to increase in step with works projects such as Fort Adams in Newport and the Blackstone Canal (both started in 1824), railroad construction (beginning in 1833), and the growing number of textile mills and metals factories.

As the state industrialized and urbanized, existing laws concerning such issues as voting were increasingly perceived to be antiquated. By 1840, for example, some 60 percent of free adult males were disenfranchised. As a result, participants in Dorr's Rebellion (led by Thomas Wilson Dorr) drafted a People's Constitution in 1841, and Dorr was elected governor in 1842. Meeting with resistance from largely rural politicians, incumbent governor Samuel Ward King was reinstated through a separate election. Dorr's response, an attempt to seize the state's arsenal in May 1842, failed and resulted in his exile. The conservative reaction to the rebellion led to a revised constitution that limited the influence of the working classes and immigrants. Those of foreign birth were disenfranchised, as land was required to hold office or to vote. This was, in many ways, one of the more nakedly nativist actions aimed largely at the Irish.

In many senses, assimilation was slow and difficult compared with the process in many other states because of this conservatism and difficulty in accessing the vote. The Know-Nothings compounded this resentment against immigrants and the "Irish problem" in the 1850s, and prejudice was fanned by the state's newspapers. In 1855, James Smith, a Know-Nothing candidate was elected mayor, and the Know-Nothings planned to raid a Catholic convent, but this attempt met with armed Irish resistance. Relative levels of disempowerment meant that many Irish did not support abolition during the Civil War, fearing competition from the freed slaves for lower-paid jobs. In the postwar years, Irish immigration remained steady but numbers fell proportionally as French Canadians, Germans, and later southern and eastern Europeans (particularly Italians) arrived in large numbers.

One of the first strikes in America occurred in Rhode Island in 1885 and resulted in messy attempts to bring in strikebreakers and riots. The factory was owned by Joseph Bannigan, a prominent businessman and philanthropist who had migrated from Ireland during the Famine and had a strong tradition of hiring Irish workers and fostering Irish community. When Bannigan was compelled to cut wages, the recently formed Knights of Labor protested at the plant and Irish religious leaders were asked to intervene. Bannigan went on to become president of the U.S. Rubber Company. Jobs at the turn of the century were provided by a variety of businesses from the state, but the large mills declined in the early twentieth century.

Intragroup tensions remained, notably between Irish communities and the Italians and French Canadians, but overall the large numbers of Catholics (Rhode Island became predominantly Catholic before 1910) began to translate into representation, and James Higgins, an Irish Catholic Democrat, was elected governor in 1906.

In general, the state has been a reliable Democratic state since the Depression years. In recent years it has been linked with the Kennedy clan, as Ted Kennedy's son, Patrick, was elected to the state House of Representatives in 1988 and has represented the state in the U.S. House of Representatives since 1995. Rhode Island is one of a number of states that signed on to the MacBride Principles, guidelines for U.S. companies investing in Northern Ireland.

The state population stood at 1,048,319 in the 2000 U.S. Census. People with Irish ancestry make up 18.4 percent of the state population, the second largest ancestry group after Italian-Americans (19 percent). As a result, the state has a high concentration of Catholicism.

Sam Hitchmough

References

Doyle, David Noel, and Owen Dudley
    Edwards, eds. *America and Ireland,*
    1776–1976: The American Identity
    and the Irish Connection. Westport, CT:
    Greenwood Press, 1980.
McLoughlin, William, *Rhode Island, A History.*
    New York: W. W. Norton, 1986.
Miller, Kerby A., *Emigrants and Exiles: Ireland*
    and the Irish Exodus to North America.
    Oxford: Oxford University Press, 1988.
Kenny, Kevin, *The American Irish.* London:
    Longmans, 2000.

ROBINSON, MARY (1944–)

Mary (Bourke) Robinson has shown the world what an Irishwoman can achieve. In a distinguished career, Robinson has displayed a new paradigm of female leadership,

With the swearing in of Mary Robinson as Ireland's first woman president, on December 3, 1990, a watershed was reached in Irish politics. After a productive seven-year tenure, she resigned from the presidency in September, 1997, to assume leadership of the United Nations High Commission on Human Rights. Since 2003, she has been president of Realizing Rights: The Ethical Globalization Initiative (New York City). (Patrick Bertschmann, Photo Bianco, 1998, Geneva. With kind permission.)

a paradigm melded from traditional Irish values of justice and activism, as well as an abiding pledge to global human rights. Foremost an advocate, Robinson launched a big public career, first in the service of Ireland and then in the service of the world. In 1990, when she famously placed a lighted candle in the kitchen window of Áras an Uachtaráin (the official presidential residence in Dublin), Robinson demonstrated a proud continuity with the rituals of an ancient race and an unwavering confidence in Ireland's rising presence on the international stage. This simple gesture was more than a beacon of hope: it was a profession of faith in Ireland and in Ireland's global role in the coming years, a role she would heartily invest with her own moral example.

Herself a child of privilege, Mary Therese W. Bourke was to become an advocate for the underprivileged. She was born in Ballina, Co. Mayo, into an educated Irish Catholic family on May 21, 1944; both parents, Aubrey de Vere Bourke and Tessa O'Donnell Bourke, were physicians. Her late father, Dr. Aubrey Bourke (Edinburgh University, 1938), was the first general practitioner to use penicillin in the west of Ireland in 1941. Mary Bourke's brothers are established professionals in the fields of medicine and law: Oliver, in medical practice in New Zealand; Henry, a barrister; and Adrian, a solicitor, who in 1991 served as president of the Law Society. (A fourth brother, Aubrey Bourke, died some years ago.) Her paternal line, the Hiberno-Norman Bourkes, has flourished in Mayo since the thirteenth century. By tradition, the Clan Bourke is decidedly political, either as rebels against the English crown or as knighted servants. Some Bourkes are linked to the Mayo Land League and the Irish Republican Brotherhood; others have been knighted by Queen Elizabeth II for meritorious colonial service. Some Bourkes have been Catholic nuns; others have been Anglicans. It fell to a talented young woman of the Bourke line to take the clan to the summit of Irish political power in the 1990s.

Mary Bourke's career was finely planned, and she had the best international training any 'comer' could garner, even if access required special handling at the highest levels of the Irish government. To matriculate at Trinity College, University of Dublin, from which Catholics were traditionally barred by order of its founder, Elizabeth I, the young Mary Bourke obtained permission from John Charles McQuaid, D.D., Archbishop of Dublin. She graduated with a law degree from the King's Inns Dublin (LLB, 1967); she then pursued further legal training in the United States, where she earned a Master of Legal Letters (LLM) at Harvard University in 1968. Shortly thereafter, she was appointed Reid Professor of Constitutional and Criminal Law at Trinity College, an enviable appointment for a young woman yet in her twenties.

Barrister Mary Bourke began her public career in law and human rights advocacy in 1969, with her election as an independent candidate to the Irish Senate (Seanad Éireann). In this role, Senator Bourke had valuable public access and an official platform from which to launch several bold campaigns for the reform of Irish law. Then, as now, she strove to liberalize and modernize her nation, and she typically aligned herself with liberal, humanitarian, and feminist issues. An attractive and vocal new presence in the national press, Bourke proved to be a forceful speaker. She advocated for women's right to participate as jurors in the legal process; for the legal and public availability of contraceptive devices (a hotly contested issue); for the admission of married women into Irish civil service; and, in one of her most controversial campaigns, for the decriminalization of homosexuality.

In 1970, Senator Mary Bourke married Nicholas K. Robinson, a lawyer, conservationist, and published authority on eighteenth-century graphic arts, especially caricature; their union produced a daughter and two sons.

As an Irish senator (1969–1989), Mary Robinson was something of an electric presence among a conservative and traditionalist body of mostly male politicians. She was more than a breath of fresh air: she was a force to be reckoned with. She served on several parliamentary committees, including the Joint Committee on European Community Secondary Legislation (1973–1989). In 1973, she was a member of the English Bar (Middle Temple). In 1979, she was elected to the Dublin City Council. In 1980, she was senior counsel, English Bar (Middle Temple). And by this time, Robinson had garnered broad media attention when she changed her status as an independent senator by joining the Labour party. From 1983 to 1985, she served on the parliamentary Joint Committee on Marital Breakdown. In 1988, Robinson and her husband founded the Irish Centre for European Law at Trinity College, Dublin University. After many years of vigorous political engagement, marked equally by victories and losses, Robinson did not seek reelection to the Irish Senate in 1989.

It was in 1990 that Robinson's career saw a huge advance. At the urging of her colleagues in the Labour Party, she decided to run for the presidency of Ireland. This was a bold and courageous decision; indeed, Robinson became the first Labour nominee for the Irish presidency and the nation's first woman candidate. After a colorful and closely reported presidential race, Robinson became the first Labour candidate, the first woman, and the first non-Fianna Fáil candidate to win the Irish presidency in the history of contested presidential elections. RTÉ (Ireland's radio and television broadcasting network), memorably celebrated Robinson's victory by preempting its usual coverage of the day's

Angelus to carry her victory speech live. President Mary Robinson was inaugurated as Ireland's seventh president on December 3, 1990; she signed her Declaration of Office with the quill pen of Eamon de Valera, third president of Ireland (1959–1973). To her formidable new responsibilities as head of state, Robinson brought broad knowledge in international law and politics, complemented by many years of regional (grassroots) activism. Ireland's new president knew the country, its urban and rural history, its mix of people, and its future challenges. Clearly, she was keen and well-positioned to shepherd Ireland into the new modern century.

In her tenure as Ireland's president, Robinson proved to be pleasantly popular, even among former contrarians. Brian Lenihan, Ireland's defense minister and Robinson's chief rival in her presidential campaign, would eventually admit that Robinson proved to be the better national leader. To her credit, she reimagined and redefined the Irish presidency, she sought out opportunities to meet with political colleagues of all hues and views, and she aimed to present Ireland as a worthy newcomer on the global stage. Her chief concerns were stemming the Irish diaspora (the sad exit of Irish to other lands, owing chiefly to Irish unemployment) and improving Irish relations throughout the globe. To these ends, in 1993, Robinson became the first Irish president to visit Queen Elizabeth at Buckingham Palace; and at her official Dublin home, Áras an Uachtaráin, she hosted visiting British royals, including Charles, Prince of Wales, as well as the Christian Brothers and the Gay & Lesbian Equality Network. In a diplomatically unacknowledged trip in 1992, Robinson visited the war-ridden zones of Northern Ireland; and in 1993 in Belfast, she was photographed publicly shaking the hand of Gerry Adams, Sinn Féin president, local MP, and reputed member of the Irish Republican Army Council.

Remarkably, Robinson was the first Irish head of state to visit Rwanda in the aftermath of its 1994 atrocities. She was also the first Irish head of state to visit Somalia after its troubles in 1992, and she received the CARE Humanitarian Award in recognition of her efforts for that country. During her tenure, she signed into law two new bills dear to her humanitarian beliefs: a bill to liberalize public access to contraceptives and a law to decriminalize homosexuality. Snarls from rivals notwithstanding, Robinson's administration drew high praise from such prominent Irish statesmen as Albert Reynolds (Fianna Fáil, 1992–1994), John Bruton (Fine Gael, 1994–1997), and Bertie Ahern (Fianna Fáil, 1997-).

Throughout a distinguished seven-year tenure as president of Ireland, Robinson made a serious contribution to Ireland's developing presence as a globally-minded country, with productive economic and political links beyond its own borders. She also placed special emphasis on the needs of developing and underdeveloped countries, thus linking the history of An Gorta Mor (The Great Hunger or The Irish Famine) to modern-day devastation. Her vision as a politician was global and humanitarian; it created bridges of partnership among developed, developing, and underdeveloped countries and their leaderships.

Robinson resigned the Irish presidency on September 12, 1997, three months before the end of her term, explaining that her vision for advancement in human rights required different measures and other opportunities, opportunities found in her pending new post in Geneva as high commissioner at the United Nations. As she said in her delivery of the Romanes Lectures at Oxford, in an address titled, "Realizing Human Rights" (November 1997), her new role with the United Nations presented daunting challenges, and she concluded her lecture with inspiring words from James Fraser's *The Golden Bough* on the harmonious intersection of destiny and ambition.

As high commissioner, Mrs. Robinson prioritized the reform proposal of Secretary-General Kofi Annan to integrate human rights concerns in all the activities of the United Nations. She also oversaw an important reorientation of the priorities of her own office by refocusing its initiatives at the country and regional levels. As part of this new focus, her first year as High Commissioner included trips to South Africa, Colombia, Cambodia, China, and other countries. A memorable moment of Robinson's tenure was her emotional report at a press conference on the staggering conditions she witnessed first-hand in the villages of Rwanda. (A political colleague judged her delivery moving and magnificent.)

In 1998, Robinson was elected Chancellor of the University of Dublin. And in September 1998, she won high praise for herself and her office as the first high commissioner to visit China, where she signed an agreement whose goal was a wide-ranging program of cooperation to improve human rights in that country. Under a similar process, Robinson and her office sent human rights workers to Indonesia and to countries in Europe and Africa. Of special significance, High

Commissioner Robinson strengthened human rights monitoring in high-conflict areas, such as Kosovo (Federal Republic, Yugoslavia). During her tenure as Human Rights Commissioner, Robinson also visited Tibet to meet with the 14th Dalai Lama, Tenzin Gyatso. Also at this time, Robinson denounced the Irish system of permits for non–European Union immigrants as "bonded labor," and she condemned the continuing use of the death penalty in the United States, which she regarded as a human rights violation. Throughout her term, Mary Robinson maintained an energetic, committed staff, which monitored human rights or provided technical assistance to more than 20 countries.

In 2001, Mary Robinson announced her intention to leave the UN Human Rights Commissioner post: "I believe that I can, at this stage, achieve more outside of the constraints that a multinational organisation inevitably imposes" (*Guardian Weekly*, March 22, 2001). In 2002, Robinson was awarded the Sydney Peace Prize for consistent support of the world's vulnerable and disadvantaged.

Dating from 2003, Mary Robinson's chief focus has been her ambitious agenda as president of the entity Realizing Rights: The Ethical Globalization Initiative (EGI), based in New York City. Some of EGI's supporters include Bishop Desmond Tutu, Jimmy Carter, and Musimbi Kanyoro, Secretary General of the World YWCA. EGI's partners, board, and advisory council include prominent business leaders, educators, and human rights theorists and practitioners throughout the world. Working as a dedicated cross-cultural team of concerned specialists, the EGI consortium

has adopted a broad agenda, driven by a three-pronged mission. It seeks to "realize human rights" and "sustainable growth" in underdeveloped countries, with an initial focus on Africa, by rectifying imbalances in global trade and development policies, global inequities in health with special focus on HIV/AIDS in Africa, and barriers to more humane international migration. "The three principal issues which inform the work of EGI invite practical opportunities to influence policy; each of these issues has reached a critical tipping-point where immediate decisions will have serious, long-term consequences for us all" (Mulvihill interview, New York City, May 4, 2005). A detailed statement of EGI's programmatic goals and its continuing results are available at the EGI website (www.eginitiave.org).

A recipient of numerous honors and awards throughout the world, Mary Robinson is Chair of the Council of Women World Leaders, the International Board of the International Institute for Environment & Development, the Fund for Global Human Rights, and the Irish Chamber Orchestra; Honorary President of Oxfam International; Vice President of the Club of Madrid; Patron of the International Community of Women Living with AIDS; a member of the Leadership Council of the United Nations Global Coalition on Women and AIDS, the Vaccine Fund Board of Directors, the Advisory Board of the Earth Institute, the Royal Irish Academy in Dublin, and the American Philosophical Society; Professor of Practice in International Affairs at Columbia University in New York City; and Extraordinary Professor, University of Pretoria, South Africa.

In 2004, Mary Robinson gave the 6th Sadat Lecture for Peace at the University of Maryland; her published address, "The Journey to Peace: Finding Ourselves in the Other," included memorable words on the United States and on individual responsibility for global human rights:

> I am . . . encouraged by examples of innovative thinking here in the United States. Some of you may be aware of a report issued last year by the Migration Policy Institute, titled *America's Challenge,* which, among other recommendations, proposes the creation of an independent national commission on integration to address the specific challenges of national unity presented by post-September 11 events and actions. . . . The challenges ahead are formidable, the familiar catalogue of problems and future obstacles remains to be faced. Yes, we have a long road to travel before human rights will be secured for all. But I am convinced that this is a time when civil society world-wide can make its voice heard as never before."

Robinson also delivered the 2005 Thomas J. Volpe lecture at St. Francis College, Brooklyn Heights, New York, where she spoke on the critical intersection of globalization, nation development, and human rights. Also in 2005, Robinson was a guest speaker at Boston College, Robsham Theatre, where she spoke on "Human Rights and Justice for Refugees," as a part of the lecture series sponsored by the Center for Human Rights and International Justice. In May 2005, she was awarded the first "Outspoken" award from the International Gay & Lesbian Human Rights Commission. On October 14, 2007, she was the keynote speaker at the University of Notre Dame conference, "Race and Immigration in the New Ireland" (October 14-October 17, 2007, Washington Hall), sponsored by the Keough-Naughton Institute for Irish Studies (http://newsinfo.nd.edu/content .cfm?topicid=24786).

In a 2005 interview, she expressed abiding optimism and a strong, forward-looking vision for humanity:

> There are, of course, many urgent and also accessible opportunities for change; there are new policies, new bills, new laws in motion—all striving to restore human dignity throughout the world. This is a tremendous, long process, one requiring broad resources, talent, and genuine sympathy. Yet, results are possible. This has been the commitment of my public life, this struggle; and with the support and direction of many valuable associates, I am following that same track now because I feel—and I see—that we're onto something good and necessary here" (Mulvihill interview, May 4, 2005).

Maureen E. Mulvihill

References

Brennan, Valerie. "Here's to You, Mrs. Robinson!" *Studies: An Irish Quarterly* 87, no. 345 (1998): 7–14.

Bresnihan, Valerie. "Symbolic Power of Ireland's President Robinson." *Presidential Studies Quarterly* 19 (1999): 250–262.

Finlay, Fergus. "Beating the Big Guys." In *Snakes and Ladders.* Dublin: New Island Books, 1998.

Finlay, Fergus. *Mary Robinson: A President with a Purpose.* Dublin: O'Brien Press, 1991.

Horgan, John. *Mary Robinson: An Independent Voice.* Dublin: O'Brien Books, 1997.

Hug, Chrystel, *Politics of Sexual Morality in Ireland.* New York: St. Martin's Press, 1999.

Kenny, Mary. *Goodbye to Catholic Ireland: A Social, Personal and Cultural History from the Fall of Parnell to the Realm of Mary Robinson.* London: Sinclair-Stevenson, 1997.

McQuillan, Mary. *Mary Robinson: A President in Progress.* Dublin: Gill and Macmillan, 1994.

Mulvihill, Maureen E. 2005. Interview with Mary Robinson. On-site, May 4th, Ethical Global Initiatives office, New York City.

O'Leary, Olivia, and Helen Burke. *Mary Robinson: The Authorised Biography.* London: Hodder & Stoughton, 1998.

O'Sullivan, Michael. *Mary Robinson: The Life and Times of an Irish Liberal.* Dublin: Blackwater Press, 1993.

Purcell, Betty. "Images of the Irish Woman." *The Crane Bag* 4, no. 1 (1980).

Quinlan, Deirdre. *Mary Robinson: A President in Progress.* Dublin: Gill & Macmillan, 1994.

Quinn, David. "An Icon for the New Ireland: An Assessment of President Robinson." *Studies: An Irish Quarterly* (Autumn 1997).

Siggins, Lorna. *Mary Robinson: The Woman Who Took Power in the Park.* Edinburgh: Mainstream Publishing, 1997.

Stewart, Bruce, compiler. "Mary Robinson." *EirData.* http://www.pgil-eirdata.org/html/pgil_datasets/index.htm (accessed September 1, 2007).

ROWAN, STEPHEN C. (1808–1890)

Stephen C. Rowan was born in Dublin, Ireland, on December 25, 1808, to John Rowan and Mary (Clegg). Appointed midshipman in the U.S. Navy on February 1, 1826, he participated in a four-year cruise aboard the *Vincennes* (1826–1830), the first time an American man-of-war had circumnavigated the globe. Upon returning to the United States, Rowan served aboard revenue cutters in New York and in the West Indies on the schooner *Shark* and the sloop *Vandalia.* In 1832, Rowan was promoted to midshipman. Actively engaged in naval operations on Florida rivers during the Seminole War, he was promoted to lieutenant in 1837.

Rowan spent the next few years on coastal survey duties, serving aboard the *Delaware,* off Brazil, and on the *Ontario,* in the Mediterranean. He took an active role in the Mexican War, serving as executive officer of the *Cyane* during the capture of Monterey on July 7, 1846, and in the occupation of both San Diego and Los Angeles.

Portrait of Stephen C. Rowan, an admiral in the United States Navy who served during the Mexican-American War and the American Civil War. (National Archives)

While operating in the Gulf of California, the *Cyane* captured 20 blockade runners and destroyed several enemy gunboats.

After the war, Rowan served as ordnance inspector at the New York Navy Yard from 1850 to 1853, returning to that post in 1858 to 1861. During the interim he commanded the supply ship *Relief* and the receiving ship *North Carolina.* He was promoted to commander on September 14, 1855.

As captain of the steam-sloop *Pawnee* at the outbreak of the Civil War, he made gallant attempts to relieve Fort Sumter and to burn the Norfolk Navy yard. During the latter engagement, he fired the first shot from a naval vessel in the war. In the fall of

1861, he helped capture the forts at Hatteras and Ocracoke inlets; then, taking command of a flotilla in the North Carolina sounds, he cooperated in the capture of Roanoke Island in February 1862. In recognition of his service and gallantry, Rowan was simultaneously promoted to captain and commodore on July 16, 1862; he then supported the Union capture of Elizabeth City, Edenton, and New Bern. During the summer of 1863, he commanded *New Ironsides* on blockade duty off Charleston, South Carolina, engaging enemy batteries at Forts Wagner and Moultrie. In August, Rowan assumed command of all Federal forces in the North Carolina sounds.

When the war ended, Rowan was promoted to rear admiral, receiving his commission on July 25, 1866. He served as commandant of the Norfolk Navy Yard until 1867, when he assumed command of the Asiatic Squadron. Returning in 1870, he was appointed vice admiral in August of that year. Rowan followed this with command of the New York Navy Yard, a position he held from 1872 to 1879. Subsequently, Rowan served as president of the Board of Naval Examiners (1879–1881), governor of the Naval Asylum in Philadelphia (1881), chairman of the Lighthouse Board (1883), and superintendent of the Naval Observatory, Washington, D.C., from 1882 until his retirement in 1889.

Vice Admiral Rowan died in Washington, D.C., on March 31, 1890. His wife, Mary Stark, had died in 1875. Rowan and his wife had one child who survived infancy, Major Hamilton Rowan of the United States Army. Rowan is buried in the Oak Hill Cemetery, Georgetown.

Tim Lynch

See also: AMERICAN CIVIL WAR

References

Ayers, S. C. *Sketch of the Life and Services of Vice Admiral Stephen C. Rowan.* Cincinnati: Legion Press, 1910.

Headly, J. T. *Farragut and Our Naval Commanders.* New York: E. B. Treat, 1867.

RYAN, ABRAM JOSEPH (1839–1886)

Abram Joseph Ryan was born on August 15, 1839 (although some conflicting reports suggest that he was born on that date in 1838) in Norfolk, Virginia. The son of Irish immigrants, he trained as a Catholic priest in New York, and was thereafter almost invariably referred to simply as "Father Ryan."

At the outbreak of the American Civil War, Ryan joined the Confederate Army in

Portrait of Abram Joseph Ryan, poet and Roman Catholic priest. His support for the Confederate Army earned him the nickname "Poet-Priest of the Confederacy." (Library of Congress)

the role of chaplain. Despite the ferocious animosities of that struggle, he became known for his willingness to tend spiritually to members of either army. During his service he wrote poetry, some of which began to attract an enthusiastic public in the South. Yet his greatest success as a poet came at the war's conclusion when, in his reaction to the defeat of the South, he wrote the poem "The Conquered Banner." It became an instant success in the South and was often sung in public gatherings, both civil and religious. Despite never again writing a poem that was equally successful, Ryan's deft poetry about the American South, and about his own theological interests, was very popular in the years immediately following the Civil War. His major collection *Poems: Patriotic, Religious, and Miscellaneous* was widely read and frequently reprinted.

After the war, Ryan engaged in both religious ministry and journalistic activity. He traveled widely in the South in the pursuance of these interests, residing at various times in New Orleans, Louisiana; Augusta, Georgia; and Mobile, Alabama. His most prominent journalistic work was done during his stay in Georgia, where he founded, and for a time edited, a weekly paper called *The Banner of the South*. During these years he also engaged in extensive lecture tours, both in the North and the South, which were well attended. It was commonly attested of his public speaking—theological or cultural—that he combined geniality, force of intellect, and personal appeal. When Ryan died on April 22, 1886, in Louisville, Kentucky, he was mourned as a loss to both the poetical and religious life of the United States.

Ryan's major contribution to America was through his poetry. Although his prominence as a poet has diminished significantly since his own time, he was once one of the most popular poets in America. He is also notable as the most popular poet of the rebellious South, and through his poetry he gave expression to much of the cultural life for which the people of the Confederacy believed they were fighting. Although he was devotedly an American southerner, he occupies an important role in an often underrepresented aspect of Irish-American life: that of the Irish-Americans affiliated with the Confederacy. Because so many Northern soldiers were proudly Irish, a misconception has arisen that the Irish Americans were united in support of the United States against the Confederacy. But Ryan, through his unparalleled popularity as a poet of the South, serves to correct this oversimplification of Irish-American participation in the Civil War.

Andrew Goodspeed

See also: AMERICAN CIVIL WAR

References
Haegney, Harold. *Chaplain in Gray*. New York: P. J. Kenedy & Sons, 1958.
Painter, Franklin V. N. *Poets of the South*. New York: American Books, 1903.
Ryan, Abram Joseph. *Poems: Patriotic, Religious, and Miscellaneous*. New York: P. J. Kenedy & Sons, 1896.
Ryan, Abram Joseph. *Selected Poems of Father Ryan*, ed. Gordon Weaver. Jackson: University and College Press of Mississippi, 1973.

RYAN, CATHIE (1959–)

Cathie Ryan is a singer and songwriter whose work, both interpretive and original, bridges traditional Celtic music and the ideas of contemporary singer/songwriters. She was chosen as the Irish Voice of the

Decade for the 1990s by the *Irish American News* of Chicago and has been called a singer of insight and originality by *The Irish Times* of Dublin, *The Wall Street Journal, Billboard* magazine, and U.S. poet laureate Billy Collins, among others. As a writer and composer she works with events and ideas of Irish and Irish-American history as well as with events and ideas of the heart's history.

Ryan was born in Detroit, Michigan, to parents who emigrated from Kerry and Tipperary in the late 1950s. They brought their music with them and passed it on to their daughter, through playing and singing along with traditional and mainstream recordings in the house, and through participating in events at Detroit's Gaelic League. Soon Ryan began singing there herself, but she was taking in other sorts of music as well. A good friend's parents came from Appalachia, so she heard that music often while growing up, as well as country music from artists such as Hank Williams and Merle Haggard. Living in Detroit, she was also exposed to the development of the Motown sound, adding a background in rhythm and groove that would emerge when as an adult she took up playing the bodhrán.

Traditional Irish music was at the heart of what Ryan was learning, though, that and an appreciation for narrative structure and story, which are carried through song and myth. Regular summer visits to Ireland to spend time with her grandparents encouraged these interests, as her grandmother Catherine Ryan was a fiddle player who loved to have ceilídhs in her kitchen and get everyone to share in the music, while her grandfather Patrick Rice was a storyteller whose vivid accounts of Irish myth and history made the events and emotions seem very real to Ryan and her sister and brother.

In her late teens Ryan began singing with traditional musician Dermot Henry's band. Ryan and Henry married and relocated to New York, where for a time Ryan time studied sean nós singing with master singer Joe Heaney from Connemara, who was then in his seventies. More importantly than the passing on of musical technique and song knowledge, he encouraged the young woman to see herself as a singer and to see songs as entities that need to be understood and courted as the singer learns from them how they should be sung. Ryan has said that Heaney's inspiration is what kept her going on with her music even when at times she found it difficult to find the right audience; though he taught her the most traditional of songs and style, his encouragement freed her to begin incorporating all her other influences and background into her own music.

Divorced and raising her son, Ryan went back to college for a teaching degree in English, but a spur-of-the-moment performance at a friend's party brought her to the attention of Joanie Madden, who was putting together a band of Irish-American women musicians called Cherish the Ladies. Through hard work and outstanding musicianship they would rise to be one of the best known, best loved, and most popular bands of any genre, known for the quality of their music and their respect for tradition. Ryan would be their lead singer for nearly eight years, during which time she would expand her gifts as a songwriter, work out her own unique style on the bodhrán, and as a singer demonstrate powerful abilities to interpret and inhabit contemporary and traditional songs in both English and Irish.

The next step for Ryan was to set out upon her own solo career, which she has pursued through four albums. Each recording comprises songs sung in Irish, familiar songs from Ireland sung in English, contemporary covers of folk-influenced music in both languages, a song or two from the American traditional folk songbook, and several original songs. Over the years, her arrangements have become more spare, cutting back almost to the bone of the melody in service to the song, and her song choices have become both more focused and more wide ranging. In her writing, she has moved from telling of characters and events of history—the struggling immigrant of "The Back Door," a track she recorded in 1992 for a Cherish the Ladies album of the same name, "Grace O'Malley," a look at Ireland's pirate queen that is just as feisty as she likely was; "Raithlin Island" (1847), an emigration song covering the history and present day of those who stayed behind; and "In My Tribe," a consideration of the connection and duality of roots and rootedness framed in the landscapes of rural Ireland and the desert Southwest of the United States—to reflections on pain, healing, and the courage it takes to do so, in the very different songs "The Farthest Wave," "Be Like the Sea," and "What's Closest to the Heart." In both words and melody Ryan explores both the light and darkness of her dual heritage and creates music that invites listeners as well to consider the sources of what it means to be both Irish and American.

Kerry Dexter

See also: Cherish the Ladies

Reference

Dexter, Kerry. "Motown Meets Tipperary." *Dirty Linen* 100 (June/July 2002): 35–38.

SADLIER, MARY ANNE (1820–1913)

One of the most popular and prolific Irish authors in the nineteenth century, Mary Anne Sadlier emigrated from Cootehill, County Cavan, to Montreal in 1844, where she met her husband and publisher James Sadlier, with whom she relocated to New York (1860). Many editions of Sadlier's works reached a far wider audience than most of the canonical texts of Anglo-Irish literature. Indeed, few nineteenth century authors could lay claim more convincingly to be populist writers in either Ireland or North America than Mary Anne Sadlier. She was, in many respects, a typical figure of the Irish emigrant community that she sought to represent and for which she wrote. During her lifetime, Sadlier published nearly 100 novels and translations, historical and religious tracts, all of which combined elements of Catholic piety, Irish nationalist fervor, and late-Victorian sentimentality and were widely sold in Irish-American communities, although by the time of her death in 1913 her literary reputation had already significantly diminished. Through her literary endeavours, Sadlier not only catered to but also effectively created and shaped the demands of a distinctly (and predominantly female) Irish American readership.

Sadlier's novels were designed first and foremost for the moral edification and religious instruction of her emigrant readership, through the inculcation of Irish Catholic values. Moreover, she also sought to provide practical advice and occupational guidance for Irish emigrant women, especially those going into domestic service, "by showing them how to win respect and inspire confidence on the part of their employers, and at the same time, to avoid the snares and pitfalls which have been the ruin of so many of their own class" (preface to *Bessy Conway; or, an Irish Girl in America*, iv). Sadlier's novels sought to resolve anxieties about the cultural retention of an Irish Catholic religious ethos in the adverse social, economic, and political circumstances that confronted Irish emigrants in urban America: various permutations of this underlying conflict provided the subject matter, sources of narrative tension, and plotlines for the thematic development of a range of social issues that were of vital concern to the Irish emigrant community as a whole, including: Irish emigrant manual labor (*Willy Burke; or, The Irish Orphan in America*, 1850), the separate, denominational "School Question" (*The Blakes and Flanagans*, 1855), Irish female domestic labor in North America (*Bessy Conway; or, The Irish Girl in America*, 1861), Irish Catholic colonization schemes for agricultural settlement in the mid-western United States (*Con O'Regan; or, Emigrant Life in the New World,* 1864), and genteel Irish, middle-class female migration to the New World (*Elinor Preston; or, Scenes at Home and Abroad,* 1861).

Although she spent most of her literary career in New York, Sadlier was also a close friend and confidante of the Irish-Canadian statesman Thomas D'Arcy McGee, and she played an instrumental role in shaping his vision and disseminating his ideas through her family's press. In fact, McGee corresponded regularly with Sadlier over a period that spanned from 1855, two years before he embarked from the United States for Montreal, until shortly before his assassination in 1868; his letters are now preserved as part of the James Sadlier collection in the National Archives of Canada. Throughout this period, McGee sought to publish much of his writing under the auspices of D. & J. Sadlier & Co; he frequently corresponded with Mary Anne Sadlier about his literary ambitions; and, after his assassination, it was Sadlier who collated and published his posthumous *Poems of Thomas D'Arcy McGee* (1869).

After the tragic deaths of both D'Arcy McGee (1868), and then her husband (1869), Sadlier returned to Montreal (1885), but there she proved unable to arrest the declining fortune of either the family's press or her own diminishing literary output, before eventually losing control not only of D. & J. Sadlier & Co. but even her own copyright in 1895. She died in straitened circumstances in Montreal in 1913, where she is buried.

Jason King

See also: McGEE, Thomas D'Arcy.

References

Howes, Marjorie. "Discipline, Sentiment, and the Irish-American Public: Mary Ann Sadlier's Popular Fiction." *Éire-Ireland* 40, no. 1 & 2 (Spring/Summer 2005): 140–169.

King, Jason. "The Feminization of the Canadian Frontier: Engendering the "Peaceable Kingdom" Myth in the Writings of Mary Anne Sadlier (1820–1913) & Isabella Valancy Crawford (1850–1887)," *The Canadian Journal of Irish Studies,* 32, no. 1: 46–55.

Lacombe, Michéle. "Frying Pans and Deadlier Weapons: The Immigrant Novels of Mary Anne Sadlier," *Essays on Canadian Writing* 29 (Summer 1984): 96–116.

McGee, Thomas D'Arcy. Letters to James and Mary Anne Sadlier, the James Sadlier Collection. National Archives of Canada. MG 24, c 16, Vol. 1, 1–52.

Sadlier, Mary Anne. *Bessie Conway; or, The Irish Girl in America.* New York: D. & J. Sadlier & Co., 1861.

Sadlier, Mary Anne (ed). *The Poems of Thomas D'Arcy McGee, with copious notes. Also an Introduction and Biographical Sketch, By Mrs. J. Sadlier.* New York: D. & J. Sadlier & Co., 1869.

SAINT-GAUDENS, AUGUSTUS (1848–1907)

Augustus Saint-Gaudens was born in Dublin on March 1, 1848, to a French father and an Irish mother. Fleeing the Potato Famine, the family sailed first to Boston, and shortly thereafter moved to New York City, where Saint-Gaudens grew up. He showed an early aptitude for art and was apprenticed to several cameo cutters; this period of apprenticeships began his later mastery of portraits. In his teens he also attended drawing classes in the Cooper Union and the National Academy of Design.

In 1867, Saint-Gaudens sailed to Paris, where he studied for a time at the Ecole des Beaux-Arts. He remained in Paris until the Franco-Prussian War turned decisively against the French; at that time he went to Rome. There he started accepting commissions, and his skills as a portraitist began to attain public notice, particularly among the affluent. While in Italy Saint-Gaudens met the woman who would later become his wife, Augusta Homer.

Despite several early lean periods in both Europe and the United States, Saint-Gaudens's breakthrough success came in 1881, when he unveiled his Admiral Farragut Monument in New York City. (Farragut was a Civil War hero for the Union.) This work caused a sensation—patriotic yet also artistic, it propelled Saint-Gaudens into the forefront of the widespread postwar market for monumental commissions. Indeed, one of his next commissions (1884) was also related to the Civil War, and it is likely his most famous single work. The subject of enormous and time-consuming effort, the Robert Gould Shaw Memorial was unveiled in Boston in 1897. This large and moving bronze commemorates both Shaw and the black soldiers he commanded, the 54th Massachusetts Regiment. Saint-Gaudens depicts an angel of benediction hovering over the men as they march to the 1863 Battle of Battery Wagner, in which they distinguished themselves with valor and were horribly slaughtered. The Gould Shaw Memorial remains one of the most admired public artworks in the country, and has inspired numerous other artists; it is the monument mentioned prominently in both Robert Lowell's "For the Union Dead" and John Berryman's "Boston Common."

Although the Farragut and Shaw memorials are likely Saint-Gaudens's most prominent works, he spent the 1880s, 1890s, and the first years of the twentieth century creating a large body of successful monumental work. Among his greater achievements were his statue of *Diana* (1881; it was removed from atop the first Madison Square Garden in 1925 and is now in the Philadelphia Museum of Art), his standing *Abraham Lincoln* (1887; Lincoln Park, Chicago), the Adams Memorial (1891; Rock Creek Cemetery, Washington D.C.), his bronze allegory *Amor Caritas* (1898; Metropolitan Museum of Art, New York), the William Tecumseh Sherman Monument (1903; Grand Army Plaza, New York), and his sculpture of a *Pilgrim* (1904; Fairmount Park, Philadelphia). He is also highly esteemed for his 1907 design for the $20 coin known as the "Double Eagle," which many numismatists consider to be the most beautiful coin ever issued by the United States.

On August 3, 1907, Saint-Gaudens died of cancer at his home in Cornish, New Hampshire. Although his fame has diminished since his death, he is still regarded as one of the most important American artists of the nineteenth century. His Civil War monuments particularly contribute to the public memory of the war in which so many of his fellow Irish Americans distinguished themselves, and in which many thousands gave their lives. Saint-Gaudens also left a lasting contribution to the city of his birth: his statue of Charles Stewart Parnell that stands at the northern head of O'Connell Street in Dublin.

Andrew Goodspeed

See also: AMERICAN CIVIL WAR

References

Dryfhout, John, and Beverly Fox. *Augustus Saint-Gaudens: The Portrait Reliefs.* Washington, DC: National Portrait Gallery, 1969.

Garnett, Jeff, and Ron Guth. *100 Greatest U.S. Coins.* Atlanta: H. E. Harris, 2003.

Tharp, Louise Hall. *Saint-Gaudens and the Gilded Era.* Boston: Little, Brown & Company, 1969.

Wilkinson, Burke. *Uncommon Clay: The Life and Works of Augustus Saint-Gaudens.* New York: Harcourt Brace Jovanovich, 1985.

SAINT PATRICK'S CATHEDRAL

The first Saint Patrick's Church in New York was established by Jesuit Father Anthony Kohlmann on June 8, 1809, at Broadway and Bowery Road (today Mott and Prince Streets). Services were in English, French, and German. Father Kohlmann later purchased land and a house on 5th Avenue between 50th and 51st Streets to establish the New York Literary Institution for boys. It was attended by both Protestants and Catholics. The area, however, was not very accessible in the early part of the nineteenth century because of its location in a yet-undeveloped area of the city, and this prevented the school from growing. Father Kohlmann was recalled to Maryland, and the Literary Institution continued, albeit haphazardly. When Napoleon was defeated and sent into exile, many French Catholics returned to France, a situation that took away the Catholic Mass from the Literary Institution.

The Institution eventually closed its doors and fell into secular hands. For several years, it was a roadside inn. In 1828 the property was purchased outright by the Trustees of Saint Patrick's and Saint Peter's to be used as a cemetery. The ground proved to be too rocky and the idea for a cemetery had to be abandoned. But most importantly, the property was back in Church hands and as an investment, it proved itself to be a very valuable piece of real estate in the heart of present-day Manhattan.

The new Saint Patrick's Church on this site was prepared for dedication in 1815. The first priest ordained at Saint Patrick's was Irish-born Father John Hughes in 1837. In 1850, Father Hughes announced the building of Saint Patrick's Cathedral, an idea many called "Hughes's Folly." He envisioned it becoming the center of Catholic life in New York. Catholics would no longer be outsiders in a mostly Protestant New York City, and such a cathedral would certainly announce their presence as a major religious group.

Architectural plans were drawn up by architect James Renwick. Father Hughes's vision came to fruition with the dedication of Saint Patrick's Cathedral in 1879. By then, Father Hughes had been dead for 15 years but his laying of the cornerstone in 1858 and the Cathedral's eventual dedication 21 years later showed New York City and the world that such a massive, mostly marble building was indeed no folly. It was a symbol of Catholic life and Father Hughes's ambitious wish. Contributions were solicited for many years before and after the construction of the cathedral, and it was finally consecrated as debt free in 1910.

Since 1948, Midnight Mass has been televised live from Saint Patrick's Cathedral. It is the first American church to have its name inscribed on the floor of Saint Peter's Basilica in Rome.

Cynthia A. Klima

See also: CATHOLIC CHURCH, the; NEW YORK CITY

References

Burton, Katherine. *The Dream Lives Forever: The Story of St. Patrick's Cathedral*. New York: Longman's, Green and Company, 1960.

Carty, Margaret. *A Cathedral of Suitable Significance: St. Patrick's Cathedral, New York*. Wilmington, DE: Michael Glazier, 1984.

Cathy, M. P. *Old St. Patrick's: New York's First Cathedral*. New York: U.S. Catholic Society, 1947.

Cook, Leland. *St. Patrick's Cathedral*. New York: Quick Fox, 1979.

SAINT PATRICK'S DAY PARADES

Saint Patrick's Day—March 17—has been observed by the Irish as both an ethnic festival and a national celebration for thousands of years on the saint's religious feast day and the anniversary of his death in the fifth century. It is not a national holiday in the United States, but it is nationally observed. The original Patrick, based on his *Confessio,* was a missionary born in Roman Britain in the first decade of the fifth century who was kidnapped, at age 16, by Irish marauders and enslaved as a shepherd for six years in Antrim. He escaped, studied for the priesthood in Gaul, and then returned to Ireland in 432 with a group of companions. Despite the many legends that grew around him, Patrick was not the first to introduce Christianity to Ireland—there is substantial evidence that it already had roots there—but he has been considered the patron saint of Ireland for 15 centuries. His writings are also the earliest extant documents written in Ireland. For these reasons, Patrick has achieved a special role in the cultural and spiritual life of the country, expressed in song, poetry, prose, prayer, and pilgrimage. Today, Saint Patrick's Day is a rowdy festival of parading, revelry, dancing, and drinking, emblazoned with shamrocks and harps, all in emerald green.

Irish immigration to the United States began as early as the eighteenth century. More than half of the soldiers who fought in the Revolutionary War had Irish ancestors, and it was in colonial America that the

Saint Patrick's Day parade in New York's Union Square, 1870. (Library of Congress)

Irish first paraded to express their identity and solidarity. In a touch of irony, those who marched in the first Saint Patrick's Day parade were Irishmen in British uniform, soldiers stationed in the colonies who were sent by King George III to preserve the crown's grip on a rebellious colony.

The first public Saint Patrick's Day celebrations outside a church in the United States were held by the Charitable Irish Society of Boston in 1737. The first parade in New York City, which is today considered the largest Saint Patrick's Day parade in the world, took place on March 17, 1762, when a group of Irish-born soldiers were on their way to breakfast on Saint Patrick's Day and staged an impromptu march through the streets of colonial New York with their regimental band. Along with their music, the parade helped the soldiers to reconnect with their Irish roots, as well as with fellow Irishmen serving in the English army.

Until 1774, military units were a special part of Saint Patrick's Day celebrations in New York. After 1783, Irish-American soldiers participated in the parade until 1812, when some societies, such as the Friendly Sons of St. Patrick, the Hibernian Society, and the Shamrock Friendly Association, joined forces to run the parade, which soon consisted of small groups, many featuring bagpipes and drums, marching from the headquarters of their organizations to the first Saint Patrick's Cathedral and other local churches. Since 1776, Boston has also had a parade. With the rise of these so-called Irish aid societies, Irish patriotism strengthened among American immigrants.

After 1820, the increase in Irish immigration brought Saint Patrick's Day parades to whatever city or community they settled in large numbers. For Irish workers,

March 17 became the day to honor their ethnic roots with the wearing of the green that symbolized their identity as they paraded their Irish pride. Later, the significance of the day was overshadowed by the commercial aspects. Along with the parades, the political celebrations, and the Irish music and dancing, a microcosm of Irish culture and folklife in one day, people wear green, one of the national colors of Ireland and one of the signs of spring. On Saint Patrick's Day, green stripes are painted on the streets where the parade will travel, flowers are dyed green, people wear green clothing and shamrocks, and many American taverns serve green beverages. However, the main attraction, the center of the events, remains the parade where political friend and enemy come together for the length of several blocks to show themselves to the thousands of cheering spectators lining the streets.

By 1870, the order of march usually imcluded a platoon of policemen, the 69th Regiment (the Fighting 69th), the Legion of Patrick, men of Tipperary, 21 divisions of the Ancient Order of Hibernians, and numerous parish benevolent societies and total abstinence units. The first floats appeared in 1875; according to reports at the time, one carried two women representing Ireland and America, and another had 32 women, one for each of the counties of Ireland.

After New York and Boston, one of the oldest and biggest parades in the United States has been held in Savannah, Georgia, a city with a long Irish history. The oldest Irish society in this country, the Hibernian Society, was formed in that city in 1812 by 13 Irish Protestants who held a private procession the next year, a forerunner to the present Saint Patrick's Day parade. The first public procession was held in 1824, and public parades have been held there since, with only six lapses: for wars, sympathy for the Irish Revolution, and for an unrecorded reason.

Other parades soon followed in Carbondale, Pennsylvania (1833), New Haven, Connecticut (1842), Chicago (1843), San Francisco (1852), Scranton, Pennsylvania (1853), Atlanta (1858), and Cleveland (1867). By the late twentieth century, there were an estimated 235 parades in 44 states. As the parades began to increase in the 1850s and the 1860s, the press began to give them more detailed coverage. One hundred years later, the parades were covered by newspapers and on radio and on television, bringing moving images and sounds of the festivities to a very large audience. By the dawn of the twenty-first century, highlights of many of these parades were available on websites and on DVDs, sometimes within hours of the parade's end. However, in the beginning, when Irish Americans in these cities paraded on Saint Patrick's Day, newspapers portrayed them in cartoons as drunk, violent monkeys, one of the many stereotypes that persisted into the late twentieth century, but the Irish soon realized that their great numbers endowed them with a political power that had yet to be exploited. They started to organize, and their voting block (the "green machine") became an important swing vote for political hopefuls. Suddenly, annual Saint Patrick's Day parades became a show of strength for Irish Americans and a must-attend event for political candidates.

In Boston, there are still memories of Mayor James M. Curley riding in the parade in a fur coat, shaking hands with priests and nuns; of Up-Up Kelly, a Curley lieutenant, punctuating the mayor's Saint Patrick's Day speech by jumping up every minute to applaud Curley's condemnation of the British and urging the audience to do likewise; and of Grand Marshall Knocko McCormack, brother of former U.S. House Speaker John McCormack, heaving his 300 pounds onto a dray horse that hauled the ashcart for the city of Boston. In 1948, President Harry Truman attended New York City's Saint Patrick's Day parade, a proud moment for the many Irish whose ancestors had to fight stereotypes and racial prejudice to find acceptance in America.

Conflicts and Controversies

A parade, by its very nature, requires incredible preparation and coordination and the participation of hundreds of organizations to make it a successful endeavor. For example, in 1868, the *Irish Citizen* protested that there were too many German bands in the parade and not enough Irish ones, which lessened the amount of Irish music that was played. This was quickly replaced by more political concerns, which continue today. For a time after the Civil War, the Fenian Brotherhood (Fenians), a wing of the Irish Republican Brotherhood, a society devoted to gaining Irish independence through revolution, headed the annual Saint Patrick's Day parades in Chicago until 1870 when the Catholic Church condemned and excommunicated them. This led to their removal from their position at the head of the Saint Patrick's Day parade; they then marched in a separate procession right before the main parade. The Fenians' chief rival was the Ancient Order of Hibernians (AOH), which required members to be of Irish birth and Roman

Catholics of good standing. They were to play a major role in Saint Patrick's Day celebrations, especially in the control they exerted in the 1980s and 1990s over what groups and organizations could march. Also, they began to attend Mass as a group on the holiday and to allow the clergy a more active role in the celebrations.

The last decades of the twentieth century saw an increase in the use of the parades to support the Northern Ireland conflict. At the 1970 New York parade, four men unfurled a banner demanding "Civil Rights for Northern Ireland" in full view of Cardinal Cooke at Saint Patrick's Cathedral. In 1972, members of the Irish Republican Aid Committee preceded the main body of the Boston parade along the march route in protest of the British presence in Northern Ireland, but despite the intervention of Northern Ireland politics into the background of the parade, the parades were carefully monitored through the rest of the 1970s for inappropriate political activity. In 1983, the choice of an alleged Irish Republican Army (IRA) sympathizer, Michael Flannery, to lead the New York parade led to demands that the parade be boycotted, and the Irish government criticized Irish Americans who supported IRA causes. Cardinal Cooke publicly declared his opposition to Flannery and refused to emerge from Saint Patrick's Cathedral until Flannery walked past.

By the early 1990s, a more serious dynamic emerged as more Saint Patrick's Day parades, mostly controlled by the AOH, reflected conservative, traditional family values. The 1991 New York parade heralded the arrival of the Irish Lesbian and Gay Organization (ILGO) who emerged from within the spectators, chanting "We're here, we're queer, we're Irish." Their attempts to publicly sanction homosexuality on Saint Patrick's Day, while supported by the mainstream media, were rejected by the official organizing committee. Instead, another Irish group in the parade, Division 7 from Manhattan, subsumed ILGO into their group and were further assisted by then Mayor David Dinkins, who marched with Division 7 instead of at the nominal head of the parade. He was booed for his efforts. The next year, after a complex series of maneuvers by both sides after ILGO was excluded again, in what was clearly a violation of New York human rights legislation, ILGO sued the AOH.

The judicial decision ruled in favor of the organizers: ownership of the invitation list belonged to the organizers. As such, they could overlook any group that they wished. In other words, although the parade was held on public streets, it was effectively a private parade, and only those who were invited could join. At subsequent parades, demonstrators who were opposed to the exclusion of gays from the event protested along the parade route on 5th Avenue, and this political statement continues today.

As the controversy in New York grew, gay and lesbian groups across the United States campaigned to be in parades and in other celebrations. In Massachusetts, the Irish-American Gay, Lesbian and Bisexual Group of Boston sought to enter that city's parade, but its organizers denied their application. Unlike their New York counterparts, they went to the U.S. Supreme Court in what was officially a case between them and the Allied War Veterans' Council of South Boston, the organizers of the parade. As in the New York situation, the organizers won. Although they were not allowed to exclude gay and lesbian marchers from the parade, they could prevent any group from participating. Commenting on the situation in New York and Boston, the *New Republic* (February 1, 1993) noted that "some Irish Americans show themselves to be narrower than their homelanders, and less festive too." However, the debate still continues over the inclusion of these groups in the parades.

Other Parade Venues

Today, Saint Patrick's Day is celebrated by people of all backgrounds in the United States, Canada (Ottawa, Quebec, Halifax, Montreal, Toronto, Edmonton, Vancouver), Australia, Argentina, Japan, Singapore, and Russia, while many leading Irish figures and politicians, including the president of the Republic of Ireland or the Irish ambassador to a particular country, often participate in the local parade. It is quite an honor for a parade to have a high Irish official within its ranks. The Dublin office of the Irish Department of Foreign Affairs receives overseas requests for government assistance in commemorating Saint Patrick's Day from expatriate Irish societies, parade organizers, and Irish embassies, consulates, and legations across the globe; Irish ambassadors and diplomats are expected to participate in a lead role.

In the United States, the best-known parades are still held in Baltimore, Boston, Chicago, New York, and Washington, D.C., where traditions of the parades reflect different celebrations, as do their counterparts in Australia, Canada, and across Ireland. In Washington, D.C., the parade, unlike its counterparts in other cities with highly defined Irish-American communities, better reflects its representation as "The Nation's Saint Patrick's Day Parade." The first Saint Patrick's Day parade in Washington, D.C., was held in 1871 and traveled along Massachusetts Avenue from Dupont Circle to the statue of Robert Emmet. In 1874, the Constitution Avenue route was established, and the march became a full-scale parade with marching bands, pipe bands, military units, and police and fire departments, as well as floats, novelty groups, and marchers wearing green. The parade is always held on the Sunday before Saint Patrick's Day. Traditionally, the parade is not a forum for political issues. Elected officials march, but those running for office are not allowed to use the parade as a campaign site. The parade is an Irish community endeavor that was started by the Irish American Club and is now held in cooperation with the U.S. Capital Park Service. The president of the Irish American Club maintains a place on the Board of Directors of the Parade Committee.

Current Situation

More than 200 years since the first Saint Patrick's Day parade was held, the event continues to be celebrated with more fanfare in the United States than in Ireland, but it has also garnered its share of criticism for a loss of religious meaning, commercialism, unfortunate displays of drinking, and increasing political activity, which has long divided the Irish community, torn between those who support their conservative, traditional values and those who embrace alternative lifestyles but also want to honor their Irish heritage. At the same time, the parade, like the Saint Patrick's Day celebration itself, has united Irish emigrants worldwide, whether in the United States, Canada, or elsewhere.

Martin J. Manning

See also: IRISH REPUBLICAN ARMY; IRISH REPUBLICAN BROTHERHOOD; NATIONALISM, IRISH-AMERICAN; POLITICAL PARTIES, IRISH

References

Barth, Edna, with Ursula Arndt. *Shamrocks, Harps, and Shillelaghs: The Story of St. Patrick's Day Symbols.* New York: Seabury, 1977.

Cronin, Mike, and Daryl Adair. *The Wearing of the Green: A History of St. Patrick's Day.* London: Routledge, 2002.

Davies, Wallace E. *Patriotism on Parade: The Story of the Veterans' and Hereditary Organizations in America, 1783–1900.* Cambridge, MA: Harvard University, 1955.

Fraser, T. G., ed. *The Irish Parading Tradition: Following the Drum.* Houndmills, Basingstoke: Macmillan, 2000.

Glazier, Michael, ed. *The Encyclopedia of the Irish in America.* Notre Dame, IN: University of Notre Dame, 1999.

Ridge, John J. *St. Patrick's Day Parade in New York.* New York: New York St. Patrick's Day Committee, 1988.

Santino, Jack. *All Around the Year: Holidays and Celebrations in American Life.* Urbana: University of Illinois, 1994.

Walkowski, Paul J., and William M. Connolly. *From Trial Court to United States Supreme Court: Anatomy of a Free Speech Case, the Incredible Inside Story Behind the Theft of the St. Patrick's Day Parade.* Boston: Branden Publishing, 1996.

SAMPSON, WILLIAM (1764–1836)

Educated at Trinity College Dublin and Lincoln's Inn, London, William Sampson frequently acted as counsel for the Society of the United Irishmen, which had been established by his friend, fellow lawyer Theobald Wolfe Tone. As a reluctant rebel, Sampson did not believe in the violent plans of the organization but acted as defense counsel for the United Irishmen after efforts to suppress the organization in the latter half of the 1790s. In the eyes of the government, he was nevertheless a rebel, and as a consequence of his pro-United Irish activities he was imprisoned with the rest of the state prisoners at Fort George; in 1805 Sampson managed to leave for the United States. He had initial difficulties setting up a law practice in New York, suffering from a lack of funds, but he was eventually successful. Sampson and Thomas Addis Emmet were the only United Irishmen who were admitted to practice law in New York, because of widespread dislike of the "fugitive Jacobins" among the predominantly Federalist law circles. Acting in accordance with his United Irish beliefs, Sampson became a lawyer heavily involved in civil rights litigation, often working on a pro bono basis. His longtime passion was the eradication of the British common law, upon which the New York legal system was based. Sampson's 1823 address to the New York Historical Society did manage to generate a lively debate in the legal circles, and for the next two years he was involved in the debate for legal reform, particularly the codification movement.

Sampson was best known as an advocate for Irish immigrants, fighting for their rights as Catholics in the justice system. His most famous case was in 1813, when he successfully defended the "priest-penitent privilege" that allowed a Jesuit priest not to disclose confessional details in court. In his cases, he also made frequent allusions to the suffering of Catholics in Ireland.

William Sampson was an avid writer on Irish affairs, and in his memoirs he wrote extensively about the 1798 rebellion and its causes. Sampson was also active in benevolent Irish circles. In 1828, along with the United Irish surgeon William James Mac-Neven, he established the Society for Civil and Religious Liberties, the main objective of which was Catholic Emancipation. With Thomas O'Connor, another United Irish exile, he founded the Association of the Friends of Ireland in New York, which collected money for O'Connell's emancipation campaign both in Ireland and Westminster.

Aki Kalliomaki

See also: O'CONNELL, Daniel

References

Madden, Richard R. *United Irishmen, Their Lives and Times.* London: 1887.

Maxwell, Bloomfield. *American Lawyers in a Changing Society, 1776–1876.* Cambridge: Cambridge University Press, 1976.

Twomey, Richard. *Jacobins and Jeffersonians: Anglo-American Radicalism in the United States, 1790–1820.* New York: Garland, 1989.

Wilson, David: *United Irishmen, United States: Immigrant Radicals in the Early Republic.* Ithaca, NY: Cornell University Press, 1998.

SAN FRANCISCO

Unlike other American metropolises, such as Boston and New York, San Francisco is not usually a city associated with the Irish in the popular imagination. However, San Francisco's Irish community, though no longer as large or as vibrant as in years past, has made its unique presence felt throughout the city's history.

Spanish priests and soldiers founded what would eventually become the city of San Francisco as a Roman Catholic mission, Mission San Francisco, on June 27, 1776. In 1834, Mexico, having won independence from Spain, closed the Catholic missions and sold their land. San Francisco was the first of the missions to be secularized. In 1846, California became part of the United States. Although some Irish had arrived in the region earlier, Irish immigrants began coming in substantial numbers when the California gold rush began in 1849, and they soon outnumbered even the Hispanics in the area.

As early as the late 1860s, a visitor wrote that while "every civilized nation is represented [in San Francisco]," "[t]he Irish predominate and dominate." Another, describing the great number and variety of religious faiths represented in the city, commented, "The Catholics, of course, are everywhere and very rich; fat lands have descended to them from the Spaniards and Mexicans; fat revenues flow to them now from the Irish." By 1880, the number of Irish had swelled to one-third of the city's population of 233,959.

One way in which the San Franciscan Irish were atypical, if not unique, among their compatriots in the United States was in their degree of financial success. In part because they were early arrivals in the city—unlike the nineteenth-century Irish in New York and Boston—and in part because of San Francisco's unusually welcoming attitude to Catholics, given the city's Spanish colonial roots, the Irish were able to prosper there from the start. In addition, as opposed to those who arrived on the East Coast of the United States, many Irish arriving in San Francisco were second-stage immigrants, having earlier immigrated from Australia to Ireland, and they had already dealt with the travails of immigrant life. Gold rush arrival Eugene Kelly made his first fortune in San Francisco before moving to New York to advise the clergy there on the building of Saint Patrick's Cathedral. San Francisco's "Silver King" and business titan John W. Mackay was born in Dublin in 1831, and fellow immigrant Peter Donahue was known as the "Father of California Industry." James C. Flood, born in New York City to poor Irish immigrants, built the city's landmark Flood Building. Flood made his initial money after moving to San Francisco during the gold rush. He later became far wealthier after investing in Nevada silver mining with his fellow Irishman and business partner, William O'Brien, and two Irish mining engineers, John Mackay and James Fair.

Among the Irish middle class, Michael Maurice O'Shaughnessy, also from Dublin, designed San Francisco's West Portal Tunnel, water system, and streetcar system. Another Irish engineer, Jasper O' Farrell, laid out the city plan for modern San Francisco. Many other Irish were proprietors of saloons, groceries, and so on, as well as common laborers. As in other U.S. cities, the Irish were also well represented among the ranks of San Francisco's police, firefighters, politicians, and Catholic clergy, frequently attaining the highest positions in those fields.

Unfortunately, the Irish in San Francisco were not immune to the ethnic hatred that infected many of their compatriots in other cities such as New York. The Chinese rivaled the Irish in numbers and visibility as one of San Francisco's largest immigrant communities. The height of Chinese immigration in the nineteenth century coincided with one of the worst economic depressions of the era, leading many white residents of San Francisco to blame the massive influx of Chinese laborers for the recession and consequent rise in unemployment. Dennis Kearney, an Irish immigrant and drayman, denounced the Chinese during a meeting of workers in San Francisco in 1877 as "shrewd, opportunist, and disloyal" to the labor cause by undercutting wages and acquiescing to poor working environments. Kearney's inflammatory rhetoric aggravated a mob of hundreds of angry, unemployed men and resulted in the San Francisco riot of 1877, which became only the most infamous of a series of violent attacks against the Chinese in nineteenth-century California.

White laborers, many of whom were Irish, roamed the streets of San Francisco for several days, searching for Chinese and other Asians to attack. Many Chinese businesses, particularly laundries and restaurants, were vandalized, robbed, and burned. Rioting became so frenzied that the National Guard, citizen volunteers, and three warships requested by Governor William Irwin were called in to try to quell the violence. However, the riots continued for several days. For more than a decade afterward, Kearney remained the leader of the struggle to expel the Chinese from California. Today, a street in San Francisco is named after him.

The Irish were not only the instigators of some attacks driven by ethnic hatred, but also the victims of them. Although San Francisco was more welcoming to the Irish than other parts of the United States in the nineteenth century, California was a hotbed of the national Know-Nothing movement of the mid-1850s, which was fueled mainly by anti-Catholic sentiment and directed at Irish and German immigrants. California was the only state to elect a Know-Nothing governor, and the party was very strong in San Francisco. In 1851, San Franciscans also turned their hostility on Australians, who were arriving by the thousands. A group of citizens made up mainly of local businessmen formed the Committee of Vigilance, which met ships at the docks so they could turn away "undesirable immigrants,: particularly those from Australia, and even hanging immigrants without trial. The majority of these "Australian" immigrants were, in fact, Irish or of Irish descent.

Despite such challenges, far more Irish Americans made positive rather than negative contributions to the cause of labor in

San Francisco and to the city generally. In 1860, the first concerted drive by labor in San Francisco was for a shorter workday, with workers campaigning for a 10-hour rather than the then-standard 12-hour day. Later, Irishman Alexander M. Kenaday, a San Francisco printer, led the campaign for an eight-hour day. Among labor leaders who opposed Dennis Kearney was his fellow Irishman Frank Roney, who had fought as a revolutionary for the Irish Republic before becoming a voluntary exile to the United States. Although Roney had been born to a wealthy family, he dedicated himself to improving the status of the average laborer in San Francisco. Roney appeared at a labor gathering with Kearney only once, denouncing the latter as a "traitor" to the workingman's cause. Another of Roney's targets were the "crimps," San Francisco's boarding house keepers who had supplied sea captains with shanghaied—that is, kidnapped slave labor—crew members since the gold rush. In 1885, Roney became the first president of the newly formed Federal Trades and Labor Council in San Francisco.

The Irish in San Francisco also distinguished themselves in political office. James D. Phelan, the son of a wealthy Irish gold rush banker and financier, became mayor in 1896 and pushed through a new city charter. The contributions of Irish Americans to civic life in San Francisco did not diminish in the next century. San Franciscan John Francis Houlihan, the son of Irish immigrants, served as mayor of the neighboring large city of Oakland in the 1960s. Irish-American Frank Jordan served as mayor in the late 1980s and early 1990s. More recently, Irish-American Gavin Newsom was elected to the office of mayor of San Francisco in 2004. The history of Irish-American politicians in

San Francisco has not been entirely positive. In 1978, a tragic event again brought tensions between the city's traditional, heavily Irish population and a growing minority group into sharp focus. Mayor George Moscone and Harvey Milk, a member of the city's board of supervisors and the nation's first openly gay elected official, were shot to death in their offices at City Hall by Dan White. White, an Irish American, was a native San Franciscan who had run for city supervisor in what was then a very conservative, working class, and Irish-Catholic neighborhood known as District 8. Although White was elected to the board of supervisors, he blamed Moscone and Milk for his later political failures. After the shock and sorrow of Moscone and Milk's murders, tensions in the city escalated, culminating in riots, when White was found guilty only of manslaughter and given a minimal sentence. Many in San Francisco, particularly in the gay community, believed White's lenient sentence was due in large part to general antigay sentiment as well as resentment of the growing political power of the city's gay community. After being released from prison in January 1985, White committed suicide in October of that year.

Today, San Francisco's Irish population is no longer as large or as visible as it once was. The city's Mission District, once largely Irish, is now home to a mainly Hispanic community drawn chiefly from Mexico and Central America. (Today, San Francisco boasts an Irish Mexican Association.) Another once predominantly Irish enclave, the Richmond District, is now called by many "New Chinatown," although it is still known for its many Irish bars. Along with other formerly prominent ethnic groups in the city, such as the Japanese, Italians, Germans, and Jews, the

Irish community in San Francisco has waned for a variety of reasons, mostly the post–World War II desire of many families to move into the suburbs and own their homes. However, a substantial minority of Irish immigrants still lives and works in San Francisco today, and one can find traces of the city's strong Irish past in many street names, its lively Saint Patrick's Day parade, its numerous Catholic churches, and its Irish bars. One of only four statues in the world of Irish patriot Robert Emmet, who was executed by the British in 1803, stands in the city's Golden Gate Park. And the legendary Irish coffee drink was invented not in Ireland but at San Francisco's Buena Vista Hotel bar. The New College of California in San Francisco is one of very few universities in the United States to offer degrees both in Irish studies and in the Irish language.

Danielle Maze

See also: NATIVISM AND ANTI-CATHOLICISM

References

Binetti, Mike. "Dennis Kearney." http://baseportal.com/cgi-bin/baseportal.pl?htx=/zpub2000/sfentries&cmd=list&range=0,50&cmd=all&Id=119 (accessed August 27, 2007).

"California as I Saw It: First-Person Narratives of California's Early Years, 1849–1900." The Library of Congress. http://memory.loc.gov/ammem/cbhtml/cbhome.html (accessed August 27, 2007).

McBroom, Patricia. "Hounded, Hunted, and Sometimes Hanged." Berkeleyan Online, Office of Public Affairs, the University of California at Berkeley, 1994. www.berkeley.edu/news/berkeleyan/1994/1109/immigrant.html (accessed August 27, 2007).

Milner, Clyde A., Carol A. O'Connor, and Martha J. Sandweiss, eds. *The Oxford History of the American West.* New York: Oxford University Press, 1994.

Morris, Charles R. *American Catholic.* New York: Vintage, 1997.

SAN PATRICIOS BRIGADE

The San Patricios were composed of deserters from the U.S. Army, the greatest single number being Irishmen and foreigners resident in Mexico. In five battles of the Mexican-American War the San Patricios Brigade bore arms for the Mexicans. It is disputed whether their principal motivation in deserting and fighting against their former comrades was to defend fellow Roman Catholics from conquest by a Protestant power and as a consequence of the nativism of their own officers, or was because of the prospects of better pay, rank, land, and citizenship offered to deserters by the numerically stronger Mexican Army. The deserters were originally organized in the border town of Matamoros by John Riley, a native of Co. Galway. He claimed that this company was formed from 48 Irishmen in the April of 1846.

On May 3, 1846, this force assisted in the artillery bombardment of the American Army at Fort Texas from Matamoros. After the Mexican withdrawal to Monterrey on May 17, more deserters were added. When Monterrey was assaulted by the American Army of Zachary Taylor on September 21, Riley and his fellow deserters are thought to have again served with the Mexican artillery. After the Mexican surrender of the city on September 26, at least 100 deserters followed Riley in the retreat. Riley was himself summoned before General Santa Anna to fashion a force of deserters and foreigners resident in Mexico into artillerymen. From November 1846 the Voluntarios Irlandeses appeared in the payroll records of the Mexican Army. At San Luis Potosi with Santa Anna's Liberating Army of the North, Riley displayed an emerald flag said in different accounts to be variously decorated with a harp, a shamrock, a cross, and an image of Saint Patrick as well as with the Mexican eagle and coat of arms. By 1847 the title of San Patricios had been given by the Mexicans to Riley's men.

At the Battle of Buena Vista on February 23, 1847, the San Patricios lost 22 men and won much praise for their heroism. Riley was promoted from lieutenant to captain. In April 1847 the San Patricios served at the Battle of Cerro Gordo against Scott's expedition to capture Mexico City. On July 1, 1847, by the presidential decree of Santa Anna, the San Patricios were transferred from the artillery to the infantry and were merged into a Foreign Legion; however, they still retained their identity as two San Patricio companies of 102 men each. Riley commanded one company and Captain Santiago O'Leary the other. On August 20, 1847, at the Battle of Churubusco, in defence of the approach to Mexico City, the two companies of San Patricios suffered 35 dead and 85 taken prisoner, including the now Brevet Major Riley. The stand of the San Patricios at Churubusco is often credited with allowing most of Santa Anna's army to escape to defend Mexico City.

The American Army now tried those captured San Patricios who had deserted from their ranks. The defense offered by many of the San Patricios was that drunkenness had led to their capture by the Mexicans, who had then coerced them into bearing arms. Riley too claimed he had been captured and forced to fight for Mexico. This has led some to argue that neither the nativism of the American officers nor the religious conscience of Catholic soldiers motivated the San Patricios. Others have drawn attention to drunkenness being an acceptable defense for desertion under the American Army's Articles of War that would save them from execution. The military judges sentenced 70 prisoners to death. General Scott pardoned five men, reduced 15 sentences, and confirmed 50 of the death sentences. Riley was reprieved because he had deserted before the declaration of war. Those San Patricios who had escaped at Churubusco and those later released from American captivity after punishment continued in the Mexican Army in what was now the Batallón de San Patricio, under the command of Riley. Despite fighting against rebels, they were suspected of involvement in one of the attempted coups that followed Mexico's defeat and were disbanded in the summer of 1848. The records are incomplete, but approximately two-fifths of the San Patricios were Irishmen; many other nationalities filled the rest of their ranks. Santa Anna stated that with more soldiers like the San Patricios he would have defeated the United States. After the war Mexico certainly remembered the San Patricios as Irish Catholics, as was soon also true in the United States and Ireland.

O. R. Butler

References

Hogan, Michael. *The Irish Soldiers of Mexico.* Guadalajara, Mexico: Fondo Editorial Universitario, 1997.

Miller, Robert Ryal. *Shamrock and Sword, The Saint Patrick's Battalion in the U.S.–Mexican War.* Norman, London: University of Oklahoma Press, 1989.

Stevens, Peter F. *The Rogue's March, John Riley and the St. Patrick's Battalion.* Washington, DC: Brassey's, 1999.

SCANLAN, WILLIAM J. (1856–1898)

Born in Springfield, Massachusetts, William Scanlan began his career as the 13-year-old "Temperance Boy Singer," appearing with temperance lecturers on the New England circuit. He eventually found his way to New York City and into vaudeville. He teamed up with Jim Cronin ("That Hibernian Wit") and later toured with Minnie Palmer. He began writing songs, and, while appearing in Bartley Campbell's *Friend and Foe* in 1882, he introduced his first success, "Midnight in Killarney." Scanlan's good looks and his abilities as a singer, actor, and songwriter attracted the attention of Augustus Pitou, an impresario with a knack for packaging talent. Pitou created a string of successful Irish musicals around Scanlan: *The Irish Minstrel* (1883), *Shane-na-lawn* (1885), *Myles Arroon* (1888), and *Mavourneen* (1891). Scanlan wrote songs for all of these shows, the most successful of which were "Peek-a-Boo," "Scanlan's Rose Song," "Peggy O'Moore," and "My Nellie's Blue Eyes" (1883), the only one to survive into the twentieth century. Dennis Morgan sang it in the 1947 film biography of Chauncey Olcott, *My Wild Irish Rose*. (William Frawley played Scanlan in the film.)

In fact, it was Olcott whom Pitou summoned to New York to take over Scanlan's role in *Mavourneen* a few months after the show opened in September 1891. Since coming to New York, the former temperance singer had adopted a lifestyle that left him trapped in dementia at the age of 35. The performer was committed to Bloomingdale Asylum in White Plains, New York, in January 1892. He died there six years later.

Although his career was short, Scanlan was an important pivotal figure in the Irish musical in America. Scanlan's stage representations had less of the vaudeville Paddy and more of the smooth, self-assured Irish American. Musically, his songs were anchored firmly in the mainstream of American popular music and had little to do with traditional Irish melody. (In fact, "My Nellie's Blue Eyes" is based on the Venetian song "Vieni Sul Mar.") In terms of their lyrics, Scanlan's songs offered Irish Americans a sense of Irishness based on romance, sentiment, and national pride that had nothing to do with famine, poverty, politics, or revolution. Scanlan helped to create the emerging genre of Tin Pan Alley Irish-American song.

William H. A. Williams

See also: OLCOTT, Chauncey

References
Fiedler, Mari Kathleen. "Chauncey Olcott: Irish-American Mother-Love, Romance, and Nationalism." *Éire-Ireland* 22, no. 2 (1987): 4–26.
Williams, William H. A. *'Twas Only An Irishman's Dream: The Image of the Irish and Ireland in American Popular Song Lyrics, 1800–1920.* Urbana: University of Illinois Press, 1996.

SCOTS-IRISH

The ethnic identifier "Scots-Irish" (sometimes "Scotch-Irish") generally refers to American descendants of Presbyterian Scots who settled in Ulster (modern-day Northern Ireland) during the seventeenth century. The Scots-Irish left Ulster for varied reasons, including neomercantilist British economic policy in the region, requirements that they (along with other non-Anglicans in Northern Ireland) pay 10 percent of their income to the Anglican Church, ongoing friction with the native Catholic Irish, and greater economic opportunity in the New World. Although the Scots-Irish settled throughout the American colonies, initially they were concentrated most heavily in Pennsylvania.

There has long been controversy surrounding the term "Scots-Irish." According to some historians the term "Scots-Irish" originated in mid-eighteenth century America to distinguish the Ulster Presbyterian emigrants of Scottish ancestry from Roman Catholic Irish settlers in the colonies. Although the significance of Scots-Irish as a religious identifier in the United States has largely faded, its religious significance remained clear well into the twentieth century. Some commentators have postulated that noted Americans of Roman Catholic Irish descent, such as famed frontiersman Daniel Boone, have been commonly identified as Scots-Irish because Catholicism and Irish ethnicity did not fit prevailing ideals of American greatness at the time.

The Scots-Irish were by far the most numerous of the early immigrant groups from Europe who settled in the United States. According to historian David Hackett Fischer, Puritan immigrants numbered about 21,000, while the Scots-Irish numbered 275,000. Scots-Irish historian Charles A. Hannah estimates that about 200,000 Protestants, mostly Presbyterians, one-third of the entire Protestant population of Ireland at that time, left Ulster between 1725 and 1768 for the American colonies. Another 30,000 came during the years 1771–1773.

Having arrived later than the English Puritans, many Scots-Irish settled in the mountain backcountry of pre-Revolutionary America, leading a hardscrabble existence. Many others, however, gained considerable success in business, politics, and other spheres. Their descendants, many of whom moved westward, include such famous Americans as Patrick Henry, George Patton, John C. Calhoun, former U.S. President Bill Clinton, writers Mark Twain and William Faulkner, infamous outlaws like Clyde Barrow, and Hollywood legend John Wayne.

Danielle Maze

See also: PRESBYTERIANISM; SCOTS-IRISH CULTURE; SCOTS-IRISH PATTERNS OF SETTLEMENT IN THE UNITED STATES; SCOTS-IRISH POLITICS

References

Cobb, Irvin S. "The Lost Tribes of the Irish in the South: An Address at the Annual Dinner of the American Irish Historical Society." New York: Office of Edward H. Daly, Secretary-General, American Irish Historical Society, 1917.

Fischer, David Hackett. *Albion's Seed: Four British Folkways in America.* Oxford: Oxford University Press, 1991.

Hanna, Charles A. *The Scotch-Irish, or The Scot in North Britain, North Ireland, and North America.* Vol. I. New York: G. Putnam's Sons, 1902.

Leyburn, James C. *The Scotch-Irish: A Social History.* Chapel Hill: The University of North Carolina Press, 1962.

SCOTS-IRISH AND MILITARY CONFLICT

Perhaps one of the most pervasive dimensions of the Scots-Irish stereotype that still exercises powerful influence at a popular level in modern America is the image of a people who were irascible, prone to feuding, and ready to take direct, violent action to settle disputes. Some of the power of this caricature relates to the notion of generational continuity back to the violence and conflicts forged in the environment of the "debatable land," which constituted the shifting border between southern Scotland and northern England, and then later in the context of the Ulster Plantation. While it might be conceded that the outlook of those who adhered to the Calvinist theology and Covenanter principles of seventeenth-century Presbyterianism shaped a culture that tended to be uncompromising rather than accommodating, we should be wary of applying too much determinism in characterizing people who were consistently mixing and changing in the British Isles and in the backcountry of colonial America. The reputation, not without some evidential foundation, the Scots-Irish attained for being dismissive of Native American rights and prone to violence in that direction, requires a little contextualization. If set in comparison to eighteenth-century Philadelphia Quakers such a judgment may seem fair, but if one looks back to Puritan New England in the previous century, it is harder to see Scots-Irish frontiersmen as particularly exceptional in their dealings with the Indians. Furthermore, as research progresses we can appreciate more and more that settlers from Ulster and their descendants enjoyed a significantly more complex relationship with native peoples, learning from and trading with the natives as well as grabbing land and plundering. Andrew Jackson, son of Ulster immigrants, and infamously associated with the forced migration of the Cherokee, both personified and compounded this negative reputation. However, a perusal of the biographical dictionaries illustrates the point that many prominent Scots-Irish figures demonstrated in their dealings with native peoples an approach which was pacific and cooperative rather than consistently antagonistic.

It is not possible to ascribe an ethnic identity to all those who engaged in the various conflicts that dotted the history of Colonial America and the United States, but the involvement of the Scots-Irish in these campaigns has usually served as a source of pride to those who celebrate this heritage. In 2004, for example, James Webb, former assistant secretary of defense under Ronald Reagan, published a volume charting the contribution of the Scots-Irish to America under the title, *Born Fighting*. Given the extent of their settlement along the expanding southern frontier of the American Colonies and their enthusiasm for and familiarity with firearms, it was to be anticipated that they would play a prominent role in the French and Indian War (1756–1763). Their forebears, after all, had originally been encouraged to settle on the frontier in both Pennsylvania and Virginia because they were perceived to be experienced in and skilled at "dealing with a native threat." The Scots-Irish pioneers of the Appalachian region were much admired for their adept guerrilla tactics in confronting both native and French forces. Epitomizing this reputation was Colonel John Armstrong, born in Brookeborough, Co. Fermanagh, around 1720 and a leading figure in the struggle in western Pennsylvania after 1756. Armstrong represented continuity between the French and Indian War and the Revolutuionary War (1775–1783), in which he was promoted to the rank of general in Washington's patriot army. The military action with which the Scots-Irish are most commonly associated in this war is the Battle of King's Mountain. Here on October 7, 1780, a body of about 1,000 "over-mountain militia," many of Ulster extraction, routed a battalion of redcoats under the command of Scots aristocrat Major Patrick Ferguson. In truth, the decisiveness of the military contribution of the Scots-Irish and the unanimity of their commitment to the patriot's cause have been prone to some exaggeration. Nonetheless, there is no doubt that they contributed significantly to the ideology underpinning the Revolution and that this acted as an inspiration for many radical Presbyterians in later eighteenth-century Ireland.

Slightly perversely those figures who perhaps came to represent the greatest martial heroes of the Scots-Irish performed their deeds of valor well after independence from Britain had been won. Andrew Jackson, the son of settlers from Ulster and in so many ways the figure taken to personify the personality, culture, and values of his people was, of course, celebrated as a military strategist before being acknowledged as a master politician. Jackson, as southern theater commander, won a stunning and decisive victory over the British forces at the Battle of New Orleans on January 8, 1815. It was symbolic of a somewhat curious conflict (1812–1815) that this victory was actually secured more than a fortnight after peace terms had been agreed between the warring parties in far-off Belgium. The other two figures, Sam Houston and Davy Crockett, both claimed Scots-Irish ancestry and had served under Jackson in the War of 1812. Yet it would be later that these men would win notoriety for their bravery and martial skill. Houston successfully commanded the Texan army to victory over Santa Anna in the Battle of San Jacinto (April 21, 1836), which led in turn to the establishment of Texan independence. Crockett, from Tennessee, was the most famous defender who surrendered his life at the Alamo (March 6, 1836) in the same cause. Crockett also reflected in his own genealogy that pride in the continuity of a warrior ethic. Allegedly, a number of Crockett's ancestors back in Ireland had served the Williamite cause in the defense of Londonderry in 1690, while two uncles had participated in the victory at the Battle of King's Mountain in 1780. This could be said to represent the Scots-Irish pedigree par excellence.

Again, somewhat curiously, one of the few books not yet written about the American Civil War is that dealing specifically with the contribution of those who could be considered ethnically Scots-Irish. No simple narrative could communicate the highly complex picture that emerges from even cursory exploration. One can accurately claim that a significantly greater proportion of the Confederate army, both officers and rank and file, was of Scots-Irish descent than was the case with the Union forces. However, several subregions within the South, across the Appalachian zone heavily settled by immigrants from Ulster in the eighteenth century, followed their leaders in opting to support the Union cause in 1861. Although there were many Confederate generals of Scots-Irish descent, Stonewall Jackson and Jeb Stuart to name two of the most noted, it was Ulysses Simpson Grant, whose maternal grandfather had been a Presbyterian immigrant from Co. Tyrone, who contributed so much to achieving the final victory of North over South. Well beyond the era of the Civil War, involvement in the U.S. military continued to play a central role in the definition of a Scots-Irish identity, just as it did for the increasing numbers of citizens who saw themselves as Irish-American Catholics.

Patrick Fitzgerald

See also: AMERICAN CIVIL WAR;
    AMERICAN WAR OF INDEPENDENCE;
    JACKSON, Andrew; PRESBYTERIANISM;
    SCOTS-IRISH; SCOTS-IRISH CULTURE;
    SCOTS-IRISH POLITICS

References

Leyburn, James, G. *The Scotch-Irish: A Social History.* Chapel Hill: University of North Carolina Press, 1962.

Marley, David, F. *Wars of the Americas: A Chronology of Armed Conflict in the New World, 1492 to the Present.* Santa Barbara, CA: ABC-CLIO, 1998.

Webb, James. *Born Fighting: How the Scots-Irish Shaped America.* New York: Broadway Books, 2004.

SCOTS-IRISH CULTURE

Immigrant groups who did not speak English on arrival, such as the Germans, tended to maintain a distinctive way of life longer in the New World. The fact that Presbyterian immigrants from Ulster spoke English gave them an immediate advantage in accessing mainstream American culture. Added to this, their tendency to move home successively over a wide area rather than remain in the first place of settlement increased their exposure to other cultural influences, making it relatively difficult to isolate a single distinctive Scots-Irish way of life. Scholars debate the extent to which Ulster Presbyterian settlers up until the middle of the nineteenth century were aware of themselves as a distinct ethnic group. Two major movements have documented and studied this group, the first associated with the establishment of the Scotch-Irish Society of America in 1889 to "preserve the history and perpetuate the achievements of the Scotch-Irish race in America," and the second, under way since the 1950s with the foundation of the Ulster-Scot Historical Society, and particularly associated now with the Ulster-Scots movement in Northern Ireland (recognized by the Belfast Agreement of 1998), which has a strong interest in the Ulster-Scots diaspora, including the Scots-Irish in the United States.

A main indicator of the varied pattern of Scots-Irish settlement in both broad belts and enclaves is the clustering of family names that are evidently of Ulster and ultimately Scottish origin (such as McKean, Read, and Thompson—signatories of the Declaration of Independence). Another indicator is the presence of place-names of Ulster origin, such as Belfast and Bangor in Maine, the towns of Londonderry and Antrim and the county of Hillsboro in New Hampshire, Orange County in what would later become Vermont, and Coleraine in Massachusetts. Economically, we may distinguish broadly between those who became increasingly successful in financial and entrepreneurial roles along the Philadelphia-Pittsburgh axis and those in the southern backcountry whose economic and political power diminished.

The Scots-Irish came from what has been called "the most relaxed landlord regimen in the British Isles." As farmers on the American frontier they engaged in much the same agricultural practices as their neighbors, learning the technique of making the V-notched log cabin from the Swedes and Finns of the Delaware Valley, and the winter foddering techniques and wagon styles from the Germans of Pennsylvania. Their main distinctiveness in western Pennylvania was involvement in linen production, which was a special craft they brought from the "old country." Representations of this way of life may be seen today in the outdoor museums of Ulster-American Folk Park at Omagh, Co. Tyrone, in Northern Ireland and the Museum of American Frontier Culture in Staunton, Virginia.

Contemporaries did not always compare the Scots-Irish favorably with their German neighbors, contrasting the indolence and carelessness of the former with the industry and neatness of the latter. There was often mutual antagonism between the groups, especially at election times, that were accounted for more by difference in social values than in farming skill. Whereas the Germans tended to remain where they first settled, the Scots-Irish tended to exploit their farms ruthlessly before moving on to others. It has been suggested that this was because migration was in a sense second nature to them. Situated mainly on the frontier, the Scots-Irish proved "hard neighbors to the Indians" and bore the brunt of Indian raids.

The main social institution of Scots-Irish frontier settlements was the Presbyterian Church—usually the forerunner of the civil authority. Colonial officials regularly appealed to Presbyterian clergy for their support in civil matters, acknowledging their role as both the secular and religious leaders of their communities. Scots-Irish settlements in the Chesapeake Bay colonies, especially on the eastern shore of Maryland, became the cradle of the Presbyterian church in America. Francis Mackemie (ca. 1658–1708), who emigrated from Co. Donegal and settled in Virginia, is regarded as the "father of American Presbyterianism."

The development of an effective network of church organization was hindered by the relatively small size of scattered rural congregations across such a wide area and poor communications among them. Although some congregations had emigrated from Ulster en masse, accompanied by their ministers, these were relatively few. The ongoing shortage of well-qualified ministers prompted regular appeals for missionaries from Ulster and Scotland. Following the Ulster tradition of founding private schools or academies, Presbyterian colleges were eventually established to help meet this need, the first being Log College at Neshaminy, near Philadelphia, which

was the seed from which the College of New Jersey (later Princeton) developed in 1746. Nevertheless, social organization was inhibited in many places on the frontier, where communities could be without a church building or pastor for years, having to rely on irregular visits of itinerant preachers. In such areas there tended to be a drift from Presbyterianism to other Protestant denominations better equipped to supply their spiritual needs, such as the Congregationalists in New England and the Baptists and Methodists in the southern colonies. At the outbreak of the American War of Independence the Scots-Irish still belonged predominantly to the Presbyterian church, but it was a church that had become, in competing actively for members, more evangelical and less insistent on the doctrine of election, which had been its distinguishing characteristic carried over from Ulster.

Against expectation perhaps, the strict Calvinism of the Scots-Irish settlers proved a barrier to their integration with the less zealous and more broad-minded New England Puritans. The relative poverty of many Scots-Irish settlers who remained in Boston and their poor reputation among Puritan Bostonians for drinking, blasphemy, and violence also proved barriers to integration. As emigrants from Ulster were mostly removed by several generations from their original family immigration to Ulster from Scotland, they tended to regard Ireland rather than Scotland as "the old country" and the Presbyterian church in Ireland as their "mother church." For the descendants of the pioneer emigrants from Ulster, their affiliation to a religious denomination generally proved more important than their experience as members of an ethnic subculture.

As well as the Presbyterian Church, the Scots-Irish also carried over the Orange Order, a social and religious as well as a political organization. The earliest instances of parading on July 12, anniversary of King William of Orange's victory at the Battle of the Boyne in 1690, date to the 1820s. The first lodge of the Loyal Orange Institution or Orange Order, founded in Ulster in 1795, was established in the United States in New York in 1867. By 1873 there was a network of nearly 100 lodges and 10,000 members, and in 1914 that number had reached 364 lodges and 30,000 members. Although open to Protestants of all ethnic backgrounds, the Institution was overwhelming Scots-Irish in membership and leadership. As late as 1919 the Orange Order held a sizable Twelfth of July parade in New York City. After the Great Depression, which brought immigration from Ulster virtually to an end, the Scots-Irish sustained a distinctive identity to a reduced extent.

Although proud of their Scottish roots, Presbyterian settlers from Ulster clearly did not think of themselves simply as Scots. Some, like Thomas Mellon, expressed strong affection for the poetry of Robert Burns and the novels of Sir Walter Scott, but for the most part they tended to have settled in different areas from the Scots and showed little interest in St. Andrew's societies or Burns suppers. To a certain extent, however, their speech continued to mark them apart. The original ancestors of the Scots-Irish who had immigrated to Ulster in the seventeenth century spoke Scots—a sibling language to English. Much effort is currently being put into recovering what is called "Ulster Scots" and into identifying more evidence of it being spoken and written in Scots-Irish areas of America, as for example by David Bruce (ca. 1760–1830), an emigrant from

Ulster to southwestern Pennsylvania, and Robert Dinsmoor (1757–1836), the son of an Ulster emigrant to southern New Hampshire, both of whom published poems in Ulster Scots in their local weekly newspapers.

The original Scots-Irish settlers arrived with, in effect, a triple identity: Scottish in religion, local dialect, and specific culture; Irish by birth, polity, and local associations; and British by ultimate political allegiance and aspects of their wider culture (e.g., educated speech, legal, and commercial procedures). To a large extent this accounts for the complex trajectory of their descendants in the United States.

Brian Lambkin

See also: PRESBYTERIANISM; SCOTS-IRISH; SCOTS-IRISH PATTERNS OF SETTLEMENT, UNITED STATES; SCOTS-IRISH POLITICS

References

Gilmore, Peter. "Scotch-Irish Identity and Traditional Ulster Music on the Pennsylvania Frontier." *Journal of Scotch-Irish Studies* 1, no. 2 (2001): 138–146.

Gilmore, Peter. "The Scots Irish: Cultural Baggage of the Presbyterian Pioneers." *Causeway* (Summer 1997): 44–49.

Griffin, Patrick. *The People with No Name: Ireland's Ulster Scots, America's Scots Irish, and the Creation of a British Atlantic World, 1689–1764.* Princeton, NJ: Princeton University Press, 2001.

Jones, M. A. "The Scotch-Irish in British America." In *Strangers within the Realm: Cultural Margins of the First British Empire,* edited by B. Bailyn and P. D. Morgan. Chapel Hill: University of North Carolina Press, 1991.

Keller, Kenneth W. "What Is Distinctive about the Scotch-Irish?" In *Appalachian Frontiers: Settlement, Society and Development in the Preindustrial Era,* edited by R. D. Mitchell, 69–86. Lexington: University Press of Kentucky, 1991.

Leyburn, J. G., *The Scotch-Irish: A Social History.* Chapel Hill: University of North Carolina Press, 1962.

Montgomery, Michael. "The Problem of Persistence: Ulster-American Missing Links." *Journal of Scotch-Irish Studies* 1, no. 1 (2001): 105–119.

SCOTS-IRISH PATTERNS OF SETTLEMENT, CANADA

The settlement patterns of the Scots-Irish and the larger population of Irish Protestant immigrants set the stage for English Canada's ethnic, economic, and political makeup in the nineteenth century. Sometimes this society was marked by conflict as Irish Protestants clashed with Irish Catholics, but for the most part the world the Scots-Irish created was rural and peaceful, and they surrounded themselves with kin and coreligionists.

Canadian historians have noted that the Scots-Irish experience in Canada was dissimilar to that of the Scots-Irish in the United States. The term is actually misleading—most Irish Protestant immigrants came to Canada a century later than the American Scots-Irish and were not of the Scottish Presbyterian faith but were in fact Anglicans of English descent. Nevertheless, some nineteenth-century Irish Canadians claimed that the country's Scots-Irish population was significant in quantity, heritage, and accomplishment. In 1891, the Reverend Stuart Acheson addressed the third congress of the Scots-Irish in America on the ethnic group's status in Canada. He claimed that one quarter of Canadians were Scots-Irish and that every province contained counties almost entirely populated by Scots-Irish, such as Colchester, Nova Scotia.

Although these population statistics were clearly false—Irish of all religions accounted for less than 25 percent of Canadians in 1871 and decreased in the following decades—they did suggest strong concentrations of people with similarities to the Ulster Presbyterians who migrated to New England and Pennsylvania in the eighteenth century. Within the larger group of Irish Protestants, Presbyterians tended to have ancestry among the Ulster Scots and remained an identifiable group in Canada at least until the late nineteenth century. They usually immigrated in group or chain migration paradigms, and despite their image as frontiersmen in America, they were more often found in Canadian areas known for their Irish Presbyterian roots.

Attempts to promote Irish immigration in the British colonies before the nineteenth century were negligible. Alexander McNutt attempted to bring Scots-Irish settlers to Nova Scotia in the early 1760s through elaborate settlement schemes, and Thomas Desbrisay tried similar projects to L'Isle St. Jean (Prince Edward Island) in the following decade. Both had little success. McNutt's emigration project was actually resisted by the English government who feared the loss of too many loyal subjects in Ireland. However, one group of Irish Presbyterian immigrants did settle in the Minas Basin area of Nova Scotia beginning in 1760. They traced roots to Ulster but actually migrated from Londonderry, New Hampshire. The settlers were in fact resettlers, inheriting cleared land, scattered buildings, and deteriorating dykes from the Acadian people who had been torn from the land by the British only a few years earlier. A census in 1766 showed 694 people in the townships of Truro, Onslow, and Londonderry: all were Protestants, and all but 16 came from Ireland or the American colonies. The community they created became part of Colchester County, which Acheson pointed to as the quintessential Scots-Irish settlement in Canada.

Serious Irish emigration to Canada did not begin until after 1815 when the British Isles experienced postwar readjustment and Ulster experienced agricultural instability. As many as 100,000 Irish left per year in the pre-Famine decades, many to Britain for seasonal labor and many others to North America. That Canada drew the majority of the latter from 1825 to 1845 was due in some part to its convenience and affordability as a channel to the United States. In the second quarter of the nineteenth century more than two-thirds of immigrants to British North America were Irish. The cause of emigration was usually economic pressure. Many Ulster Presbyterians who experienced the instability of the Ulster linen industry saw opportunity in Britain's sparsely populated North American colonies. Because of the high cost of transatlantic fares immigrants were rarely impoverished and were usually farmers and skilled tradespeople such as weavers seeking a life as agricultural settlers.

Two general patterns of settlement emerged in the nineteenth century. The Scots-Irish community in Colchester is an example of a chain migration settlement that remained largely atypical in the British Atlantic region. Instead, most Atlantic colonies attracted Catholics from the south coast of Ireland whose immigration routes were paved before the Famine by the Atlantic fishery trade. Conversely, in the Saint John Valley and Central Canada the timber trade formed the most important migration channels for Ulster Protestants and immigrants from enclaves in the south of Ireland. The use of merchant vessels for passenger transport

created the popular but rather exceptional story of immigrants arriving in "coffin ships." A more reliable trend demonstrated by trade route migration is that many Irish were subsequently found in the areas most crucial to these industries.

The early history of the Irish Presbyterians in what would become Canada is difficult to uncover. The historical literature on the subject is scarce, conflicting, and sometimes embellished. Donald MacKay argued that three-quarters of Irish emigrants to British North America were Presbyterian when the postwar Ulster emigration began. Of 4,000 farmers and linen weavers who left Belfast for British North America in 1818, only 20 percent were Anglican and most of the others were Presbyterian. If this was an early trend among Irish migrants it was short lived. Over the next few decades Anglicans outnumbered Irish Presbyterians, and it is clear that Presbyterians in Canada were either converting to other denominations, continuing on to the United States, or ceasing to immigrate in such magnitude.

Although Protestants in Ulster were more than half Presbyterian in the mid-nineteenth century, less than one quarter were Presbyterian in Canada at Confederation. Protestant immigration to Canada originated in many parts of Ireland, including the southern areas, which were predominantly Anglican. Ulster Presbyterian emigrants were more likely to join their fellow Scots-Irish in the United States, but some established migration routes existed between Derry and Canadian ports like Saint John. New Brunswick's Irish Presbyterians, therefore, accounted for more than the national average with 38 percent of the Irish Protestant immigrants and even 31 percent of the Protestants who claimed Irish ethnicity in 1871.

Statistical software and increasingly available samples from the late nineteenth century manuscript censuses allow detailed studies of Irish Canadians—most of whom are second- and third-generation immigrants by this period. The Reverend Acheson exaggerated when he claimed that Colchester, Nova Scotia, was almost entirely Scots-Irish, but he did identify a community with unusually strong Irish Presbyterian roots. The 1881 Census of Canada recorded 5,520 Irish Presbyterians, who made up 64 percent of the county's Irish population. The Baptists were the second largest group of Irish with only 16 percent of the population. The Methodists were a distant third, followed by Roman Catholics and Anglicans. A sample of the 1901 census reaffirms these concentrations and indicates that they remained consistent, with 64 percent Presbyterians and 15 percent Baptists.

In Ontario, English Canada's population center, the story was much different. Whereas the Colchester Irish Presbyterians were present in the late eighteenth century and assumed farms that were taken from Acadians during a prosperous golden age, Ontario's Irish Presbyterians came later, with less organization, to unbroken land and in disputed numbers. According to the 1871 census, Ontario's Irish were only 16.4 percent Presbyterian. This low representation was despite the fact that Protestants made up two-thirds of the Irish in Ontario. Anglicans and Methodists accounted for most of the Irish Protestants, but Methodists were only 1 percent above Presbyterians among the Irish born in Ontario. Methodism was popular among Irish pioneers and their descendants, and its circuit riders were more successful than the Presbyterian or Anglican missions.

The Irish Presbyterians in Ontario remained consistent in 1881 at 16.5 percent of the Irish population. Thirty percent of Ontario's Irish Presbyterians lived in the eastern counties in 1881, compared with 34 percent of the province's Irish. By this time the western counties were experiencing more rapid population growth than the counties of the east. For instance, Euphrasia township in Grey County was settled largely by Ulster Protestants who had lived elsewhere in Ontario, which demonstrates their transience in Ontario and the popularity of resettlement in the western counties. Irish Protestants from Ontario represented the first of their group to settle the Canadian west in large numbers, because few Irish immigrated directly to the fur-trading region in earlier decades.

Interestingly, Irish Presbyterian groups can be identified in the late nineteenth century—in a particularly concentrated area or an Irish Presbyterian church—though they were not as apparent as Acheson claimed. In Eastern Ontario, for instance, four adjacent counties between the Ottawa and St. Lawrence rivers had unusually high concentrations of Irish Presbyterians, around 25 percent of the local Irish population. Compared with Colchester, these are small concentrations, but for a province whose Anglican and Methodist Irish populations usually outweighed the Presbyterian, the numbers are significant. Dundas County's Irish were more than 26 percent Presbyterian in 1881. The 1,899 Irish Presbyterians formed the largest religious group among the Irish in that region and almost half of the county's Presbyterians. The county's Irish were less than 15 percent Anglican.

Dundas County is an interesting case study because it was one of the earliest settlements of English-speaking immigrants in Ontario. Loyalists were the first of these settlers in the late eighteenth century and were mostly Germans accompanied by a few Scottish Presbyterians. A riverfront county like Dundas was typically settled first along the lots on the St. Lawrence. Gradually, younger generations and later arrivals began moving into the northern townships. Almost two-thirds of the county's highly Presbyterian Irish population lived in the two western townships: 28 percent were in Matilda, the riverfront township, and more than 36 percent were in Mountain to the north. If Irish Presbyterians settled early and permanently in Dundas it was most likely on the county's western riverfront lots, and if later migration or land shortages for inheriting children made the northern townships more attractive to the Irish, the Presbyterians greatly preferred Mountain. The scattered centers of Irish Presbyterianism in Eastern Ontario demonstrate that this identification was important to Irish immigrants and their children when they chose where to live.

Economically, the Scots-Irish differed very little from their neighbors. The 1881 census reveals that, like the rest of Canadians Irish, Presbyterians were mostly farmers and overwhelmingly rural—more than half of the Irish Presbyterians and Anglicans were farmers in Eastern Ontario. Methodists, Wesleyans, and Episcopal Methodists were each roughly 60 percent farmers, as were almost half of the Irish Catholics in the region. The unusually high amount of home-manufactured linen in the Dundas area suggests that the traditional Scots-Irish occupation of linen weaving might have perpetuated itself among Irish Presbyterian descendants. The county produced more than 20 percent of Ontario's homemade linen in 1871, and with Russell, Dundas' highly Irish Presbyterian neighbor, it produced one-third of the province's linen in 1881. Ulster households had long been central parts of a linen industry, and early Irish Presbyterian immigrants to Canada, like those in Colchester, were skilled in flax cultivation and linen weaving.

However, the linen produced in Dundas in 1871 did not belong to the Irish Presbyterians, nor was it ethnically neutral: 64 percent of the linen was produced in the township least favored by Irish Presbyterians, and more than 71 percent of the producers were of Dutch and German origin. The Irish, predominately Anglicans, were a distant second at 14 percent. The second-highest linen production occurred in Mountain, the most Irish Presbyterian township, but the producers there were mostly English Anglicans and Methodists. The paucity of linen among the Irish in Dundas demonstrates that their geographical distinctiveness did not necessarily imply a rigid connection with other parts of their collective heritage.

Before Canada became a place that spoke to the world about multiculturalism it hosted many culturally disparate and often acrimonious bedfellows. Religious and ethnic strife formed one of the more infamous parts of the early Scots-Irish experience in Canada. Occasionally, a report of Orange and Catholic violence or threats of violence would involve the regions of concentrated Irish Presbyterians. In some cases Irish Presbyterians were specifically mentioned, and in many cases Ulster Protestants in general were implicated. The first major confrontations in Ontario took place in Murphy's Falls (now Carleton Place, Lanark) and Shipman's Mills (now Almonte, Lanark) in the 1820s. The aggressors in the former were supposedly some Irish Catholics known as the Ballygiblins who started a bar fight with a group of influential Scottish immigrants that developed into a street battle between armed posses. The bar owner was Alexander Morris, an Ulster Orangeman, but most of the Protestants involved were Scottish.

Occasionally, Orange violence erupted in reply to large-scale Irish Catholic immigration. Peter Robinson, a superintendent of colonization schemes in what would become Ontario, was well aware of the danger these confrontations posed to his immigrant communities and attempted to locate his settlements a safe distance from Ulster settlements. Later in the century the meeting of Irish Catholics with established Ulster Protestants in cities such as Saint John resulted in a series of violent outbreaks and riots. Orange activities cannot simply be explained as reactionary and xenophobic, however. They were more often symptomatic of political movements and localized attempts to create space and identity for established immigrants.

Orange demonstrations were often connected to churches known to be Irish Presbyterian and were found in larger cities like Toronto and Kingston. Displays of ethnic and denominational pride were regular and often peaceful, but more importantly they identified the close connection between the Orange Lodge and Irish Presbyterians. The latter were also intimately—though not always happily—connected by doctrine to the Scottish Presbyterians in Canada. On many occasions, and especially in rural places, Irish Presbyterians shared congregations with their Scottish coreligionists. At other times, the distinct identity shared by the Irish Presbyterians was enough to split their churches along ethnic lines. Because of the smallness of Irish Presbyterianism in Canada, they relied on the Scottish United Presbytery for ministers. Some believe Irish Presbyterians were accustomed to a more active and evangelical ministry than the Scots. The complicated relationship between the two groups and the ecclesiastical work of Irish Presbyterians remains an uncharted section of Canadian history.

Josh MacFayden

See also: PRESBYTERIANISM; SCOTS-IRISH; SCOTS-IRISH AND MILITARY CONFLICT; SCOTS-IRISH CULTURE; SCOTS-IRISH POLITICS; SCOTS-IRISH PATTERNS OF SETTLEMENT, UNITED STATES

References

Akenson, Donald H. *The Irish in Ontario: A Study in Rural History.* Kingston, ON: McGill-Queen's University Press, 1984.

Elliott, Bruce. *Irish Migrants in the Canadas: A New Approach.* Kingston, ON: McGill-Queen's University Press, 1988.

Houston, Cecil J., and William J. Smyth. *Irish Emigration and Canadian Settlement: Patterns, Links, and Letters.* Toronto: University of Toronto Press, 1990.

Mackay, Donald. *Flight From Famine: The Coming of the Irish to Canada.* Toronto: McClelland and Stewart, 1999.

Murphy, J. M. *The Londonderry Heirs: A Story of the Settlement of the Townships of Truro, Onslow, and Londonderry.* Middleton, NS: Black Print Co., 1976.

Wilson, Catharine. *A New Lease on Life: Landlords, Tenants, and Immigrants in Ireland and Canada.* Montreal: McGill-Queen's University Press, 1994.

Wilson, David. *The Irish in Canada.* Canada's Ethnic Groups series, Booklet No. 12. Ottawa: Canadian Historical Association, 1989.

SCOTS-IRISH PATTERNS OF SETTLEMENT, UNITED STATES

Before 1725

The first concerted effort by Presbyterians from Ulster to emigrate across the Atlantic came in 1636 and was directed toward New England. The voyage, however, was aborted when mid-Atlantic storms were taken as a signal of divine disfavor and the vessel, *Eagle Wing,* returned eastward for Scotland. This episode appears to have dampened enthusiasm for emigration amongst Ulster Presbyterians for at least a generation. However, by the final quarter of the seventeenth century there is evidence of a renewed interest in transatlantic migration from Ulster. Reconstructing the precise patterns of emigration in the half century up to 1725 is problematic, but relative to later movement, it appears fairly diverse in terms of the destinations selected. Even before 1700 modest Scots-Irish settlement could be identified in Delaware, eastern Maryland, the lower Hudson Valley, and New Jersey. A significant acceleration in the pace of emigrant departures from Ulster occurred in the years after 1717. The great majority of vessels departing were destined either for the ports of New England or Delaware. While the significance of migration toward the Delaware River in this early phase of migration may have been underrepresented in the past, it remains the case that migration to New England was most significant in the decade before 1725. Theological disputes and a hunger for land helped fan out Scots-Irish settlers from Boston, the main port of entry, toward the New England frontier. They moved west within Massachusetts toward Worcester, and north toward New Hampshire and Maine. Ultimately, significant numbers of first- and second-generation settlers moved to Vermont and Rhode Island also.

1725–1775

Although migrants and hosts shared an enthusiasm for what one historian has described as "a hotter kind of Protestantism" there were numerous objections by the dominant Congregationalists of New England to these Ulster Presbyterians, and differing ethnicity, English versus Scottish/Irish, added to the animosity. Thus, emigrants from Ulster increasingly directed their attentions south toward the Delaware ports. Here, indentured servitude offered a mechanism by which those of modest means could hope to establish a foothold on the land in the New World.

In the years after 1717, migrants from Ulster coming into the Delaware ports settled in significant numbers in Chester and Lancaster counties near Philadelphia. As the population grew and competition for land increased on the fertile Pennsylvania Piedmont the Scots-Irish increasingly moved westward toward the frontier or backcountry. This westward settlement was to some degree sponsored by tidewater colonial governors nervous about a threat from native peoples and sensing that these Scots-Irish could provide an effective defensive buffer. Moving up the Delaware Valley and then beyond the Susquehanna River, in the 1730s and 1740s they came increasingly to occupy the Cumberland Valley. The physical barrier of the Allegheny Mountains, combined with growing friction with Native Americans and uncertain land titles, all served to deflect the further spread of settlement south toward western Maryland and in particular into the Shenandoah Valley of Virginia. Throughout the middle decades of the eighteenth century, the Valley of Virginia, flanked to the west by the Appalachian Mountains and to the east by the Blue Ridge Mountains, would come to represent the crucial artery carrying migrants from Ulster south and west toward the expanding settlement frontier. Scots-Irish settlement became particularly concentrated in the central counties of Augusta and Rockbridge but a continuing stream of fresh arrivals from Ulster and the sons and daughters of Scots-Irish settlers continued to move on. The Great Wagon Road, which stretched from Philadelphia in the north down through the Valley of Virginia and out into the Carolina backcountry, remained busy in the decades before the Revolutionary War with thousands of Conestoga wagons. The families they carried were predominantly from the north of Ireland and Germany. In the backcountry of North and South Carolina and in western Georgia settlers from Ulster who had traveled south from the Delaware were met by other Scots-Irish migrants who had entered the colonies through Charleston, South Carolina. Many of these people had been induced to settle the southern frontier by a bounty scheme operated in the 1730s and 1760s by colonial governors keen to maintain the proportion of white European Protestants peopling the colonies.

While the bulk of Scots-Irish settlers in the colonial era were to be found peopling the southern Appalachian backcountry we should remain conscious of slowly expanding urban populations in cities like Philadelphia, Charleston, or New York as well as other pockets of rural settlement in places like western upstate New York. In attempting to characterize their settlement in colonial America, two particular features have been identified in relation to the Scots-Irish: high rates of mobility and scattered or isolated settlement. Throughout the period these settlers showed a particular propensity to uproot and move on. There is much evidence to support their traditional association with the expanding frontier. In addition wherever they settled in the backcountry, when land was plentiful, they often sought out settlement at a natural spring that offered a comfortable distance from their neighbours.

After 1775

The American Revolutionary War checked immigration from Ulster for the seven seasons after 1775, but as soon as the Atlantic reopened to emigrant shipping a strong flow of migration recommenced. The ports of what had been the middle colonies, Philadelphia and Baltimore, in particular, continued to receive those who might come to see themselves as Scots-Irish. Increasingly after 1815, however, there was a shift in the flow of migration, increasingly emanating from all over Ireland, it was directed toward northern ports such as New York and Boston. The evolving role of Liverpool as the dominant port of departure from the British Isles and the evolving timber trade served to draw the maritime Canadian ports into the orbit of the emigrants from Ireland. After American independence, Ulster Protestants were more likely to migrate to British North America, particularly to Upper Canada, which would become Ontario. From the core heartlands of Scots-Irish settlement before the Revolutionary War, western Pennsylvania and the Valley of Virginia, came the westward flow of subsequent generations of settlers who carried settlement through the iconic Cumberland Gap and on into Kentucky,

Tennessee, and across the American South. In addition, there was expansion west into Ohio and beyond. Classically, the pattern of Scots-Irish migration and settlement is depicted as petering out around 1820 as Catholic migration became predominant, but this division is somewhat distorted. Very significant numbers of Protestants from Ulster—Presbyterians, Anglicans, Methodists, Quakers, and others—continued to migrate to and settle in the United States. The so-called "Orange riots" that convulsed New York City in July 1870 and 1871 were a graphic reminder of this presence. By no means would all of the parading Orangemen in Manhattan have considered themselves Scots-Irish, but many had their origins in the province of Ulster.

Patrick Fitzgerald

See also: PRESBYTERIANISM; SCOTS-IRISH; SCOTS-IRISH AND MILITARY CONFLICT; SCOTS-IRISH CULTURE; SCOTS-IRISH PATTERNS OF SETTLEMENT, CANADA

References

Blethen, H. Tyler, and Curtis J. Wood, eds. *Ulster and North America: Transatlantic Perspectives on the Scotch-Irish.* Tuscaloosa: University of Alabama Press, 1997.

Fischer, David Hackett, *Albion's Seed: Four British Folkways in America.* Oxford: Oxford University Press, 1989.

Fitzgerald, Patrick, and Steve Ickringill, eds. *Atlantic Crossroads: Historical Connections between Scotland, Ulster and North America.* Newtownards, Northern Ireland: Colourpoint Books, 2001.

Jackson, Carlton, *A Social History of the Scotch-Irish.* Lanham, MD: Madison Books, 1993.

Jones, Maldwyn A. "The Scotch-Irish in British America." In B. Bailyn and P. D. Morgan, eds. *Strangers Within the Realm.* Chapel Hill: University of North Carolina Press, 1991.

Leyburn, James, G. *The Scotch-Irish: A Social History.* Chapel Hill: University of North Carolina Press, 1962.

SCOTS-IRISH POLITICS

The contribution of the Scots-Irish to America political life parallels that of their military contribution. Before the 1760s they were relatively powerless, and their settlements (then largely mid-Pennsylvanian) were underrepresented in government. In the period 1763–1800 they came from the colony's political margins to the center of state events. Except in New England they entered the American mainstream, pioneering the abandonment of ethnic enclaves for full assimilation and acculturation. Presidents Andrew Jackson, James Buchanan, and Chester A. Arthur were all sons of immigrants from Ulster, and James K. Polk, Andrew Johnson, Ulysses S. Grant, Grover Cleveland, Benjamin Harrison, William McKinley, Theodore Roosevelt, and Woodrow Wilson were of Scots-Irish descent.

The Presbyterians in Ulster constituted one of the largest blocs of Protestant dissent in the British Isles. This helps to explain the ease with which, as immigrants, they fit into the American drive for republicanism and religious disestablishment within a broadly Calvinist framework. However, their attitudes to the American War of Independence were determined more by their local conditions in the New World than in the Old. They were divided in their allegiances as patriots and loyalists, and a substantial proportion struggled to remain neutral. In Pennsylvania the Scots-Irish largely supported independence, motivated strongly by their hostility to the Quaker oligarchy in Philadelphia. Their relations with other Irish groups were complicated: many opposed the proposal drafted by Dublin-born Protestant George Bryan (1731–1791) for the abolition of slavery in Pennsylvania, while others served alongside

Irish Catholics in a loyalist regiment in Philadelphia known as the Volunteers of Ireland. There were similar divisions between the Scots-Irish in New England and the Carolinas. In the towns and cities the Presbyterian Ulstermen were able to make their political debut, obtaining local political offices that in the colonial period had been largely the monopoly of the Quakers and Anglicans.

The failure of the United Irishmen rebellion of 1798 resulted in an emigration of between 100 and 200 political refugees and their families, Catholic and Anglican as well as Presbyterian, including the Presbyterian clergyman Thomas Ledlie Birch. These exiled United Irishmen, with their enthusiasm for revolutionary France, engaged in American politics on the side of Thomas Jefferson and his Republican supporters against the Federalists. Their example was followed by many urban Scots-Irish who joined in Republican clubs and militia units. On the frontier the Scots-Irish were also strongly Republican. Such was their perceived influence that the Naturalization Act of 1798 was introduced "to prevent the indiscriminate admission of wild Irishmen and others to the right of suffrage." They voted in strength for Jefferson in the election of 1800. Later a majority of Scots-Irish inclined to the Democrats, influenced among other factors by the example of Andrew Jackson, son of Scots-Irish immigrants from Carrickfergus, Co. Antrim. Later still, the examples of James K. Polk and James Buchanan, both of Scots-Irish descent, exercised a similar influence.

Continuing immigration to America from Ulster, interrupted during the War of Independence, was perceived as "a prodigious influx of indigent foreigners" and revived earlier anxieties about a growing burden on towns. While many immigrants from Ulster between 1783 and 1812 joined the Scots-Irish settlements on the frontiers of Pennsylvania, Virginia, and the Carolinas, many others settled in the cities of the eastern seaboard, especially Philadelphia, Baltimore, New York, and Pittsburgh, which became the main Scots-Irish center in the United States. In the first quarter of the nineteenth century the Scots-Irish made up a gradually declining majority of immigrants to America from Ireland and were content to be described and to describe themselves as simply "Irish." In politics they cooperated with Catholic Irish and shared membership of benevolent organizations such as the Friendly Sons of St. Patrick and the Hibernian Society. The term "Scots-Irish" or "Scotch-Irish" is not well attested between the end of the American War of Independence and the Great Famine. The Famine-induced influx of Catholic Irish coincided with anti-Catholicism becoming dominant in American nativism, and the Scots-Irish interpreted this new situation as a challenge to differentiate themselves as Protestant Irish. In the 1850s many Ulster Presbyterians shifted to the new Republican party. What one commentator calls their "discovery of Scotch-Irishness" was part of a nativistic reaction, including the Know-Nothing movement of the 1850s, to the waves of poor southern Irish Catholics immigrating after 1835 and the continuing dominance of the New England elite.

Many Scots-Irish sympathized with Unionist opposition in Ulster to Home Rule between the 1880s and 1914. During the War of Independence in Ireland (1918–1922), organizations like the Orange Order sought to refute the arguments of Nationalist organizations like the Friends of

Irish Freedom. During World War II the stationing of U.S. troops in Northern Ireland was interpreted by many Scots-Irish as an endorsement of the partition of Ireland. The effect of the conflict in Northern Ireland during the 1970s was mainly to distance Scots-Irish from "the old country." On visits to the United States, the Reverend Ian Paisley, as a leader of extreme Unionism and Protesantism, was received less warmly by the Scots-Irish than by southern fundamentalist churchmen who saw him as an anticommunist crusader. Scots-Irish organizations, such as the Scotch-Irish Foundation, the Loyal Orange Order of the United States, Ulster American Loyalists, and the Northern Ireland Service Council, lobbied the U.S. government on behalf of Northern Ireland during the 1970s and 1980s. They extolled the Scots-Irish record in America, drawing attention to Ulster's role in World War II and contesting allegations of discrimination against Catholics in Northern Ireland, all of which indicated a continuing survival of political influence by this ethnic group.

Today about 8 million Americans are identifiable as having some Ulster Protestant background, but few have much sense of it, mainly as a result of their closeness to the dominant English culture against which their ancestors occasionally fought. The Scots-Irish for the most part joined settlers of English heritage in forming the social basis of the emerging American nation. Their need to promote a distinct Scots-Irish identity seems to have passed after World War I in an age of mass culture and economic individualism. It remains to be seen how current efforts to promote increased awareness of historic links between the Scots-Irish diaspora in the United States (and elsewhere) and its Ulster homeland will play into the unfolding story of how ethnic identity is negotiated on both sides of the Atlantic.

Brian Lambkin

See also: PRESBYTERIANISM, SCOTS-IRISH; SCOTS-IRISH AND MILITARY CONFLICT; SCOTS-IRISH CULTURE; SCOTS-IRISH PATTERNS OF SETTLEMENT, CANADA; SCOTS-IRISH PATTERNS OF SETTLEMENT, UNITED STATES

References

Doyle, David N. "Ulster Migrants in an Age of Rebellion." *Irish Economic and Social History* 22 (1995): 77–87.

Ickringill, Steve J. S. "The Scotch-Irish and the American Revolution." In *The Ulster-American Connection,* edited by J. W. Blake, 19–25. Coleraine: New University of Ulster, 1981.

SCULLY, WILLIAM (D. 1885)

William Scully, an Irish journalist and businessman, was the owner and editor of the *Anglo-Brazilian Times* of Rio de Janeiro, and founder of the Sociedade Internacional de Imigraçao. According to genealogical sources in Ireland, William Scully was born in Buolick, south Co. Tipperary, into a family of minor Catholic landlords. The family entered hard times during the Famine, and William arrived in Brazil in the 1850s or early 1860s. In Rio de Janeiro he made his living as a teacher of calligraphy. He married into an English Protestant family in Rio and then worked as a shipping agent for British lines. In 1872 he was the agent for the National Bolivian Navigation Company, which owned the majority of the Madeira-Mamoré Railway Company.

Scully's most important undertaking was the *Anglo-Brazilian Times,* which was published weekly from February 7, 1865, to September 24, 1884. The masthead described the *Times* as being a "Political, Literary, and Commercial" newspaper, and among its intentions were "to point out, and seek remedies for grievances and defects in the commercial and political intercourse of England and Brazil, and to promote a good understanding between the two countries" (from the first issue). The editor argued that Irish immigration to Brazil was a potentially viable means of upgrading the country's levels of economic productivity. As immigration and shipping businesses were complementary and beneficial to his interests, Scully both advertised Irish immigration in Brazil and promoted it in Great Britain.

The *Times* contained general Brazilian news and political comments, commercial reports, market prices, and maritime and immigration news. Although the paper received a subsidy from the Brazilian government, it was capable of criticism. When the local aristocracy—of which Scully was disdainful—promoted restrictions to the immigration of Protestants, the *Times* editor opposed them. Scully's newspaper was also critical of the British consul, claiming that he failed to help its destitute nationals. However, the legation believed Scully influenced the emperor and noted that Brazilian papers reprinted articles from the *Times*, believing it to be free of political bias. Foreign papers, including the influential London monthly *Brazil and River Plate Mail*, reproduced articles from the *Times*.

The International Society for Immigration represented William Scully's material support to the Brazilian government. The first meeting was held in February 1866, and Scully strongly recommended that the society be independent of the government. The society was active for the next two years. Although Great Britain forced Brazil to reduce its slave labor force from Africa, the Brazilian economy depended heavily on slaves. Arrangements were made for the slaves employed in the Northeastern provinces to be transferred to the burgeoning coffee production areas, especially in São Paulo and Rio de Janeiro. Plans for an increase in the employment of European immigrants began to multiply. However, Irish immigration was, in Scully's words, "nipped in the bud" and was never successful in Brazil. The episode that marked its failure was the collapse of the Irish colony Príncipe Dom Pedro's in Santa Catarina, which was suddenly deprived of funds and support between 1868 and 1869.

When the British minister William D. Christie published his *Notes on Brazilian Questions* (1865) in London, Scully had to appease most Brazilian leaders in power, and the emperor in particular, by criticizing very strongly the way Christie expressed his views on the slavery issue. The Irish newspaperman apparently delighted in trying to mend the badly damaged relationship between England and Brazil, to the point of verging on a pro-slavery stance, so as to dismiss the charges made public by Christie and thereby please the Brazilian political establishment.

William Scully also published the guide *Brazil: Its Provinces and Chief Cities; the Manners and Customs of the People; Agricultural, Commercial and Other Statistics, etc.* (various editions in 1865, 1866, and 1868), as well as *A New Map of Brazil* in 1866. The *Anglo-Brazilian Times* was published until September 1884, and William Scully died in Pau, France, on February 14, 1885.

Edmundo Murray

See also: BRAZIL

References

Alexandre de Araujo Neto, Miguel. "An Anglo-Irish Newspaper in Nineteenth-Century Brazil: The Anglo-Brazilian Times, 1865–1884." *Newsletter of the Brazilian Association for Irish Studies* 8 (August 1994).

Marshall, Oliver. *The English-Language Press in Latin America.* London: Institute of Latin American Studies, University of London, 1996.

SHACKLETON, ERNEST (1874–1922)

Ernest Shackleton spent the first six years of his life on a farm near his birthplace at Kilkea House, Co. Kildare, but then moved with his family to Dublin and later to suburban London. His father's family was Anglo-Irish, originally from Yorkshire. His mother's family was Irish, from counties Cork and Kerry.

Shackleton attended Dulwich College, but he was more interested in maritime adventures and left school at 16 to join the Merchant Navy. From 1890 to 1901 he sailed on numerous voyages across the Atlantic and Pacific, rising in rank from ship's boy to second mate to third officer.

In 1897 he met Emily Dorman, with whom he shared a love of poetry. While courting Emily, Shackleton decided to improve his situation. Accordingly, when he learned that Robert Scott was leading an expedition to Antarctica in 1901, Shackleton signed on as third lieutenant. His responsibilities included maintaining the ship's provisions and arranging the expedition's

Ernest Shackleton leaves for the Shackleton-Rowett Expedition aboard the Quest. *(Library of Congress)*

entertainment. He was also one of two crew members to join Scott on the unsuccessful sledge drive toward the South Pole in 1902, reaching the furthest point south anyone had ever traveled.

Shackleton returned to England in 1903, and he was appointed secretary of the Royal Scottish Geographical Society (RSGS). With this enhanced status, Shackleton married Emily in 1904, and they moved to Edinburgh. Always looking for new adventures, Shackleton agreed to stand as the Liberal Unionist Party candidate for Parliament. The Liberal Unionists opposed Home Rule for Ireland, presumably an ironic stance for the Irish-born Shackleton, who spoke with a slight brogue. Shackleton lost not only the election in 1906, but also his position with the RSGS, which felt he was neglecting his official duties.

The lure of Antarctica was still strong, so in 1907 Shackleton organized another expedition, hoping to reach the South Pole with the help of Manchurian ponies. Shackleton came within 97 miles of the Pole in 1909, but then turned back, fearing that no one would survive if he pushed forward. He returned to England a hero and was knighted for having reached the furthest point south.

Shackleton's published account, *The Heart of the Antarctic* (1909), brought him further acclaim, including a lecture tour and honors throughout Europe, the United States, and Canada. By all accounts, Shackleton was an engaging public speaker—bold and charming, but also modest and completely credible. He was especially admired by American audiences, who appreciated his Irish wit and manner of speaking. "Even [Shackleton's Irish] accent [. . .] was received as a breath of fresh air. Knight and unionist he might be,

but democratic America was impressed" (Shackleton and MacKenna 2002, 130).

When Roald Amundsen and Robert Scott both reached the South Pole in 1910–1911, Shackleton's dream was dashed, but he soon made plans for another adventure: the first transcontinental crossing of Antarctica. In 1914, Shackleton and 27 other men sailed on the *Endurance*, hoping to reach the head of the Weddell Sea, and then travel east across the continent. However, floes of pack ice first trapped and then crushed the *Endurance*, forcing Shackleton to abandon not only his ship but his entire mission. In three small boats, the crew reached remote Elephant Island; from there Shackleton and five others set off for help on South Georgia, 800 miles away, through some of the roughest waters on earth. That they were able to reach this destination in 17 days is considered one of the greatest nautical feats, but their boat was badly damaged when it landed on South Georgia's western shore. To reach the whaling station on the island's eastern shore, Shackleton and two other men walked for 36 hours up and down jagged mountain peaks and treacherous glaciers. No one had ever crossed South Georgia by land before, and no one would ever do it again, until a group of expert climbers with professional equipment managed the feat in 1955.

The fact that Shackleton's Imperial Trans-Antarctic Expedition never succeeded has in retrospect seemed less important than the endurance and survival of all crew members. Several films, exhibitions, and publications in the early twenty-first century have greatly enhanced Shackleton's reputation, particularly in the United States, where business executives have admired his ability to hire an effective team, create a spirit of camaraderie, overcome obstacles, and lead effectively in a crisis. Unfortunately, Shackleton never lived to receive this acclaim. While heading south in 1922 to conduct an extensive mapping expedition of Antarctica, he died of a heart attack in South Georgia.

James I. Deutsch

See also: FALKLAND/MALVINAS ISLANDS

References

Alexander, Caroline. *The Endurance: Shackleton's Legendary Antarctic Expedition.* New York: Knopf, 1998.

The Endurance: Shackleton's Legendary Antarctic Expedition. Directed by George Butler. Produced by Discovery Channel Pictures and FilmFour, 2000.

Fisher, Margery, and James Fisher. *Shackleton.* London: Barrie, 1957.

Huntford, Roland. *Shackleton.* London: Hodder and Stoughton, 1985.

Lansing, Alfred. *Endurance: Shackleton's Incredible Voyage.* New York: McGraw-Hill Book Co., 1959.

Mill, Hugh Robert. *The Life of Sir Ernest Shackleton.* London: W. Heinemann, 1923.

Morrell, Margot, and Stephanie Capparell. *Shackleton's Way: Leadership Lessons from the Great Antarctic Explorer.* New York: Viking Penguin, 2001.

Shackleton, Jonathan, and John MacKenna. *Shackleton: An Irishman in Antarctica.* Madison: University of Wisconsin Press, 2002.

Shackleton: The Greatest Survival Story of All Time. Written and directed by Charles Sturridge. Produced by A&E Television Networks with Channel 4 Television, 2002.

SHAW, GEORGE BERNARD (1856–1950)

George Bernard Shaw was born in Dublin, Ireland. He received little formal education, going to school only until he was 13 years old and never attending college. However, he read voraciously from an early age and was provided with a thorough introduction to music by his mother's music teacher,

Portrait of playwright George Bernard Shaw, who, during the course of his career, wrote over 60 plays. He won the Nobel Prize for Literature in 1925 and an Oscar in 1938. (Library of Congress)

George John Vandeleur Lee, who lived with the Shaw family. Additionally, Shaw frequented the theater in Dublin.

At age 20, one year after his mother left his father and moved to London with her music teacher, Shaw followed. There, he tried his hand at a number of writing ventures with little initial success. He ghostwrote music criticism, attempted to compose short fiction and drama, and penned five unsuccessful novels. He also developed an interest in social and political reform, and in the 1880s he became a vegetarian, a socialist, a compelling public speaker, and a driving force behind the Fabian Society. He earned a reputation for his biting wit as a book reviewer for the *Pall Mall Gazette* (1885–1888); a music critic for the *Dramatic Review* (1886) and then for the *Star* (writing under the name

"Corno di Basseto"; 1888–1890); and later, a drama critic for the *Saturday Review* (1895–1898).

As a drama critic, Shaw attacked the shallow hypocrisy he found in the theater of the day and sought to replace it with a theater of ideas like the one he lauded in the "new drama" of Henrik Ibsen in his 1891 book *The Quintessence of Ibsenism*. Toward this goal, he began writing his own plays, ultimately becoming the most significant dramatist of his time. Shaw's plays were unique from the start, evincing a distinctive writing style and addressing issues and characters deemed by many to be inappropriate for dramatic representation. Repudiating the "well made" plays that were currently most popular, Shaw wrote about social topics such as prostitution, war, religion, family strife, and economics. Action was secondary to thought in his dramas, which encouraged audiences to reconsider their values. Despite the seriousness of their subjects, Shaw's works avoided stodginess by using comedy and witty dialogue. This blending of social relevance, intelligent dialogue, and lively wit came to define the adjective "Shavian."

Shaw's socialist beliefs, public speeches, and challenging plays were not widely accepted at first, and many considered him to be a subversive influence. His early dramas, *Widowers' Houses* (1892), *Mrs. Warren's Profession* (1893), and *The Philanderer* (1893), were not seen publicly but were instead offered only in private club performances. Shaw's first work to be publicly produced was *Arms and the Man,* which was staged at the Avenue Theatre in 1894. His unqualified success in the theater can be dated to the 1904 Vedrenne-Barker production of *John Bull's Other Island* at the Royal Court Theatre. This play, originally commissioned by W. B. Yeats for presentation on the Abbey stage in Dublin (although the Abbey directors refused to produce it), included a comic Englishman who was every bit as buffoonish as the stage Irishman that was frequently dramatized at the time. Between 1904 and 1907, the Royal Court Theatre had enormous success maintaining 10 of Shaw's plays in repertory. Shaw was highly prolific; a complete list of his works would be laborious. Some of his more important plays are *Fanny's First Play* (1911), *Androcles and the Lion* (1913), *Pygmalion* (1914), *Heartbreak House* (1920), *Back to Methuselah* (1922), *Saint Joan* (1923), *The Apple Cart* (1929), *Too True to Be Good* (1932), *Geneva* (1938), and *King Charles's Golden Days* (1939). For the publication of each of these plays, Shaw provided carefully crafted prefaces and line notes that explained how the plays should be performed and what they mean.

Shaw's reputation in the United States mirrored his success in England. The same year *Arms and the Man* was first seen in London, it was also produced to general acclaim at the Herald Square Theatre in New York. *The Devil's Disciple,* when performed at the 5th Avenue Theatre in 1897, established Shaw's reputation abroad and provided him with sufficient revenue to devote himself to playwriting full time. Many of his plays had their world premieres in the United States, including *Heartbreak House* and *Saint Joan.* Shaw received numerous awards for his work, including the Nobel Prize for Literature in 1926 and Hollywood's Academy Award for best screenplay for his adaptation of *Pygmalion* in 1938.

Robert I. Lublin

See also: FEDERAL THEATRE PROJECT; YEATS, William Butler

References

Dukore, Bernard. *Shaw's Theatre*. Gainesville: University Press of Florida, 2000.

Holroyd, Michael. *Bernard Shaw*. New York: Random House, 1988. 4 vols.

Innes, Christopher. *The Cambridge Companion to George Bernard Shaw*. New York: Cambridge University Press, 1998.

Mander, Raymond and Joe Mitchenson. *Theatrical Companion to Shaw*. London: Rockliff, 1955.

Weintraub, Stanley. *Bernard Shaw: A Guide to Research*. University Park: Pennsylvania University Press, 1992.

SHERIDAN, JIM (1949–)

Born to a working-class family in Dublin, Jim Sheridan came of age in an Ireland of rampant poverty that was only beginning to wake from years of self-imposed isolation from the outside world. Despite being best known as a cinematic director, Sheridan began his artistic career as a theater director and playwright, founding the Project Arts Centre in Dublin's Temple Bar district in 1967 with his brother Peter. The project rapidly became (and remains) one of the most reputable avant-garde theater houses in the Irish capital. The urban, gritty, and frustrated aesthetic that dominated Sheridan's early work at the project in plays such as *Mobile Homes* (1976), which deals with low-income families who live on a mobile home site, cast light upon the dark underbelly of a rapidly modernizing Ireland. Sheridan resigned from the project, however, when the Dublin City Council pulled the company's funding over a play that dealt openly with homosexuality.

Sheridan relocated with his family to New York City in 1981, where, after a brief stint as a student at New York University's film school, he became director of the Irish Arts Center. Sheridan's time in New York had immense effects on his future work, exposing him not only to American filmmaking but also to the complex cultural relationship between Ireland and America. This would become an important theme in several of his later films.

Sheridan returned to Ireland in 1989 at the behest of Noel Pearson, who had convinced Sheridan to make a movie based on Christy Brown's memoir of growing up with cerebral palsy in working-class Dublin. *My Left Foot* (1989) was a breakthrough not only for Sheridan but also for the Irish film scene in general. The movie was nominated for five Academy Awards, and leads Daniel Day-Lewis and Brenda Fricker won Oscars for Best Actor and Actress.

Over the next decade, Sheridan's film work explored various and disparate forms of the Irish experience. *The Field* (1990), an adaptation of Jack B. Keane's well-known play from the 1960s, depicts Bull McCabe's (played by Richard Harris) maniacal fight with an Irish American (played by Tom Berenger) for the farmland McCabe's family has possessed for generations. The film radically reinterprets the theme of John Ford's *The Quiet Man* (1952), which also dealt with the Irish-American "return" to the land in a much more nostalgic, sentimental way. This filmic dialogue with Ford would continue in Sheridan's screenplay *Into The West* (1992), in which a group of Irish Traveler (or Gypsy) children embark on a journey into the west of Ireland inspired by westerns they have watched on television. The film makes important parallels between the Irish and American notions of the "West," and Sheridan's exploration of the racism leveled at the Irish Traveler community mirrors Ford's own depiction of American racism toward Indians in films such as *The Searchers* (1956).

In the 1990s, Sheridan turned his attention to the Northern Irish Troubles in a series of critically acclaimed films. *In The Name of the Father* (1993), which Sheridan directed and cowrote with Terry George, starred Day-Lewis again as the real-life Gerry Conlon, who was falsely imprisoned along with his father Giuseppe (played by Pete Postlethwaite) as one of the "Guildford four," a group charged with the 1975 Irish Republican Army (IRA) bombing campaign in London. The film was nominated for seven Academy Awards. *The Boxer* (1997), again starring Day-Lewis, is the story of ex-IRA man Danny Flynn, who takes up boxing after spending 15 years in prison in Belfast. His love affair with Maggie (played by Emily Watson), whose husband is still serving time for paramilitary activities, brings a critical lens to bear on the sexual politics of republican nationalism.

Recently, Sheridan's work has increasingly focused more explicitly on the transatlantic connections between Ireland and America. The semiautobiographical *In America* (2002) is the story of Johnny and Sarah, an Irish couple, and their two children, who move to New York in the 1980s so that Johnny can pursue his acting career. The film offers a modern version of the trauma of immigration, a mainstay of the Irish-American experience for more than a century and a half. His forthcoming project *The Emerald City* will continue to document this Irish-American immigrant experience, exploring the criminal underbelly of the predominantly Irish Hell's Kitchen neighborhood in New York City.

Sheridan remains a powerful force in Irish filmmaking whose work has consistently demonstrated, in its broad choice of material, a dynamic mind equally at home investigating the cultural particularities of his own country or in probing the complex interplay of the transatlantic relationship between Ireland and America.

Michael P. Jaros

See also: DAY-LEWIS, Daniel; HARRIS, Richard; FORD, John; PEARSON, Noel

References

Barton, Ruth. *Jim Sheridan: Framing the Nation.* Dublin: Liffey Press, 2002.

Cavanagh, Dermot. "Nation and Narration: Rewriting 'The Field.'" *Literature/Film Quarterly* 31, no. 2 (2003): 93–98.

Cullingford, Elizabeth Butler. *Gender and Ethnicity in Irish Literature and Popular Culture.* Notre Dame, IN: University of Notre Dame Press, 2001.

McCloone, Martin. *Irish Film: The Emergence of A Contemporary Cinema.* London: British Film Institute, 2000.

Pettit, Lance. *Screening Ireland. Film and Television Representation.* Manchester, UK: Manchester University Press, 2000.

SHERIDAN, PETER (1792–1844)

Peter Sheridan, a merchant and pioneer sheep breeder in Argentina, was born in Co. Cavan, brother of Richard and Hugh Sheridan. Sheridan arrived in Argentina in 1817 and opened Sheridan Bros., a textile merchant house in Buenos Aires. With his partner John Harrat from England he also established a felt factory and a meat-curing plant. In 1824 they purchased 100 merino sheep imported by the government of Buenos Aires from the Rambouillet breeders. In 1830, they founded Los Galpones ranch in Ranchos, near Luján, where Sheridan was appointed as member of the city council. The owners of Los Galpones produced large quantities of premium wool from the favored merino breeds, Saxony and negrete.

Sheridan was an important employer of Irish workers. Irish settlers employed by Sheridan businesses, usually younger unmarried men, were ditchdiggers or factory workers. Sheridan employed more Irish workers than other Irish businessmen in Buenos Aires, like Thomas Armstrong, Patrick Browne, John Mooney, or Patrick Bookey, who formed a group of immigration sponsors. Sheridan did not want to be part of this group as he considered their strategy as expensive and short term. As a result of Sheridan's refusal to sponsor immigration, his home area of Co. Cavan never became a source of Irish immigration to Argentina, whereas Armstrong's and Browne's areas did.

In the 1820s and 1830s, cattle raising to obtain hides and tallow was the primary rural business among large landowners in Buenos Aires province. When Sheridan and Harrat began their production, sheep farming was secondary, but a few years later it became the principal activity for hundreds of newly arrived Irish and other shepherds who were employed by ranchers. Frequently, Irish immigrants started up with salaried jobs to pay the cost of their journey. When they married and were able to add the labor of wife and children (and often brothers and cousins), they worked in halves or thirds as shepherds or *posters* (in charge of a *puesto*, an outpost in the ranch's limits). The wool industry, which Sheridan pioneered with an integral vision of the production cycle all the way from sheep farming to exports, became a primary industry in Argentina. Two decades after Sheridan established his methods the turnover was so important that many Irish managed to acquire their own means of production, that is, sheep and land, in about 10 years after their arrival.

One of Sheridan's frequent contacts was with the governor of Buenos Aires province, Juan Manuel de Rosas, who sometimes solicited his advice on sheep farming and cattle ranching. With his brothers Richard and Hugh (a physician), Peter Sheridan established a meat-processing plant and opened a store in Ranchos. They were also involved in the import and export trade. In 1832 he was appointed inspector of the Riachuelo harbor. Sheridan was a founding member of the Strangers Club of Buenos Aires.

Sheridan died on January 8, 1844, in Ranchos. At the time of his death, he owned 40,000 purebred and *mestizo* head grazing on 16 outposts of Los Galpones. His son Enrique Sheridan (1836–1864) was a celebrated landscapist whose paintings of the pampas became popular in England.

Edmundo Murray

See also: ARGENTINA

References

Coghlan, Eduardo A. *Los Irlandeses en la Argentina: Su Actuación y Descendencia.* Buenos Aires: Author's Edition, 1987.

Murray, Thomas. *The Story of the Irish in Argentina.* New York: P. J. Kenedy & Sons, 1919.

Sabato, Hilda, and Juan Carlos Korol. *Cómo fue la inmigración irlandesa en Argentina.* Buenos Aires: Plus Ultra, 1981.

Slatta, Richard. *Gauchos and the Vanishing Frontier.* Lincoln: University of Nebraska Press, 1992.

SMITH, ALFRED EMMANUEL "AL" (1873–1944)

Alfred E. Smith, better know as Al Smith, is one of the key figures of twentieth-century Irish-American cultural history. By the early twentieth century Smith's fate had become so indelibly linked to that of the Irish-American community that, after his death on October 4, 1944, the *New York Times* would write of his Irish roots: "Governor

Smith was fortunate in his ancestry and his upbringing. They fitted him for honor and he in turn conferred it on them."

Al Smith was born on December 30, 1873, to Alfred Emmanuel Smith and Catherine Mulvihill on South Street on the Lower East Side of New York. Named after his father, whose heritage is presumed to be Italian and German (but not by Al), Al's Irish connections came from his mother's side; she was the daughter of an Irishman. However, it seems, more than his mixed parentage, the neighborhood in which Al grew up formed and confirmed his ethnic identity. As the *New York Times* said of Smith's early New York parish, "it was a little Ireland of God-fearing people." One of only two children, his early childhood was relatively untroubled: his father was a truckman, and they lived in a five-room flat in the shadow of the Brooklyn Bridge. The young Al served as an altar boy in Saint James Church and attended the local parish school, where he was considered an average student. He did, however, win a citywide oratory contest at age 11, with an oration on the death of Robespierre. The next year his father died, and the family's fortunes changed for the worse. Al was soon forced to drop out of school and take the first of a succession of odd jobs. By the age of 20, Al Smith would come to realize that the road to overcoming his social conditions lay in politics.

Smith had become friendly with a local saloon owner and Democratic precinct leader, Tom Foley. After successfully defeating the Tammany candidate for the 4th District's congressional seat in 1894, Tom Foley rewarded Al Smith, who had helped him achieve his victory, with a clerkship in the office of the commissioner of jurors. In 1903, after repairing his relations with Tammany

Hall, Foley had Smith put forward as the Democratic candidate for state assembly of New York. By this time Smith had married Catherine Dunn, an Irish woman from the Bronx. They would go on to have five children together: Alfred Emmanuel, Emily, Catherine, Arthur, and Walter.

Although initially ignored by both Republican and Democratic assembly members, by becoming an expert in assembly procedures and the structure of government Smith eventually established a reputation for himself as a hardworking and progressive legislator. It was well-known that he read the annual appropriation bill, a 300-page document, very carefully each year, becoming familiar with every item in it. His commitment to progressive legislation for the working-class people of New York gained national prominence in 1911, when a fire at the Triangle Shirtwaist Company killed 146 people, mostly young women. Smith sponsored legislation for an investigating committee to examine working conditions in New York, a committee on which he would be vice chairman. The committee's shocking findings in 1915 gave Smith the opportunity to sponsor much of the social legislation it recommended: sanitary, health, and fire laws; regulations on worker's compensation; and regulations on the working conditions for women and children. The opportunity this committee afforded Smith, of working with some of the best social reformers and thinkers of the time, broadened his own ideas (such as changing his view on women's suffrage to one of support) and his reputation, allowing him to transcend the taint of Tammany's machine-style politics. He was subsequently elected to a two-year term as sheriff of New York City, a position offering an income of $60,000 a year.

By 1918 Smith was one of the most popular New York Democrats, and with support from both Tammany politicians and independent reform groups, he was chosen over William Randolph Hearst as the Democratic candidate for the governorship of New York. Never simply a "Tammany man," Smith selected talented, progressive thinkers for his campaign staff, regardless of their affiliation or sex, and, in a Republican year, he managed to beat the incumbent governor, Charles S. Whitman, by 15,000 votes.

The first of four terms as governor of New York, Smith's 1919–1920 gubernatorial term set the pattern for his progressive, constructive reform of municipal state politics. Despite strong opposition from Republicans and businesspeople, Smith fought for a 44-hour workweek for labor, developed low-cost housing projects, and sponsored the temporary extension of rent controls. In an effort to defend civil liberties, he opposed anti-sedition legislation, which sought to curtail the civil liberties of Socialists. He reformed New York's state government by eliminating overlapping agencies and reducing costs. He also sought, unsuccessfully, to repeal prohibition. In 1920 a rising conservative tide swept him from government, but he easily regained the governorship in 1922; after this victory, he served three consecutive terms.

By 1920, Smith's national standing had risen enough for his name to be mentioned as a potential Democratic candidate for president; however, it was not until the 1924 presidential elections that Smith would become a serious contender for the Democratic candidacy. Noted for Franklin Delano Roosevelt's speech, which named Smith the "happy warrior," the 1924 Democratic convention was dominated by a resolution put forward by the northeastern representatives to condemn the Ku Klux Klan (an organization Smith had successfully outlawed in New York during his term as governor). This resolution implacably divided the convention and nomination process between the rural, dry, Protestant wing, centered in the South and West and represented by William McAdoo, and the urban, wet, northeastern wing, represented by Smith. After nearly two weeks of deadlock, both Smith and McAdoo (who had led Smith all the way in the balloting) withdrew, and weary delegates chose John W. Davis of Virginia as a compromise candidate. Davis was easily defeated in the presidential election by the Republican candidate, Calvin Coolidge.

By 1928, Smith's four terms as governor had made him the foremost Democrat in public office. This, combined with his four years of planning and publicity, made Smith the outright candidate for the Democratic presidential nomination. However, opposition to him was still strong from certain sectors of the Democratic Party, particularly in the South. This opposition was based on three grounds: his Roman Catholicism, his assumed association with Tammany Hall, and his opposition to prohibition. Smith's religious affiliations were directly challenged by Charles C. Marshall, a lawyer and prominent Episcopalian, in a letter published in the *Atlantic Monthly,* which questioned whether Smith's Catholicism, in view of the historical policy of that church, did not effectively disbar him from being elected president. Smith's reply, published in the *Atlantic Monthly,* was seen to capture the American Catholic viewpoint: he emphasized his belief in the total separation of church and state, and pronounced that thus he could see no conflict of duties between his role as a Catholic and any potential future role as president. Smith's early Tammany associations, his "wet," anti-prohibition leanings, and his Catholicism would deny him unanimous endorsement as Democratic candidate, four southern states refusing to vote for him.

These issues would affect his campaign for president. The Republican Party selected Herbert C. Hoover, secretary of commerce, to run against Smith; he was an experienced and conservative Republican who not only saw prohibition as the "noble experiment" but also believed America would not elect a Catholic with Tammany associations in a time when its economy was booming. He got it right. In a campaign dogged by bigotry and agrarian distrust of big-city politics, and hampered by Smith's inability to augment his regional appeal, Smith polled 15 million votes to Herbert Hoover's 21.4 million, and the electoral votes were 87 to 444. While Smith did poll more votes than any former Democratic presidential candidate, he was abandoned by the voters of his own state. In a personally devastating campaign, awakening Smith to the full extent of bigotry still present in America, the loss of New York hit him particularly hard.

Disillusioned with politics and becoming ever more conservative, Smith went into private business after his defeat. He became president of the Empire State Building Corporation at a salary of $50,000. He moved to a luxury 5th Avenue apartment and became a celebrity and friend to New York's rich and famous. As his friends became more conservative, so did his politics: he moved away from the progressivism of his early political life. This move reflected in part his changing attitude toward his former friend and political ally, Franklin Delano Roosevelt (FDR). However, the growing disunion between Smith and FDR had a more personal origin: FDR, now governor of New York, had begun to disassociate himself from Smith, not consulting him or appointing any of Smith's associates to his administration. In 1932, when FDR made a run at the Democratic nomination for president, Smith made his own bid for the nomination, possibly in an attempt to thwart FDR. Ill organized, Smith's campaign was easily defeated by FDR. After this, Smith's politics continued to harden conservatively, and he became an outspoken opponent of FDR's New Deal. In 1936, Smith abandoned his allegiance to the Democratic Party and supported Alf Landon, the Republican candidate for the presidency, over FDR. He had finally broken with his former friends and supporters, betraying not just them but also his earlier political ideals. With the approach and outbreak of World War II, Smith and FDR overcame their differences and began to talk to each other again; Smith even visited the White House on at least two occasions. In May 1944 Smith's wife, Catherine, died. They would not be separated long; by October of that year Smith too was dead.

See also: CATHOLIC CHURCH, the; NEW YORK CITY; TAMMANY HALL

References

"Alfred E. Smith." *New York Times,* October 4, 1944, early edition: 18.

Burner, David. "Alfred Emmanuel Smith." *Dictionary of American Biography.* Supplement 3: 1941–1945. New York: American Council of Learned Societies, 1973.

Burner, David. *The Politics of Provincialism: The Democratic Party in Transition, 1918–1932.* Cambridge, MA: Harvard University Press, 1986.

"Career of Alfred E. Smith, Presidential Nominee of 1928 and Four Times New York Governor." *New York Times,* October 5, 1944: 12.

Handlin, Oscar. *Al Smith and His America*.
Boston: Little, Brown, 1958.

Josephson, Matthew, and Hannah Josephson.
Al Smith: Hero of the Cities. Boston:
Houghton Mifflin, 1969.

Shannon, William V. *The American Irish: A
Political and Social Portrait*. Amherst:
University of Massachusetts Press, 1966.

Smith, Alfred E. *Up to Now: An Autobiography*.
New York: Viking Press, 1929.

SMURFIT, SIR MICHAEL W. J., KBE (1936–)

In a legendary business career spanning five decades to date, Sir Michael W. J. Smurfit, KBE, chairman and former chief executive officer of Jefferson Smurfit Group (Dublin, Ireland), may well be the world's first "Celtic Tiger."

By any standard, Sir Michael has distinguished himself as one of Ireland's wealthiest and most successful business professionals. He effectively turned the Jefferson Smurfit Group (JSG) into the largest worldwide maker of paper and packaging materials for cardboard boxes; at one time JSG owned, and operated in, some 600 facilities globally. JSG is also a major wastepaper recycler. Dating from the 1970s, Smurfit introduced fresh ideas to modernize Irish business at a time when the Irish economy and talent pool were provincial and uncompetitive. His seasoned entrepreneurial skills and international experience soon contributed to Ireland's new status as Europe's Celtic Tiger. Smurfit's vision for an enlarged Irish role in the world economy helped reposition Ireland as a 'comer' of surprising potential on the world stage. An Englishman by birth, Smurfit holds dual Irish and British citizenship. He was reared in Ireland, and educated in Ireland and America, the dual base of his big career. And it has been to Ireland, as well as to America, that Smurfit has given generously of his resources,

In a celebratory luncheon on February 10, 1998, at the Merrion Hotel in Dublin, Michael Smurfit was fêted Entrepreneur of the Year. This distinction would be followed in 2005 by an even grander one: Knight of the British Empire. Often called the first Celtic Tiger, Smurfit is Chairman and former CEO of Jefferson Smurfit Group, Dublin, and owner of the five-star golf venue and spa resort: K Club, County Kildare. (© Frank Fennell, Photographer, 1998. With kind permission.)

business acumen, and educational commitment. In his global business dealings and broad philanthropic contributions, Michael W. J. Smurfit continues to be a prominent presence in Ireland's economic growth and an important voice in Irish-American relations.

Born in 1936 in St. Helen's, Lancashire, England, Michael W. J. Smurfit was the first of eight children of John Jefferson Smurfit, a master tailor from Sunderland, and Veronica Magee, from Belfast. Sir Michael acknowledges his father as his role model and career model: "Why, my father was working from the age of 12, an awe-inspiring individual. His ethics, integrity, his sheer ability to focus and move forward—all of this drove me" (Mulvihill 2005). The family first resided in Lancashire where, in the 1930s, the Smurfits began their lifetime association with paper packaging, owing initially to the Magee family's interests in a box factory in Rathmines, Dublin. After some experience in the industry, the Smurfits relocated to Dublin, just after World War II, where they launched their own modest packaging concern. The first machines were manually constructed and assembled by John Smurfit himself. Understandably, early profits were unstable. Sir Michael recalls, "We went from huge houses in Killiney to rented places in Rathmines; my father went from success to close to bankruptcy, and then back again to success" (Thesing 2003). Money issues notwithstanding, the Smurfits valued education and enrolled their first son in the exclusive Jesuit boarding school, Clongowes Wood College, Co. Kildare. During this interval, the family business began to prosper and eventually became the incorporated entity Jefferson Smurfit & Sons Ltd. So busy and promising was the fledgling company that young Michael Smurfit was asked in 1952 to leave school and join his father and brothers on the factory floor at the age of 16, thus missing the experience of third-level (university) training. As he recalls: "Yet, the results speak for themselves; I may not have had the ambition I had, had I gone on to university" (Thesing, 2003). Seeking to expand his skills, Smurfit then trained in management at the Continental Can Corporation in Connecticut, and shortly thereafter set up his own carton factories in Lancashire: Jefferson Smurfit Packaging. But when his father's Dublin company went public in 1966, Michael Smurfit returned to Ireland to assume the helm. The sale of Smurfit's United Kingdom company to his father's Irish company effectively ensured his financial future (and

fortune). By 1977, Smurfit's developing aptitude for business was manifest, and he was appointed chairman and chief executive of the company known worldwide as Jefferson Smurfit Group (JSG).

A corporate acquisitions spree by JSG throughout the 1960s and 1970s was swift and savvy, leading to a relative paper-and-packaging empire for JSG. A new international presence followed fast in the 1980s and 1990s. In 1986, Smurfit dramatically asserted its corporate muscle with the acquisition of Container Corporation of America at $1.2 billion. In 1994, Smurfit acquired the French company, Cellulose du Pain, for about $1.6 billion, making Smurfit the premier packaging group in Europe. By about 1995, JSG had more than doubled its sales base in Europe, owing primarily to its acquisition of the paper-and-packaging operations of the French company Saint-Gobain. In 1998, JSG brokered the merger of its U.S. associate, Jefferson Smurfit Corporation, with Stone Container Corporation, now forming the Smurfit Stone Container Corporation, an entity of unprecedented size in the industry. This merger gave JSG and its associates more than 70,000 employees and 600 facilities as well as a presence in some 30 countries.

In the opening years of the new millennium, Smurfit and JSG had become the doyen of the paper industry. Poised for a profitable acquisition, the company was bought out and privatized by Madison Dearborn Partners in November 2002. Following the dispersal of JSG's North American assets, the company's chief focus is now South American and European markets. In 2004 alone, company sales amounted to approximately €4 billion. Madison Dearborn spun off the North American operations, leaving JSG to focus on expansion in Latin America and Europe. By the second half of the twentieth century, Smurfit had become an industry brand, owing mostly to strategic buy-outs of smaller packaging entities in the United Kingdom, the United States, Latin America, and more recently continental Europe. "The one regret I have in my business career," said Michael Smurfit in 2003, "is not finishing the development in Asia before Madison Dearborn came along; that was the last outpost which I was developing" (Thesing 2003). The recent buyout of JSG notwithstanding, Smurfit recently retired as chairman of JSG. Presently entering his eighth decade, Smurfit is however only semiretired, at work on a memoir, and developing a rapidly expanding business venture in Florida: Carsmedics (presently, a 20-unit operation).

Complementing his achievements in business, Michael Smurfit has built an impressive record of educational and cultural patronage on both sides of the Atlantic, thus contributing to his long record of success in the United States. Well beyond the relatively huge employment opportunities his facilities and operations have offered Irish and Americans these many decades, Smurfit and his company have made large contributions to several Irish and U.S. universities. His chief educational legacy is founding in the 1990s the Michael Smurfit Graduate School of Business, a 25-acre campus at University College Dublin. Smurfit's school enjoys the distinction of being the first educational entity in Ireland to offer an MBA degree. The school's Corporate Partners Program and its longstanding hospitality to American students, in particular, through various student exchange programs, have contributed to continuing good relations between Ireland and the United States. Smurfit has also been a major contributor to the Keough Program in Irish

Studies, based in Dublin and at Notre Dame University in South Bend, Indiana, to whose Irish literature collection, housed at Notre Dame's Hesburgh Library, Smurfit has generously contributed. His sensible goal of bridging the two spheres of academia and business is also the vision of the Jefferson Smurfit Center for Entrepreneurial Studies at St. Louis University in Missouri.

Smurfit's long record as an educational patron is broadly acknowledged. He is a fellow of the International Academy of Management and holds honorary doctorates from Irish and American colleges and universities: Trinity College Dublin, the National University of Ireland, University College Galway, the University of Scranton in Pennsylvania, and Babson College in Boston. Smurfit is also the honorary Irish consul to Monaco, and he has been honored for his achievements by the governments of France, Italy, Venezuela, Colombia, Spain, the United Kingdom, and the Republic of Poland. In June 2005, Queen Elizabeth II of England conferred upon Smurfit his most distinctive public honor, to date: Knight Commander of the Most Excellent Order of the British Empire (KBE) for his "services to British business and charitable interests" (RTÉ News online, June 11, 2005; Mulvihill correspondence with British Embassy, Dublin, June 13, 2005). On this occasion, Sir Michael said, "I am proud to be Irish; it is, however, a wonderful privilege to be honoured by my country of birth."

When asked for his thoughts regarding the present and future health of Irish-American relations, Smurfit had to admit that Ireland's rising consumerism and multinational/multicultural presence in the twenty-first century was changing the island's identity and Irishness: "Why, Dublin's looking a bit more like New York

City these days!" (Mulvihill 2005). While a good mix of talent and ethnicities can enrich the talent pool and strength of any nation, Smurfit is concerned about the continuing Irish identity of the island. As for Irish-American relations, in particular, he urges business and educational leaders to "hold steady" and to accelerate their current practice of business partnerships, charitable giving, and educational exchange programs.

Smurfit is the father of six children (four sons, two daughters) and has 12 grandchildren. He has resided in Monaco since 1986. His present hobbies and nonbusiness interests include sport (horse racing, horse breeding, golf), wine connoisseurship, and membership in several élite social clubs in France, the United Kingdom, the United States, and Ireland. He recently purchased control of the K Club, a hotel and golf resort in Straffan, Co. Kildare, Ireland. He developed these facilities for JSG as a long-term vision to help put Ireland on the map as a premier golf venue. K Club is the home of the Smurfit European Open Golf Championship and the venue for the 2006 Ryder Club matches.

Smurfit is a great credit to Irish business and Irish success; but more than this, he has used his resources humanely to improve the quality of life, especially in Ireland and America, the twin hubs of his continuing ventures.

Maureen E. Mulvihill

References

The K Club Hotel & Golf. Straffan, Co. Kildare, Ireland, *http://www.kclub.ie/default.asp* (accessed June 3, 2005).

Lavery, Brian. "Irish Financial Regulator Faces Its First Major Test." *New York Times,* April 1, 2005: C2.

Lavery, Brian, and Timothy L. O'Brien. "Insurers' Trails Lead to Dublin." *New York Times,* April 1, 2005: C1–C2.

Mulvihill, Maureen E. Interview with Smurfit by Maureen E. Mulvihill. Transatlantic telephone call. April 26, 2005. Monaco to New York City.

Mulvihill, Maureen E. "Wall Street Irish." *The World of Hibernia,* Summer 1995, 140–159. With photos.

Thesing, Gabi. "Man of Paper, Man of Power." Interview with Michael W. J. Smurfit. *Business & Finance.* November 20, 2003: 16–21.

University College Dublin. "Smurfit School of Business." Smurfit School of Business and Smurfit Collection in Irish Studies, Notre Dame University, www.library.nd.edu/.

SOCCER, EARLY ARGENTINE

The first Argentine soccer club was the Buenos Aires Football Club, founded on May 9, 1867, by a group of British players. Matches were organized in the field of the Buenos Aires Cricket Club in Palermo. In this period, playing soccer was associated with cricket and British social institutions, of which some Irish settlers were members. Among the first players was James Wensley Bond (b. 1846) of Co. Armagh. Bond played in a match on June 29, 1867, that lasted two and a half hours. Another player in the same match was Richard Henry Murray of Dublin, auditor of the Buenos Ayres British Clerk's Provident Association.

In the beginning, the rules of the game were not clear, and soccer was similar to today's rugby. Only in the 1880s did soccer and rugby begin to effectively separate. However, the players of both sports belonged to the same social circle, which also participated in cricket and rowing and, in the countryside, horse racing and polo.

In the 1890s, soccer extended to other English-speaking circles, especially in the rural areas of Buenos Aires. On July 3, 1892, a group of Irish Argentines and others founded the Lobos Athletic Club. Among the founding members were Tomás McKeon, Tomás P. Moore, Tomás Garrahan, Edmundo and Patricio Kirk, Santiago F. MacKeon, Eduardo Burbridge, Eugenio Seery, Juan Geoghegan, José Garrahan, Lorenzo Owens, Felix Dolan, Hugo Lawlor, Eduardo Walsh, William Weir, José Joyce, Eduardo Slamon, and Eduardo Burbridge, Jr. Tomás P. Moore was selected as their first team captain. The games were very popular among the native population, who gathered to watch the *ingleses locos* playing soccer. The club developed successfully, and in 1900 it merged with the English High School club, whose ex-pupils later formed the famous Alumni, winner of nine league championships from 1900 to 1911.

The most famous player of Lobos Athletic Club was Paddy McCarthy. Born in 1871 in Cashel, Co. Tipperary, McCarthy arrived in Argentina in 1900 and was hired to teach athletics in the Escuela Nacional de Comercio, whose director was James Fitzsimons (1849–1944), son of the schoolmaster Patrick Fitzsimons. When his colleagues decided to merge Lobos with the English High School, McCarthy went to play with Club Atlético Estudiantes, founded in 1898. In 1900 he also played for Central Athletic Club, and then he was hired by Gimnasia y Esgrima in 1904. The following year the Boca Juniors hired him to train the enthusiastic teams of younger players. McCarthy was also one of the pioneers of professional boxing in Argentina.

Many of the soccer clubs in the 1890s and 1900s were associated with schools, alumni associations, and British railway companies. Some of the first clubs were St. Andrew's, Old Caledonians, English High School, Buenos Aires al Rosario Railway, Belgrano Football Club, Buenos Ayres Football Club, Lomas Athletic, Flores Athletic, and Lobos Athletic. On February 21, 1893, the Argentine Association Football League was founded, and the Scottish schoolmaster Alexander Watson Hutton became its first president. On July 20, 1902, the first international match was played between Argentina and Uruguay—Argentina won, 6–0. Among the first-division players at that time were Eduardo Duggan, Ernesto Brown, Edward Morgan, Juan Moore, and Jorge Brown. Other famous players of Irish origin were Miguel Murphy, a grandson of John James Murphy, and Carlos Lett. Most of these players came from Porteño Athletic Club, the institution founded by members of the Irish community, who proudly perceived themselves as the first Argentine-born players. Porteño started on July 28, 1895, and in the beginning a majority of the founding members were Irish Argentines: Tomás Hagan, José I. O'Farrell (brother of Dr. Santiago O'Farrell), Gerardo R. Kenny, Tomás Cavanagh, and Francisco Geoghegan. The club's original name (Capital Athletic Club) was changed when the first members won a good amount of money through gambling on horse races, so that they could purchase balls and other equipment (Porteño was the name of the winning horse). Besides soccer, members played cricket and enjoyed other athletic disciplines.

In 1899, Porteño had 42 members, and the president was Santiago G. O'Farrell (1861–1926), national member of Parliament and president of the Irish Catholic Association, who served as member of the board in several British-owned companies. That year there was a concert to collect funds to purchase a playing field. The club rooms were at the grounds of the Irish Orphanage in Caballito. In 1901 the first playing grounds were inaugurated in Palermo. Between 1899 and 1906, Porteño's "first eleven" played in the second division. The club was promoted to the first division of the Football League in 1907 and won its first national championship in 1912. Some of the first Porteño players were Miguel A. Kenny, G. and E. Hearne, J. Tormey, M. A. Tyrrell, E. Rugeroni, A. Chopitea, J. McDonald, T. and F. Geoghegan, J. Oates, T. Cavanagh, J. Gahan, J. J. MacLoughlin, J. McAllister, and A.C. Hugues. During a match against Alumni, Porteño's famous goalkeeper, Juan José Rithner, saved 67 shots. By the late 1930s there were no more Irish names among the members of Porteño, and soccer was gradually replaced by rugby as its main activity.

As opposed to the sport of hurling in Argentina, many Irish Argentines who played soccer in those years belonged to traditional landowning families, followed Anglo-Argentine lifestyles and entertainments, and often revealed pro-British attitudes. Significantly, the Irish Argentines of Porteño Athletic Club founded their own institution and perceived themselves as "a group of Argentines," therefore giving an indication that their loyalties were more with Argentina than with England or Ireland.

Edmundo Murray

See also: FITZSIMONS, Patrick; HURLING IN ARGENTINA; MURPHY, John James

References

Frydenberg, Julio David. "Prácticas y Valores en el Proceso de Popularización del Fútbol, Buenos Aires 1900–1910." *Entrepasados* 6, no. 12 (1997): 7–27.

Mastropietro, Guillermo. *Misceláneas Lobenses.* Buenos Aires: Author's Edition, 2002.

Olivera, E. *Orígenes de los Deportes Británicos en el Río de la Plata.* Buenos Aires: Talleres Gráficos Argentinos, 1932.

Raffo, Victor, and Alfredo Yanes. *Un Pionero Llamado Banfield: Origen del Club Atlético Banfield y de la Comunidad Británica de Lomas de Zamora.* Buenos Aires: Author's Edition, 1999.

SOMERVILLE, EDITH ŒNONE (1858–1949)

The comic Irish short fiction of Edith Somerville and Martin Ross (Violet Martin) gained popular appeal, especially among sporting circles, in the United States after the publication of the Hitchcock edition of the Irish R.M. (resident magistrate) series in 1927. Following the successful introduction of Somerville and Ross's writing into the United States, Edith Somerville toured the United States and exhibited her artwork in 1929 and 1936. She published an account of her initial visit to the southern states, New England, and New York City in *The States through Irish Eyes* in 1930. The travel book provides a significant connection between the Irish big house and the American southern plantation. Drawing various comparisons to Ireland, Somerville concentrates on riding to hounds, architecture, landscaping, and the manners of black servants in the various homes she visits. The Irish writer's connection to the United States continued with her sales of Irish horses to Americans up until 1939.

From her early years in West Cork, Edith Somerville was attracted by the rough glamour of the American West. She admired Mark Twain's writing, and her earliest publication, *The Mark Twain Birthday Book* (1885), compiled quotations from Twain's fiction. She became interested in the art of horse whispering when studying John Leech's illustrations of a visiting American horse tamer in London, John S. Rary, in *Punch* magazine. In 1886, Somerville met her second cousin, Violet Martin from Galway; they shared an interest in horses and writing and eventually discovered critical acclaim with the publication of *The Real Charlotte* in 1894. Somerville and Ross's popular short fiction, *Some Experiences of an Irish R.M.* (1898), *Further Experiences of an Irish R.M.* (1908), and *In Mr. Knox's Country* (1915), deal with the comic escapades of the members of the Irish Hunt in West Cork. The stories provide lively and accurate treatment of the Hiberno-English, and Somerville's illustrations ensured their broad appeal. Her extended visits to Paris to study art in the 1880s and 1890s included tuition by the American illustrator Cyrus Cuneo. An accomplished sportswoman and activist for women's rights, Somerville was master of the West Carbery Foxhounds, 1903–1908, and president of the Munster Women's Franchise League in 1913. She was thus very happy to be the guest of another female master of the foxhounds, Mrs. Thomas Hitchcock, on her initial visit to America.

In some of their writing, Somerville and Ross suggest that Irish America promotes a rabid form of Catholic nationalism that contributes to the upstart notions of the Irish peasantry, but they admired the independence and spirit of the American people. After Martin's death in 1915, Somerville continued to publish writing under their joint names with a few exceptions, including her travel book on the United States. She believed Martin continued to collaborate with her through supernatural means (achieved through automatic writing). One suspects, however, that enthusiasm

for the United States belonged more to Somerville than it did Martin.

Julie Anne Stevens

Reference

Somerville, Edith and Martin Ross. *Happy Days*. London: Longmans, Green, 1946.

SOUTH CAROLINA

The majority of Irish immigration to South Carolina took place between 1730 and 1775. As in other southern states at the time the vast number of immigrants were Scots-Irish or Ulster Protestants. Although there were some Irish Catholics, the state's hostility to Catholicism proved a deterrent to their settling there. One of the first settlers in South Carolina was Captain Florence O'Sullivan, who was originally from Kinsale in Co. Cork. Sullivan's Island was later named after him. During this colonial period there were two Irish governors of South Carolina. The first, Richard Kyrle of Cork, died shortly after his appointment, and the second, James Moore, served as governor from 1700 to 1703. Later, with the arrival of Irish Quakers and their settlement at Mulberry, the colony made several plans to attract groups of Irish Protestants to come and settle in South Carolina. In the years before the American Revolution, the number of Irish entering the state reached its height. With the War of Independence the Irish in South Carolina played an important role, and two of the state's four signatories of the Declaration of Independence were of Irish ancestry.

In 1749, the Irish Society of Charleston was formed, and it preceded the establishment of the Friendly Sons of St. Patrick in 1773. After the Revolutionary War, the Friendly Brothers of Ireland was formed in 1786. Then, one year after the United Irishmen's Rebellion of 1798, the

Hibernian Society of Charleston was founded. In a similar fashion to its work in other states, its membership was largely composed of local men of property and business, and it raised funds and provided financial assistance for needy compatriots. The flurry of Irish organizations set up at this time continued with the establishment of the Irish Volunteers Company of Charleston in 1799 and the formation of St. Patrick's Benevolent Society in 1817.

Roman Catholic Bishop John England, who had been born in Cork in 1786, was consecrated as bishop of Charleston in 1820. He responded to Daniel O'Connell's condemnation of slavery, saying that although he disapproved of it, he also recognized the impossibility of abolishing it in the southern states. Another prominent citizen of South Carolina who was of Irish extraction was John C. Calhoun, whose father had been born in Donegal. Calhoun recognized his Irish background and showed this by joining the Irish Emigrant Society of New York in 1844.

In the 1820s, as was the case in many other states, the construction of canals and railroads led to an increase in the number of Irish emigrating to and settling in South Carolina. With the Great Famine in the 1840s many of the Irish associations in South Carolina raised funds to send to Ireland. Although there was a trickle of Irish immigrants from the northern cities, there was not the same level of immigration as there was in other states. With the outbreak of the Civil War, the Irish formed units to fight for the Confederacy. The Irish Volunteers of Charleston joined the Confederate army. Bishop Patrick Lynch of Charleston, who had been born in Clones, Co. Monaghan, became a representative of the Confederacy in Europe, where he defended slavery. With the end of the Civil War and the defeat of the South, there was not the same level of immigration from Ireland to South Carolina as there had been in the antebellum period. In spite of this there were some success stories. including that of Michael Patrick O'Connor, the son of an emigrant from Charville, Co. Cork, who was elected to Congress as a Democrat in 1878. Following the Irish Parliamentary Party leader Charles Stewart Parnell's address to the House of Representatives, he traveled the country speaking in support of Irish land reform. Parnell was not the only Irish leader who had an effect on South Carolina. In April 1920, Eamon de Valera, the president of the Irish Republic, visited the city of Charleston, where the city's mayor, John P. Grace, received him. In a 1980 census 14 percent of the population of South Carolina claimed that they were of Irish ancestry. The Ancient Order of Hibernians continues the Irish presence today with its branches in Charleston, Columbia, and Myrtle Beach, South Carolina.

David Doyle

References
Gleeson, David T. *The Irish in the South, 1815–1877*. Chapel Hill: University of North Carolina Press, 2001.
Mitchell, Arthur. *The History of the Hibernian Society of Charleston, South Carolina, 1799–1981*. Charleston: Hibernian Society, 1982.

SOUTH DAKOTA

South Dakota was originally inhabited by the Sioux (Dakota, Lakota, Nakota) and Arikara tribes. A portion of the area was first explored by Europeans in the mid-eighteenth century before the entire region was purchased from Napoleon as part of the enormous land sale in the Louisiana Purchase of 1803. The famous Lewis and Clark expedition of 1804–1806, which commenced in St. Louis to explore and chart the newly acquired land, ventured into sections of what would become South Dakota. White settlements grew primarily around trading interests: the first fur trading post was established at modern-day Fort Pierre in 1817, and there was subsequent activity by the American Fur Company. By the 1830s, the Sioux had become dominant and had largely pushed the Arikara from the land, and in 1858 a group of Sioux signed over much of eastern South Dakota to the U.S. government. Many, however, would fiercely resist white westward expansion.

The first sizable numbers of white settlers arrived in the 1850s, many from Minnesota and Iowa; land companies were established and towns were planned. The Dakota Territory, with Yankton as capital, was organized in 1861 and encompassed both present-day Dakotas as well as part of Wyoming and Montana. Insect plagues, droughts, and the threat of conflict with local Indians resulted in a relatively depressed number of new immigrants, although the arrival of rail lines to Yankton in 1872 began to increase the number, mostly Irish, German, Scandinavian, and Russian. These first three groups still represent the largest ancestry groups in present-day South Dakota.

Incoming numbers would be further helped by the discovery of gold reported by a military expedition led by George A. Custer in 1874. Prospectors and miners subsequently spilled into the Black Hills. The bulk of this region had been promised to the Sioux in the Treaty of Fort Laramie in 1868, and this sudden white encroachment represented a breach of the treaty. The government attempted to purchase the Black Hills, but owing to its highly sacred character, the offer was refused. Piqued, the government ordered the tribe to vacate and the situation descended into warfare, most famously known for the defeat of Custer at the Battle of Little Big Horn in 1876 (present-day Montana).

Wounded Knee creek in South Dakota would witness what is commonly regarded as the end of Native American resistance in the nineteenth century, when approximately 200 men, women, and children were massacred by Custer's former regiment, the 7th Cavalry.

In the late nineteenth century, cattle and mining fueled a steady growth, and the years 1878–1886 witnessed a land boom that saw a 300 percent increase in the population. Irish Catholics began to move steadily into the area—the religion had already been established in the state by French Catholics who had arrived and founded the first permanent mission in 1867. Other groups arriving included Germans, Norwegians, Swedes, Danes, and smaller numbers of Italians, facilitated by the arrival of the railroad from Sioux City, Iowa. Indeed, the white population rocketed to 82,000 by 1880 and 348,600 in 1890. Railroad construction attracted settlers and boosted the economic prospects of the state, but the boom came to a halt as agricultural difficulties in the late 1880s forced many to reconsider the area's potential, and many settlers migrated out of state. Statehood was attained in 1889: the Dakotas were separated and admitted on the same day, and Pierre became the capital of South Dakota.

With its strong agrarian and farming interests, South Dakota became involved, as many western and southern states did, in the Populist Party phenomenon in the

1890s. Often known as the People's Party, it represented a position of protest born out of increasing frustration after a series of events and issues, including droughts, agricultural hardship and debts, national financial policies, and resentment against the railroad (they lobbied for government ownership). South Dakota elected Andrew E. Lee, running on the Populist ticket, as governor in 1896, but in 1900 he lost to the Republicans when running for Congress, a loss that saw the rapid decline of the Populists in the state.

From 1900 to 1930, immigration generally rose; settlers arrived from Scandinavia, Russia, much of mid-Europe, China, and Ireland. However, new agricultural difficulties (drought, 1910–1911) prompted some to move on to different states. Others turned once again to a more radicalized politics in the guise of the Progressives, reflected in the election of Peter Norbeck and Frank Byrne, the son of Irish immigrants; both were elected as state senators and subsequently governors.

Further population losses occurred during the Great Depression decade (around 50,000), and many farmers with relatively small holdings were pushed out of business after World War II as agricultural techniques reshaped the character of farming in the state into large, consolidated farms. (The state has suffered a recurrence of out-migration at the turn of the twenty-first century.) Service industries began to establish centers in the state in the 1980s, and with the boom in Indian gaming, the state has witnessed a growth in casinos. The state also draws significant amounts of money through tourism to the Badlands National Park and the state's most famous landmark, Mount Rushmore.

Sam Hitchmough

References

Doyle, David Noel, and Owen Dudley Edwards, eds. *America and Ireland, 1776–1976: The American Identity and the Irish Connection.* Westport, CT: Greenwood Press, 1980.

Kenny, Kevin. *The American Irish.* London: Longman, 2000.

Miller, Kerby A. *Emigrants and Exiles: Ireland and the Irish Exodus to North America.* Oxford: Oxford University Press, 1988.

Schell, Herbert. *History of South Dakota.* Pierre: South Dakota State Historical Society, 2004.

SPELLMAN, ARCHBISHOP FRANCIS JOSEPH (1889–1967)

Born in Whitman, Massachusetts, Francis Joseph Spellman was the eldest of five children of William and Ellen (Conway) Spellman, both of whom were the children of Irish immigrants. During one of his visits to Ireland Spellman recalled how all four of his grandparents had immigrated to America from the counties of Cork, Carlow, Tipperary, and Limerick. After graduating from Fordham College in New York, he entered the seminary at the North American College in Rome, where he studied at the Urban College of Propaganda. He was ordained in Rome on May 14, 1916, and he returned to Boston, where he became an assistant pastor at All Saints' Church in Roxbury, Massachusetts. He became assistant chancellor of the Boston archdiocese in 1922 and an archivist a year later. In 1925, Spellman was appointed to the position of vatican secretariat of state by Pope Pius XI. He was made a monsignor and was appointed auxiliary bishop of Boston in 1932 and became pastor of Sacred Heart parish in Newton Center. Following the death of Cardinal Patrick Hayes, on April 15, 1939, Spellman was appointed archbishop of New York, a position he would hold until his death, making him the longest serving person to hold that position. In addition, he was also military ordinary, or bishop, over the armed forces. In 1946 he was elevated to cardinal. After the war he became a vociferous opponent of communism, and for a while he embraced the anticommunism of Senator Joseph McCarthy. During this time he also bemoaned the decline of censorship in American films. In Christmas 1965 he visited American soldiers in Vietnam and expressed his support for their presence there, viewing the war as part of the fight against communism. Spellman died in New York on December 2, 1967, and was interred in the crypt under the altar of Saint Patrick's Cathedral in New York.

Although Cardinal Spellman was conscious of his Irish ancestry he always identified himself as an American, correcting his biographer when he referred to him as an Irishman. In 1931, he had paid a visit to Ireland, the highlight of which was his time in Clonmel, where his grandfather had been born in 1831. The following year he accompanied the papal legate, Cardinal Lauri, as his official secretary and translator, to the International Eucharistic Congress in Dublin. He met Archbishop Edward J. Byrne of Dublin; the newly elected taoiseach, Eamon de Valera; and the lord mayor of Dublin, Alfred Byrne. He read the English translation of the papal bull in Saint Mary's Pro-Cathedral in Dublin. In 1942, during World War II, Spellman revisited Ireland, where again he met de Valera as well as Archbishop John Charles McQuaid at the American Embassy. On February 11, 1944, he made a third and final visit to Ireland, during which he landed at Shannon Airport, where he was met by Irish government officials and members of the Irish hierarchy before celebrating mass at Saint John's Cathedral in Limerick. After the mass he recalled how his maternal grandmother had left Limerick more than a century before to immigrate to America, eventually settling in Whitman, Massachusetts. Afterward, he traveled to Killarney by train where, following a trip to the Gap of Dunloe, a state dinner was held in his honor with the taoiseach once again present.

The anticommunism espoused by the cardinal at the height of the Cold War affected his relations with Ireland. In September 1957, Ireland's minister for foreign affairs, Frank Aiken, announced in New York that Ireland would support a motion to discuss China's admission to the United Nations at a time when communist China was not recognized by the United States and Taiwan held the Chinese seat at the United Nations. A representative of Cardinal Spellman called the Irish delegation to inform them that the cardinal would boycott a reception planned for that evening rather than accept hospitality from a friend of communist China. According to Conor Cruise O'Brien, a member of the Irish delegation at the time, the cardinal's efforts to dissuade the Irish delegation from supporting the Chinese entry were rebuffed, and Ireland eventually voted for discussion of China's entry to the United Nations.

David Doyle

References

Cooney, John. *The American Pope: The Life and Times of Francis Cardinal Spellman.* New York: Times Books, 1984.

Gannon, Robert I. *The Cardinal Spellman Story.* London: Hale, 1963.

O'Brien, Conor Cruise. *To Katanga and Back.* New York: Grosset & Dunlap, 1966.

STOKER, ABRAHAM "BRAM" (1847–1912)

As acting manager of the Lyceum Theater, Bram Stoker became involved in the first large-scale acting tours of the United States by a British acting company. From 1884 until 1903 the company traveled across America on a series of visits. Stoker's enthusiastic interest in the social and political life of the United States became apparent in a lecture given in England upon return from his first visit and entitled "A Glimpse of America." He consequently became fascinated by the life and times of Abraham Lincoln and wrote an extended lecture on Lincoln, slavery, and the American Civil War in 1886, which he presented in both the United States and England. Stoker published a number of articles on American theater in early 1900, and although he had been publishing fiction from the 1870s onward, his most significant works followed upon his long involvement in the theatrical world. His melodramatic study of the Irish gombeen man in *The Snake's Pass* (1890) and his popular treatment of the vampire in *Dracula* (1897) recall British and American theater of the late nineteenth century.

Stoker was born in Dublin and educated in Trinity College, where he was introduced to the poetry of Walt Whitman. Initially, he worked as a civil servant until 1879, when he took over the business dealings of London's Lyceum Theater. The theater company's regular American tours (1883–1884, 1884–1885, 1887–1888, 1896, 1899, and 1903) featuring the most prominent English actors of the day, Henry Irving and Ellen Terry, and complete with stage sets, costumes, performers, and technicians, indicate the popularity of English productions in the United States. Based on

Portrait of Irish author Bram Stoker, who is best known for his 1897 novel Dracula. *(Hulton-Deutsch Collection/Corbis)*

his travels and research, Stoker's *Glimpse of America* concentrates on the effect of climate and topography on the development of the American national character. The author provides an introduction to the nature of the American political system, the manners and dress of the people, attitudes toward women, and the practical approach of American citizens to matters of injustice.

Stoker met Whitman during the theater company's initial tour, and his lecture on Lincoln relies in part on the poet's observations of the American statesman in "Memoranda During the War" in *Two Rivulets* (1876), which Stoker had read while in Trinity. Stoker also researched contemporary biographies on Lincoln. His lecture elaborates on the growth of the American nation, the events leading up to and throughout the Civil War, and the central figure of Lincoln, who manifests the ideals of democratic freedom as expressed by the northern states. Though Stoker initially depicts Lincoln as a man of the people, he soon elevates him as a hero. He illustrated his lectures with casts of Lincoln's face and hands made by Augustus Saint-Gaudens. The lecture did not attract sufficient audiences in the United States after 1887, but Stoker continued to present his lecture in England up until 1893. Stoker's writings on America demonstrate the extent of his interest in its history and his intent to improve Anglo-American understanding.

Julie Anne Stevens

See also: SAINT-GAUDENS, Augustus

References

Havlik, Robert J., ed. "Bram Stoker's Lecture on Abraham Lincoln." *Irish Studies Review.* 10, no. 1 (April 2002): 5–27.

Stoker, Bram. *A Glimpse of America, A Lecture Given at the London Institution, 28 December 1885.* London: Sampson Low, Marston, 1886.

SULLIVAN, JOHN L. (1858–1918)

John L. Sullivan was a second-generation Irish American who ushered boxing into the modern era of sport as the heavyweight champion of the world from 1882 to 1892. Sullivan, who was born in 1858 to Irish immigrant parents, was a product of his Irish working-class culture. He claimed to have finished school and attended Boston College for a brief period, although he actually left school with a ninth grade education and quickly fell into the laboring professions typical of Irish Americans of that time.

With a fiery temperament, unsuited to conventional labor, Sullivan soon took to entering and winning boxing tournaments to gain repute and money. At 19, after knocking out Tom Scannel, a boxer of local repute, Sullivan began fighting in Boston theaters and music halls. After defeating three well-known opponents in quick succession and securing a victory over John Donaldson, the "champion of the West," in his first prizefight, Sullivan was regarded as a possible challenger for the champion bare-knuckle boxer, Paddy Ryan. Ryan, however, spurned the challenge, and Sullivan began a cross-country tour where he offered $50 to anyone who would stand up against him for four rounds. This tour and Sullivan's bombastic self-promotion (a harbinger of the modern game) secured his national reputation.

Ryan finally agreed to fight Sullivan on February 7, 1882, in Mississippi City. The extensive newspaper exposure this fight received did much to foster the development of modern sports coverage. The fight itself lasted only nine rounds—Sullivan won easily, and earned himself the sobriquet of John the Great. At age 23 he had become the heavyweight champion; over the next decade he was to become one of the best-known public figures in the world.

As heavyweight champion, Sullivan began to dispense with the London Prize Ring code of bare-knuckle boxing, which had made boxing an illegal activity in America and had caused Sullivan no end of trouble with the law, choosing to fight instead under the Marquis of Queensbury rules, in four-round exhibition fights. Under these new rules, a round consisted of three minutes of fighting with a minute's rest between rounds. As well as allowing Sullivan to evade prosecution (because four-round exhibition fights were not covered by America's anti-prizefight law) and avoid unnecessary injuries (through the use of gloves and the elimination of wrestling), this decision ushered in the era of modern boxing as we now know it. Sullivan fought all comers and contenders under these rules, except for Peter Jackson—a black Australian fighter who probably presented the most formidable challenge to his dominance—drawing the color line as justification for his refusal.

After extensive exhibition tours, including a "World Tour" of Great Britain (where he received a rousing welcome in Ireland), Sullivan was forced to defend his title in a prizefight on July 7, 1889, against Jake Kilrain. Sullivan's years of heavy drinking had taken a serious toll on his health, and his fans had grown doubtful of his continued ability to defend his title. However, after enduring an intensive training program, Sullivan fought and defeated Kilrain in a 75-round fight that lasted two hours and 16 minutes, regaining his fans' unquestioning adoration. This was the last heavyweight championship fought under London Prize Ring Rules.

By the time Sullivan fought Jim Corbett, on September 7, 1892, he had slipped back into his old carousing ways and had not trained in any substantial form. It was to be the first fight of the modern era of heavyweight boxing—fought with gloves, under the Marquis of Queensbury rules, and inside the Olympic Club of New Orleans—and the last fight of John L. Sullivan's long career. He lost to Corbett in 21 rounds. Though retaining his celebrity status until his death, Sullivan filed for bankruptcy 10 years after losing his title, and he died on February 2, 1918, aged just 59.

James P. Byrne

References

Chidsey, Donald Barr. *John the Great: The Times and Life of a Remarkable American, John L. Sullivan.* New York: Doubleday, 1942.

Fleischer, Nat. *John L. Sullivan: Champion of Champions.* New York: G. P. Putman's Sons, 1951.

Sullivan, John L. *Life and Reminiscences of a Nineteenth Century Gladiator.* Boston: Jas. A. Hearn & Co., 1892.

TALLCHIEF, MARIA (1925–)

Though prima ballerina Maria Tallchief is most often associated with the Native American ancestry of her father, who was of the Osage tribe, she shares Irish background as well. Her mother, Ruth, was of Scottish and Irish descent. Tallchief describes her in her autobiography as a "true pioneer." Part of that pioneering spirit must have been passed on to her daughters, Betty Marie and Marjorie. Both were interested in dance, and specifically in ballet, from a young age, at a time when that was not a common or easy career aspiration for young women from Native American tribes. Betty Marie, later Maria, was born in Fairfax, Oklahoma, and spent much of her young life there with her father's people. Her mother, however, wanted to support and advance her daughters' talents beyond what was available to them on the rural lands of the Osage tribe, and she spearheaded a family move to California, where the young ballerinas studied with Bronislava Nijinska. Maria adapted to the discipline required of a ballet dancer and began to show the grace, fire, and originality that would distinguish her work in later years. At 17, she auditioned in New York for the Ballet Russe de Monte Carlo and was accepted into the corps de ballet, supporting such world-renowned ballerinas as Alexandra Danilova as the company toured

the world. Tallchief herself soon became a featured soloist with the company. Though she was barely in her early twenties, the power and individuality of her stage presence caught the eye and the imagination of famed choreographer George Balanchine.

Tallchief soon joined Balanchine's company, the New York City Ballet. A master choreographer, Balanchine found in Tallchief a professional and, for a time, a personal partner for his vision. Tallchief's interpretation of Balanchine's choreography for *The Firebird* in 1949 allowed her talents to come full force to national and international attention and became a signature moment for both their careers. She also created the role of the Sugar Plum Fairy in Balanchine's reinterpretation of the holiday ballet *The Nutcracker*. She also enthralled audiences with her performances in *Swan Lake, Pas De Six,* and *Orpheus,* among other works. The pair were married from 1946 to 1951, and Tallchief continued to dance with the company until 1960, when she joined the American Ballet Theater.

Her graceful moves, her subtlety and delicacy of interpretation, and her strong sense of self expressed through the classical strictures of professional ballet drew audiences to Tallchief's work. The fact that she was not only an American prima ballerina at a time when that was not common, but also a Native American one at that, brought more attention to her work. In 1953 President Eisenhower named Tallchief Woman of the Year. That same year, she was also recognized by her native state Oklahoma as Wa-Xthe-Thomba, or "Woman of Two Worlds."

Tallchief did not want to dance past her prime, and professional ballet is physically very demanding, so, in her early forties, she retired. She became a well-respected teacher and leader in the arts. She was artistic director and teacher at the Chicago Lyric Opera Ballet in the 1970s. With her sister Marjorie, who had also become a top ballerina, she founded the Chicago City Ballet and was its artistic director until 1987. Both Maria and Marjorie Tallchief were inducted into the Oklahoma Hall of Fame in recognition of their achievements. Tallchief remarried twice after her divorce from George Balanchine. With her third husband, Henry Paschen, she had a daughter, Elise, who became a poet. In 1996, Tallchief was given one of the highest artistic recognitions the United States gives its artists, the Kennedy Center Honors.

Kerry Dexter

References

Gourley, Catherine. *Who Is Maria Tallchief?* New York: Grosset & Dunlap, 2002.

Kaplan, Larry. *The Art of Maria Tallchief.* 1954. Reprint, New York: Video Arts International, 2003.

Tallchief, Maria, with Larry Kaplan, *America's Prima Ballerina.* New York: Henry Holt, 1997.

TAMMANY HALL

On May 12, 1789, Irish-born upholsterer William Mooney founded the Society of Saint Tammany in New York City. The society was created as a patriotic, benevolent, and nonpolitical organization to counteract the aristocratic influence of the Order of Cincinnati. Tammany's name is derived from legendary Delaware chief Tamanend and patterned after the prerevolutionary Sons of Saint Tammany as a fraternal society. Tammany Hall became a power in Democratic Party politics during the Jacksonian era of the 1830s. When Fernando Wood was elected mayor in 1854, city hall became and generally remained a Tammany fiefdom until Fiorello La Guardia took office in 1933.

Although a few similar short-lived societies were founded in other states, New York is where the name Tammany took on significant historical meaning. In 1805, the New York Society was incorporated as a benevolent society and built its first "wigwam" or hall in 1811. The Tammany Society was a secret organization with secret handshakes and elaborate rituals that supposedly had Native American origins. The organization was divided into tribes named by the "sachem after a specific animal." The sachems acted as the chief officials and a grand sachem was the absolute authority. Other officials included a "sagamore" or master of ceremonies and a "winskinkie," or doorkeeper. New York was the number one wigwam and served as the headquarters for the national eagle tribe. As new states were admitted to the United States they were also given tribal names. However, except for the first 15 years, the Tammany Society was not a truly national organization.

The Tammany Society did not resemble the well-known political organization until Matthew Davis negotiated the rental of its New York wigwam to the Tammany Hall General Committee, which laid the groundwork for political control and opportunism.

Tammany Hall, located on West 14th Street in New York City, ca. 1914. Tammany Hall was the meeting place for, and popular name of, the Democratic Party political machine that dominated much of New York City's political life until 1933. (Library of Congress)

Thereafter, the Tammany Society and the Tammany Hall General Committee were nearly synonymous. Overall, Tammany Hall's power came from its ability to organize citywide. Each ward or assembly district had a boss or leader who controlled the local committee that in turn sent representatives to the General Committee whose leaders made up the Executive Committee.

Almost from the beginning Tammany was actively engaged in politics. Although its early membership was strongly Federalist, the group supported Thomas Jefferson's Democratic-Republican Party in the 1800 election and sided with the Aaron Burr faction in New York City, which opposed De Witt Clinton's largely Irish following.

As a result, the Federalist members resigned from the society as Tammany lost all pretense of nonpartisanship.

It was during the 1820s—when the Democratic-Republican Party, with Tammany's support, passed legislation to extend male suffrage and abolish imprisonment for debt—that the organization became increasingly less Protestant and less elitist. In addition, after 1827, Tammany fought for reducing the five-year period necessary for naturalization. Thereafter, foreign-born immigrants gradually played a more prominent role in both the Tammany Society and Tammany Hall. Moreover, throughout the 1830s and 1840s the society expanded its political control by earning the loyalty of New York's ever-expanding immigrant community and by helping newly arrived foreigners obtain jobs, find a place to live, and even attain citizenship so that they could vote for Tammany candidates in city and state elections. By 1842, Irish gangs regularly used physical violence at election time, thereby becoming a source of Tammany political strength.

The money Tammany Hall garnered for itself and its leaders came from an assortment of activities. For example, they blackmailed corporations that preferred to purchase peace rather than fight bogus charges or corporations that desired to operate city concessions. In addition, money came from such purveyors of vice as liquor dealers, gambling establishments, and prostitution operators, who historically functioned at the mercy of the party in power or whose business was easily hampered by police, vigilant officeholders, and moralistic political candidates.

By 1854, all of these factors had combined to make Tammany the political force in New York City, conferring immense power on the society's "bosses" and allowing them to enrich themselves and their associates through corruption and administrative abuse. Most of the New York City board of aldermen during the 1850s were Tammany men who earned the title of the Forty Thieves. Corruption was elevated to a science when William Marcy Tweed rose to grand sachem of the Tammany Society in 1863. Tweed's leadership made it a well-organized, powerful political machine that served as the model for the "big city" machines to follow. Although nobody knows how much money was actually stolen, the city's bonded debt increased from $36 million in 1869 to $97 million in 1871 at a time when New York City borrowed an additional $20 million in floating loans.

Tammany became the prototype of the all-pervasive corrupt city machine. "Honest" John Kelly fine-tuned Tammany into an efficient, autocratic organization that dominated New York City politics for several generations. Kelly's successor, Richard Croker, lasted until 1901, then gave way to other important leaders or beneficiaries of Tammany Hall like Alfred E. Smith, James J. Walker, and William O'Dwyer. The New York Society was oftentimes charged with corrupt political practices that involved working with gangster elements in its control of municipal politics. As a result, from time to time investigations were undertaken by federal, state, and local groups. Foremost among the early muckrakers were Samuel Tilden, Thomas Nast, and *Harper's Weekly* in the 1880s, along with the comprehensive and trend-setting Seabury Investigation of 1932 and the televised Kefauver Investigation of 1950 to 1951.

In 1932, Tammany Mayor James J. Walker was brought up on corruption charges before Governor Franklin D. Roosevelt and forced to resign. In retaliation, the Tammany leaders refused to support Roosevelt's bid for the Democratic nomination for president, and as a result, the Roosevelt faction funneled federal patronage to New York City through the reform mayor, Fiorello La Guardia. Thereafter, Carmine G. De Sapio briefly revived Tammany Hall in the 1950s but lost control of his district to reformers in 1961, when the New York County Democratic Committee dropped the Tammany name.

Mark Connolly

See also: KELLY, "Honest" John; SMITH, Alfred Emmanuel "Al"; TWEED, William "Boss"

References

Allen, Oliver. *The Tiger: The Rise and Fall of Tammany Hall.* Reading, MA: Addison-Wesley, 1993.

Erie, Steven. *Rainbow's End: Irish-Americans and the Dilemma of Urban Machine Politics, 1840–1985.* Berkeley: University of California Press, 1988.

LaCerra, Charles. *Franklin Delano Roosevelt and Tammany Hall of New York.* Lanham, MD: University Press of America, 1997.

Mushkat, Jerome. *The Evolution of a Political Machine, 1789–1865.* Syracuse: Syracuse University Press, 1971.

Myers, Gustavus. *The History of Tammany Hall.* New York: Ben Franklin Press, 1968.

Riordan, William L. *Plunkitt of Tammany Hall: A Series of Very Plain Talks on Very Practical Politics.* New York: Amereon House, 1982.

TENNESSEE

As in many other states, early Irish immigration to Tennessee was mostly composed of Scots-Irish, and later mid-nineteenth-century settlement was made up of Irish Catholics. The first Scots-Irish migrated to Tennessee in the 1760s and 1770s, where they were instrumental in founding towns such as Knoxville and Nashville. All three of Tennessee's U.S. presidents, Andrew Jackson, James K. Polk, and Andrew Johnson, were of Scots-Irish ancestry, as were other notable figures, such as Davy Crockett and Sam Houston. Although there had been an increase in the number of Irish Catholics in Tennessee in the 1820s with the establishment of some Catholic parishes, there was a sharp rise in their numbers with the mass exodus from Ireland during the Great Famine in the 1840s. By this stage many of the earlier Scots-Irish immigrants had now become accepted as successful people of property and business, and the newer immigrants formed a poorer laboring class. Between 1850 and 1860, Tennessee saw the largest increase in its Irish population in all of the southern states and was in seventh position nationally. During this time, the Irish population in Knoxville, Nashville, and Memphis increased four times, with new towns called Erin and McEwen and areas known as "little Ireland." This increase in the number of Irish brought success to some: Michael Burns, who had been born in Sligo, became the director of two railroads and banks and served in the state legislature. However, although some Irish prospered, most lived in poor and overcrowded slums. With a rise in hostility toward the new immigrants, as expressed by the Know-Nothing movement, the Irish were forced to band together for solidarity.

At the outbreak of the Civil War the Irish showed their loyalty to their new home by volunteering for and forming various units to fight for the Confederacy. The Second Tennessee Volunteer Infantry, which was nicknamed the "Irish Regiment," the 10th Tennessee Infantry Regiment, also known as "the Sons of Erin," and the Third Cavalry, which was led by Nathan Bedford Forrest, were all composed of Irishmen. By the end of the Civil War this newly found pride and confidence on the part of the Irish in Tennessee found expression in the establishment of a number of Irish organizations in the state. By 1868, a branch of the Ancient Order of Hibernians had been organized in Nashville, along with the Hibernian Benevolent Society and the Parnell Branch of the Irish National League. However, it was to be with the Irish separatists—the Irish Republican Brotherhood, known as the Fenians—that the next phase of Irish involvement in Tennessee occurred. There had been a history of Fenians in Tennessee: leading member John Mitchel settled in east

Tennessee with his family in 1855 and later moved to Knoxville, where he edited a pro-slavery newspaper, *The Southern Citizen*. In 1866 the Fenians planned an invasion of Canada; their members in Tennessee assembled in Memphis and then traveled north by train, but the invasion itself was a complete failure.

After the end of the Civil War, with newly freed blacks competing with the Irish for low-paid jobs, a three-day riot broke out in Memphis, which left 48 dead. A congressional investigation later discovered the extent of Irish control of the different services of the city; they controlled more than 90 percent of the police, 60 percent of city officers, and the office of mayor. Gradually, the position of the Irish in the city and the state began to change; some migrated to other states, while those who remained found their power restricted after the return of the old elites in the Reconstruction era. The standard of living rose for those who remained and they subsequently moved from the inner-city slums in which they had first settled to the suburbs. Recently, however, there has been a greater awareness of Irish ancestry among those currently living in Tennessee. In the 1990 census, one in five people living in Tennessee claimed that they were of Irish ancestry. As a way of expressing these ties, which bind Tennessee and Ireland together, in 1995 Nashville and Belfast were twinned as sister cities.

David Doyle

References

Gleeson, David T. *The Irish in the South.* Chapel Hill: University of North Carolina Press, 2001.

Gleeson, David T., ed. *Rebel Sons of Erin.* Indianapolis: 1993.

Kennedy, Billy. *The Scots-Irish in the Hills of Tennessee.* Belfast: Ambassador Press, 1995.

TEXAS

The story of the Irish pioneer settlers in Mexican Texas is one of hardship, tragic loss of life, endurance, and ultimate triumph. They came from the United States and directly from Ireland in pursuit of land and a new life. They suffered from cholera, shipwreck, Indian depredations, and the destruction of their property at the hands of the Mexican army. Those who survived and stayed on made a powerful contribution to the independence of Texas and to the building of communities. In so doing, they prospered in the developing ranching industry and in business and commerce.

After Mexico gained independence from Spain in 1821, Coahuila y Texas was the northern state most vulnerable to the influx of American squatters. Fear of the Americanization of Texas led to the recruitment of European settlers, especially Catholic Irish; and two pairs of Irish merchants were contracted as *empresarios* (agents) to establish mixed Irish and Mexican settlements. In 1830, John McMullen and James McGloin established the town of San Patricio de Hibernia on the Nueces River, and in 1834, James Power and James Hewetson founded Refugio on the site of the old Spanish mission a few miles inland from the port of El Copano. The Mexican government offered generous land grants to encourage settlement: each family received 4,428 acres of pasture and 177 acres of arable land.

The Irish families that settled in San Patricio were mostly recruited from New York, Philadelphia, and New Orleans, while others came directly from Co. Tipperary. The Irish in Refugio—mostly small tenant farmers—were brought directly from Co. Wexford and other southern counties. Two ships, the *Prudence* (with

81 listed passengers) and the *Heroine* (with 71 adult passengers), sailed in the spring of 1834 from Liverpool to New Orleans, where they encountered a cholera epidemic that killed some of the passengers of the *Prudence.* Many others died from cholera, and others died when some of the schooners taking them to the Texas coast were shipwrecked.

The survivors acquired their land grants during the period 1834–1835 but were soon engulfed in the war between Texas and Mexico (1835–1836). At first San Patricio sided with Mexico, while Refugio stood for Texan independence. After the Mexican army, commanded by General Urrea, destroyed the two settlements, both communities fought for Texas. Some of the Irish who enlisted in the Texan army were killed alongside American volunteers at the massacres of Goliad and at the Alamo in March 1836. Others, including Thomas O'Connor, nephew of James Power, fought in the decisive battle of the war, under Sam Houston, at San Jacinto in April 1836. Texas won its independence.

The Irish colonists were evacuated from the war zone in 1836. They faced an insecure future and threats from attacking Comanches and Mexican bandits, until 1845, when the families were allowed to return to their burnt-out homesteads. Thomas O'Connor had stayed all through the war and its aftermath and began to build up a ranching estate that was eventually to make him the "cattle king" of Refugio County. At his death in 1887, he had amassed 500,000 acres and 100,000 head of cattle, much of the land having formerly been in the possession of fellow colonists; it remains in the family to the present time. In 1934 oil was discovered on the O'Connor estate.

Irish families owned a third of all ranches and inherited the Hispanic ranching tradition in the coastal bend area of south Texas. From the 1840s, Irishmen were also prominent as judges, merchants, and bankers in Corpus Christi, Victoria, and San Antonio.

Graham Davis

See also: SAN PATRICIOS BRIGADE

References

Davis, Graham. *Land!: Irish Pioneers in Mexican and Revolutionary Texas.* College Station: Texas A & M University Press, 2002.

Flannery, John Brendan. *The Irish Texans.* San Antonio: University of Texas Institute of Texan Cultures, 1995.

TITANIC, IRISH ON THE

When the *Titanic* left Queenstown on April 11, 1912, the third Home Rule Bill was going through Parliament, and England was experiencing the National Coal Strike of 1912. Emigrants were leaving Ireland in search of a better life abroad, continuing the flood of emigration that had already transported millions of Irish across the Atlantic. Some of those emigrants left on the *Titanic* from Queenstown, now known as Cobh. Two-thirds of them did not reach their destination.

The *Titanic* was built in Belfast's Harland and Wolff shipyard by a Protestant workforce for the White Star Line. One impetus for building the *Titanic* and its sister ships, the *Olympic* and the *Britannic,* was to cope with the competition from the Cunard Line's popular *Lusitania,* which had been built in 1906. The *Titanic* was constructed in 36 months. It was 882 feet long, and 46,329 tons. The boat, fully equipped, cost £1.5 million sterling.

However, a few aspects suggested problems when the ship left Ireland. There was a serious fire in one of the boiler rooms, and there were no binoculars on the lookout known as the crow's nest. Moreover, there were not enough lifeboats. Despite that fact, and with full knowledge of it, the British Board of Trade deemed *Titanic* seaworthy on April 1, 1912.

The ship's departure from Belfast on April 2, 1912, was witnessed by thousands. Before its arrival in Queenstown on April 11, the *Titanic* picked up passengers in Southampton, England, and Cherbourg, France. It docked two miles from shore off the southern Irish coast and awaited passengers. They were transported to the *Titanic* on the tenders *Ireland,* for first-class and second-class passengers, and *America* for the third-class passengers. A substantial amount of mail, almost 1,400 bags, was also brought to the ship, and mail was returned to shore on the tenders.

Ships leaving Queenstown were a common sight, as it had been the port of departure for emigrants for decades. The town had a number of boarding houses that accommodated passengers while they waited for passage. However, the visit of the *Titanic* was different. Great excitement greeted the enormous steamship. The Deepwater Quay in Queenstown was decorated with bunting. People from Cork City traveled around the harbor to see the ship at a distance out in the ocean. The crowds included *Cork Examiner* photographer Thomas Barker. Barker took photographs of passengers departing from the dock, and one photograph shows uilleann piper Eugene Daly, who reportedly played "Erin's Lament" as *Titanic* left Ireland. A flotilla of boats traveled out to sell souvenirs, such as Irish linen and lace, to the passengers.

Some of the Queenstown passengers had intended to go on a smaller ship whose voyage had been canceled because of the English coal strike. They now were to travel on the much bigger and more luxurious *Titanic.* The White Star Line had requisitioned coal from the *St. Louis* and the *Philadelphia* (belonging to American Line) and from their own *Majestic* so they would have enough fuel for the *Titanic* to sail across the Atlantic. The first-class passengers boarding at Queenstown consisted of Dr. Minahan, his wife, and his sister from Wisconsin. There were seven second-class passengers, five of whom were Irish and the other two Canadian and American (a priest). However, the bulk of the passengers who boarded at Queenstown were the 113 third-class Irish, consisting of 55 men and 58 women. There were also five children; the Rice brothers were all under 10. They were accompanying their mother home to Spokane, Washington. They had been back to Ireland for a visit after the death of their father.

Some of the passengers were in groups. The largest group of 14 was from Co. Mayo. The third-class passengers included couples, families, and a number of single people. Apparently, one couple had eloped. Senan Molony's extensive research on the Irish passengers in *The Irish Aboard the Titanic* indicates that some of the passengers were returning emigrants and others were going out to join brothers and sisters or other relatives with the purpose of getting employment as domestic servants and laborers. These Irish were housed in third-class accommodation, and the single men and women were in opposite ends of the ship.

There were those who, for one reason or another, decided against the trip to the

United States and disembarked at Queenstown. Irishman John Coffey, who embarked at Southampton, had signed up as a stoker for the entire journey but did not continue across the Atlantic. The Odells, who included the future Jesuit Father Francis Browne, also disembarked. Browne was the nephew of the Catholic bishop of Cork, who presided over the cathedral that overlooked Queenstown harbor. The bishop had given Browne a present of a first-class ticket from Southampton to Queenstown via Cherbourg. Browne took numerous photographs of his voyage. These subsequently appeared in newspapers all over the world and now represent an invaluable visual reflection of the last few days of the *Titanic.*

When the *Titanic* departed from Ireland, in the early afternoon, at 1:55 p.m., it was watched from various coastal points by Irish people who wanted a glimpse of the famous ship. Those on the ship also watched as it sailed around the headlands of southern Ireland, their last view of Europe. The ship struck an iceberg on April 14 at 11:40 p.m. and sank on April 15 at 2:20 a.m. It is now accepted that the ship split into two, based on reports at the time and the Ballard expedition in 1985. There were two inquiries after the disaster. One was carried out by the United States Senate (April 19 to May 25, 1912) and the other by the British Board of Trade (May 2 to July 3, 1912). Most of the statistics on the number of deaths and survivors have been obtained from these reports. Books and articles written since the disaster have slightly different statistics. Apparently, differences in numbers can be explained by the following factors: some people traveled under pseudonyms, for one reason or another; some who may have disembarked at

Queenstown were not taken off the passenger list; the lists were sloppy, and there were at least two instances of female names being changed to male names. Nevertheless, the following seems to be reasonably accurate based on an assessment of the different primary and secondary sources, and Senan Molony's research in particular. Of the 710 total third-class passengers, 536 died; 74 of the 113 Irish third-class passengers who departed from Queenstown were lost. These included the Rice children and at least 10 of the group from Co. Mayo. Dr. Minahan and five of the Irish second-class passengers were also lost. A handful of Irish-born passengers who got on at Southampton and a number of Irish-born crew members also died. According to the U.S. Senate investigation, 60 percent of first-class passengers were saved while only 25 percent of third-class passengers lived.

Clearly, the Irish third-class passengers were disadvantaged by their economic and colonial status. There has been debate in the literature on whether or not Irish passengers drowned because they were Irish. They were disadvantaged because most of them were poor and thus in third class and on the lower decks. For a period after the collision it seems they were told there was nothing to worry about and to go back to their cabins. Moreover, there were reports of some of them encountering locked doors and passageways and even loaded guns. However, according to the British enquiry into the disaster, "Irish emigrants were not discriminated against." The U.S. Senate investigation does not comment on the matter and merely reports on the statistics of the deaths.

The survivors were rescued by the *S.S. Carpathia* and taken to New York City, where they arrived on April 18. Irish newspapers followed events and reported when someone's death or survival was confirmed. They also gave simultaneous and equal coverage to the passing of the third Home Rule Bill. Those who survived were helped by the American Red Cross in New York City. They were provided with clothes and money. Survivors later received compensation from the White Star Line for goods they had lost (clothes, money, and luggage). Eugene Daly lost his uileann pipes and received compensation of $50.

The survivors always had this calamity in their history. Some lived for decades, others a few years. Danny Buckley from Kingwilliamstown, now known as Ballydesmond, joined the U.S. Army, and died on the last day of World War I. A neighbor of his in Kingwilliamstown, Nora O'Leary, later Herlihy, returned to her Irish home and lived until 1975.

Cliona Murphy

See also: EMIGRATION

References
Ballard, Robert D. *The Discovery of the Titanic*. New York: Madison Press Books, 1987.
Butler, Daniel Allen. *"Unsinkable": The Full Story*. Mechanicsburg, PA: Stackpole Books, 1998.
Cameron, Stephen. *Titanic Belfast's Own*. Dublin: Wolfhound Press, 1998.
Lynch, Donald. *Titanic: An Illustrated History*. London: Hodder and Stoughton, 1995.
Molony, Senan. *The Irish Aboard Titanic*. Dublin: Wolfhound Press, 2000.
O'Donnell, E. E. *The Last Days of the Titanic*. Dublin: Wolfhound Press, 1997.

TRAVEL PATTERNS FROM IRELAND TO SOUTH AMERICA

For the emigrants from the British Isles, traveling to South America was very different from traveling to North America. The differences in places of origin, transport means, and areas of settlement made each experience unique, and in some way determined the social profile of the emigrants and the probability of their successful settlement and integration in the local societies.

Most Irish emigrants to South America came from two areas, south-east of Wexford (16 percent), and a sector on the Westmeath-Longford-Offaly central region (61 percent). They immigrated mainly to the River Plate (at that time comprising Argentina, Uruguay, and regions of Brazil and Paraguay). Moreover, scattered merchants, soldiers, servants, and professionals came frequently from Irish cities and settled in northern Brazil, Chile, Colombia, Peru, and Venezuela.

The River Plate countries were attractive to Irish emigrants because of their reputation as a place where land was relatively easy to acquire. By the mid-nineteenth century, migration networks had been gradually established by Irish landowners, merchants, and Catholic priests. All of them were highly regarded by the local bourgeoisie for their condition of *ingleses* (i.e., English speakers). The established immigrants hired family members, friends, and neighbors in Ireland to help them in their sheep farms in the pampas or in their businesses in other South American countries.

During the highest peak of emigration (1840–1880), most emigrants from the Irish midlands would travel to Dublin; cross to Liverpool; sail to Rio de Janeiro, Montevideo, and Buenos Aires; and then head for the major Irish settlements scattered over the pampas. Before this period, they would travel along the trading routes between Europe and North America and then journey on from the United States to the Caribbean, the Brazilian coast, and the

River Plate. (A few would go to Panama to board ships to Peru and Chile.) After the 1880s, other transit ports were frequently used by emigrants, particularly Cork and Southampton. However, Dublin was the nearest port for emigrants from the midlands.

From the beginning of the nineteenth century, to reach Dublin emigrants would use canal barges towed by horses. Later, from about 1848, they used the railway. Poorer emigrants would use less expensive means of transport or would simply walk. Most of them paid for their tickets, and some were reimbursed by their employers in Buenos Aires. In 1806, the Royal Canal reached Mullingar from Dublin. The Longford branch was opened in January 1830. The journey from Mullingar to Dublin took around 13 hours in the early years of the canal service. By the 1840s, faster boats (the "fly boats") had cut journey times to eight hours. Canal barges lumbered along sedately at three or four miles per hour. The journey was relatively comfortable, even if one had to sleep on deck. But as emigration increased during the Famine years, the boats were often overcrowded. Some emigrants would have traveled by the Grand Canal, which was older and busier than the Royal Canal. Two boats left daily, and the fare for the Mullingar-Dublin section (41 miles) was 12 shillings and sixpence in first cabin and seven shillings and seven pence in second cabin.

In 1848, the railway reached Mullingar, and in 1851 the line extended to Athlone. The railway age signaled the demise of the canal. By 1855 the train arrived in Longford, and the railway replaced the canal as the main means of transport to Dublin, with a journey time of about two hours. For those emigrants who lived at a distance from the railway, the journey to the station was made by coach. By the late 1840s, Bianconi coaches, each capable of carrying up to 20 passengers, provided the means by which emigrants could reach Longford, Mullingar, and Athlone from the countryside and from the small rural villages and townlands of Westmeath and Longford. Horse-drawn stagecoaches moved at about eight miles per hour, with frequent stops to rest horses and passengers. Bianconi coaches connected with the Royal Canal boats to Dublin and intermediate stages. Fares from Ballymahon to Mullingar were six shillings and 11 pence (state or first class) and five shillings and nine pence (back or second class). Emigrants to South America were advised to bring a revolver and a saddle.

Once in Dublin, emigrants would stay a night at a local hotel. The fare for one bed for one person in a room containing two or more beds was two shillings and two pence. At least three boats daily crossed the Irish Sea from Dublin to Liverpool, and the journey took from 12 to 14 hours. For emigrants from Wexford steamboats were available to Liverpool. Departures were every Thursday at 6.00 a.m. and Saturday at 7.00 a.m., with an estimated journey time of 12 hours. In Liverpool, emigrants landed in Clarence Dock. Since most of them would already have purchased their sea passages in Ballymahon, Mullingar, or Wexford town, their money was secured and they just had to take care of their lodging until the boarding time. During the days of sailing ships, vessels were "expected any day now" and, if the wind was against them, they could be up to three weeks late.

Once the emigrants managed to get on board the ships, the Atlantic crossing followed. It was not an easy voyage. It was long, taking usually between six weeks and three or up to six months. The sea was a strange environment for most emigrants, especially for those coming from rural areas. Owing to insurance requirements, the ships sailing from Liverpool to the River Plate were mostly first and second class, that is, surveyed and judged to be of best or good quality in terms of age, condition, and seaworthiness, unlike many ships on the North American routes in the 1840s, which were third class (the infamous "coffin ships"), a status that prohibited any but short voyages. Fares to Brazil and the River Plate varied with company and class, ranging from £10 to £35, with an average of £16 (half of an Irish farmhand's annual salary in Argentina).

The second half of the nineteenth century was marked by iron and steel sailing ships, and later by steamships. The length of the journey was reduced from three months to four weeks. Steamships were far superior vessels, to such a degree that the last sailing ships were built by 1855. The transition from sail to steam was radical. During the 1860s, which saw the highest peak in Irish immigration to South America (with the exception of the *City of Dresden* in 1889), the most active company was Lamport & Holt. In 1863 they began sailing to and from Rio de Janeiro, Montevideo, and Buenos Aires. By 1892 the direct voyage took 22 days. Before the 1880s, the most important ship in terms of quantity of Irish emigrants carried was *La Zingara,* the smallest vessel of Thomas B. Royden & Co. She was a barque built in 1860 in Liverpool, sheathed in yellow metal fastened with copper bolts (287 tons). The captain was George Sanders. Tickets on *La Zingara* were cheaper than those of other vessels such as *Raymond* from Dublin (Captain Lenders). In 1889 the *City of Dresden* carried

the largest number of passengers (1,774) ever to arrive in Argentina from any one destination on any one vessel, the result of a deceitful immigration scheme managed by Argentine government agents in Ireland, later called the Dresden Affair.

Upon their arrival, the vast majority of the Irish in Argentina, Brazil, and Uruguay settled in rural areas. Temporary lodging for English-speaking guests in Rio de Janeiro and Buenos Aires cost about eight shillings a day. The change of climate was a major concern for travelers, who were advised to rise early, take a cold bath every morning, and avoid walking in the sun.

To cover the immense extension of the Argentine pampas, immigrants had to ride horses for days, sometimes weeks. Routes and bridges were almost nonexistent and during the rainy season in winter, floods and rivers prevented any attempt to travel. In the 1870s a few coach services were inaugurated, but still most of the travel was done on horseback. The railway definitively changed the carriage of passengers and cargo in the pampas. In 1892, Mercedes, one of the Irish parishes, was reached in three hours from Buenos Aires in the Western and Pacific Railway, and Fortín de Areco (called "Fourteen" by the Irish), 90 miles northwest of Buenos Aires, in six hours. Salto was connected to Arrecifes, on the Pergamino railway line. The journey to Lincoln (180 miles west of Buenos Aires) took one day, and to Venado Tuerto, a major Irish settlement in southern Santa Fe, eight hours from Rosario. Some Irish estancieros sold or donated their land to build railway stations, therefore originating some Irish place names: Murphy, Hughes, Duffy, Cavanagh, Maguire, Ham, Gahan, Kenny, Gaynor, Dennehy, Duggan, and Heavy. Some of these places, like Gahan or

Murphy, are today flourishing villages, and others are solitary railway stations or abandoned wasteland.

Edmundo Murray

See also: DRESDEN AFFAIR

References

Howat, Jeremy N. T. *South American Packets 1808–1880*. York, UK: Postal History Society, 1984.

Illingworth, Ruth, ed. *When the Train Came to Mullingar*. Mullingar: Author's Edition, 1998.

Murray, Edmundo. "The Irish Road to Argentina: Nineteenth-century Travel Patterns from Ireland to the River Plate." *History Ireland* (Autumn 2004): 28–32.

TULLY, JIM (1888–1947)

Irish-American writer Jim Tully may be said to have embodied the Horatio Alger legend—from abject poverty to fabulous Hollywood riches—leaving in his wake a series of proletarian novels that have at times been compared with the opus of Maxim Gorky. Born in a rural log cabin near St. Mary's, Ohio, on June 3, 1891, Tully was the third son of immigrants James Denis Tully and Marie Bridget Lawler, a grade-school teacher. When he was seven his mother died and his alcoholic ditchdigger father cast his three sons into St. Joseph's Orphan Asylum in Cincinnati, Ohio. At 11 he was fostered out to a farmer who beat him, keeping him in near-starvation until he fled at 14, becoming a roving tramp. He crossed the continent three times by rail, occasionally finding work at odd jobs: dishwasher, newsboy, porter, circus roadie, tree surgeon, eventually settling into the trade of chain maker. During his wanderings the law dumped him in jail for vagrancy five times. At 21 he pursued a featherweight boxing career and, after several successful bouts, he was knocked unconscious for almost 24 hours. When he came to, he decided it might be more prudent to become an observer of the boxing scene and made great efforts to establish a career as a sportswriter, but he more often worked as an advertising salesman for newspapers.

In 1911 Tully married Florence Bushnell and had two children, but the marriage failed in 1924. For eight years the self-educated Tully labored on his first novel, *Emmet Lawler* (1922); the manuscript was a single rambling paragraph of about 100,000 words. Despite Tully's ignorance of elementary grammar, Rupert Hughes at Harcourt Brace tutored Tully, editing the manuscript to publication, thus launching the literary career of a personality larger than bourgeois life. Receiving reviews and magazine commissions, Tully turned to the writing life, often plucking at the typewriter 16 hours a day.

Tully's next book, *Beggars of Life* (1924), written in six weeks, limns a picaresque dramatization of his seven years as a tramp. Populated by outrageous characters from the underclass, these gripping adventures are so completely devoid of literary sensibility that they testify as one of the few authentic chronicles of tramp life in America. Maxwell Anderson rushed to fashion a play adaptation, *Outside Looking In* (1925), the first stage vehicle for the young tough-guy actor James Cagney (film version, 1928). *Beggars of Life* was the first of five autobiographical novels Tully called "the Underworld Edition," also including his roustabout experience in *Circus Parade* (1927); his family background, *Shanty Irish* (1928); the difficulties of incarceration and the inhumanity of the death penalty, *Shadows of Men* (1930); and his passionate farewell to literature, *Blood on the Moon* (1931), his most eloquent book.

Tully wrote more than a dozen self-indulgent, garrulous potboilers, from which his reputation never quite recovered. The most notable of these is the first Hollywood novel, the satire *Jarnegan* (1925), praised by H. L. Mencken. In 1925 Tully married Margaret Myers, but she had a difficult time adjusting to the presence of Tully's old tramp friends in their Spanish-style Hollywood mansion and disliked sleeping on couch or floor to accommodate their drunken slumbers—the marriage ended in divorce (1930). Tully, the highest-paid Hollywood interviewer, prided himself on exposing the shallow lives of Hollywood celebrities. For 18 months he worked as publicist for Charlie Chaplin, writing a biography of him, but they parted bitterly. Tully collaborated on a number of screenplays, his most notable success being the 1935 version of Poe's *The Raven* with Bela Lugosi. Inventing the Hollywood fanzine (ghostwriting complete issues, including letters to the editor), Tully weathered the Depression in high style.

Tully's books brim with authentic hard-boiled dialogue; although this was popular in his day, literary tastes have changed, preferring sophisticated ironies and less raw emotion. Some of Tully's interviews and magazine work continue to fascinate, and his collection of character sketches, *A Dozen and One* (1943) remains indicative of this work. There is still a body of unidentified work, even as his books are now being reprinted as they fall into public domain.

Kevin T. McEneaney

References

Anderson, David. "A Portrait of Jim Tully: An Ohio Hobo in Hollywood." *Society for the Study of Midwestern Literature Newsletter* 23, no. 3 (Fall 1944): 8–14.

Dawidziak, Mark, and Paul Bauer. *Jim Tully: A Biography*. Tucson, AZ: Dennis McMillan, 2006.

Fanning, Charles. *The Irish Voice in America*. Lexington: University Press of Kentucky, 2000.

TUNNEY, JAMES JOSEPH "GENE" (1898–1978)

Born in New York City's Greenwich Village on May 25, 1897, to Irish immigrants John Tunney, a longshoreman, and Mary (Lydon), James Joseph "Gene" Tunney was one of five children. He grew up in modest circumstances, learning to fight on the streets and in the social clubs of New York City. At age 16 he began sparring with professional boxers at the Village Athletic Club; from July 1914 to 1916 he fought sporadically as a professional in New York and New Jersey, although he was not interested in pursuing pugilism as a profession.

In 1918, after having been rejected earlier because of an arm injury, Tunney enlisted in the Marine Corps. He was sent to France but did not see any action at the front. While overseas, he was persuaded to engage in service boxing and soon became the middleweight and heavyweight champ of the camp and the light heavyweight champ of the entire American Expeditionary Force. At this point, Tunney decided to become a full-time boxer upon his return to civilian life.

Tunney began to fight seriously in November 1919 and, under the tutelage of manager Frank "Doc" Bagley, won his first 24 fights. His success caught the eye of famed promoter Tex Rickard, who matched Tunney with notable opponents. On January 13, 1922, Tunney beat "Battling" Levinsky at Madison Square Garden to win the light heavyweight title. On May 23,

1922, Tunney suffered the only defeat of his career, losing to Harry Greb at Madison Square Garden. Tunney returned to the ring, winning his next three bouts and a close rematch against Greb on February 23, 1923. Later that same year, he successfully defended his title against Greb, winning their third bout convincingly. Tunney fought a dozen bouts in 1924, winning all but a draw with Greb. Among his victories was a thrilling 15th-round knockout of Georges Carpentier on July 24 at the Polo Grounds. Despite standing only six feet one inch and weighing only 180 pounds, Tunney was quickly being touted as a serious contender for the heavyweight crown held by Jack Dempsey.

On September 23, 1926, Tunney moved up to the heavyweight division to battle Dempsey before 120,000 spectators in Philadelphia. Dempsey had not fought in over three years, and his performance showed the effect of his sustained layoff. Tunney delivered a one-sided beating and won the title by decision. The fight garnered nearly $2 million in gate receipts and led, inevitably, to a rematch.

The two fought again in Chicago on September 22, 1927, before 100,000 fans (and another 50 million listening on radio). Tunney was knocked down—for the only time in his career—in round seven, but was saved by the long count when Dempsey had to be escorted to a neutral corner. Tunney regained his senses and eventually won by decision in what is still considered to be one of boxing's most controversial fights.

Tunney's relative intellectualism, reticence in public, and scientific boxing style distanced him from fight fans and the press. He was an extremely intelligent fighter who carefully studied his major opponents and adapted strategies designed to exploit their weaknesses. Fleet of foot, he was an excellent defender, adept at sidestepping and blocking punches. Despite this lack of contemporary acclaim, Tunney is remembered as a great fighter and one of the best strategists and quickest thinkers in the history of boxing.

Tunney retired in 1929 with a professional record of 65–1–1. Soon after his last bout, he married Mary Lauder, heiress of the Carnegie fortune. The couple lived near Stamford, Connecticut; they had four children, one of whom served as a U.S. senator from California. In his retirement, Tunney had a long and successful business career. He served on the boards of many corporations and as director of the Boy Scouts of America and the Catholic Youth Organization. Tunney died in Greenwich, Connecticut on November 7, 1978, and was posthumously inducted into the International Boxing Hall of Fame in 1990.

Tim Lynch

See also: DEMPSEY, Jack

References
Fleischer, Nat. *Gene Tunney: The Enigma of the Ring*. New York: The Ring Athletic Library, 1931.
Van Every, ed. *The Life of Gene Tunney: The Fighting Marine*. New York: Dell Publishers, 1926.

TUOHY, PATRICK J. (1894–1930)

Patrick Tuohy was born in Dublin, the only son of John Joseph Tuohy and Mary Murphy. His father was a prominent surgeon and both of his parents were ardent Irish nationalists. Despite being born with the fingers on his left hand not fully formed and despite the fact that there was no tradition of painting in the Tuohy family, he showed an early talent for drawing. After being educated by the Christian Brothers, at the age of 14 he attended St. Enda's, the school that was founded and run by Patrick Pearse who, along with his younger brother Willie, was executed for his role in the 1916 Easter Rising. At this time he began painting, and while at St. Enda's he was encouraged by the art teacher and sculptor Willie Pearse to develop his talent. He also attended evening classes at the Metropolitan School of Art, where he later enrolled as a full-time student. His teacher William Orpen regarded Tuohy as one of his finest students. In 1913 he was awarded a scholarship by the Department of Agriculture and Technical Instruction, and he was present in the General Post Office with his father during the 1916 Easter Rising. Escaping afterwards, he traveled to Spain, where he spent more than a year working as a teacher and continuing to paint. His time in Madrid greatly influenced the future development of his art; the work of the Spanish painter Diego Velazquez in particular had a great impact upon him. In 1918 he was appointed, along with fellow painter Justin Keating, as a part-time teacher at the Metropolitan School of Art, and his work was later exhibited at the Royal Hibernian Academy. At this time he painted portraits of General Richard Mulcahy, Archbishop William Walsh, and the writer James Stephens. He also painted a number of religious works commissioned by various churches in Dublin. In 1922 his work was included in the Paris exhibition L'Art Irlandais, which had been organized by Maud Gonne on the occasion of the foundation of the new Irish state. Through James Stephens he was introduced to James Joyce in Paris. He painted two portraits of

Joyce, and the writer also commissioned him to paint his father, John Stanislaus Joyce, while in Dublin. This painting was eventually hung in Joyce's house in Zurich. Later Tuohy would continue his relationship with the Joyce family by sketching a portrait of Joyce's mother as well as one of Joyce's daughter, Lucia.

In 1927 Tuohy immigrated to America; he settled in South Carolina, where relatives on his mother's side had moved some years before. His first commission there was to paint a portrait of the governor of South Carolina, John G. Richards. He was unpopular in South Carolina as a result of his criticisms of the treatment of African Americans in the state. He was diagnosed as manic-depressive before moving to New York, where he was one of the founders of the Irish University Club. In New York Tuohy lived in an apartment on Riverside Drive overlooking the Hudson River. He traveled to Ireland for a brief holiday before returning to New York when his work was included in the first exhibition of contemporary Irish painting in America held at the Helen Hackett Gallery. The exhibition was a great success and Tuohy's work was praised, particularly by Henry McBride, the art critic of the *New York Sun*. He lectured on art and was held in high regard by both critics and collectors. However, he began to suffer increasing bouts of depression, and he frequently spoke to his friends about contemplating suicide. A second exhibition of Irish painting took place at the Hackett Gallery in 1930, at which four of his paintings were exhibited. At the time of his death his portrait of the actress Claudette Colbert remained unfinished. He died, apparently the result of suicide, by gas poisoning in his apartment in September 1930. After his body was embalmed, it was taken back to Ireland and removed to the Pro-Cathedral in Dublin before being buried in Glasnevin Cemetery.

David Doyle

See also: JOYCE, James Augustine Aloysius

References

Kennedy, Christina. "Patrick J. Tuohy." In *The Encyclopedia of the Irish in America,* edited by Michael Glazier. Notre Dame, IN: University of Notre Dame Press, 1999.
Mulcahy, Rosemary. *Patrick J. Tuohy, 1894–1930.* Belfast: 1991.
Murphy, Patrick J. *Patrick Tuohy: From Conversations with His Friends.* Dublin: Townhouse, 2004.

TWEED, WILLIAM "BOSS" (1823–1878)

The most notorious example of Tammany Hall–style corruption in the U.S. political system, "Boss" Tweed represented everything inimical about Irish immigrants without even being Irish. Though caricatured by his Republican opponents as a coarse, hard-drinking Irishman, Tweed was, in fact, born in Manhattan, the son of third-generation Scots Protestants and a virtual teetotaler. Early in his career, Tweed was a brush and chair maker and a member of the local, mostly Irish, volunteer fire brigade. In 1850, he was elected foreman of the brigade and became the Democratic candidate for the post of assistant alderman in the Seventh Ward. He lost this election but quickly won the next one. In 1852, he was elected a Democratic alderman in New York; a year later he entered Congress. In 1856, he became chairman of the New York Board of Supervisors and School Commissioner. In 1867, he was elected a state senator, a position he retained until he was exposed for corruption in 1871. Finally, in 1870 he was appointed commissioner of public

Harper's Weekly *cartoon lambasting William "Boss" Tweed. (Library of Congress)*

works for the city, a seemingly innocuous position from which he wielded virtually complete control over the city.

His association with Tammany brought about both his rapid rise to power and his headlong crash into public infamy. Originally the kind of society in which young men from good families could meet up, get drunk, and sing patriotic songs, by Tweed's time Tammany was fast becoming the most important organized faction within the Democratic Party of New York. As a New York Democrat, Tweed would have long been recognized as an ally of the Tammany Society, but he did not actually become a member until 1859. His rise to the top was swift: he gained power throughout the 1860s, until he eventually became leader of the organization. He was appointed the grand sachem in 1868.

Though in its early years Tammany had been ambivalent toward the issue of mass immigration, it had long since recognized the benefit of cultivating the immigrant vote. During Tweed's reign Tammany perfected a method of registering and mobilizing the immigrant vote that both confounded and outraged their Republican opponents. Not only was Tammany naturalizing immigrants at the rate of three per minute, according to horrified Republican observers of 1867, but once they were naturalized Tammany kept the immigrants loyal to the Tammany cause by giving public jobs to loyal constituents and issuing free fuel to the Tammany wards in the winter.

By 1870 the Tweed Ring, consisting of Boss Tweed (commissioner of public works), Peter "Brains" Sweeney (city chamberlain), Richard "Slippery Dick" Connolly (city comptroller), A. Oakey Hall (mayor), and John T. Hoffman (governor), had gained virtually total control over the city's public institutions and municipal works and were siphoning off staggering sums of money from the hundreds of city projects under their control. Much of the time this was done by the simple device of having contractors pad their bills and slip the overcharge back under the table. The symbol of this type of corruption for the public became the New York County Courthouse, renowned as "Tweed's Courthouse." Begun in 1858, it was supposed to have cost $350,000; 12 years later, however, the cost had risen to $12 million and was still rising. When the accounts were uncovered, the extent of Tammany's corruption was revealed by the *New York Times*. In just one instance, 11 thermometers had been charged at $7,500.

Through lampooning and attack in the *Times* and *Harpers Weekly*, Tweed quickly became the scapegoat for Tammany corruption. He was indicted on three counts of fraud on December 15, 1871. In the winter of 1875, trying to avoid a civil suit, Tweed escaped from his warders while on a home furlough and fled to Spain. However, he was quickly recaptured by the Spanish police—after being recognized by a series of lampooning cartoons that had appeared in *Harpers Weekly*—and returned to prison. On April 12, 1878, he died of pneumonia in Ludlow Street Jail (built under his tenure in public office), penniless and broken.

James P. Byrne

See also: TAMMANY HALL

References

Burrows, Edwin G., and Mike Wallace. *Gotham: A History of New York City to 1898*. New York: Oxford University Press, 1999.

Hershkowitz, Leo. *Tweed's New York: Another Look*. New York: Anchor Press, 1977.

Lynch, Denis Tilden. *The Story of a Grim Generation: "Boss" Tweed*. 1927. Reprint, New Brunswick: Transaction Publishers, 2002.

Mandelbaum, Seymour J. *Boss Tweed's New York*. New York: John Wiley & Sons, 1965.

U

U2

U2 is a Dublin quartet that has gained and sustained worldwide popular and critical acclaim from the 1980s onward. Representing and influencing contemporary Ireland, U2 has become the voice and sound of the nation as perceived by the rest of the globe. Despite sometimes grandiose ambitions that threatened to derail the band and undermine their (at times) messianic

Studio portrait of the rock group U2, (left to right) Larry Mullen Jr., The Edge, Bono, and Adam Clayton during the Joshua Tree *tour in 1987. (Corbis)*

message, U2 has endured as a force of not only musical but also economic expansion; their efforts to broaden the social and the sonic realm have revitalized the Temple Bar section of Dublin, raised funds for charity, and heightened first world awareness of third world inequalities.

Larry Mullen, Jr., (drums, born October 31, 1961, Artane, Dublin) recruited the members of what was first called Feedback, a cover band playing Beatles and Rolling Stones tunes, and then the Hype, in 1978. Malahide's Adam Clayton (bass, born March 13, 1960, Chinnor, Oxfordshire); Dave Evans ("The Edge," guitar, keyboards, vocals, born August 8, 1961, Barking, East London); and Dave's brother Dick ("Dik Prune," guitar, born 1958) joined Ballymun's Paul Hewson ("Bono Vox," vocals, guitar; born May 10, 1960, Stillorgan, Dublin) at Mount Temple school to form the band. As the nation's first nondenominational, coeducational comprehensive school, Mount Temple attracted students from all over North Dublin's suburbs: a diverse, and substantially Protestant, student body. This emphasis on a nonsectarian, inclusive, and broadly Christian (as opposed to Catholic) influence marked the band as well. Its members' families were not only Irish

Catholic but also Welsh Presbyterian, and Church of Ireland. The group's themes of acceptance, struggle, and spiritual and ethical choices gained them an early and loyal following, an audience open to new musical experimentation and lyrical appeals in the aftermath of punk.

The name U2 was suggested by Steve "Rapid" Averill of the Dublin band Radiators from Space. Stories differ on its origin: its suggestion of spying or its ability to be translated into any language suggest why it appealed to the band. Winning a Harp lager talent contest in Limerick, the four members (Dik had left to join the Virgin Prunes) were still at Mount Temple when Paul McGuinness, manager of the Stranglers, offered to direct them. Although failing a CBS Records audition, U2 issued an Irish-only extended play, *U2:3,* which topped the national charts but failed to attract English attention. In early 1980, after "Another Day" gained the notice of Island Records, the band signed and recorded its debut album, *Boy,* for release that autumn.

Produced by Steve Lillywhite, this record and the next two albums he would craft with the band, *October* (1981) and *War* (1983), would shape the alternative rock sound of the decade. With The Edge's arpeggios and ostinatos, Mullen's thunderous beat, Clayton's propulsive drive, and Bono's combination of operatic, folk, and popular vocal styles, the band revised the familiar four-piece rock sound into a style of presentation of yearning for grand statements, in the words sung and the emotions conveyed. Steady touring of the United States and Britain gained them initial exposure on college radio and among the postpunk fans of new wave music; the rise of MTV in the early 1980s brought "I Will Follow" and "Gloria" to a wider audience. With video, U2 was one of the first bands to find success.

On *War,* the political concerns of "New Year's Day" and "Sunday Bloody Sunday" capitalized on the Troubles in the North of Ireland and established the band as spokesmen for an end to Irish Republican Army–motivated violence. This stance attracted worldwide interest, and Irish Americans embraced the group as it steadily increased its popularity in the United States and Britain. Their *War* tour concert at Red Rocks amphitheater in Colorado appeared on VHS and an extended play, *Under a Blood Red Sky* (1984), while appearances at Band Aid (1984) and Live Aid (1985) further promoted the band's activist stance.

The Unforgettable Fire (1984) featured a blurred Irish castle on its cover, but the album's hit, "(Pride) In the Name of Love," became their first number one song in Britain and first Top Forty charting in the United States. Commemorating Martin Luther King, Jr., this anthem revealed a band eager to adopt American themes (along with Elvis's legacy) through a more expansive production under Brian Eno and Daniel Lanois. Two songs from their U.S tour appeared on a follow-up extended play, *Wide Awake in America* (1985). *The Joshua Tree* (1987), with its attacks against American intervention in Central America, continued to preach from the pulpit of international rock music. Although it topped the U.S. charts and brought the band the arena-rock concert success for which their sound had always been suited, its lyrical self-righteousness irritated many critics. Nevertheless, U2 made the cover of *Time* magazine and the group was deemed the conscience of rock music.

The band's sound shifted, as its success in the United States grew, to American roots influences. Working with B. B. King and Harlem choirs, and integrating rhythm and blues and soul strains, *Rattle and Hum* (1988) documented their Joshua Tree American tour on film and record. The predictable backlash now weakened sales for both versions, and the band took a break.

Returning with an electronic emphasis, and energized by the atmosphere in Berlin after the collapse of the Iron Curtain, *Achtung Baby* (1990) moved U2 into a catchier pop-rock hybrid that continued through the 1990s. This album debuted at number one throughout the world. The Zoo tour over the next three years portrayed a looser delivery of both message and media through a presentation, headed by Bono as "The Fly" and then "MacPhisto," which satirized and celebrated technological saturation and rock star excess. As their albums *Achtung Baby,* the techno-driven *Zooropa* (1993), and *Pop* (1997) continued the legacy of chameleon-like David Bowie (who at the start of U2's career had worked in Berlin with Eno), so their concerts glorified a band less intent (at least on stage) with saving than selling the world through multimedia entertainment.

Although their musical direction has shifted, with *All That You Can't Leave Behind* (2000) representing an amalgam of U2's musical styles, the band's support of humanitarian causes has earned them respect; Bono pursued efforts to aid Africa, end land mines, and cancel third world debt. In 2000, the members along with McGuinness were made honorary freemen of Dublin city, while the band's financial clout has made them one of Ireland's most valuable exports. Windmill Lane Studio and the Clarence Hotel attract fans and tourists alike because they are owned by the band. A deal in 1998 with Polygram reportedly netted $50 million for the band, as greatest hits releases have appeared: *The Best of 1980–1990* (1998) and *The Best of 1990–2000* (2002).

John L. Murphy

See also: MICHIGAN; MUSIC IN AMERICA, IRISH

References
Bordowitz, Mark, ed. *The U2 Reader.* Milwaukee, WI: Hal Leonard, 2003.
Chatterton, Mark, ed. *U2: The Complete Encyclopedia.* 2nd ed. London: SAF/Firefly, 2004.
Dunphy, Eamon. *The Unforgettable Fire: The Definitive Biography of U2.* New York: Warner Books, 1987.
Gittis, Ian. *U2: The Best of Propaganda: 20 Years of the U2 Magazine.* New York: Thunder's Mouth Press, 2003.
Parra, Pimm Jal de la. *U2 Live: A Concert Documentary.* London: Omnibus, 2003.
Stockman, Steve. *Walk On: The Spiritual Journey of U2.* Lake Mary, FL: Relevant Books, 2001.
Stokes, Niall, ed. *U2: All For One—The Best of Hot Press: 1990–2003.* Dublin: Hot Press Books, 2003.
Waters, John. *Race of Angels: Ireland and the Genesis of U2.* Belfast: Blackstaff Press, 1994.

UNITED IRISH LEAGUE OF AMERICA

The United Irish League of America (UIL) was founded in 1900 first in the New York area, but it rapidly spread throughout the country. Its organizers patterned the group on the original United Irish League, which served as the chief support organization for the Irish Parliamentary Party, supplying parliamentary candidates and election funds for the party in its quest for a Home Rule government in Ireland.

Though not directly administered by Irish party leaders, like its counterparts in Ireland and Great Britain, the UIL functioned as the chief fund-raiser for the Irish Parliamentary Party and the Home Rule movement in the United States and Canada during this time as well as a source of moral and political support for the Home Rule cause. The American organization developed quickly enough to hold a national meeting by 1902, but enthusiasm waned during its first decade because of a lack of progress on the Home Rule issue. A high level of member interest returned after 1910 when Home Rule became an active political issue in the British parliament.

During this critical period, Michael Ryan, city solicitor of Philadelphia, held the office of national president; Thomas B. Fitzpatrick of Boston served as national treasurer; and John O'Callaghan acted as national secretary. The United Irish League suffered its first major organizational setback when O'Callaghan died in July 1913. O'Callaghan had served as national secretary since the body's origin. League President Ryan called him "the soul of the League movement" and described him as nearly irreplaceable. His successor, Michael J. Jordan, possessed none of the organizational skill, ambition, or standing among Irish Americans that O'Callaghan had. Organizational effectiveness and loyalty to the nationalist leadership in Ireland, however, remained strong into 1914. Ryan and the leadership backed Irish Party leader John Redmond when he accepted the controversial principle of temporary exclusion of six northern counties from Home Rule in March 1914 and when he exerted party authority over the paramilitary Irish Volunteers in June. Ryan even forwarded $100,000 in American pledges to Redmond in July 1914.

The onset of World War I, however, exposed fundamental disagreements between the Irish and American organizations, which doomed the league in America. In 1914, Redmond's decision to support Irish enlistment in the British army in exchange for a promise of Irish self-government after the war devastated UIL unity and Irish-American support for Redmond's party. Most of the American UIL's leaders and members harbored much stronger anti-British sentiments than Irish Party leaders did and they refused to back Britain in a war while the United States remained neutral.

Internal disagreements about Ireland's proper role in World War I wracked the league. UIL President Michael Ryan of Pennsylvania, whose wife was German American, had reacted as much of Irish America did to Redmond's call for support of Britain in the war, calling for public neutrality and even privately praising Germany. He and league treasurer Fitzpatrick ceased their active support of the Irish Party after the start of the war, and only the national secretary, Michael J. Jordan, remaining loyal among the leadership.

In October 1914, Ryan privately informed Redmond that with the final passage of a suspended Home Rule Act in Parliament the previous month the Irish Party leader ought to consider the United Irish League work in America completed. Starting that month all UIL funds from America evaporated. Ryan and Fitzpatrick favored shutting down the organization's headquarters in Boston for the remainder of the war to cut expenses. National secretary Michael J. Jordan, the most recent and least influential of the organization's leadership, opposed this move as a sign of defeat and irrelevance. Leading members of the New York UIL joined Jordan in vocal opposition to this shutdown, though ironically the prewar organization had drawn its most active support from the states of Massachusetts and Pennsylvania. John Redmond, however, directed his followers in America to avoid a public breach and approved of the UIL's decision to postpone its national convention indefinitely, based on the hope of a relatively short war and the benefit of at least the semblance of Irish-American unity.

As a result, the UIL became largely defunct by 1915 and faded into insignificance once the Easter Rebellion of 1916 radicalized nationalist opinion in Ireland and the United States, undercutting all demands for a moderate Home Rule settlement.

Joseph P. Finnan

See also: EMMET, Thomas Addis; PRESS, The ETHNIC IRISH

References

Carroll, F. M. *American Opinion and the Irish Question, 1910–1923*. Dublin: Gill and Macmillan, 1978.

Dangerfield, George. *The Damnable Question: A Study in Anglo-Irish Relations*. Boston: Little, Brown and Company, 1976.

Finnan, Joseph P. *John Redmond and Irish Unity, 1912–1918*. Syracuse, NY: Syracuse University Press, 2004.

URUGUAY

Known as Banda Oriental until the 1900s, Uruguay was part of the Spanish colonial vice royalty of Rio de la Plata, together with Argentina, Paraguay, and Bolivia. In 1814, José Artigas and other leaders broke with the junta in Buenos Aires and struggled for independence until annexed by Brazil in 1821. The republic was constituted in 1830.

In 1762, Irish-born Captain MacNamara led a British force to occupy Colonia del Sacramento, a stronghold alternatively held by the Portuguese and the Spanish, but failed and lost his life together with most of his men. Brigadier General Samuel Auchmuty occupied Montevideo in 1807 with a regular force of British and Irish officers and rank and file. The British rule in Uruguay lasted 14 months, a period in which prominent merchants from the British Isles settled in the city and influenced its culture. One of the Irish soldiers, Peter Campbell (1780–ca. 1832), enlisted in the 71st regiment and later remained in the River Plate serving the patriot ranks. He served under Artigas and was appointed deputy governor of Corrientes province. Campbell is acknowledged as the founder of the Uruguayan navy.

Sometimes perceived by English and Irish press as a part of the same country of Argentina and Paraguay, Uruguay started to receive a steady flow of Irish immigration in the decades after independence. The interior countryside, especially in Rio Negro department, was settled by some Wexford sheep farmers from around Kilrane. Paysandú, in the same department and near the Argentine province of Entre Ríos, was occupied by immigrants from Westmeath and Longford.

In the 1840s, after Juan Manuel de Rosas's dictatorship in Buenos Aires, which was favorable to British settlements, many Irish sheep farmers moved from Uruguay to Buenos Aires province and leased or purchased land in departments like Carmen de Areco, Salto, and Pergamino, and later Nueve de Julio and Lincoln. Landowners like James Gaynor (1802–1892) and John Maguire (d. 1905) moved to Argentina, but maintained their holdings in Uruguay and when they died left important ranches there. Other Irish settlers worked in Entre Ríos (Argentina) and Rio Negro (Uruguay). William Lawlor (1822–1909) of Abbeyleix, Co. Laois, married in Gualeguay, Entre Ríos (Argentina), and died at his ranch, Las Tres Patas, in Uruguay. It is likely that other Irish ranchers owned land on both sides of the Argentine-Uruguayan border, speculating with the prospects of political and financial stability in each country. However, the simultaneous management in both sides of the River Plate did not start off the immigration chains from Ireland as it did in Argentina. Distinguished Irish physicians in Uruguay were Constantine Conyngham (1807–1868), who rendered important services during the epidemic of 1856 in Montevideo, and Dublin-born Louis Fleury, surgeon-general to the army, who attended in Charity Hospital. Among the rural settlers were J. Hughes in Paysandú and several Irish managers working for Robert Young in what is today Young City in Rio Negro department. In the 1870s, Young purchased 10 square leagues of land in Estancia Bichadero and planted a magnificent quadrangle of *ombúes* (a typical tree of the pampas) near the house. In 1875 he owned 100,000 sheep and horned cattle, and he applied improved methods for farming and agriculture.

Edmundo Murray

See also: MULHALL, Michael George; O'BRIEN, John Thomond; O'LEARY, Juan Emiliano; RE-EMIGRANTS WITHIN THE AMERICAS

References

Coghlan, Eduardo A. *El Aporte de los Irlandeses a la Formación de la Nación Argentina.* Buenos Aires, 1982.

Murray, Thomas. *The Story of the Irish in Argentina.* New York: P. J. Kenedy & Sons, 1919.

Pyme, Peter. *The Invasions of Buenos Aires, 1806–1807: The Irish Dimension.* Research Paper 20. Liverpool: University of Liverpool, Institute of Latin American Studies, 1996.

Ryan, Hugh Fitzgerald. *In the Shadow of the Ombú Tree.* Dublin: Chaos Press, 2005.

VENEZUELA

Relations between Ireland and Venezuela have been limited chiefly to the latter country's engagement in the nineteenth-century war of independence from Spain. As a result of an appeal by Simón Bolívar for British volunteers, recruitment began in Ireland and Britain in 1817. Over the next two and a half years, 53 ships left Irish and British ports carrying some 6,500 men for service in South America, until pressure by the Spanish ambassador in London forced the British authorities to put an end to it in late 1819. Of those who left, some 5,300 landed in Colombia or Venezuela, most of them Irish. Many of these were former soldiers in the British army who were being demobilized as the Napoleonic wars had come to an end.

In November 1817, the first group of 800 officers and men set out but were depleted through mutinies and shipwreck; only 240 arrived in South America. Known as the first Venezuelan Rifles, and put under the command of Kerryman Arthur Sandes in 1819, these served right through the war of independence and were only disbanded in 1830. Another officer, John Devereux, actively recruited in Ireland and sent about 2,000 men to Venezuela, who were enlisted in the Irish Legion. The flag of the Legion was a golden harp on a green ground encircled by the stars of Venezuela and Colombia. The first contingent landed in Margarita between September and December 1819, and the rest arrived in Angostura (today's Ciudad Bolívar) in April and May 1820. From the beginning the expedition was plagued with problems as they were given little food and no pay. Most of the men had to be evacuated after suffering a number of mutinies, and particularly after an attack on the Legion in Rio Hacha soon after they landed. Thirty or 40 officers refused even to remain in Venezuela and returned to Ireland in the same vessels in which they had come.

Remnants of the various groups in the Irish Legion, the first Venezuelan Rifles, and others were reorganized in what became an Anglo-Irish Legion. Hundreds of Irish took part in the decisive battles of Boyacá (Colombia) and Carabobo (Venezuela). In the latter battle the Irish Legion was said to number 350, and of those, 11 officers and 95 men were killed and 50 were wounded. All of the survivors were awarded the Order of the Liberator, and the legion was renamed the Carabobo Battalion, which still exists in the Venezuelan army.

A junior officer from Co. Cork, Daniel Florence O'Leary, won Bolívar's esteem and an appointment as his aide-de-camp. O'Leary attained the rank of brigadier general and played a key role in plotting political and military strategy. After retiring from the army, O'Leary wrote his memoirs, which were published in Caracas by his son. His extraordinary compilation of eyewitness accounts, correspondence, and documents has proved an indispensable resource for every subsequent biographer and historian of the independence period. O'Leary died in 1854 in Colombia, and the Venezuelan government removed his remains to Caracas. He was laid to rest with high public honors in the national pantheon.

Edmundo Murray

See also: O'LEARY, Daniel Florence

References

Hasbrouck, Alfred. *Foreign Legionaries in the Liberation of Spanish South America.* New York: Columbia University, 1928.

Kirby, Peadar. *Ireland and Latin America: Links and Lessons.* Dublin: Trócaire, 1992.

McGinn, Brian. "Venezuela's Irish Legacy." *Irish America* 7, no. 11 (November 1991): 34–37.

VICUÑA MACKENNA, BENJAMÍN (1831–CA. 1886)

Benjamín Vicuña Mackenna was a Chilean writer, journalist, and historian. Born in Santiago on August 25, 1831, he was the son of Pedro Félix Vicuña and Carmen Mackenna, and grandson of General John MacKenna of the war of independence.

Benjamín Vicuña Mackenna studied in Santiago and joined the school of law in 1849. From the beginning of his career he contributed to *La Tribuna* newspaper, writing political articles. In 1851 he participated in the revolution of Pedro Urriola against the government but was imprisoned during the attack on the headquarters of Chacabuco Regiment. On July 4, Vicuña Mackenna and Roberto Souper managed to escape from the prison disguised as women. In 1852 he was exiled in the United States, and from San Francisco he traveled through Mexico and Canada. A year later he studied agronomy in England, and then visited many parts of Europe, including Ireland.

Back in Chile in 1856, Vicuña Mackenna graduated as a lawyer from the University of Santiago. Although he did not practice as a barrister, his political and other writings were solidly based on legal knowledge. Together with Isidoro Errázuriz, in 1858 Vicuña Mackenna started the newspaper *La Asamblea Constitucional.* He was expelled by the government and exiled in England, but he was allowed to return in 1863. He began contributing to *El Mercurio* newspaper this same year. In 1865 he was in New York as envoy of the Chilean government and founded *La Voz de América* newspaper. Elected national senator for a six-year term, in 1872 Vicuña Mackenna was also appointed mayor of Santiago. His political career was interrupted in 1875 when he was defeated by Errázuriz in the elections for president of Chile. He dedicated himself to journalism and writing, and in 1880 edited *El Nuevo Ferrocarril* and *La Nación.* His most important works are *El Sitio de Chillán* (1849), *La Agricultura Aplicada a Chile* (1853), *Chili* (1855), *Tres Años de Viajes* (1856), *Ostracismo de los Carrera* (1857), *Historia de la Revolución del Perú* (1860), *Ostracismo de O'Higgins* (1860), *Diego de Almagro* (1862), *Historia de la Administración Montt* (1861–1862), *Vida de Don Diego Portales* (1861–1862), *Historia de Santiago* (1868), *Historia de Chile*

(1868), *Historia de Valparaíso* (1868), *La Guerra a Muerte* (1868), *Francisco Moyen* (1868), and dozens of other novels, history books, and political essays, the most popular being *El Santa Lucía, La Unión Americana, El Cambiazo, Seis Años en el Senado de Chile,* and *El 20 de Abril.*

Like his contemporary Bartolomé Mitre in Argentina, Vicuña Mackenna represented an intellectual class belonging to the South American landed elites. They started the mainstream historiography in their countries, and selected and immortalized the national discourse that served those elites to envision the model of national values to be imitated by the middle and working classes.

Edmundo Murray

See also: MACKENNA, John

Reference

Figueroa, Pedro Pablo. *Apuntes históricos sobre la vida y las obras de don Benjamín Vicuña Mackenna.* Santiago, Chile: Imprenta Victoria, 1886.

VIRGINIA

During the colonial period, the practice of Catholicism was prohibited in Virginia. This, along with the fact that it had an economy that was heavily dependent upon slavery, meant that it was not a popular destination for Irish immigrants. In 1786, however, after the American Revolution and under the leadership of the Virginian Thomas Jefferson, Virginia became the first state to formally separate church and state with its Statute of Religious Liberty. Following this move there began to be a slow increase in the number of Irish immigrants arriving in the state, seeking work, and then settling there. In the 1790s, George Washington's aide-de-camp, Colonel John Fitzgerald, who had been born in

Rathdowney, Co. Laois, led a campaign to found the first Catholic parish in Alexandria, Virginia. Meanwhile, in nearby Norfolk, there was a small Irish community, some members of which had settled there after the 1798 rebellion in Ireland. Although the Holy See had considered creating a new diocese of Richmond under an Irish bishop, Patrick Kelly from Waterford, the plan was eventually shelved. And it was not until 1841 that Richard Vincent Whelan, who had been born in Baltimore of Irish parents, was consecrated bishop of Wheeling. Virginia was second only to California as the state that was most dependent on priests from overseas. In practice, overseas meant Ireland—many priests from All Hallow's seminary in Dublin were transferred to Virginia to minister to Catholic communities there.

With increasing numbers of Irish settling in Richmond to work on the railroad connecting the town with Lynchburg, there was a need for institutions to fulfill their religious requirements. Father Timothy O'Brien, who had been born in Co. Mayo, ministered to their needs by creating a second parish and by inviting the Sisters of Charity to come to the city. At this time, as well as working on the railroads, many of the Irish in Richmond worked in flour mills and tobacco warehouses, while in Norfolk they formed the bulk of the workers in the shipyard. After the yellow fever epidemic and the Know-Nothing movement, both of which threatened the position of the Irish in the state, the Civil War provided an opportunity for Virginia's Irish to demonstrate their loyalty toward their new home. However, attitudes to the war among the Irish were sharply divided. Although some Irish formed the Montgomery Guards and the First Virginia Infantry Regiment, others sought exemptions because of their foreign-born status. In the years immediately after the war, unlike in some other southern states, the Irish continued to settle in Virginia. This presumably had much to do with its location as the most northerly of the all the states that had formed the Confederacy. As before the war, it was still the railroads that provided the principal source of employment for Irish laborers.

By the 1920s, most Irish immigrants in Virginia had become assimilated into mainstream American life and did not think of themselves as a self-conscious ethnic minority with some of the restrictions that implied. The result was a situation where the Irish in Virginia did not seek political power in the same way they had done so in a state like New Jersey, where they created political machines. Instead, they realized it was only by working with those of other religions and backgrounds that they could hope to survive politically in Virginia. In terms of religious vocations, not much had changed over the years: Virginia is still very reliant on priests from Ireland and from other American dioceses.

David Doyle

References

Bailey, James H. *A History of the Diocese of Richmond: The Formative Years.* Richmond: Chancery Office, Diocese of Richmond, 1956.

Fogarty, Gerald P. "Virginia." In *The Encyclopedia of the Irish in America,* edited by Michael Glazier. Notre Dame, IN: University of Notre Dame Press, 1999.

Gleeson, David T. *The Irish in the South, 1815–1877.* Chapel Hill: University of North Carolina Press, 2001.

WALL, EAMONN (1955–)

Eamonn Wall, the poet and critic, was born in Enniscorthy, Co. Wexford, in 1955. He immigrated to the United States in 1982 and now lives in Missouri. He has a BA from University College Dublin, an MA from the University of Wisconsin-Milwaukee, and a PhD from the City University of New York (1992). He was associate professor of English at Creighton University from 1992 to 2000. In addition to teaching courses in creative writing and Irish literature, he was director of the Creighton Irish Summer School. He is currently the Smurfit-Stone Professor of Irish Studies at the University of Missouri-St. Louis.

Wall first published poems in the Gorey Arts Festival magazine. Since then, his poetry has been published widely in Ireland and in the United States. A recurring theme in his poetry is the desire to integrate the Irish and American elements of his experience. His books include *The Celtic Twilight* (1974), *Fire Escape* (1988), *The Tamed Goose* (1990), *Dyckman–200th Street* (1994), *Iron Mountain Road* (1997), *The Crosses* (2000), and *Refuge at DeSoto Bend* (2004). He is also the author of a study of Irish diaspora to the America, *From the Sin-é Café to the Black Hills* (2000), which was co-winner of the Durkan Prize from the American Conference for Irish Studies for excellence in scholarship. In addition to poetry, Wall regularly contributes book reviews and articles on Irish fiction to *The Washington Post, The Chicago Tribune, The Review of Contemporary Fiction,* and other newspapers and journals. He has been influential in the New Irish Writers movement, which advocates a more contemporary and realistic assessment of emigrant Irish writers in the United States. He has published essays on this topic in *Forkroads.* He also contributed to *Ireland in Exile: Irish Writers Abroad* (1993), edited by Dermot Bolger. He is widely regarded as an important critic of both Irish-American and Irish-in-America writing. In 2005, he became president of the American Conference for Irish Studies, the first Irish-born scholar to be elected to this position.

Aoileann Ní Eigeartaigh

See also: AMERICAN CONFERENCE FOR IRISH STUDIES

References

Glazier, Michael ed. *The Encyclopaedia of the Irish in America.* Notre Dame: University of Notre Dame Press, 1999.

Pierce, David, ed. *Irish Writing in the Twentieth Century: A Reader.* Cork: Cork University Press, 2000.

WALLACE, WILLIAM VINCENT (1812–1865)

William Wallace, the Irish-born composer of English-language operas and virtuoso piano music, was one of the most frequently performed opera composers of his day, and a U.S. citizen from 1853. The son of a Scottish military bandmaster stationed at Ballina, Co. Mayo, Wallace was taught a number of musical instruments by his father and played second violin in the orchestra of the Theatre Royal, Hawkins Street, Dublin, from 1827. He took the additional name Vincent in 1830, when he fell in love with a Roman Catholic girl, Isabella Kelly, while working as an organist and teacher at Thurles. Her father would not agree to a marriage without Wallace changing his faith, which he duly did in the autumn of 1830. At age 22 he made his debut as a composer, playing a violin concerto of his own at a concert at the Dublin Anacreontic Society.

In July 1835, Wallace immigrated with his wife and sister-in-law to Hobart, Tasmania, but quickly moved on to Sydney, Australia, in January 1836. He made a career in Australia as a performer and teacher, opening the first Australian Music Academy and becoming, in retrospect, the first composer of international stature to have resided in Australia. Wallace left Sydney (including his family and £2,000 of debt) in February 1838 to begin an adventurous journey, in which he reportedly fought against the Maoris of New Zealand and visited India, but the next established fact is a recital in June 1838 in Valparaiso, Chile, whence he explored the South American continent in musical travels via Buenos Aires, Lima, Jamaica, and Cuba, conducting an Italian opera season at Mexico City in 1841, proceeding to

Sheet music for The Flag of Our Union, *an American patriotic song by William Vincent Wallace. (Library of Congress)*

New Orleans (1841), Philadelphia (1842), and Boston (1843), and then reaching New York in June 1843 with the reputation of "decidedly the first violinist and pianist in this country." After travels to Germany and the Netherlands (1844) he became resident in London, where he produced his greatest operatic success, *Maritana,* in 1845. *Maritana* was played all over the English-speaking world for decades, reaching New York and Philadelphia as soon as May 1848, but although Wallace composed at least five other operas, he was never able to repeat its success.

From 1849 Wallace again traveled the American continent, including several years at New York from 1850, where he married for a second time (the German pianist Helene Stoepel) and gained U.S. citizenship. He lived at various places in central Europe from 1858 while being more or less based in London, and in 1864 he retired to the south of France on account of increasing illness. Wallace died in the care of his wife Helene in the following year and was buried at Kensal Green, London. Of his two wives, Helene died in New York in 1885 and Isabella in Dublin in 1900.

Together with his compatriot Michael William Balfe, Wallace was the most successful composer of English-language operas in the nineteenth century. His fluent style was full of memorable melodies that made his works instantly popular, and prints of the most popular songs appeared in multiple editions. He was one of the first composers to integrate elements of South American traditional music into Western art music. He also shared with Balfe the fate of largely falling into obscurity after the 1930s, but he has regained critical attention in recent years.

Axel Klein

See also: BALFE, Michael W.; MUSIC IN AMERICA, IRISH

References

Klein, John W. "Vincent Wallace (1812–1865): a Reassessment." *Opera* 16 (1965): 709–716.

Phelan, Robert. *William Vincent Wallace. A Vagabond Composer.* Waterford: Celtic Publications, 1994.

White, Eric Walter. *The Rise of English Opera.* 1951. Reprint, New York: Da Capo, 1972.

WALSH, MARÍA ELENA (1930–)

María Elena Walsh, an Argentine poet, singer, and writer, was born in Ramos Mejía in the greater Buenos Aires, on February 1, 1930. Her father was a son of Irish and English settlers and worked in the local branch of the railway company.

Walsh studied in the Escuela Nacional de Bellas Artes. During this time, she worked on her poems, and in 1947 she published her first book of poetry, *Otoño Imperdonable,* which was an immediate success in the literary circles. She visited the United States with the Spanish writer Juan Ramón Jiménez and met Ezra Pound, Pedro Salinas, and Salvador Dalí. Walsh returned to Argentina and published her second book of poems, *Baladas con Angel* (1952), amidst the difficulties created for intellectuals by the Peronist regime.

Having decided to seek voluntary exile out of Argentina, Walsh met the singer Leda Valladares in Panama, with whom she settled in Paris. The duo "Leda y María" began singing Argentine folkloric songs in the Parisian Latin Quarter and recorded their first LP, *Le Chant du Monde.* Walsh also began writing poems and songs for children.

The Walsh-Valladares duo went back to Argentina, but they could not find a place in the folkloric scenario of the time, in which the stereotyped musical groups were always formed by gauchos (men). Walsh launched a music hall for children, "Los sueños del Rey Bombo" (1959), and published *Tutú Marambá* (1960), a book of children's stories. In 1962, her famous *Canciones para Mirar* appeared both in recordings and in the theater and was a great success; it was later produced in France and the United States. By 1965, when "Hecho a Mano" appeared, Walsh was publishing poetry and children's stories, singing in theaters, and recording. Her music show for adults *Juguemos en el Mundo/Show para Ejecutivos* (1968) was launched in the Teatro Regina in Buenos Aires and ran for one year. Given her general popularity and success with children, the censors of the military government were not willing to ban her protest songs.

The film *Juguemos en el Mundo* was launched in 1971, with a screenplay written by Walsh and María Herminia Avellaneda. It was an economic failure, and Walsh began presenting music hall shows in many Latin American cities. In Buenos Aires, she presented *El Viejo Variété* and *El Buen Modo*. In 1974, Walsh was diagnosed with cancer and had to undergo operations and chemotherapy treatments. However, neither her poor health nor censorship were reasons enough for Walsh to remain inactive during the military dictatorship of 1976–1983, which took power after Perón's death in 1974.

On August 16, 1976, Walsh published in *Clarín* newspaper the polemic article "Desventuras en el País Jardín de Infantes," including an explicit disapproval of the authoritarian military rule. Walsh's whole body of work was immediately banned, although her immense popularity probably saved her life. Her song "Como la Cigarra" became a musical symbol of the resistance against the military junta. A tireless advocate of the rights of women, Walsh struggled during her entire life against male oppression, and among her targets were Perón, Fidel Castro, and Latin American military dictators.

Further works by Walsh were published as anthologies in 1984 and 1994. In 1997 she published a book of short stories, *Manuelita ¿Dónde vas?*—the title of one of her most famous songs. Among the awards Walsh received are those of the Argentine Society of Authors, Fundación Konex, and the *honoris causa* doctorate of the Universidad de Córdoba.

When Bill Meek of RTÉ interviewed María Elena Walsh in 1987, he inquired about her awareness of Irish culture through her poems and songs. She replied, "It is important to be bred up with two languages and I inherited this English tradition, and I think the Irish sense of humor . . . I think Irish and Andalusian is a very good combination for poetry and for fantasy" (*Voices from the Camps,* sound files).

Edmundo Murray

See also: ARGENTINA

References
Dujovne Ortiz, Alicia. *María Elena Walsh.* Madrid: Ediciones Júcar, 1982.
Sibbald, Kay. "Tradición y transgresión en la poética de María Elena Walsh." In *Poéticas de Escritoras Hispanoamericanas al Alba del Próximo Milenio,* edited by Trempe L. Rojas and Catharina Vallejo. Miami: Ediciones Universal, 1998.
Walsh, María Elena. *Las Canciones.* Buenos Aires: Seix Barral, 1994.

WALSH, RAOUL (1887–1980)

Raoul Walsh was born Albert Edward Walsh on March 11, 1887, in New York. His father, Thomas Walsh, was born in Ireland but emigrated to America in the 1870s, where he prospered in the garment industry. His mother, Elizabeth (Brough) Walsh was of Spanish-Irish descent.

One of four children, Raoul was raised in a comfortable, middle-class household. According to his autobiography, *Each Man in His Time* (1974), Walsh left home while still a teenager to work as a sailor in Cuba; he would later work as a ranch hand in Texas and Mexico. By 1910, he had become an actor, working for stock theater companies in minor roles. In 1912 he signed with the Biograph Film Company and caught the eye of the era's most important director, D. W Griffith, who employed him as an actor and assistant. Under Griffith's tutelage, Walsh learned acting and directing skills that would prove invaluable in his long and varied career. Although Walsh was a competent actor, he had his sights set on directing, and by 1912 he was shooting scenes for the semi-documentary film, *The Life of General Villa* (codirected with Christy Cabanne). He continued directing films while also working for Griffith: in 1914 he was cast in the role of John Wilkes Booth in Griffith's controversial epic, *The Birth of a Nation*.

In 1915 Walsh signed a contract with Fox studios, where he got the opportunity to direct a number of prestigious films. One of his earliest surviving films—and one that anticipates some of the films he directed in the 1930s—was *Regeneration*, a crime melodrama filmed on the Lower East Side and featuring Rockliffe Fellowes and Anna Q. Nilsson, two major stars of the 1910s. Walsh's attention to realistic detail, the authenticity of his tenement setting, and his sophisticated handling of action make the film one of his finest works. While under contract to Fox, Walsh proved himself a versatile director, equally adept at directing big-budget star vehicles (e.g., *Carmen* with Theda Bara); society dramas (e.g., *Should A Husband Forgive?*); delicate art films (e.g., *Evangeline*); and gritty crime films (e.g., *The Honor System*).

In the first 10 years of his career Walsh turned out more than 40 films, establishing himself as an important director. His importance was underscored when he was chosen to direct Douglas Fairbanks in a lavish 1924 production of *The Thief of Bagdad*, one of the most visually arresting films of the 1920s. Walsh continued to work steadily as a director throughout the 1920s, achieving big successes such as *What Price Glory?* (1926), while also taking occasional acting jobs, the most significant of which was his appearance with Gloria Swanson in *Sadie Thompson* (1928). In 1929, while filming *In Old Arizona,* he was involved in a car accident that cost him an eye. Undeterred, Walsh soon returned to directing and made a smooth transition to sound films.

Walsh worked well with actors, most notably James Cagney, Humphrey Bogart, Errol Flynn, and John Wayne. Although John Ford has often been credited with discovering John Wayne, it was Walsh who cast the actor in his first starring role in *The Big Trail* (1930). Throughout the 1930s, 1940s, and 1950s Walsh directed films in a range of genres, particularly excelling at action films (*Under Pressure*, 1935; *Objective, Burma!*, 1945), gangster films (*The Roaring Twenties*, 1939; *High Sierra*, 1941; *White Heat*, 1949), and westerns (*They Died with Their Boots On*, 1942; *Colorado Territory*, 1949).

Walsh continued to direct well into his seventies. He retired soon after the release of his final film, *A Distant Trumpet,* made in 1964. He was the subject of many retrospectives and awards in Europe and America, and in 1974 he published his autobiography, *Each Man in His Time*, a highly colorful, often fanciful, account of his career. He died in California on December 31, 1980.

Gwenda Young

See also: CAGNEY, James; FORD, John; WAYNE, John

Reference
Hardy, Phil, ed. *Raoul Walsh*. Edinburgh: Vineyard Press/Edinburgh Film Festival, 1974.

WALSH, RODOLFO (1927–1977)

Rodolfo Walsh was the son of Miguel Esteban Walsh (1894–1947) and Dora Gill and the great-grandson of Edward Walsh

(1832–1903), who was probably from Ballymore, Co. Westmeath, and who immigrated to Argentina around 1853. Born in Choele-Choel, Rio Negro province, Walsh was sent to a Catholic orphanage. Walsh created the genre of investigative journalism in Latin American literature. In *Operación Masacre,* the account of a summary execution of 34 Peronists, Walsh combined detective suspense with nonfiction narrative techniques. Other works of investigative journalism include *¿Quién Mató a Rosendo?* (1969) and *El Caso Satanovsky* (1973).

Walsh began writing articles as a journalist, and from 1959 to 1961 he worked for the agency Prensa Latina in Cuba. Back in Buenos Aires, he wrote for *Panorama, La Opinión,* and *Confirmado.* His political activity led him to operate in the hard-line Montoneros group, where he acted as their top intelligence officer. Walsh played a key role in the bombing of the cafeteria at the police headquarters in July 2, 1976. On the first anniversary of the military dictatorship, March 24, 1977, Walsh condemned the military junta in an open letter, which Nobel Prize–winner Gabriel García Márquez considered one of the jewels of universal literature. But the next day three army tanks demolished his home in San Vicente (Buenos Aires), and Rodolfo Walsh was murdered in downtown Buenos Aires by a military death squad. Their instructions were to capture him alive, but they had to kill him when he pulled a gun to return their fire. His dead body was taken to the Navy Mechanics' School and was never seen again.

Among his published works that have survived are: *Diez Cuentos Policiales* (1953), *Cuentos para Tahúres, Variaciones en Rojo* (1953), *Antología del Cuento Extraño* (1956), *Operación Masacre* (1957), *Secuencia Final,* the plays *La Granada* and *La Batalla* (1965), *Los Oficios Terrestres* (1965), *Un Kilo de Oro* (1967), and *Un Oscuro Día de Justicia* (1973).

Edmundo Murray

See also: LITERATURE, IRISH-ARGENTINE

References

Geraghty, Michael John. "Rodolfo Walsh: An Argentine Irishman." *Buenos Aires Herald* (29 March 2002).

McCaughan, Michael. *True Crimes: Rodolfo Walsh, the Life and Times of a Radical Intellectual.* London: Latin America Bureau, 2002.

WASHINGTON, D.C.

The seat of the United States government, Washington, D.C., is officially known as the District of Columbia, which makes it more than a city but less than a state. Because Washington has never been an industrial or commercial center, it did not attract as many European immigrants as other metropolitan areas on America's Atlantic seaboard, but it nevertheless has been an important place for Irish Americans to settle.

Even before the federal government moved to Washington from Philadelphia in 1800, Irish laborers were helping to build the U.S. Capitol and the White House. The latter was designed by architect James Hoban, born in Co. Kilkenny, who modeled it after Leinster House in Dublin and who also supervised its construction. To serve these Irish laborers, as well as other Roman Catholics, Saint Patrick's Parish was established in 1794 in what would become Washington's downtown.

The Irish population continued to increase in the early nineteenth century. By

1802, there were reports of Irish Americans parading on Saint Patrick's Day with shamrocks in their hats. That same year, James Hoban founded the Society of the Sons of Erin in Washington. More Irish arrived as new federal buildings were constructed, and particularly after August 1814, when British troops burned the White House, the Capitol building, the Navy Yard, and more. Irish laborers—primarily from Belfast, Cork, Dublin, and Liverpool—also played a major role in constructing the Chesapeake and Ohio Canal during the 1820s and 1830s.

Because of the Great Famine, many more Irish immigrants came in the 1840s and 1850s, making the Irish the largest ethnic group in Washington: 48 percent of the foreign-born population in 1850 and 58 percent of the foreign-born population in 1860. According to city directories from the 1850s, the Irish were employed primarily as laborers, grocers, and government clerks, and they resided in some of the poorer districts.

The reaction of other ethnic groups to the Irish was not always favorable. As one resident recalled, "In the extreme western part of the town . . . dwelt the Irish, a wild-looking, undisciplined and turbulent people, different in every way from their countrymen amongst us at the present day" (quoted in McGirr 1949, 93). The xenophobic Know-Nothing Party sparked riots in 1856 and 1857 in Washington in which several members of the Irish community were killed. These ethnic tensions relaxed significantly after the upheaval of sectional violence during the American Civil War.

New postwar construction in Washington brought more jobs and higher pay to Irish laborers during the 1870s and 1880s. By 1900, many Irish families that had lived in Washington for two or three generations had established small businesses and increasingly were members of skilled or semiskilled occupational groups. Religious and community organizations—including the Knights of St. Patrick, Sons of St. Patrick, St. Patrick's Total Abstinence Benevolent Society, and six branches of the Hibernian Society—were prospering in Washington.

In the twentieth and twenty-first centuries, Washington's Irish community has been very much part of the mainstream, and therefore less conspicuous within American society. The community makes itself known primarily on Saint Patrick's Day each year, when Washington's Irish pubs serve traditional corned beef and cabbage, though not green beer. Another Saint Patrick's Day tradition, which began in 1956, is to place a shamrock on the grave of George Washington Parke Custis (1781–1857), the adopted grandson of George Washington and father-in-law of Robert E. Lee. Custis founded the Washington Benevolent Society in 1826 to encourage solidarity with the citizens of Ireland and their struggle for independence.

Traditional Irish culture, music, and dance are promoted today by the Greater Washington Céili Club, established in 1985. The club sponsors céilis, workshops, dinners, concerts, and other programs for the Washington community at large.

James I. Deutsch

See also: HOBAN, James; CANALS AND THE IRISH INVOLVEMENT; NATIVISM AND ANTI-CATHOLICISM

References

Hickey, Matthew Edward. "Irish Catholics in Washington up to 1860: A Social Study." Master's thesis. Washington, DC: Catholic University of America, 1933.

MacGregor, Morris J. *A Parish for the Federal City: St. Patrick's in Washington, 1794–1994.*

Washington, DC: Catholic University of America Press, 1994.

McAleer, Margaret. "'The Green Streets of Washington': The Experience of Irish Mechanics in Antebellum Washington." In *Washington Odyssey: A Multicultural History of the Nation's Capitol,* edited by Francine Curro Cary, 42–62. Washington, DC: Smithsonian Books, 1996.

McGirr, Newman F. "The Irish in the Early Days of the District." *Records of the Columbia Historical Society of Washington, D.C.* 48–49 (1949), 93–96.

O'Neill, Michael J. "Friend of the Irish." *Washington Star,* March 15, 1959: 14–15.

Proctor, John Clagett. "Irish Have Played Important Parts in History of Washington and Nation." *Washington Star,* March 17, 1940: C4.

WAYNE, JOHN (1907–1979)

John Wayne, nicknamed "the Duke," was born Marion Robert Morrison on May 26, 1907, in Winterset, Iowa. His parents, Molly and Clyde Morrison, were both part Irish: Molly's mother was born in Cork in 1848 and Clyde's great grandfather, Robert Morrison, was born in Co. Antrim in 1782.

Clyde Morrison was a drug store clerk who, in 1914, abandoned his profession to embark on a new career as a farmer on a small farm near Lancaster, California. The venture was not a success, and in 1916 the family moved to Glendale, where Clyde resumed his career as a druggist. The young Marion Morrison grew up in Glendale, a city that was a popular location for film productions, particularly western shoots. Marion attended Glendale High School from 1921–1925, where he excelled at sports. Soon after his graduation from high school he entered the University of Southern California on a football scholarship. During his college years he began working part-time at the nearby Hollywood film studios. His first appearances as a film extra date from 1926 (*Brown of Harvard* and King Vidor's *Bardleys the Magnificent,* both produced by MGM). However, it was his work as a props assistant at Fox studios that caught the eye of leading American director, John Ford, who cast him in small extra roles in *Mother Macree* and *Hangman's House* in 1928.

For the next year Morrison worked prolifically in the film industry, mainly as an extra or in bit parts. During that time he landed a leading role in Raoul Walsh's epic production, *The Big Trail* (released in 1930) and changed his name to John Wayne (prompted by Walsh, who suggested the surname "Wayne" after "Mad" Anthony Wayne, a U.S. Army general in the American War of Independence). Wayne's biographer, Gary Wills, credits Walsh as the discoverer of Wayne; certainly he was the first director to cast him in a major role. Despite his starring role in *The Big Trail,* Wayne seemed unable to capitalize on the publicity, and for the next eight years he went back to playing small roles at Columbia and Warner Brothers and larger roles for "Poverty Row" studios Mascot and Monogram. By the mid-1930s Wayne had appeared in a number of serials and in a recurring role as "Stony Brook," the hero of a series of westerns made for Republic studios.

The turning point in Wayne's early career was his reunion with John Ford in 1939 for an "A" budget western, *Stagecoach.* Wayne's performance as the Ringo Kid not only proved that he could hold his own among a fine ensemble cast that featured Claire Trevor and Thomas Mitchell, but it also renewed Hollywood producers' interest in the charismatic actor. In 1940,

Wayne played leading roles in four major productions: *Dark Command*, which saw him reunited with Raoul Walsh; *Seven Sinners* (the first of several pairings with Marlene Dietrich); *Three Faces West*, a romantic drama directed by future blacklist victim Bernard Vorhaus; and *The Long Voyage Home*, John Ford's adaptation of Eugene O'Neill's play.

Wayne's career continued to flourish during World War II, and he often took starring roles in war films (*Back to Bataan; They Were Expendable*), despite his lack of involvement in active war service. Wayne's output was prolific in the 1940s—he made 33 films in less than a decade—and saw him work with some of Hollywood's most important directors, including John Ford, Rauol Walsh, Henry Hathaway, and Cecil B. De Mille. When Howard Hawks was casting for his first western, *Red River* (made in 1946), he chose Wayne to play the role of the aging western hero, Tom Dunson, alongside Montgomery Clift as Dunson's adopted son, Matthew Garth. Hawks' unusual casting (Clift was not a typical western hero) and his revisionist approach to the genre presented a challenge to Wayne, who delivered a complex, multi-layered performance in an often unsympathetic role. By the time the film was released in 1948, Wayne had already embarked on the first of three westerns for John Ford (*Fort Apache*, 1948; *She Wore a Yellow Ribbon*, 1949; *Rio Grande*, 1950). The films were collectively known as the cavalry trilogy, and their success reinforced the public's association of Wayne with the western genre.

The 1940s also saw a hardening of Wayne's right-wing politics: He was a leading member of the conservative Motion Picture Alliance for the Preservation of American Ideals, an organization founded in 1944 by director Sam Wood to help the House Un-American Activities Committee in its fight against communism. In 1948 Wayne became the head of the alliance, and his commitment to conservative cold war politics found expression in his starring roles in the anticommunist films *Jet Pilot* (made in 1950 but released in 1957), *Big Jim McLain* (1952), and *Blood Alley* (1955), and in his ultra-patriotic war film, *The Sands of Iwo Jima* (1949).

In 1952, Ford began production on a long-cherished project, an adaptation of Maurice Walsh's novel *The Quiet Man*. Having secured funding from Republic studios, he cast Wayne in the leading role of Sean Thornton, with Maureen O'Hara taking the role of Mary Kate Danaher, the red-haired Irish girl Thornton falls in love with. The film was shot around Cong, Co. Mayo, and the cast featured many Ford stalwarts. It met with considerable success upon its release in 1952 and remains perhaps the most popular of the Ford-Wayne films. Wayne teamed up with Ford again on *The Searchers* (1956), in which he delivered an outstanding performance as the complicated, cantankerous Ethan Edwards, a man driven by an obsession that extends beyond the ostensible task of finding his kidnapped niece. *The Searchers* is still regarded by many critics as one of the most complex of all westerns, and Wayne's Ethan represents a clear challenge to the notion of an "unproblematic" western hero.

In 1960 Wayne's directorial ambitions found expression in *The Alamo*, in which he directed himself in the role of Davy Crockett. The film was panned by critics and did not perform well at the box office. Wayne's association with the western genre continued in the 1960s, and during that decade he worked again with Ford (*The Man Who Shot Liberty Valance* and *The Horse Soldiers*) and Hawks (*Rio Bravo, Rio Lobo,* and *El Dorado*). Although Wayne remained popular with the American public throughout the 1960s, his conservative stance on the Vietnam War, expressed in the ultra-right-wing film, *The Green Berets* (1968), alienated him from many.

By the late 1960s Wayne was struggling with recurring bouts of cancer and his last westerns mixed sentiment, pathos, and humor. His performance as Rooster Cogburn in *True Grit* (1969) won him an Oscar (he had been nominated twice before), while art mirrored life in his final film, *The Shootist* (1975), in which he starred as a gunfighter battling cancer. Wayne succumbed to lung and stomach cancer on June 11, 1979. His third wife, Pilar Wayne, and seven children survived him.

Gwenda Young

See also: FORD, John; O'HARA, Maureen; WALSH, Raoul

References

Roberts, Randy, and James Olson. *John Wayne: American.* New York: The Free Press,1995.

Shipman, David. "John Wayne." In *The Great Movie Stars.* New York: Da Capo, 1982.

Wills, Gary. *John Wayne's America.* New York: Simon & Schuster, 1997.

WEBB, RICHARD DAVIS (1805–1872)

Richard Davis Webb, an Irish Quaker printer and reformer, was a friend to many of America's most influential abolitionists, most notably William Lloyd Garrison, Lucretia Mott, and Henry Clark Wright. Of equal importance is the practical support his printing business allowed him to extend to visiting reformers and antislavery speakers, especially Charles Lennox Remond and Frederick Douglass.

Richard S. Harrison offers a comprehensive account of Webb's life and suggests that "Webb kept open a small window of humanity on the world outside of Ireland" (Harrison 1993, 1). This impulse stems from his desire to highlight the many issues that required reform in the early Victorian era: temperance, the peace movement, and especially antislavery. Webb, like Garrison, but unlike other abolitionists, believed he should not confine himself to one reform topic, but should argue on behalf of causes as they arose. He was very aware of conflicts outside his immediate surroundings and his refined sense of conscience and extensive knowledge of world affairs is rooted in the practice and connections that were part of the Quaker world. These connections can be traced across the Atlantic as Webb and his fellow reformers discussed and debated reform topics in their extensive correspondence.

While this transatlantic perspective was confined to an elite group, Webb moved beyond this and undertook the practicalities of reform work. He helped to establish reform organizations and regularly attended meetings. In 1840, Webb attended the first World Anti-Slavery Convention in London. Here he met Lucretia Mott, whom he described as the "Lioness of the Convention" (Harrison 1993, 24) and was one of the first to openly sympathize with her when she was not allowed to take her place as a delegate. He also met Garrison, and they became firm friends. Webb enjoyed their correspondence and was inspired by Garrison's ideals. However, it was his position as a printer that allowed Webb to be of great value to the spread of the antislavery message in the British Isles. He organized and printed many pamphlets of a reform nature during his career, but the assistance he gave three individuals positions him as an important player in the transatlantic network of reform and change.

Inspired by the World Anti-Slavery Convention of 1840, Webb and James Haughton organized an address to the Irish people of America. They wished to inspire Irish Americans to engage with the work of the abolitionists in their newly adopted home and to challenge them not to become involved with the ownership of slaves. They collected 60,000 signatures, including that of Daniel O'Connell. These Webb gave to Charles Lennox Remond in 1841 as he returned to America. Remond had undertaken a nationwide tour of speaking engagements in Ireland, which was organized by Webb.

In 1845, Frederick Douglass, the American fugitive slave, visited Ireland and England. This was necessitated by the publication of his autobiography *Narrative of the Life of Frederick Douglass, An American Slave, Written by Himself,* which exposed him as a fugitive and revealed his whereabouts to his owner. The autobiography acquires deeper significance in an Irish context. Sales of the narrative were to finance Douglass's lecturing tour; such was its popularity, Douglass had to have it republished twice in Ireland, and Webb undertook the task. These Irish editions reveal the newly acquired control that Douglass could now exercise over the presentation of his story and, by extension, the representation of his emerging selfhood.

Webb was an astute observer of the political situation in Ireland and was very aware of the complexities and contradictions that motivated the nationalist and establishment structures. However, he was quick to assist in cases that he deemed grossly unjust. The Young Irelanders organized a minor and very unsuccessful insurrection in August 1848. The leaders—William Smith O'Brien, Patrick O'Donohoe, Thomas Francis Meagher, and T. B. McManus—were charged with high treason and sentenced to be hanged. Webb helped to organize a petition for clemency; 25,000 signatures were collected and presented to the lord lieutenant. Eventually, the sentences were commuted to penal servitude for life.

Ann Coughlan

See also: ABOLITIONISM AND SLAVERY; DOUGLASS, Frederick; MEAGHER, Thomas Francis; MOTT, Lucretia Coffin

References

Harrison, Richard S. *Richard Davis Webb: Dublin Quaker Printer (1805–1872).* Cork: Red Barn Publishing, 1993.
Sweeney, Fionnghuala. " 'The Republic of Letters': Frederick Douglass, Ireland, and The Irish *Narratives.*" *Éire-Ireland* 36, no. 1 & 2 (Spring/Summer 2001): 47–65.

WELLMAN, WILLIAM A. (1896–1975)

William Augustus Wellman was born in Brookline, Massachusetts, on February 29, 1896. His father, Arthur Wellman, born in Boston on April 8, 1858, was of English descent, and his mother, Celia Guinness McCarthy, born in Boston on July 13, 1869, was descended from the famous Guinness family of Dublin.

Wellman attended Newton High School, where he excelled at athletics. He graduated in 1914 and went to work as a "lumper" in a lumberyard in Waltham, Massachusetts, but his sights were on a career in aviation. When he was refused entry into the U.S. Aviation Service in 1917, he traveled to France and there joined the Lafayette Flying Corps, an offshoot of the famous Lafayette Escadrille. Over the next year, Wellman experienced all the dangers, injuries, and excitement associated with life as an aviator, and he would often use this period of his life as material for his films.

By March 1918, he was back in America, employed by the U.S Air Service as a flying instructor at Rockwell Field in San Diego. He also found time to publish a record of his French experiences (entitled *Go, Get 'Em)* and marry a young film actress, Helene Chadwick. Chadwick had a contract with the Goldwyn studios in Los Angeles and Wellman followed her there in 1919.

Wellman's first involvement in films was in a minor acting role in a Douglas Fairbanks film, *The Knickerbocker Buckaroo* (1919), but he soon found that he was more interested in staying behind the camera than appearing in front of it. He became an assistant propman on a number of Will Rogers films, all of which were directed by Clarence Badger. In 1921 he became Badger's assistant director on *A Poor Relation* and, following his move to Fox studios in 1922, he served as an assistant director to Bernard Durning. Wellman made his directorial debut in 1923 with the release of *The Man Who Won,* a western starring Dustin Farnum. For the next three years, Wellman worked steadily as both a director and an assistant director for a variety of film studios.

Soon after his move to Paramount Studios in 1926, Wellman began production on an action film entitled *Wings,* starring Clara Bow, Charles "Buddy" Rogers, Richard Arlen, and Gary Cooper. Drawing on his own experiences as a pilot, Wellman fashioned an action-packed saga detailing the lives of two American flyers (played by Arlen and Rogers) in World War I. Upon its release in 1927, it was greeted with critical acclaim and box office success, catapulting Wellman from the ranks of contract director to star director. Wellman followed it up with another aviation film, *Legion of the Condemned,* and a crime melodrama, *Ladies of the Mob.* One of his most unusual films, *Beggars of Life,* based on Jim Tully's hobo novel and starring Louise Brooks, was released soon after the coming of sound and, with its theme of outsiders living on the margins of society, it anticipated his later Depression-era films, such as *Wild Boys of the Road* (released in 1933).

By 1930, Wellman had left Paramount and signed with Warner Brothers. Over the next four years he directed some of his most powerful work, including the seminal gangster film, *The Public Enemy,* which helped launch the career of James Cagney, and several hard-hitting melodramas that exposed the seedier side of American society, such as *The Star Witness* (1931), *Night Nurse* (1932), and *Heroes for Sale* (1933). Despite his reputation as a maverick director (his nickname was "Wild Bill"), Wellman proved himself both efficient and effective as a director, bringing his films in on schedule and usually on budget. He worked steadily throughout the 1930s and 1940s for most of the major studios, and he produced some of the key examples of Hollywood genre filmmaking, including screwball comedies (*Nothing Sacred* [1937]), action dramas (*Beau Geste* [1939]), westerns (*The Ox Bow Incident* [1943]; *Buffalo Bill* [1944]), and war films (*The Story of G.I. Joe* [1945]). His last film,

Lafayette Escadrille, paid tribute to the famed French air corp and was released in 1958.

Wellman married four times and had seven children with his fourth wife, Dorothy Coonan, whom he married in 1933. He published his autobiography, *A Short Time for Insanity,* in 1974. He died in Los Angeles, California, on December 9, 1975.

Gwenda Young

See also: CAGNEY, James; TULLY, Jim

References

Schickel, Richard. *The Men Who Made the Movies.* New York: Atheneum Books, 1975.
Thompson, Frank. *William A. Wellman.* Metuchen, NJ: Scarecrow Press, 1983.

WILSON, THOMAS WOODROW (1856–1924)

Of Scots-Irish ancestry, Woodrow Thomas Wilson became the 28th president of the United States. Born in Staunton, Virginia, in 1856, Woodrow Wilson was the third child of the Reverend Dr. Joseph Ruggles Wilson and Janet Woodrow. His father, a Presbyterian minister who could trace his ancestry back to Strabane, Ireland, bequeathed to Woodrow both the high moral scruples that would characterize his presidential reputation (if not, at times, his private life) and the outstanding oratorical ability that would set him apart from other contemporary political candidates.

Though originally from Ohio, Wilson's parents were confederate sympathizers during the Civil War. At age eight he watched as captured Confederate president Jefferson Davis was led through town in chains; this and other experiences of the Civil War would later affect his response to the great conflict of his own presidency—World War I. Suffering from what many historians now believe to be a form of dyslexia, Wilson was a poor student in early life. To overcome his scholastic difficulties, his father spent many hours teaching him the art of debate, and he succeeded in teaching himself the new art of shorthand. At 17, he entered Davidson College, transferring a year later to Princeton University, before graduating from there in 1879. Next he studied law at the University of Virginia and practiced it briefly before returning to academia, earning a PhD in political science from John Hopkins University. The success of his published dissertation—*Congressional Government*—landed him teaching jobs at Bryn Mawr College and Wesleyan College; he finally returned to Princeton in 1890, as a professor of jurisprudence and economics. He remains the only U.S. president to date to have gained a doctoral degree.

On a trip to Rome, Georgia, he met Ellen Louise Axson, marrying her in 1885. They would have three daughters: Margaret (1886), Jessie (1887), and Eleanor (1889). At Princeton, he established a reputation as a brilliant teacher and scholar, and in 1902, he became its 13th president. His tenure as president of Princeton was marked by educational reform and expansion for the university. However, it was also dogged by strong division, as many Princeton trustees, alumni, and students staunchly opposed many of Wilson's reforms. After eight years, he was forced to resign. In 1910 Wilson was elected governor of New Jersey on the Democratic ticket. Expected by his gubernatorial backers to be largely conservative, Wilson instead aligned himself with the reform movement, pushing a series of political and economic reforms through the legislature, such as workmen's compensation and regulation of public utilities. By 1912, Wilson's accomplishments and outstanding oratorical ability had made him popular with the progressive element in the Democratic party, and he became the Democratic Party candidate for president. Helped by a split in the Republican Party nomination—between William Taft's party regulars and Theodore Roosevelt's Bull Moose party—Wilson gained a commanding majority in the Electoral College and was elected as the first Democratic president in 20 years.

Wilson had ridden to power on a platform of "New Freedom," arguing that social justice could best be served by abolishing special privileges and restoring competition. Once elected, he went straight to work on his pledge, experiencing early successes with his antitrust laws and tariff reform. The Underwood Tariff (1913), the Federal Reserve Act (1913), the Federal Farm Loan Act (1916), and the Adamson Act (1916) are all parts of Wilson's domestic legacy, aimed at redressing the growing economic and social gap between the haves and the have-nots in America. In 1913, Ellen Wilson developed a serious kidney problem and died within a year. Woodrow was left in a state of deep despair, just as the world was entering World War I. Up until now, apart from a brief squabble with Mexico, Wilson's foreign policy had been largely nonexistent. With the outbreak of war in Europe, Wilson determined on a policy of neutrality as the best course of action for America. This policy became increasingly difficult to maintain, as Republicans called for tougher policies toward Germany, and a German submarine sank the British liner *Lusitania* in 1915. In December of this year, he married Edith

Bolling Galt—a widow and 15 years his junior—and gained a new lease on life.

In 1916, Wilson ran for presidential reelection on an antiwar platform, with the now infamous slogan: "He kept us out of the war." He won reelection, defeating the Republican nominee—Charles Evan Hughes—277 electoral votes to 254. On April 2, 1917, just a month after his inauguration, Wilson went back on his implied election pledge and asked Congress for a declaration of war to "make the world safe for democracy." Although revived German U-boat activity in 1917 has been ascribed as the reason for Wilson's action, many now believe he entered the 1916 presidential election privately knowing he would eventually be forced to lead America to war. As commander-in-chief of the largest army the United States had raised to date, Wilson was an able leader and administrator. However, he was already dreaming of a just and lasting peace. On January 8, 1918, with the war not yet over, Wilson issued his Fourteen Point plan for postwar reconstruction. Some of the items contained within this plan were an end to secret treaties; freedom of the seas in war and peace; removal of trade barriers; the evacuation, restoration, and readjustment of certain countries and boundaries; and the creation of a League of Nations to prevent future international conflicts. Armistice was declared on November 11, 1918, and less than four weeks later Wilson sailed for Europe to attend the Versailles Peace Conference. Though he was initially revered and celebrated as a savior of humanity, Wilson's early glory in Europe was soon to be replaced by disappointment and even embitterment at the allies squabbling over territory and refusing to embrace his principles at Versailles. As the months dragged on, Wilson saw his vision of "peace without victors" being gradually eroded as he was forced to concede on point after point. He managed to salvage his concept of the League of Nations, but by this time he was facing much opposition to it at home.

In 1919 Wilson was awarded the Nobel Peace Prize. On July 10, 1919, he presented the Treaty of Versailles to the Senate for ratification, but he could not persuade the necessary two-thirds of the Senate to ratify the treaty. Asked by a group of senators, known as the "reservationists" and led by Henry Cabot Lodge, to modify the treaty—particularly aspects pertaining to U.S. participation in the League of Nations—Wilson refused. Instead, he went on a cross-country speaking tour in an effort to garner public support for the treaty and his cause. Unfortunately, at Pueblo, Colorado, on September 25, he collapsed and soon after suffered a paralytic stroke. Cared for by his second wife, Edith, who restricted all access to the president and kept the true extent of his invalidity secret, Wilson remained in office until the end of his term. He also remained adamant in his opposition to any modifications of the treaty, issuing appeals from his sickbed that the treaty be ratified. However, the Senate refused to ratify the treaty, and with the election victory of Republican Warren G. Harding in November 1920, Wilson's last hope of U.S. participation in the League of Nations faded. Wilson remained in Washington after his retirement from the residency in 1921, forming a law partnership with Bainbridge Colby; however, his fading health prevented him from actively working. He died in February 1924; his legacy, however, survived him, in both Franklin Delano Roosevelt's New Deal proposals and today's United Nations.

James P. Byrne

See also: COHALAN, Daniel F.; DEVOY, John; PRESBYTERIANISM; SCOTS-IRISH; SCOTS-IRISH POLITICS

References

Clements, Kendrick A. *The Presidency of Woodrow Wilson.* Lawrence: University Press of Kansas, 1992.

Clements, Kendrick A. *Woodrow Wilson.* Washington, DC: CQ Press, 2003.

Clements, Kendrick A. *Woodrow Wilson, World Statesman.* Boston: Twayne, 1987.

Heather, Derek Benjamin. *National Self Determination: Woodrow Wilson and His Legacy.* Basingstoke, UK: Macmillan, 1994.

Heckscher, August. *Woodrow Wilson: A Biography.* New York: Scribner, 1991.

Hoover, Herbert. *The Ordeal of Woodrow Wilson.* London: Museum Press, 1958.

Link, Arthur S. *Wilson.* Princeton, NJ: Princeton University Press, 1947.

Olasky, Marvin. *The American Leadership Tradition: Moral Vision from Washington to Clinton.* New York: The Free Press, 1999.

Walworth, Arthur. *Woodrow Wilson.* Baltimore: Penguin Books, 1965.

WINCH, TERENCE (1945–)

The great wave of Irish immigration to America had slowed when Terence Winch's parents arrived in New York City in the 1930s, where they met and married. Growing up in the East Bronx, then a very Irish neighborhood, Winch experienced the vibrancy of the old urban Irish-American culture before its precipitate decline. His father, Paddy, played tenor banjo, and Winch and his brother Jesse accompanied their father at gigs and house parties. Winch eventually settled on the button accordion as his instrument. This period in the Bronx became the subject for Winch's first collection of poetry, *Irish Musicians/ American Friends,* which won the American Book Award in 1986. Whatever nostalgia there is in the book is kept firmly in check by a gritty, comic sense of realism. However, in his songs, *When New York Was Irish, Saints* (a litany of Irish Catholic schools), and *The Irish Riviera* (Rockaway), he is unabashedly sentimental. Whereas the immigrant generation used to sing nostalgic songs about the Emerald Isles, Winch writes in celebration of the lost world of Irish America.

Winch seemed destined for an academic career, when he abandoned his doctoral studies at Fordham to join his brother Jesse in Washington, D.C., in 1971. After playing in various folk bands, the Winch brothers discovered that the traditional Irish music with which they had grown up was becoming popular. Celtic Thunder, the band they formed with flutist Linda Hickman in 1977, became one of the most prominent Irish bands on the New York-Washington corridor. The band's *Light of Other Days* won the INDIE award for the best Celtic album for 1986.

Celtic Thunder was unique in that it had its own in-house poet. Not only did Winch write songs for the group, but performances were punctuated with readings of his poetry. Winch was and remains very active in Washington's poetry scene. In the 1970s there were weekly readings above the Community Book Shop just off Dupont Circle. The sessions eventually produced *Mass Transit,* a magazine that Winch edited. Among the many poets Winch read with was Michael Lally, another prominent Irish American. Over the years Winch's poems have appeared in numerous periodicals and anthologies. His published collections include *Rooms* (1992), *The Great Indoors* (1995), and *The Drift of Things* (2003). He has received grants and fellowships from the Maryland State Arts Council and from the National Endowment for the Arts. He has been interviewed on National Public Radio and in turn frequently interviews other writers.

In addition to his poetry Winch has published a collection of short stories, *Contenders* (1989), and his memoirs of the musician's life, *That Special Place* (2004). In most of these short pieces, some peculiar character or strange event seeps through the borders of the mundane to reveal an Irish appreciation for the humorously grotesque.

However, the Irish quality of Winch's work is not to be found only in those pieces about music, immigrant life, and occasional trips back to Ireland, subjects that clearly establish him as one of the major Irish-American writers of his generation. Most of his poems deal not with Irishness but with the universal themes of love, desire, loss, and death. Yet amid the surreal images etched with paranoia and irony, one hears echoes from deep within the Irish experience. Native-born son of the Bronx, Winch has somehow fully incorporated into his imagination the immigrant's sense of loss. In many of his poems there is the sense of something missing. This is perhaps inevitable for one whose grandfather Winch, a German living in Britain, was incarcerated as a enemy alien during World War I. Terence's grandmother was left for a time to raise the family alone in Mayo. More immediate was the death of Terence's mother, Bridy, when he was a teenager. In "Non-Possession is One-Tenth of the Law," Winch gives himself the ironic advice: "Hide precious items from yourself /Then forget where you have hidden them/This will promote non-attachment to things" (from *The Drift of Things,* 2001). Things, perhaps, but attachment to lost faces and places and love remains clear and painful in

Winch's poetry. There is the haunting sense that, no matter how good things may get, the world will still break your heart.

William H. A. Williams

References

Morgan, Jack. "Memory and Music: An Interview with Terence Winch." *Irish Literary Supplement* 21, no. 2 (Fall 2002): 24.

Retallack, Joan. "Local Ex-Centrisms: The Dupont Circle School." *GW Washington Studies* 1986.

Winch, Terence. *The Drift of Things*. New York: Figures, 2001.

WRIGHT, THOMAS CHARLES JAMES (1799–1868)

Thomas Charles Wright was an officer in Simón Bolívar's army and founder of the Ecuadorian naval school. Wright was born in Queensborough, Drogheda, on January 26, 1799, son of Thomas Wright and Mary Montgomery. In 1810 he was sent to the naval college at Portsmouth, and two years later joined HMS *Newcastle* under the command of George Stewart. In her he sailed to serve with the squadron under Borlase Warren, which was engaged in blockading the Atlantic coast of the United States. He was promoted and went home on leave in 1817. Since that time Wright seems to have been under the influence of radical and republican ideas such as had so influenced the French Revolution.

In November 1817, Wright enlisted as officer in Bolívar's British Legion. He sailed in the brigantine *Dowson* with 200 other volunteers and valuable ammunition, and after a series of delays, dangers, and adventures landed on Margarita Island off the Venezuelan coast on April 3, 1818. Nine years later Wright and another Irishman were the only survivors of the 32 officers who left in the *Dowson*.

At Angostura (now Ciudad Bolívar) Wright first met Bolívar, for whom he quickly developed boundless admiration. His first action was at Trapiche de Gamarra on March 27, 1819. His victory here inspired Bolívar to undertake his astonishing New Granada campaign and the march over the Andes.

Wright played important roles in the battles at Pantano de Vargas and Gamesa in July 1819, and in the decisive victory of Boyacá in August of the same year, after which he was promoted to captain. In 1820 he was sent back with his Rifles regiment to the coastal plain to operate in the jungle east of the Magdalena against the Spanish forces based at Santa Marta. The battle at Ciénaga de Santa Marta on November 10, 1820, resulted in the fall of this town. Convoyed by sea to Maracaibo, the Rifles participated on June 21, 1821, in Bolívar's decisive victory of Carabobo. Cartagena was taken and the Rifles were brought in boats up the Magdalena en route for Popayán. They formed part of the contingent led by Bolívar in the second of his legendary Andean campaigns. After winning the battle at Bomboná on April 7, 1822, Wright was twice mentioned in Bolívar's order of the day for his exceptional skill and courage. From February 1822 Wright was acting lieutenant colonel, a rank that was confirmed early in 1823, when he was serving under Sucre, who joined forces with Bolívar at Quito, Ecuador.

Wright was sent to Guayaquil to improvise a naval force and patrol northward between that Ecuadorian city and Panama. In September 1824, after Bolívar's great victory at Junín and Sucre's at Ayacucho, the Spanish made their last bid to turn the tide and sent a fleet to break the republican blockade in the Peruvian stronghold of Callao. Wright had had a busy year ensuring the arrival of supplies by sea for Bolívar's and Sucre's armies. He had greatly impressed Bolívar, who had appointed him commodore of the Pacific squadron that joined the patriot naval force off Callao. Trying to force their way out, the royalist ships became closely engaged with the blockaders. The brigantine *Chimborazo* sustained three waterline hits and was in a collision with the ship of the line *Asia,* but by consummate skill Wright maneuvered free and avoided being driven ashore. In January 1826 Callao capitulated and the Spanish rule in South America was over. Meanwhile Wright, in *Chimborazo,* had ferried Bolívar from port to port all down the liberated Pacific coast to the frontier of Chile.

Wright settled in Guayaquil in 1826, and founded there the nautical school that still exists. In 1828 the Peruvian government sent the corvette *Libertad* to blockade Guayaquil. Wright had intimately studied the unique swells and currents of the Gulf of Guayaquil, and he used his knowledge to drive off the *Libertad.* Wright's *Guayaquileña* had 60 casualties out of 96 aboard.

Wright took part at sea and on land in the fighting that ended with the delimitation of the Ecuador-Peru boundary, and he was specially commended by Sucre after the victory of Portada de Tarqui. Ecuador had been independent since August 8, 1830, and Wright became one of the new republic's leading citizens. He married María de los Angeles Victoria Rico, the niece of Vicente Rocafuerte, president of Ecuador (1835–1839 and 1843–1845). Wright converted to Roman Catholicism before the wedding. After María's death, Wright took her sister Pepita as his second wife. He was now commander of the Ecuadorian navy and governor of Guayaquil. His courage during a yellow fever epidemic in 1840 was remarkable.

A military plot in 1845 overthrew the liberal regime supported by Wright, and he went into exile in Chile for 15 years. In Chile he met and became a great influence upon the Ecuadorian exile Eloy Alfaro, who would be president in 1897–1913. Wright went back to Ecuador in 1860 and joined various liberal conspiracies against the despot Moreno. With his house still surrounded by police, Wright died on December 10, 1868.

Edmundo Murray

See also: O'LEARY, Daniel Florence

References

Hasbrouck, Alfred. *Foreign Legionaries in the Liberation of Spanish South America.* New York: Columbia University, 1928.

Ireland, John E. de Courcy. "Thomas Charles Wright: Soldier of Bolívar; Founder of the Ecuadorian Navy." *The Irish Sword* 6, no. 25 (Winter 1964): 271–275.

Y

YEATS, JOHN BUTLER (1839–1922)

John Butler Yeats was born on March 16, 1839, in Tullylish, Co. Down, where he spent the first 10 years of his life. He was then sent to a school near Liverpool, which he disliked; after two years he moved to the Atholl Academy, on the Isle of Man. In 1857 he entered Trinity College Dublin, from which he graduated in 1862. At about this time he met Susan Pollexfen, whom he married in 1863. Although he was called to the Irish Bar in 1866, he did not practice, and in 1867 he abandoned law, moved to London, and studied art.

For most of the next three decades he and his growing family led an erratic existence, moving among London, Dublin, and the Pollexfen home in Sligo. Although Yeats concentrated on portraiture—for which he had real talent—he received too few commissions to establish a reliable income for his family. His fortunes were also hurt by his temperamental reluctance to treat art as a commercial endeavor; he gave away drawings, sketched acquaintances for little or no payment, and frequently reworked paintings that were, to other eyes, complete.

Beginning in the 1880s and 1890s, and continuing throughout the remainder of his life, Yeats felt an artistic father's ambiguous pride in being eclipsed by his children. Although one of his sons (Robert) died of croup as a child, his remaining children developed an imposing variety of talents. His son William became Ireland's foremost poet; daughters Elizabeth (called Lolly) and Susan (called Lily) were distinguished textilists and publishers; and son Jack became one of Ireland's most inventive and accomplished painters.

After his wife died in 1900, Yeats settled again in Dublin, continuing his art and gaining a reputation for being a fine conversationalist. He took an active interest in the culture of the city and, in 1907, delivered a famous speech in defense of John M. Synge's then-controversial play, *The Playboy of the Western World*. (W. B. Yeats wrote warmly of his father's speech in the poem "Beautiful Lofty Things"). A year later Yeats accompanied Lily on what was intended to be a brief visit to the United States, yet he remained in Manhattan for the rest of his life.

In New York Yeats led a life similar to that he had enjoyed in Ireland: he chatted often, dined well, enjoyed many friendships, and sold too few works to support himself. Yet in New York he had as friend and patron the lawyer John Quinn, whose financial assistance proved invaluable in keeping Yeats afloat. Despite growing exasperation with his elderly ward, Quinn never fully cut him off from financial rescue; and it was a commission from Quinn to paint a self-portrait that occupied the Irishman's last years. Yeats was also pleased and surprised by the popularity of several collections of his letters that were published: *Passages from the Letters of John Butler Yeats* (1917, edited by Ezra Pound) and *Further Letters of John Butler Yeats* (1920, edited by Lennox Robinson). He died in Manhattan on February 3, 1922, of heart weakness compounded by influenza.

Yeats's American years were not notably productive, although he continued his Dublin habit of drawing fine informal sketches of friends and acquaintances. His significance for Irish-American relations lay in his unofficial role as a conduit into America for Irish cultural influence. Because he knew many of the artists and writers of prominence in Ireland, Yeats's opinion on Irish matters was sought and valued by American benefactors, collectors, and journalists. By combining this cultural knowledge with personal likability, Yeats became one of the central figures of Irish New York between 1909 and 1922.

Andrew Goodspeed

See also: RESEARCH COLLECTIONS, IRISH, IN CANADA; RESEARCH COLLECTIONS, IRISH, IN THE UNITED STATES; YEATS, William Butler

References

Archibald, Douglas N. *John Butler Yeats.* Lewisburg, PA: Bucknell University Press, 1974.

Jeffares, A. Norman. "John Butler Yeats." In *In Excited Reverie: A Centenary Tribute to William Butler Yeats,* edited by A. Norman Jeffares and K. G. W. Cross. New York: Macmillan & Co., 1965.

Murphy, William M. *Prodigal Father: The Life of John Butler Yeats.* Ithaca, NY: Cornell University Press, 1978.

Yeats, John Butler. *Essays Irish and American.* Dublin: The Talbot Press, 1918.

Yeats, John Butler. *Letters to his Son W. B. Yeats and Others,* edited by Joseph Hone; abridged by John McGahern. London: Faber, 1999.

YEATS, WILLIAM BUTLER (1865–1939)

Born in Dublin in 1865, William Butler Yeats was the son of the artist John Butler Yeats and Susan Pollexfen. The Yeats family was somewhat unsettled in his youth, and he grew up variously in London, Sligo, and Dublin. Later in life he became a passionate advocate of continuity, tradition, and rootedness, both in personal life and in the cultural life of Ireland.

In 1884, he began study at the Metropolitan School of Art in Dublin. Although he had some rudimentary skill as a painter, the greater talent in visual art belonged to his brother, Jack. William, however, had demonstrated unusual ability in verse, and soon began publishing his writings. His early volumes reveal both extraordinary talent and a fascination with mythology and the Irish landscape. His 1889 narrative poem "The Wanderings of Oisin" is a particularly accomplished debut, and subsequent books (*Crossways* [1889]; *The Rose* [1893]; *The Wind Among the Reeds* [1899]; and *In the Seven Woods* [1904]) established him as the foremost young poet in Ireland. His early poetry is perhaps most notable for its technical virtuosity, by which he creates moving evocations of love or of mythological Irish heroes with an apparently effortless, and often memorable, lyrical beauty. Of these early poems perhaps "The Lake Isle of Innisfree" is his most widely known.

Portrait of poet William Butler Yeats, who was an integral driving force behind the Irish Literary Revival. (Library of Congress)

In the 1880s and 1890s, Yeats undertook extensive research in matters that interested him. He made several trips through the rural countryside of Ireland, recording and preserving folk tales and fairy stories. These trips he conducted with a new acquaintance, Lady Augusta Gregory; her house (Coole), her person, and her work were to be emblematic for Yeats of the aristocratic continuity he most valued in the Irish cultural nobility. Her home also provided him with a quiet place in which to think and work, and many of his poems began, or were wholly written, in Coole. Their folkloric work, if somewhat unusual, has real value. Of less apparent value was the research Yeats also began into theosophy, mysticism, and the supernatural. He spent a lifetime fascinated by ghosts, fairies, and seances, and he evolved elaborate systems to communicate with mystical voices and explain multigenerational cycles of birth, death, and rebirth. These matters, although easy to simplify unfairly, had a great importance to Yeats; it is a tribute to his skills as a poet that their appearances in his verse are rarely repellent to those who disbelieve his mysticism.

In 1889, Yeats met the young Maud Gonne, whose immediate impact and subsequent influence on his poetry is perhaps comparable only to that of Beatrice on Dante. Gonne was attractive, spirited, and devoted to Irish culture and Irish freedom. Most importantly for Yeats, she was also, for years, passionately friendly but (to him) sexually unobtainable. He wrote many of his most moving love lyrics for her, and he created an extensive and beautiful mythology around her. Her eternally radical Irish republicanism helped to encourage his own political interests. His belief in the desirability of Irish independence was deep but envisioned nothing like the violence Gonne would tolerate, and it finds expression in some highly skilled symbolic plays, most notably *The Countess Cathleen* (1892), and *Cathleen ni Houlihan* (1902).

In 1899, Yeats inaugurated the Irish Literary Theatre, based on his conviction that Ireland required and deserved a world-class national theater. This later became the Abbey Theatre, of which Yeats was a director for most of the rest of his life. In the early days the Abbey (which opened in 1904) drew largely from its own highly talented founders, producing original plays by Yeats, Lady Gregory, and John M. Synge. In 1907 Synge's *The Playboy of the Western World* provoked civic disturbances, which offered Yeats an opportunity he relished to denounce the rowdies for attacking real artistic achievement by an Irishman. He was to repeat this denunciation of rioters at a later Abbey scandal when, in 1926, the theater premiered young Sean O'Casey's play *The*

Plough and the Stars, which provoked similar uproar. Through much of his later life the difficulties and pleasures of the Abbey Theatre were to occupy his time and his interests.

As Yeats grew older, he achieved an unusual metamorphosis in his poetry; what had often been evocative, symbolic, gentle, hushed, or remorseful in his earlier work was sharply displaced by passionate public and philosophical verse of astonishing force and amazing vigor. In later verse collections (most notably: *Responsibilities* [1914]; *The Wild Swans at Coole* [1919]; *Michael Robartes and the Dancer* [1921]; *The Tower* [1928]; *The Winding Stair and Other Poems* [1933]; and *New Poems* [1938]) Yeats wrote with impeccable clarity and resonant beauty of exceptionally complex philosophical and political questions. He also asserted himself ever more as a subject of his own poetry, writing more powerfully and explicitly of his thoughts, sexual desires, and meditations than he had done as a youth (when he often referred to himself in verse as "the poet" or "he"). Moreover, he returned in his later verse to a series of self-referential mythological symbols, such as a tower, Byzantium, and a sword presented to him by a Japanese admirer named Junzo Sato. This later work bears some influence of the rising Modernists, particularly Ezra Pound, whom Yeats befriended; yet Yeats was not wholly convinced of the Modern emphasis on disjunction and never entirely embraced the movement. His accomplishment in modernizing his verse is almost wholly his own.

The Easter Rising of 1916 had been led by several men whom Yeats knew, although he was out of the country when they rebelled, and he had not been in sympathy with a violent rising. He nonetheless embraced the notion of an independent Irish state when it arose, and later he served for several years as a senator. During this time he made an important speech on abortion and headed the committee that chose the design for the new Irish coinage. In 1917, he married Bertha Georgina "George" Hyde-Lees, with whom he had two children, Anne (1919) and Michael (1921). It was also with George that he engaged in extended attempts to contact spiritual advisers through automatic writing experiments, which had an enormous influence on Yeats's thought, both about poetry and about the supernatural. The family bought and renovated a Norman tower in Co. Galway that Yeats called Thoor Ballylee and that he declared to be his symbol; aside from its symbolic value, it was prone to floods and cold winds and was uncomfortable. In 1923 he attracted world attention when he was awarded the Nobel Prize in Literature.

Yeats spent his last years based in Dublin, while occasionally visiting London, Italy, and the south of France. His income, although never enormous, was aided by a benefaction presented in admiration by Irish Americans, primarily in New York City. A late exuberance for sex led him to have several affairs, yet he never seems to have given thought to leaving his wife. He also had a brief interest in what became an Irish political party with views that resembled fascism; this has resulted in a widespread but mistaken notion that Yeats was himself a fascist or sought to promote fascism. He died in 1939, in the south of France, but was later reburied, according to his wish, in Drumcliff, Co. Sligo.

Yeats had several connections with the United States. His father spent his last years in New York City, which gave William a personal contact in America's artistic circles.

His father's financial imprudence, however, also placed an unwelcome financial burden on him, and to discharge the debt he sold many of his manuscripts to the American patron and collector John Quinn (who essentially paid for J. B. Yeats's life in America). W. B. Yeats himself visited the United States on several occasions, in connection with fund-raising for the Abbey Theatre or on lecture tours of his own: he undertook lecture tours in 1903, 1914, 1920, and 1932 and an Abbey fund-raising tour in 1911. These tours were lucrative for Yeats and helped him through several difficult economic periods.

Although Yeats does not appear to have been heavily influenced by American culture (with the exception of western novels, which he read avidly), he astutely understood that Ireland's world importance was enormously magnified by the affection and interest Americans felt for the smaller nation. He therefore took care to speak about cultural and literary matters that he felt would increase American understanding of Irish culture and politics. A rather slight volume entitled *Letters to the New Island* gathered early essays that originally appeared in U.S. newspapers. His works remain widely studied in American and Canadian universities. W. B. Yeats likely had a greater impact on twentieth-century Irish artistic culture than any other individual.

Andrew Goodspeed

See also: COLUM, Padraic; CUSACK, Cyril; ELLMANN, Richard David; GOGARTY, Oliver St. John; RESEARCH COLLECTIONS, IRISH, IN CANADA; RESEARCH COLLECTIONS, IRISH, IN THE UNITED STATES; MOORE, Marianne; YEATS, John Butler

References

Brown, Terence. *The Life of W. B. Yeats.* Oxford: Blackwell, 1999.

Foster, R. F. *W. B. Yeats: A Life—The Apprentice Mage.* Oxford: Oxford University Press, 1997.

Foster, R. F. *W. B. Yeats: A Life—The Arch-Poet.* Oxford: Oxford University Press, 2003.

Jeffares, A. N. *W. B. Yeats: The Critical Heritage.* London: Routledge & Kegan Paul, 1977.

Yeats, William Butler. *Autobiographies.* London: Macmillan, 1955.

Yeats, William Butler. *The Plays, Vol. II of The Collected Works,* edited by David R. Clark and Rosalind E. Clark. New York: Scribner, 2001.

Yeats, William Butler. *The Poems,* edited by Daniel Albright. London: Dent (Everyman's Library), 1994.

INDEX

ABOUT THE EDITORS

James P. Byrne is visiting assistant professor at Wheaton College, Norton, MA. A Fulbright scholar to the University of Massachusetts, Amherst in 2000, he received his PhD from the National University of Ireland, Cork in 2002, and was IRCHSS Government of Ireland Fellow at Trintiy College Dublin from 2004–2006. He has published several articles on Irish-American cultural identity in both American and Irish journals, and is currently completing a book on the comparative literary study of Irish American and Jewish American ethnic identity.

Philip Coleman, PhD, is a lecturer in English Literature specializing in American literatures and director of the MPhil in Literatures of the Americas program in the School of English, Trinity College Dublin, Ireland. He has edited *"After thirty Falls": New Essays on John Berryman* (Rodopi, 2007) and *On Literature and Science: Essays, Reflections, Provocations* (Four Courts, 2007), and he is the executive editor of *IJASonline,* the official journal of the Irish Association for American Studies. He has published articles on various aspects of modern American poetry and fiction.

Jason King is a graduate of McGill University (BA), Simon Fraser University (MA), and the National University of Ireland, Maynooth (PhD). He has lectured at the National University of Ireland, Maynooth, and the National University of Ireland, Cork, and is currently an assistant professor in the English department and the Centre for Canadian Irish Studies, Concordia, Montreal. His research specializes in the literary culture of the Irish diaspora, Irish theatre, the Irish novel, and immigrant writing in Ireland. He has published numerous articles about Irish diasporic writing in journals and edited collections on both sides of the Atlantic.